Fundamentals of Auditing

S.K. Basu
St. Xavier's College, Kolkata

PEARSON

ISBN 978-81-317-2885-7

First Impression, 2009

Published by Pearson India Education Services Pvt.Ltd,CIN:U72200TN2005PTC057128.
Formerly known as TutorVista Global Pvt Ltd, licensees of Pearson Education in South Asia

Head Office: 7th Floor, knowledge Boulevard, A-8(A) Sector-62, Noida (U.P) 201309, India

Registered Office: Module G4, Ground Floor, Elnet Software City, TS -140,Block 2 & 9
Rajiv Gandhi Salai, Taramani, Chennai, Tamil Nadu 600113.,Fax: 080-30461003,
Phone: 080-30461060, www.pearson.co.in email id: companysecretary.india@pearson.com

Typeset by ACE BPO Services Pvt. Ltd, India.

Digitally printed in India by Repro India Ltd. in the year of 2015.

Contents

Preface

Auditing is a multi-dimensional subject. The scope of auditing is not only restricted to financial audit under the Companies Act, but has also been extended to cost accounting aspects, managerial policies, operational efficiencies and system applications and audit under Computer Information System environment. It also covers social implications of business organisations and environmental issues. This book, *Fundamentals of Auditing*, covers all these aspects and also describes the modern tools and techniques of auditing. It explains the principles of auditing in a simple and lucid language.

This book is based on the syllabus of undergraduate colleges of different universities in India. It will also be useful for students pursuing CA, BBA, MBA and other professional courses. Even a layman interested in knowing the basics of auditing will be able to use this book.

I am confident that readers will find this book very useful and I will appreciate their valuable suggestions and comments for the further improvement of the book.

I express my gratitude to the renowned authors of this subject from whom references have been taken while writing this book. I am also grateful to Pearson Education for publishing this book. If my work is appreciated by readers, I will consider it as my best reward.

S. K. Basu

Chapter 1

Nature of Auditing

1.1   INTRODUCTION

The development of modern accountancy and the growth of auditing profession in India, and, indeed, in the world as a whole, must be seen in the context of the enormous expansion of industry and commerce which has taken place since the Industrial Revolution. While business enterprises were comparatively small, and were managed by their proprietors, there was little need for the development of complex accounting procedures. When the scale of operations increased and capital was invested in joint stock companies by shareholders who took no part in the management of such companies, it becomes necessary for the managers to present accounts to the shareholders at regular intervals by means of annual accounts. However, the managers (or directors) of unsuccessful companies had an obvious vested interest in hiding the lack of success of their companies from the shareholders; this led to fraudulent accounting and resultant scandals. Governments therefore made provisions for the accounts of companies to be reported by persons other than the directors. In this way auditing was developed. The continuing increase in the size of enterprises and the greater complexity of their accounting procedures, have made increasing demands on the skill of auditors. Hence, it is required that accounts shall only be audited by qualified accountants, who are members of recognised professional bodies.

1.2   ORIGIN OF THE WORD 'AUDIT'

The word 'audit' is derived from the Latin word 'audire', which means 'to hear'. The origin of 'audit' can be traced back to olden times, but auditing as its existing form was established only in the middle of the 19th century.

In olden times, the method of accounting was so crude and the number of transactions was so small that every individual was in a position to check all the transactions recorded by himself or by his employees. Whenever the owner of the business suspected frauds or misappropriation of funds, he appointed an official to check the accounts. Such a person would meet the concerned employees and hear whatever they had to say in connection with the accounts. The person appointed to examine the accounts came to be known as the 'auditor'.

1.3   EARLY HISTORY OF AUDIT

Historical evidence reveals that soon after the ancient states and empires acquired a coherent organisation, systems of checks were applied to their public accounts as testified by ancient records. The ancient Egyptians, the Greeks and the Romans utilised systems of checks and counter checks among the various financial officials. The duties of the auditor in ancient times were thus limited.

The last decade of the 15th century witnessed a great impetus in trade and commerce, inspired by the Renaissance in Italy. This led to the evolution of a system of accounts capable of recording completely all kinds of business transactions. The principles of double entry system were published in 1494 in Venice by Luca Pacioli, although the system had already been in existence in the preceding century. The author of the principles also defined and described, for the first time, the duties and responsibilities of an auditor in detail. Since then, the duties and responsibilities of an auditor have increased enormously.

The Industrial Revolution was another landmark in the history of trade and commerce. It resulted in large scale production requiring huge amount of capital investment. Individuals were not in a position to provide adequate capital, because of their limited finances. It was at this time that the company as a form of business organisation came into existence, and this widened greatly, the possibilities of raising capital for industry from the general public by the issue of shares with a limited liability.

In this type of organisation, the shareholders delegated the management of the undertaking to a board of directors and periodically the board submitted the accounts of the company to the shareholders so that the shareholders were in a position to have a true and fair picture of the financial position and the profit & loss of the undertaking.

With the rapid growth in the number of companies, professional accountants came in the picture. In 1880, the Queen of United Kingdom granted a charter, which incorporated the various societies of accountants into a single body, the Institute of Chartered Accountants of England and Wales. By early 1990s, the concept of audit had developed to a stage where professional accountants became prominent as auditors. The objectives of audit were also changed during this time. Apart from detecting frauds and errors, the auditors also started verifying and reporting on the accuracy of the financial records and documents as well as the financial statements. The verification and attestation of financial statements became the primary objective of company audit. Detection of errors and frauds became incidental to the attainment of this objective. The Companies Act of 1948 in U.K formalized this position.

Being under the British rule, the developments in the U.K had a profound effect on the company legislation in India. The Joint Stock Companies Act of 1857 contained provisions for voluntary annual audit of company accounts. The Companies Act, 1913 made the audit of company accounts compulsory in India. The Act also prescribed, for the first time, the powers and duties of the auditors and the procedures of their appointment. In 1949, the Parliament of India passed the Chartered Accountants Act, under which a body of professional accountants, viz., The Institute of Chartered Accountants of India, was established. The Institute is an autonomous body, which regulates the profession of chartered accountants throughout India. In 1956, a new Companies Act replaced the Act of 1913. The Act now contains elaborate provisions regarding qualifications and disqualifications of auditors, the method of appointment of auditors and their powers and duties.

1.4 EVOLUTION OF AUDITING

Prior to AD 1500, nearly all accounting was concerned with accounting for the activities for the government and the only form of auditing was the keeping of separate records by two different scribes. The objective of maintaining such records was primarily to detect fraud, e.g., to prevent defalcations within the treasuries, to minimise the erroneous recording of transactions and to ensure the honesty of those responsible for the custody of resources. Internal controls were nonexistent, although there was recognition that standardised systems of accounting could reduce the possibility of fraud.

The industrial revolution (1750–1850) was the catalyst of a great period of economic growth in Great Britain, one feature of which was the passing of management from owners to professional managers. This led, in the period 1850–1905, to an increased demand for auditors who were independent of management and who were engaged to detect not only clerical errors, but also management fraud. Consequently, auditors began to periodically report on the work they had performed to the owners of an entity and thus the concept of what is now referred to as the 'independent auditor's report' emerged.

It was during this time that the concept of 'testing' evolved. That is, auditors selected 'a few haphazard cases', where it was not economically feasible to physically examine all transactions that took place. The use of testing is recognised as one of the limitations of a modern day audit. Also, controls over cash were first recognised during this period as was the control inherent in double entry bookkeeping. However, the recognition of the benefits of such controls did not affect the extent of auditor's procedures.

From 1905–1930, there was an independent progression of British and American audit objectives. In the USA, the audit objective gradually changed during this period from the detection of fraud to reporting on 'the actual condition of an entity' and there was considerable use of testing it. In Great Britain, however, the primary objective continued to be detection of fraud and error and the prominence of detailed checking (as opposed to testing) remained to the fore. Although auditors now recognised the benefits on internal control procedure, this recognition still had little, if any effect on the nature, timing and extent of auditors' procedures.

During the period 1933–1940, there was as acceptance by auditors of somewhat 'softer' audit objectives and the wording of the standard auditor's report on the financial statements reflected this change. In the USA, the auditors reported as to whether financial statements 'present fairly' the state of affairs of an entity, rather than the more precise 'present a true and fair view' used in Great Britain. (It was not until the 1980s that Great Britain (and many British Commonwealth Countries) adopted the wording used in the USA).

By 1940, testing was the rule and detailed checking the exception. There was also a general recognition that the adequacy of 'internal checks' (as internal controls were then called) could reduce the extent of testing by auditors. The relevance of effective internal controls, since that time until the present day, has been increasingly recognised by auditors as an important factor in the determination of the nature, timing and extent of audit procedures.

From 1940 onwards, it became increasingly accepted by the auditing profession, although not necessarily by the general public, that the primary objective of an audit was the provision of an opinion on the financial statements and that the detection of fraud and error was very much a secondary objective.

Since 1960, the auditing profession throughout the world experienced significant increase in wages' costs. This, combined with the increasing complexity of business and the proliferation of computerized information systems, led to an increased demand for more efficient and effective methods of auditing. During the period 1960–1980, an assessment of the reliability of the internal control became the accepted method of determining the nature, timing and extent of many audit procedures. This leads to the extensive use of what was called 'system-based auditing'. Also, statistical methods were introduced to determine the extent of testing, although their use was not widespread. Around 1972, the concept of audit risk was recognised in the professional literature.

Since 1980, increasing fee pressure accentuated the need for audit to be both effective and efficient. As a result, there was, and still is, increasing recognition of the importance of the audit risk concepts in audit practice. Audit firms adopted what is generally called a 'risk based approach' in auditing. This approach involves a particular way of determining the nature, timing and extent of audit procedures. It is based on an explicit evaluation of the risk of the financial statements containing a material misstatement.

Although the objectives of an audit have remained unchanged since about 1940 pressure from the public to widen audit objectives to embrace, for example, the detection of fraud continues.

1.5 AUDITING DEFINED

The word 'Audit' is derived from the Latin word 'audire', which means, "to hear". In olden times, whenever the owners of a business suspected fraud, they appointed certain persons to check the accounts. Such persons sent for the accountant and 'heard' what they had to say in connection with the accounts.

The dictionary meaning of audit is official examination of accounts. Obviously the person who examines the accounts must be a person who knows what to examine, how to examine and to whom his examination report and observations to be submitted. In brief, it can be said that auditing is the process by which competent independent individuals collect and evaluate evidence to form an opinion and communicate his opinion to the person interested through his audit report.

From the above it is clear that the auditing process involves three components. These are:

i.   Books of accounts,

ii. Auditor and

iii. Techniques and procedures of audit.

Montgomery, a leading American accountant, defines auditing as: "a systematic examination of the books and records of a business or other organisations, in order to check or verify and to report upon results thereof."

The ICAI has defined auditing in its Standards on Auditing- 200 (SA- 200) as "the independent examination of financial information of any entity, whether profit oriented or not and irrespective of its size or legal form, when such an examination is conducted with a view to express an opinion thereon."

From the above definitions, it is seen that an auditor has not only to see the arithmetical accuracy of the books of accounts but has to go further and find out whether the transactions entered in the books of original entry are correct or not. This function is possible to be performed by inspecting, comparing, checking, reviewing, scrutinising the vouchers supporting the transactions in the books of accounts and examining the correspondence, minute books of the shareholders' and directors' meeting, memorandum of association and articles of associations etc.

1.6   NATURE OF AUDITING

The basic function of accounting is to record the economic events that have the effects in changing the financial position of an organization and to prepare the financial statements at the end of a particular accounting period. The objectives behind these functions of accounting are to know the financial result and the financial position of that organisation in a particular accounting period and at the end of the accounting period. The users of the financial statements include the management, the shareholders, creditors, investors, loan-providing financial institutions and the public in general.

Auditors are appointed in these organisations to check the authenticity and reliability of the books of accounts maintained by these organisations and the relevant documents preserved in order to support the transactions. After checking the books of accounts and relevant documents, the auditors are required to submit a report to the owners of the organisation. In this report, the auditors have to state as to whether the books of accounts maintained by the organisation give a true and fair view of the state of affairs of the organisation as disclosed in the financial statements. If the books of accounts fail to give a true and fair picture of the financial activities of that organisation, the auditors will report accordingly.

In the light of these two concepts about the functions of accounting and auditing, it can be said that auditing is a technique of accounting control. In keeping the books of accounts or maintaining documents through proper recording of economic events of an organisation, the accountants may do mistakes, i.e., 'accounting error' may be there or they may adopt unfair practices to manipulate accounts to mislead the users, i.e., 'accounting fraud' may be there. If there are accounting errors and frauds in the accounting records and documents, the books of accounts will not disclose the true and fair view of the financial position of the organisation. In conducting audit, an auditor has to go through the entries recorded in the books of accounts and relevant supporting documents to ensure him about the truth and fairness of the financial statements prepared on the basis of books of accounts maintained. If he finds any inconsistency and irregularity in the books of accounts, he will raise objections and report accordingly. As a result, the persons involved in maintaining the books of accounts and relevant documents become very cautious in discharging their duties. Because they know that if there is any irregularity in maintaining the books of accounts, the auditor will report against the irregularity. So, the employees engaged in the maintenance of the books of accounts want to be regular in keeping their books of accounts. Hence, it can be rightly stated that accounting work is under the control of auditing work and thereby auditing is a technique of accounting control.

1.7 ESSENTIAL FEATURES OF AUDITING

The following are the essential features of auditing:

Accounting Control
Audit is an instrument of accounting control. The truth and fairness of the accounting information is controlled and checked by auditing activities.

Safeguard
Audit acts as a safeguard on behalf of the proprietor/s (whether an individual or a group of persons) against extravagance, carelessness or fraud on the parts of the proprietors' agents or servants in the realization and utilization of his/their money and other assets.

Assurance
Audit assures on the proprietors' behalf that the accounts maintained truly represents facts and expenditure has been incurred with due regularity and propriety.

Assessment
Audit assesses the adequacy of the accounting system in order to ascertain its effectiveness in maintaining accounting records of an organization.

Review
Audit carries out a review of the financial statements to know whether the accounting records are in agreement with those statements.

Reporting Tool
Audit is a tool for reporting on the financial statements as required by the terms of the auditors' appointment and in compliance with the relevant statutory obligations.

Practical Subject
Auditing is a practical subject. It is something that people do. How it is done today is a result of long history of marginal changes and responses to new commercial and legal developments over the centuries with the most rapid progress in the last few years.

1.8 WHY IS THERE A NEED FOR AN AUDIT?

The problem that has always existed when the managers report to owners is the credibility of the report.
   The report may:
   i.   contain error
   ii. not disclose fraud

iii. be inadvertently misleading

iv. be deliberately misleading

v. fail to disclose relevant information

vi. fail to conform to regulations.

The solution to this problem of credibility in reports and accounts lies in appointing an independent person called an auditor to investigate the report and report on his findings.

A further point is that modern companies can be very large with multi-national activities. The preparation of the accounts of such groups is a very complex operation involving the bringing together and summarizing of accounts of subsidiaries with different conventions, legal systems and accounting and control systems. The examination of such accounts by independent experts trained in the assessment of financial information is of benefit to those who control and operate such organizations as well as to owners and outsiders.

Many financial statements must conform to statutory and other requirements. The most notable is that all company accounts have to conform to the requirements of the Companies Act. In addition all accounts should conform to the requirements of Accounting Standards. It is essential that an audit should be carried out on financial statements to ensure that they conform to these requirements.

1.9 OBJECT OF AN AUDIT

The original object of an audit was principally to see whether the personnel involved in accounting had properly accounted for the receipts and payments of cash. In other words, the object of audit was to find out whether cash had been embezzled and if so, who embezzled it and what amount was involved. Thus, it was only an audit of cash book. But, at present, the main object of audit is to find out, after going through the books of accounts, whether the balance sheet and profit and loss account are properly drawn up accordingly and whether they represent a true and fair view of the state of the affairs of the concern. This is possible when he verifies the accounts and the statements. While performing his duties, the auditor has also to discover errors and frauds.

The ICAI in its "Statement on objective and scope of the audit of financial statements" (SA-200A) enumerates the following as the objectives of auditing the financial statements:

i. The objective of an audit of financial statements, prepared within a framework of recognized accounting policies and practices and relevant statutory requirements, if any, is to enable an auditor to express an opinion on such financial statements.

ii. The auditor's opinion helps determination of the true and fair view of the financial position and operating results of an enterprise.

The auditor should be an independent person who is appointed to investigate the organization, its records and financial statements prepared from them and thus form an opinion on the accuracy and correctness of the financial statements. The primary aim of an audit is to enable the auditor to conform that the accounts show a 'true and fair view' or that they do not.

So, the primary object of an audit is to promote efficiency and accuracy in accounting and to place before the shareholders and management accurate information of the financial condition of the business, which may serve as an aid to overall administration of the business entity. For the fulfillment of the primary objects of an audit, the following subsidiary objects are to be realised:

i. Detection of errors.

ii. Detection of frauds.

iii. Prevention of errors.

iv. Prevention of frauds.

Again, errors, which arise out of innocence and carelessness, are of three types:

i. Clerical Errors.

ii. Compensating Errors.

iii. Errors of Principles.

Also, Clerical Errors may be of two types:
(i) Errors of Omission, (ii) Errors of Commission.

On the other hand, frauds which arise out of some intention to gain something through some manipulating devices are of three types: (i) Misappropriation or Embezzlement of Cash. (ii) Misappropriation of Goods, (iii) Manipulation of Accounts.

The objects of auditing can be presented in the following chart:

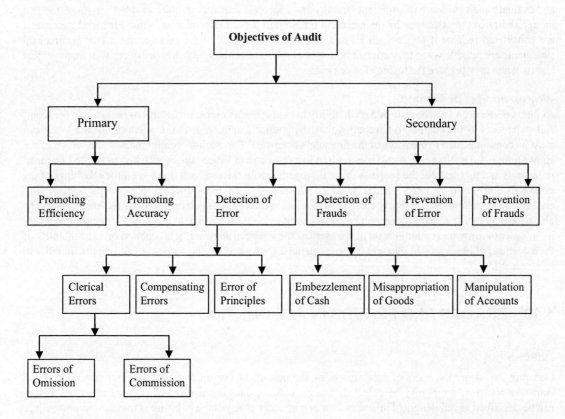

So, the overall objective of the audit of the financial statements of an entity is to gather and evaluate audit evidence of sufficient quantity and appropriate quality in order to form and communicate to the users of the financial statements an audit opinion on the reliability of the assertions of management inherent in those financial statements for the purpose of adding credibility to those assertions.

How the objective is achieved?

The principal objective noted above might be expended by including a reference as to how the objective is achieved. Auditors achieve their objective by gathering and evaluating audit evidence. The evidence needs to be such quantity and quality that the auditor is able to form an opinion on the financial statements. Thus, it may be stated that the objective of audit of the financial statements of an entity is to gather and evaluate audit evidence of sufficient quantity and appropriate quality in order to form an opinion on the financial statements prepared by management. The 'quality' term refers to the relevance and reliability of the evidence and 'entity' includes entities such as partnerships, trusts, government departments, and quasi-government organisations as well as corporate entities. The objective of audit of financial statements is the same, irrespective of the entity to which the financial statements relate.

Financial statements are simply a collection of assertions

For example, the expression "inventory, at cost of Rs. 1,000 in a set of financial statements is in fact an assertion by management that, inter alia, inventory actually exists, that it is owned by the entity at balance date, that it costs Rs. 1,000 and that is no other inventory. The objective of an audit can thus be expanded to gather and evaluate audit evidence of sufficient quantity and appropriate quality in order to able form an opinion on the reliability of the assertions by management inherent in those financial statements. Financial statements are considered reliable if they are, in all material aspects, complete, valid and accurate. That is, financial statements are reliable when they contain no material misstatements, which are, in effect, what management asserts when they prepare the financial statements.

Why an audit is performed?

Auditors perform an audit so as to add creditability to management's inherent assertions included in the financial statements. If the audit is to have any value, the auditor's opinion as to the reliability of the assertions must be communicated to the users of the financial statements. The auditor 'communicates' the results of the audit through the audit report, a document, often just one page in length, that is attached to audited financial statements and that sets out the scope of the audit together with the auditor's opinion on the reliability of the assertions inherent in the financial statements. Financial statement 'users' include such groups as shareholders, suppliers, customers, lenders, borrowers, potential investors and regulatory authorities. Accordingly, the objective may be expanded to gather and evaluate audit evidence of sufficient quantity and appropriate quality in order to form, and communicate to the users of the financial statements, an opinion on the reliability of the assertions of management inherent in those financial statements for the purpose of adding creditability to those assertions.

1.10   ERRORS AND FRAUDS IN ACCOUNTING

ERRORS

Generally errors are the result of carelessness on the part of the person preparing the accounts. During the course of auditing, errors may be detected, though auditing does not ensure detection of all errors. Errors can be described as unintentional mistakes. Errors can occur at any stage in business transaction processing: transaction occurrence, documentation, record of prime entry, double entry record, summarizing process and financial statement production. Errors can be of any of a multitude of kinds: mathematical or clerical or in the application of accounting principles.

Accounting errors, which are possible to be detected through auditing, can be of the following types:

Errors of Omission

When a transaction is omitted completely or partially from the books of accounts, such errors are known as errors of omission. This type of error is not reflected in the trial balance and hence more difficult to detect.

Example

i. Omission of purchases from Purchases Day Book.

ii. Ignoring depreciation on fixed assets completely.

Errors of Commission

When entries made in the books of original entry or ledger are either wholly or partially incorrect, such errors are known as errors of commission. Some of these errors may not affect trial balance.

Example

i. Wrong amount recorded in the books of original entry, e.g. sale of goods of Rs. 15,000 recorded as Rs. 1,500 in Sales Day Book. This error will not affect trial balance.

ii. Posting to the wrong side of an account. In place of debiting, e.g. an amount of Rs. 150 is credited. This error will affect the trial balance.

Compensating Errors

When an error offsets the effect of another error, such errors are known as compensating errors. These errors do not affect the agreement of the trial balance, hence cannot be located by it.

Example

i. A debit balance is undercast by Rs. 100 and credit balance is undercast by the same amount of Rs. 100.

ii. Sales return of Rs. 500 is posted to the Return Inward A/c as Rs. 5,000 and similarly purchase return of Rs. 500 is posted to the Return Outwards A/c as Rs. 5,000.

Errors of Principles

When principles of book-keeping and accountancy are not followed, such an error is known as errors of principles. Such errors may be committed intentionally to understate asset and to over-state liability and to inflate and deflate profit as and when circumstance dictates.

Example

i. Treatment of capital expenditure as revenue expenditure, e.g. purchase of machinery treated as purchase of goods.

ii. Valuation of stock on the basis of wrong principle.

FRAUD

Misstatements in the financial statements can arise either from error or from fraud. The term 'fraud' is defined in Standards on Auditing (SA)-240 in the following way: "Fraud refers to an intentional act by one or more individuals among management, those charged with governance or third parties, involving the use of deception to obtain an unjust or illegal advantage".

In other words, the performance of fraud within an entity is the intentional performance by a person or persons including management, other employee or third party, of an action, other than theft, that derives from the entity a benefit to which the person or persons is/ are otherwise entitled.

The primary objective of an audit of the financial statements of an entity is to form (and communication to the financial statement users) an opinion on management's assertions inherent in the financial statements. This implies that the audit objective includes the detection of misstatements in management's assertions, irrespective of whether or not the misstatements arise from fraud. Auditors argue, however, that bearing in mind they only examine a selection of transactions and that perpetrators of fraud often conceal their fraud, it is not possible to offer reasonable assurance that an audit will detect misstatements arising from fraud. This argument is reinforced by the fact that:

- Fraud often involves the use of sophisticated techniques, such as printing bogus suppliers' invoices and other stationery.
- An employee involved in fraud will often make fraudulent representations to the auditor.
- The fraud may involve collusion between two or more persons.
- The fraud may be perpetrated by a member of management who unbeknown to the auditor overrides internal control procedures.

Nevertheless, auditors identify and assess the risk of material misstatement due to fraud when planning an audit. To do this, auditors obtain a detailed understanding of the nature of the entity's business, the reporting and supervisory responsibilities within the organisation and the types of fraudulent misstatements that are likely to occur.

Whether or not an auditor is responsible for detecting a specific fraud depends on the circumstances. On the one hand, it depends on the complexity of fraud (the greater the complexity, the lesser the responsibility) and on the other hand, it depends on the adequacy of the auditor's planning, performance and judgement (the lesser the adequacy, the greater the responsibility). In many jurisdictions, the final decision rests with the judiciary.

Therefore, fraud means false representation or entry made intentionally or without belief in its truth with a view to defraud somebody. Detection of fraud is considered to be one of the important duties of an auditor. The term 'fraud' is used for several sins including:

i. Fraud, which involves the use of deception to obtain an unjust or illegal financial advantage.

ii. Intentional misstatements in or omissions of amounts or disclosures from an entity's accounting records or financial statements.

iii. Theft, whether or not accompanied by misstatements of accounting records or financial statements.

The following are the main ways in which fraud may be activated:

Embezzlement of Cash
Defalcation of cash is possible irrespective of the size of the business-small or large. The possibility of the misappropriation of cash is small in a small business organisation, where the proprietor has a direct control over the cash receipts and disbursement. The chances are greater in case of large business organisations. There are different methods of misappropriation of cash defalcation, out of which "Teeming and Lading" procedure is usually followed by the employees involved in the misappropriation of cash.

Misappropriation of Goods
Misappropriation of goods is another type of fraud. It may happen that the valuable goods of an organisation may be stolen by the employees or workers. It may also happen that the storekeeper is in collusion with the works manager may sell the goods illegally to some third party. Such frauds are very difficult to locate or identify.

Manipulation of Accounts
Accounts are manipulated through falsification of accounts. These are fraudulent manipulation through accounts and arise generally through passing of false entries with the motive of misappropriating fund slowly and steadily. Unlike misappropriation of cash and goods, this type of fraud is done by sophisticated personnel of an organisation.

1.11   ROLE OF AUDITORS IN DETECTING ERRORS AND FRAUDS

There is a difference of perception between the public and the auditing profession in relation to an auditor's duty regarding errors and fraud.

The auditor sees his duty as:

"The independent examination of and expression of opinion on, the financial statements of an enterprise by an appointed auditor in pursuance of that appointment and in compliance with any relevant statutory obligation".

While certifying the final accounts of the concern, the auditor, has to face a specific problem. He has to certify in his report as to whether the profit and loss account reflects the true profit or loss for the financial year concerned and the balance sheet exhibits a true and fair view of the state of affairs at the end of the financial year. The emphasis is on financial statements. However the public, including much of the business community, tend to see an auditor's duties in terms of the detection and possibly prevention of error and fraud.

Accordingly, he has a duty to ascertain frauds and errors to justify the correctness of the accounts. This duty of detecting and preventing errors and frauds can be analysed in the following ways:

Detection of Errors and Frauds

It is desirable that the auditor should exercise reasonable care and skill, so that he may detect errors and frauds. If he carries routine checking and vouching more carefully and checks the books of accounts thoroughly, he may be successful in his duty. Whereas, in doing so, if he is not successful but he himself feels that he has not shown any negligence in his duty, then he cannot be held responsible for any error or fraud which remains undetected in accounts. Hence, an auditor is not an insurer.

Prevention of Errors and Frauds

The auditor has no authority to introduce remedial measures for the prevention of errors and frauds. All that he can do is to advise his client and suggests the ways and means to prevent them.

1.12   RELATION BETWEEN BOOK-KEEPING, ACCOUNTANCY AND AUDITING

Book-keeping

It is concerned with systematic recording of transactions in the books of original entry and their posting to the concerned ledger accounts. In fact, book-keeping involves the following activities:

  i.   Journalise the transactions,
 ii.   Posting them into respective ledger accounts,
iii.   Casting the total of ledger accounts, and
 vi.   Finding the balances.

Accountancy

Accountancy is concerned with the checking of arithmetical accuracy of ledger accounts as prepared by the book-keeper and preparing the trial balance from the balance available of different ledger accounts. Finally from the balances, profit and loss account and balance sheet are prepared to know the financial result and financial position of the concern. In short, accountancy involves the following activities:

  i.   Preparation of Trial Balance.
 ii.   Incorporation of adjustment entries and passing entries for rectification.

iii.   Preparation of Profit and Loss Account.

iv.   Preparation of Balance Sheet.

Auditing

When the accountancy work is completed, an auditor is invited to check the accounts prepared by the accountants. That is why, it is said that "Auditing begins where accountancy ends". It is the duty of the auditor to critically examine and verify the accounts. In no case, it is the duty of the auditor to prepare accounts. After completing his work, the auditor has to submit a report of the fact whether or not the profit and loss account exhibits a true and fair financial result of the organisation and also the balance sheet reflects the true and fair financial position of the organisation.

Accountancy vs. Auditing

The difference between accountancy and auditing can be outlined in the following way:

POINTS OF DIFFERENCE	ACCOUNTANCY	AUDITING
1. Scope	The scope of accountancy is limited to the preparation of financial statements.	In auditing, the auditor is concerned with the checking of accounts.
2. Objectives	The objective of accountancy is to know the financial result and financial position.	The objective of auditing is to verify the truth and fairness of the accounts.
3. Status	An accountant is an employee of the organization.	An auditor is an independent outsider.
4. Qualification	Accounting work requires no formal qualification.	To be company auditor, he should be qualified chartered Accountant.
5. Tenure of Service	Accountant is usually a permanent employee of the organization	Auditor can be changed from year to year.
6. Knowledge in other subjects	An accountant is not expected to have knowledge in other subjects.	An auditor must have good knowledge not only in accountancy, but also in other related subjects.
7. Ranking of activities	Accountancy is not dependent on auditing work.	Auditing can be started only after the completion of accountancy work.
8. Time period of work	Accounting work is carried out throughout the year.	Auditing is usually carried out at the end of the year.
9. Professional control	There is no professional control over accountancy.	There are professional rules and regulations regarding the auditing work.

NATURE OF AUDITING | **1.13**

POINTS OF DIFFERENCE	ACCOUNTANCY	AUDITING
10. Nature of work	The nature of accountancy work is constructive.	Auditing work, on the other hand, is mostly analytical.
11. Submission of report	No report is required to be submitted at the end of the accounting work.	A report on the final accounts is required to be submitted by the auditor at the end of his work.
12. Accountability	The accountant is account-able to the management.	The auditor is accountable to the shareholders.

1.13 BASIC PRINCIPLES GOVERNING AN AUDIT

Standards on Auditing-200 (SA-200) describes the basic principles which govern the auditor's responsibilities and which should be complied with whenever an audit is carried out:

Integrity, Objectivity and Independence
The auditor should be straight forward, honest and sincere in his approach to his professional work and should maintain an impartial attitude.

Confidentiality
The auditor should respect the confidentiality of information acquired in the course of his audit work.

Skills and Competence
The audit should be performed and the report should be prepared with due professional care by persons who have adequate training, experience and competence in auditing.

Documentation
The auditor should maintain documents which are important in providing evidence that the audit was carried out in accordance with the basic principles.

Planning
The auditor should plan his work to enable him to conduct an effective audit in an efficient and timely manner.

Audit Evidence
The auditor should obtain sufficient appropriate audit evidence to enable him to draw reasonable conclusions therefrom on which to base his opinion on the financial information.

Accounting System and Internal Control
The auditor should reasonably assure himself that the accounting system is adequate and that all the accounting information which should be recorded has in fact been recorded.

Audit Conclusions and Reporting
The auditor should review and assess the conclusions drawn from the audit evidence and submit a report that contains a clear written opinion on the financial information of the organization.

1.14 SCOPE AND PROCEDURES OF AUDIT

The scope and procedures of audit for a particular organisation will be determined by the auditor on the basis of the terms of engagement, the requirement of relevant legal formalities and the pronouncement of the Institute. The term of engagement cannot, however, in any way reduce the scope and procedures of audit which are prescribed by the legal provisions or by the pronouncement of the Institute.

To express an opinion on the financial statements of an organisation, the auditor should satisfy himself first whether the information contained in the given accounting records is authentic, reliable and adequate as a basis for the preparation of the financial statements. The audit procedure should be designed in such a manner to cover sufficiently all aspects of the organisation as far as they are relevant to the financial statements. In forming his opinion, the auditor should also decide whether the relevant information is properly disclosed in the financial statements on the basis of its statutory requirements.

The Principal areas to be covered in an audit include the following:

Accounting and Internal Control
An examination of the system of accounting and internal control to ascertain whether it is adequate and appropriate for the concerned organisation or not.

Arithmetical Accuracy
An overall checking of the arithmetical accuracy of the books of account by the method of posting, casting and balancing procedures.

Authenticity of Transactions
A proper verification of the validity and authenticity of the transactions entered into by checking the entries with the supporting documents.

Distinction between Capital and Revenue Items
An effective scrutiny over the distinction between the items of capital and of revenue nature of income and expenditure correspond to the accounting period.

Verification of Assets
A detailed verification of the ownership, existence and value of the assets appearing in the balance sheet.

Verification of Liabilities
A proper verification of the liabilities of the organisation as stated in the balance sheet.

Comparison of the Financial Statements
A comparison of the balance sheet and profit and loss account or other statements with the available records in order to see that they are in accordance therewith.

Truth and Fairness of Financial Statements
An effective checking of the results as shown by the profit and loss account to see that the results shown are true and fair.

Statutory Requirements
A concrete confirmation about the fulfillment of the statutory requirements and legal formalities in recording the financial transactions and in preparing the financial statements.

Appropriate Reporting

An appropriate reporting to the concerned persons to explain whether the statements of accounts examined do reveal a true and fair view of the state of affairs and of the profit and loss of the organisation.

1.15 ADVANTAGES OF AUDITING

The tasks of an auditor are of great importance to all concerned. The auditor must prepare his audit report impartially and effectively based on facts and actual figures. If this is done, the following advantages can be expected from auditing, in its real sense:

FROM LEGAL POINT OF VIEW

Filing of Income Tax Return

Income tax authorities generally accept the profit and loss account that has been prepared by a qualified auditor and they do not go into details of the accounts.

Borrowing of Money from External Sources

Money can be borrowed easily on the basis of audited balance sheet from external sources. Most of the financial institutions sanction loan on the basis of audited financial statements.

Settlement of Insurance Claim

In case of fire, flood and the like unexpected happenings, the insurance company may settle the claim for loss or damages on the basis of audited accounts of the previous year.

Sales Tax Payments

The audited books of accounts may generally be accepted by the sales tax authorities.

Action Against Bankruptcy

The audited accounts serve as a basis to determine action in bankruptcy and insolvency cases.

FROM INTERNAL CONTROL POINT OF VIEW

Quick Discovery of Errors and Frauds

Errors and frauds are located at an early date and in future no attempt is made to commit such frauds as one is rather careful not to commit an error or a fraud as the accounts are subject to regular audit.

Moral Check on the Employees

The auditing of accounts keeps the accounts clerks regular and vigilant as they know that the auditor would complain against them if the accounts are not prepared up to date or if there is any irregularity.

Advice to the Management

The management may consult the auditor and seek the advice on certain technical points although it is not the duty of the auditor to give advice.

Uniformity in Accounts

If the accounts have been prepared on a uniform basis, accounts of one year can be compared with other years and if there is any discrepancy, the cause may be enquired into.

FROM EXTERNAL AFFAIRS POINT OF VIEW

Settlement of Accounts
The audited accounts would facilitate the settlement of accounts of a deceased partner.

Valuation of Assets and Goodwill
If the business is to be sold as a going concern, there may not be much difficulty regarding the valuation of assets and goodwill as the accounts have already been audited by an independent person.

Future Trend of the Business
The future trend of the business can be assessed with certainty from the audited books of accounts.

1.16 LIMITATIONS OF AUDITING

Truly speaking, an audit should have no limitations of its own. It is designed to protect the interest of all parties who are interested in the affairs of the business. If there be any shortcoming arising therefrom, it may be due to its narrow scope of application in its related field of operation and un-extended definition of the concept.

The audit suffers from the following shortcomings:

Want of Complete Picture
The audit may not give complete picture. If the accounts are prepared with the intention to defraud others, auditor may not be able to detect them.

Problems of Dependence
Sometimes the auditor has to depend on explanations, clarification and information from staff and the client. He may or may not get correct or complete information.

Post-mortem Examination
Auditing is a post-mortem examination. There is no use of such examination when events have already been occurred.

Existence of Error in the Audited Accounts
It is not possible for the auditor in all cases, to check each and every transactions of an organisation. As a result, there may be error in the audited accounts even after the checking by the auditor.

Lack of Expertise
Auditor has to seek opinion of experts on certain matters on which he may not have experts' knowledge. The auditor has to depend upon such reports which may not be always correct.

Diversified Situations
Auditing is considered to be a mechanical work. Auditors may not be in a position to frame audit programme, which can be followed in all situations.

Quality of the Auditor
Success of audit depends on the sincerity with which the auditor has performed his duties. The same audit work can be done by two different auditors with difference in sincerity.

Existence of Defective Policies
The auditor can only report on the truth and fairness of the financial statements. But other defects, i.e., defects relating to management and control may not be possible to be covered by the auditor.

1.17 RELATIONSHIP BETWEEN AUDITING WITH OTHER SUBJECTS

Auditing is a multi-dimensional subject. The subject has its origin from accounting and take the assistance of different other subjects to enrich the content of it. In order to develop different techniques in the conduct of audit, it has adopted the sampling techniques of statistics in the one hand; the behavioural scientific approach has also to be understood by the auditors to deal with the employees and management of the organisation in which the auditors are conducting audit on the other. Various subjects which are interrelated with the subject of auditing and extend assistance in developing the auditing subject over a period of time are the following:

Auditing and Accounting

The basic function of accounting is to record the economic events that have the effect in changing the financial position of an organisation and to prepare the financial statements at the end of a particular accounting period. On the other hand, auditors are appointed in the organisation to check the authenticity and reliability of the books of accounts maintained by the organisation and the relevant documents preserved to support the transactions. After proper checking, the auditor is supposed to submit a report to the owners of the organisation to state whether the books of accounts give a true and fair view of the state of the affairs of the organisation as disclosed in the financial statements.

In the light of the above two functions of accounting and auditing, it can be said that auditing is a technique of accounting control. The accountants know that if there is any irregularity in maintaining the books of accounts, the auditor will report against that irregularity.

Auditing and Statistics and Mathematics

The application of statistical and mathematical tool in conducting audit is very important from the point of view of auditor's effectiveness in discharging his duties. Due to paucity of time, it is not possible for the auditor to conduct in depth checking of different transactions in an organisation. Test checking is the only way out and the technique of test checking is basically based on one of the statistical tool, i.e., sampling. Different other mathematical and statistical techniques are adopted in conducting audit in the areas of vouching, verification and routine checking to make the audit procedures effective.

Auditing and Behavioural Science

The auditor should know the organisation as well as the employees and staff working in it to discharge his functions properly. The auditor is required to interact with the employees of the organisation at the time of conducting audit in order to know the fact, to read in between the lines entered in the books of accounts and also required to get clarifications about certain matters in the process of his auditing work. The behavioural aspects of the auditor with the employees and staff members are very important in this context. Most of the employees of the organisation take the auditors as the 'fault-finders' and not as facilitators. How to get the required information from the organisation by interacting with the employees and staff members of the organisation is the subject matter of the behavioural science and the auditor should develop the required skills of behavioural science to discharge his duties efficiently.

Auditing and Law

The discipline of regulatory framework is very closely linked with the work of auditing. In conducting audit, particularly in case of statutory audit, the auditor is supposed to ensure the organisation that all the legal formalities which are required to be complied by the organisation has been complied with. In order to give this assurance, the auditor is supposed to know all the legal aspects governing the maintenance of accounts as well as the functioning of the organisation. In case of company audit, the maintenance of accounts and the functions of the auditors are governed by the Companies Act and the auditor is required to ensure that all the provisions as contained in the Companies Act are duly adhered to in maintaining the books of accounts as well as in conducting the audit of the company form of organisation. The knowledge of taxation laws is also very important for the auditor in discharging his duties effectively. Different other regulatory framework including Contract Act, Negotiable Instrument Act, Banking regulations Act etc. are also to be known by the auditors for discharge of effective audit for the organisation.

Auditing and Economics

The auditor is required to be familiar with the present economic condition of the country as well of the industry in which the organization belongs to perform his functions in a better way. In accounting, only those transactions are recorded in the books of accounts, which have any economic impact on the organisation. To assess the economic impact of any event, it is necessary for the auditor to understand the theories of economics to a certain extent and if he can understand the economic logic behind a transaction he will be able to conduct the audit of that transaction more accurately. As the auditor is concerned with the accumulation and presentation of data relating to economic activity, he is expected to be familiar with the overall economic environment in which the organisation is operating.

Auditing and Management

Auditing is also closely connected with different field of management, particularly the financial management and the production or operational management of the organization. In most of the organisations, financial services play an important role and dominate most of the activities of the organisations. The decisions taken and implemented by the organizations are governed by the financial implications of the actions. Besides, the auditor is expected to have a fair idea about various financial techniques as well as different components of financial markets to improve the quality of his audit work. Again, if the operational process part of the organisation is not known to the auditor, it will be difficult for him to track the flow of activities within the organisation and ultimately he will not be able to perform his auditing functions with confidence.

Auditing and Computer Application

There is a tremendous switch over from manual accounting to computerized accounting by the organisation in the last few years. The auditors are required to conduct audit in computer information system environment. Different advanced accounting software are used by the organisations for recording the economic activities of the organisations. In order to cope up with the changes in the auditing environment, the auditors are now supposed to know the computer application to a comfortable level. The auditors are also in a position to adopt different computer aided audit techniques in the present days to conduct the audit in less time as well as in a systematic manner. Hence, the relationship between auditing and computer application is very close.

In addition to the subjects mentioned above, auditing is also directly or indirectly related to a number of subjects. As the area of auditing has extended to a large extent, the subjects which are becoming important for the auditor are also increasing day by day. For example, environmental audit is a serious concern in the present day context. In order to conduct environmental audit efficiently, the auditor is supposed to know the content and concern of environmental science.

1.18 QUALITIES OF AN AUDITOR

Only a chartered accountant can be appointed as auditor of a limited company. Besides the statutory requirement about the qualification of an auditor, he must possess the following qualities:

i.   An auditor must possess the necessary technical ability and knowledge to audit accounts.

ii. He must be conversant with the relevant provisions of the companies and other regulations and with both best current accounting practices and current auditing practices.

iii. He must be objective both in formulating his opinions and in expressing them without bias.

iv. He must have integrity. Once he has formed his opinion, he must be prepared to express it clearly without fear and favour.

v. He must be methodical in his work. An auditor who leaves loose ends will find himself open to allegations of negligence.

vi. He should have an inquiring mind. An auditor must recognise suspicious circumstances, and once his suspicion has been aroused, he has a duty to probe matters to the bottom.

vii. He also needs to be tactful and practical in his dealings with his clients.

viii. An auditor must be independent and must be careful not to compromise his independence. .

1.19 AUDITING AND OTHER SERVICES

Auditing firms do not describe themselves as auditors. They describe themselves as Chartered Accountants or in some cases just as accountants. Auditing firms are composed of accountants who perform audit for their clients. They also perform other services. The small firms especially may spend more time on other services than on auditing.

The other services may include:

i. writing up books

ii. balancing books

iii. preparing final accounts

iv. tax negotiations

v. government form filling

vi. management and system advice

vii. financial advice

viii. liquidation and receivership work

ix. investigations

x. risk management

xi. corporate governance.

CASE STUDY 1

Arun, Badal and Chavan are partners in a firm of constructions business. Since commencing in business in 15 months ago they have been fairly successful. Arun who has a Diploma in Business Management as well as in building constructions has kept the books and Arun has also prepared the first year's accounts.

Three partners are discussing these accounts, which show a profit in excess of drawings. Badal and Chavan suggest that they could draw out the excess but Arun counsels caution, talking about working capital needs, which confuses the others.

Chavan questions Arun on his interpretation of the partnership agreement, which is a fairly complicated document and suggests that they should pay to have the accounts audited. Arun becomes heated and says that would be a waste of money and he is perfectly capable of maintaining the accounts and makes no charge to his partners for his work.

Discussion

a. What benefits would the partners get from employing an independent auditor?

b. Where would they find a suitable auditor?

◆ Suggested questions

A   Short-type questions

1. Offer your comment on the following statements—

   (a) Auditing may be defined as an 'Accounting Control'.

   (b) Fraud does not necessarily involve misappropriation of cash or goods.

   (c) Auditing is a dynamic social science.

   (d) Accounting is a necessity to business organisation but auditing is a luxury.

   (e) Accountancy begins where book keeping ends and where the work of an accountant ends, the work of an auditor begins.

   (f) An auditor is not an insurer.

   (g) The relationship of auditing to accounting is close, yet their natures are different. They are business associates, not parent and child.

   (h) Auditing has its principal roots not in accounting which it reviews, but in logic on which it leans heavily for ideas and methods.

   (i) Auditing does not mean ticking or checking totals.

   (j) Auditing is a dynamic social science.

2. Define and explain the term 'Auditing'.

3. What are the principles of Auditing'?

4. Discuss the objectives of Auditing.

5. What is the difference between Audit and Accountancy?

6. Define and explain the terms 'Fraud' and 'Error'.

B.   Essay-type questions

1. Define 'Auditing'. Discuss the scope and procedure of Audit.

2. What are special and general qualifications that an auditor should possess and why?

3. "Detection and prevention of errors and frauds are the main objectives of auditing'— discuss it fully and explain the duties of auditor in this regard.

4. Discuss the advantages of audit (a) to the management (b) to the Government (c) to the shareholders and (d) to the society.

5. Discuss the different aspects of social object of Audit.

6. Discuss various classes of error and state in each case the effect they might have on the trial balance being discovered.

7. "It is nothing to the auditor whether the business is run prudently or imprudently, profitable or unprofitably".—Do you agree? Give reasons for your answer.

8. Why are auditors generally required to express an opinion on the truth and fairness of the accounts and why they are not required to certify the accounts?

9. "Audit of the accounts of the sole-proprietor is not compulsory. However, he may get his books of accounts audited for various reasons".—Discuss.

10. Write a brief outline of the development of audit profession in India.

Chapter 2

Types of Audit

2.1 INTRODUCTION

Auditing is a multi-dimensional and comprehensive subject. An effective insight into the nature of auditing can be obtained by understanding the various types of audit, which, together, constitute the auditing discipline. Auditing can be classified from various viewpoints. In this chapter, the detailed classification of audit will be discussed.

2.2 CLASSIFICATION OF AUDIT

An audit can be classified under different groups on the basis of different categories.

2.2.1 CLASSIFICATION OF AUDIT ON THE BASIS OF ORGANISATION

Audit is not legally obligatory for all types of business organisation. On the basis of organisational structure, audits may be of two broad categories.

Audit Required Under Law

This type of audit is also known as statutory audit. The organisations, which require audit under law, are the following:

Company Audit

Audit of accounts of companies, registered under the Companies Act, is compulsory. As the control of the company is vested with the directors of the company, the need for the protection of the interest of the shareholders arises. The introduction of Companies Act, 1956, which outlines the procedure of audit work, the different books of accounts to be maintained, rights, duties and liabilities of the auditor was definitely a right step towards the protection of shareholders' interest over the company.

Bank Audit

Audit of banking companies is made compulsory under the statute, since it is governed by the Banking Companies Regulation Act, 1949. The objective of bank audit is not only to check the financial result and financial position, so far as its truth and fairness are concerned, but also to review whether the banks engage only in the businesses prescribed in the Act and whether they follow the regulations to operate the banking business as per the regulations given in the Act.

Electricity Company Audit

The electricity companies are governed by the Electricity Supply Act, 1948. The books of accounts that are to be maintained by the electricity companies are given in the provisions of the said Act. The auditor will examine the details of the books of accounts and check the reliability of the internal check system of these companies. The prescribed forms for the presentation of accounts should be used as per the requirements of the Act.

Co-operative Society Audit

Audit of co-operative societies is conducted by the Co-operative Department of the State Government or by the Registrar of Co-operative Societies, as the case may be. The co-operative societies are governed by the Co-operative Societies Act, 1912, which gives the detailed procedures of audit for a co-operative society. These types of societies engage in a good number of financial transactions. So, these types of organisations have the statutory obligation to introduce audit for their better performance.

Audit of Trusts

The income of the properties of the trust is distributed by the trustees among the beneficiaries as per Trust Deed. As the beneficiaries of the trust, in most of the cases, do not know the techniques of reading the books of accounts, the chances of being defrauded by the trustees cannot be avoided. So, this type of audit protects the beneficiaries of the trusted properties against the possible financial misdeeds by unscrupulous trustees.

Insurance Audit

The Insurance Companies that are governed by Insurance Act, 1938, includes fire, marine and other miscellaneous insurance businesses. The books of accounts that are to be maintained by the insurance companies are governed by the provisions of the said Act. The auditor will examine the details of the books of accounts and check the reliability of the internal check system. The audit of insurance companies, in fact, enhances the confidence of the policyholders.

Specified Entities as per Income Tax Act

According to the various provisions of the Income Tax Act, certain entities are required to perform audit of their accounts to fulfil the requirement of the Income Tax regulations. These entities are required to appoint a qualified auditor to conduct audit of their financial statements in order to get exemptions and deduction from income of the entity.

Audit of Government Departments and Government Public Utilities

Different government departments and public utilities are also subject to independent financial audit. The requirement for such audit is contained in the Constitution of India. In addition to this requirement, government departments and public utilities also have an internal audit system of their own.

Audit of Registered Clubs, Societies etc.

Though it is not compulsory in all cases, the audit of societies, clubs etc., which are registered under the Societies Registration Act, 1960, conduct audit of their activities to continue registration. In addition to that, different government grants and loans are given to these societies, clubs etc. on the basis of their application along with the audited Income and Expenditure Account and the Balance Sheet. It is the responsibility of the secretary of the society or the club to submit the audited financial statements to the members in the annual meeting of the society or club.

Audit of Other Organisations Not Covered by Any Law

There is no basic legal requirement of audit in respect of certain organisations. These organisations may require audit as a matter of internal rules. Some may be required to get their accounts audited on the directives of government for various purposes like sanction of loan, grants etc. These organisations include the following:

Audit of Sole Proprietorship Firms

The sole proprietorship firms are not required to have their accounts audited under any specific statute. But the sole proprietary businesses, in which the number of transactions are large and huge amount is involved in the business, get their accounts audited. The proprietor himself takes decision about the scope of audit and the appointment of auditor. In fact, under this type of audit, the auditing work will depend upon the agreement of audit and the specific instructions given by the proprietor.

Audit of a Partnership Firm

There is no legal compulsion to get partnership accounts audited. But in partnership, there are possibilities of mistrust and dissatisfactions among the partners. As such, an independent external auditors' view regarding the correctness of accounts is desirable in this type of an organisation. Usually, the partnership deed includes the provision of audit of their accounts. In conducting partnership business audit, the auditor has to refer to the partnership deed. But in absence of partnership deed or any aspect, which is not included in the deed, the auditor may refer to the Partnership Act, 1932.

Hindu Undivided Family Business Audit

In respect of accounts of businesses of Hindu Undivided Family, there is no basic legal requirement of audit. But the important motive for getting the accounts of this type of family business to be audited lies in the inherent advantages that follow from an independent professional audit. If there will be any dispute or mistrust among the members of the Hindu Undivided Family regarding accounts, it can be settled through the audited accounts.

Audit of Association of Persons

Though it is not legally required to get their accounts audited, the association of persons, for example the Bengal Chamber of Commerce, is interested to appoint qualified auditors and get their accounts audited for different reasons. In case of availing exemptions of their income from income tax liability, they are required to submit their audited accounts to the Income Tax Authority. In conducting this type of audit, the auditor has to refer the constitution of the association.

Audit of Non-Profit Seeking Organisations

Certain non-profit seeking organisations, such as colleges, libraries, hospitals, clubs and charitable institutions, get their accounts audited. The basic purpose of audit of this type of organisation is to locate error or fraud committed by the staff members. The governing body of this type of organisation usually appoints the auditor. This type of organisation usually depends on government grants and other aids from different bodies. Audited accounts are helpful in getting this type of grants and aids.

2.2.2 CLASSIFICATION ON THE BASIS OF FUNCTION

The function of auditors depends on their role, i.e., in which capacity the auditor is conducting the audit work. So, on the basis of function, auditing can be of the following types:

External Audit

External audit is conducted by an independent external auditor. This type of audit is usually conducted to fulfil the requirement of the provisions of law. The qualified chartered accountants who are not connected with the preparation of accounts or management of the organisation can be appointed as external auditor.

The auditor who conducts such an audit is 'independent' of the enterprise under audit, i.e., he is an independent professional who does not have any such relationship with the enterprise as might adversely affect his ability to form an objective judgment about the financial statements. The various matters relating to the procedures of audit, rights, duties and liabilities of the auditor, their appointment procedures and presentation of reports are provided in the concerned statute.

Features of External Audit

i.   External audit is usually conducted by an independent qualified auditor.

ii. In the normal course, this type of audit is conducted periodically.

iii. The purpose of external audit is to see whether financial statements give a true and fair view of financial position and result of the concern.

iv. The external auditor can work independently and enjoys better status.

v.   The Indian Companies Act, 1956 and other statutes provide the area of responsibilities and functions of the external auditors.

vi. In cases, where external audit is being conducted due to legal compulsion, the auditor must have a professional qualification.

vii. This type of audit is conducted mainly for safeguarding the interest of owners, shareholders and other parties who do not have knowledge of day-to-day operation of the organisations.

viii. The Act always provides for the norms regarding the appointment of auditor. The auditor must not be disqualified as per the provision of the law.

Independent financial audit is undoubtedly the most common type of audit. It is generally conducted to ascertain whether the balance sheet and profit and loss account give a true and fair view of the financial position and financial performance respectively of the enterprise under audit.

Internal Audit

Internal audit is conducted by specially assigned staff within the organisation. It is an audit through which a thorough examination of the accounting transactions as well as the system according to which these transactions have been recorded is conducted. The internal audit is undertaken to verify the accuracy and authenticity of the financial accounting and statistical records presented to the management. As per Standards on Auditing-610 (SA-610), the scope and objectives of internal audit vary widely and are dependent upon the size and structure of the entity and the requirements of its management.

Features of Internal Audit

i.   The internal audit system is considered to be a part of the management control system and not merely as an assistant thereto.

ii. The scope of internal audit depends on the requirement of the management.

iii. The nature and extent of checking also depends on the size and type of the business organisation.

iv. It embraces not only the operational audit of various operational activities in the organisation but also includes the audit of management itself.

v.   The function of internal audit can be considered as an integral part of the internal control system.

vi. Internal audit is continuous in nature. The work of internal auditor starts after the transactions are completed.

vii. Generally the internal audit is conducted by the permanent staff of the organisation. Sometimes outside agencies may be asked to conduct internal audit.

viii. The existence of internal audit is a help to the external auditor.

The difference between independent financial audit and internal audit can be outlined in the following ways:

POINTS OF DIFFERENCE	INDEPENDENT FINANCIAL AUDIT [EXTERNAL AUDIT]	INTERNAL AUDIT
1. Nature	It is conducted for reporting on the reliability and fairness of the financial statements.	It is conducted with a view to checking adherence to norms and established procedures and protecting the assets of the organisation.
2. Qualifications	The external audior must possess specific qualification as prescribed by the respective statute.	No specific qualification is required to be possessed by the internal auditor.
3. Scope of work	This type of audit must be complete in all respects. Its scope cannot be curtailed in any way by the management.	The scope of work of the internal audit is determined by the management.
4. Purpose	The objective of this type of audit is to protect the interests of the owners and other parties related to the enterprise.	The basic objective of internal audit is to improve performance, efficiency and profitability of the enterprise.
5. Appointment of Auditor	The external auditors are usually appointed by the owners and in some cases by the government.	The internal auditor is appointed by the management.
6. Status	The auditor is an outsider and independent person. He is not bound by any rules and regulations of the organisation.	The internal auditor is an employee of the organisation. He is bound by the rules and regulations of the organisation.
7. Continuity	The external audit may be periodical or continuous in nature.	The internal audit is continuous in nature. It is carried out throughout the year.
8. Advice or recommendation	Giving advice or recommendation is not part of external auditor's duty. He will only report on the financial statement as prepared by the management.	The internal auditor may give advice to the management for taking some corrective measures against irregularities in the organisation's accounts.

2.2.3 CLASSIFICATION ON THE BASIS OF PRACTICAL APPROACH

On the basis of requirements of audit, the approach to auditing may differ. So, on the basis of practical approach for conducting the audit work, the audit can be classified under the following types:

Continuous Audit

A continuous audit or a detailed audit involves a detailed examination of the books of accounts at regular intervals, of say, one month or three months. The auditor visits his clients at regular or irregular intervals of time during the financial year and checks each and every transaction. At the end of the year, he checks the profit and loss account and the balance sheet.

According to R. C. Williams, "A continuous audit is one where the auditor or his staff is constantly engaged in checking the accounts during the whole period or where the auditor or his staff attends at regular or irregular intervals during the period."

Applicability

Continuous audit is applicable to the following circumstances:

  i.   Where it is desired to present the accounts just after the close of the financial year.

 ii.   Where the volume of transactions is very large.

iii.   Where periodical statements are required to be presented to the management.

Advantages

1. Easy and Quick Discovery of Errors

As the auditor starts checking just after the completion of the transaction, it becomes easier for the auditor to detect fraud and errors quickly.

2. Moral Check on the Client's Staff'

As the auditor visits frequently and checks the accounts at regular or irregular intervals, it also acts as a moral check on the employees of the organisation.

3. Preparation of Interim Accounts

Under continuous audit system, interim accounts can be prepared without much delay in time. It will help the board of directors to declare interim dividend.

4. Up-to-date Accounts:

Due to continuous pressure from the auditors, the efficiency of accounts department's staff will increase and their work will be up-to-date and accurate.

5. More Knowledge of Technical Details

Continuous audit will help auditor to understand the technicalities of the business. This will help the auditor to make valuable suggestions for the improvement of the business.

6. Audit Staff Can Be Kept Busy Throughout the Year

The auditor can make his audit plan in a systematic manner. He can evenly spread his work to the audit staff throughout the year. It will help the auditor to keep his staff busy throughout the year.

7. Quick Presentation of Accounts

Audited accounts can be presented just after the end of the financial year as the auditor has already completed most of his routine audit work.

8. Efficient Audit Due to More Time

Since the audit is carried out throughout the year, sufficient time is available for detailed checking. It will result efficient audit.

Disadvantages

1. Expensive System of Audit

As the auditing work is required to be carried out throughout the year, it becomes an expensive system. Small organisations cannot afford to adopt this expensive system of audit.

2. Alteration of Figures Already Checked

After the accounts have been checked, the staff of the client may fraudulently alter the figures.

3. Dislocation of Client's Work

Frequent visits by the auditor for checking the books of accounts and related documents may prove to be a hindrance to the work flow of the organisation.

4. Queries May Remain Outstanding

As the work is not completed at a time, the auditor may lose continuity and certain questions and inquiries may remain unanswered.

5. Unhealthy Relationship

Frequent visit and disturbance in the daily work may provide scope for unhealthy relationship between the audit staff and the client staff.

6. Reviewing of Work Already Done

Before starting the audit work, a review of findings of previous audit work should be made to establish link with the past work done.

Ways and Means of Removing the Drawbacks of Continuous Audit

In a large enterprise, continuous audit is a must for proper and timely completion of audit. So some special measures have to be taken for avoiding the limitations of continuous audit as far as practicable. The following measures can be taken to overcome the shortcomings of continuous audit:

1. Use of Audit Note Book

The auditor must record in his notebook the work completed by him and his assistants from time to time, material errors detected and rectified, queries raised by him and his staff and explanations given by the client. Before starting the work each time, the auditor should refer to the notebook and books of accounts to know the extent of work completed up to last visit or whether any query remains unanswered or whether any alteration has been made.

2. Use of Special Ticks in Checking

The auditor may use a different tick for checking the figures altered before audit. Such variation in tick mark should be slight and unnoticeable. This will enable the auditor to identify whether any unauthorised alteration has been made subsequent to audit.

3. No Change in Audit Staff

The duties of audit staff should not be changed in order to maintain the flow of work undisturbed and to ensure follow-up of unresolved points. However, to avoid monotony in work, the nature of duty of the audit staff may be changed after completion of annual audit.

4. No Change in Audited Figures

Clear instruction must be given to the client for not changing any audited figure. If any extraordinary situation requires such a change, it should be done with prior intimation to the auditor and with the help of rectification entry only.

5. Casting in Ink

The casting of periodical total of the various books of accounts should be written in ink as and when they are checked.

6. Incomplete Work

Checking of each part of work, whenever undertaken, should be completed in one visit and should not be left incomplete to be completed during the next visit.

7. Sound Audit Programme

There should be well-framed audit programme indicating the extent of work to be completed, allocation of work and time schedule of various works. This will make the continuous audit very effective.

Periodical or Final or Complete Audit

Periodical audit is taken up at the close of the financial period, when all the accounts have been balanced and final accounts have already been prepared. It may also commence before the final accounts are prepared and continue till the audit is completed even after the close of financial period.

According to Spicer and Pegler, "A final or complete audit is commonly understood to be an audit which is not commenced until after the end of the financial period and is then carried on until completed."

In case of this type of audit, the auditor visits his client only once a year and checks the accounts until the audit work for the whole of the period is completed.

Applicability

   i.   Where the volume of transactions of the organisation is small.

   ii.   Where there is no urgency to present the audited accounts within a certain period of time.

   iii.   Where internal control system is very effective.

   iv.   Where interim statements of accounts are not required by the management for review or for some other purposes.

Advantages

1. Inexpensive

It is a less expensive system as compared to continuous audit system. Hence, the method of auditing is suitable for small business organisations.

2. Quick Completion of Audit

Periodical audit can be finished quickly within reasonable time.

3. Minimum Chances of Alteration

There is minimum chance of alteration of figures after they have been checked as the auditor completes his work on a continuous basis.

4. Less Disturbance in Client's Work

Client's daily office work is not unnecessarily disturbed because auditors visit only once a year.

5. Preparation of Audit Schedule

The auditor will not face any problem in preparing his audit schedule.

6. Requirement of Small Establishment

The auditor is not required to maintain a big establishment for this purpose.

Disadvantages

1. Delay in Presentation of Accounts

This type of audit can be satisfactorily applied in case of small organisations. But in case of large organisations, it takes more time to complete the audit work and hence presentation of accounts to the shareholders is delayed.

2. Preparation of Interim Accounts

Under periodical auditing system, it is not possible to prepare interim accounts. As a result, no interim dividend can be paid without the availability of audited interim accounts.

3. Possibility of Undetected Errors and Frauds

The auditor may not be able to check and verify all the transactions. As such, there is every chance that some of the errors and frauds may remain undetected.

4. Fixation of Audit Programme

If the auditor has several clients, whose financial year ends on the same date, it may be difficult for the auditor to complete the work of all the clients within the scheduled time.

Distinction between continuous audit and periodical audit

POINTS OF DIFFERENCES	CONTINUOUS AUDIT	PERIODICAL AUDIT
1. Publication of annual report	It ensures early publication of annual report.	Publication of annual report may be delayed.
2. Period of audit work	Audit is carried out throughout the year.	Audit is carried out only once at the close of the accounting period.
3. Work coverage	Detailed checking of the books of accounts is possible because of the existence of sufficient time at the disposal of the auditor.	Detailed checking is usually not possible. In most of the cases, the checking of the books of accounts is limited to test checking.
4. Alteration of figures	Alteration of audited figures is possible due to the long gap between the two consecutive visits of the auditor to his client.	Alteration of figures is not possible as there is no break in the process of auditing work.
5. Cost involvement	It is very expensive to operate this system.	It is economical.
6. Applicability	It is applicable to a large business organisation.	It is applicable to a small business organisation.
7. Audit process	The audit staff visits and checks the accounts frequently.	The audit staff visits the client's business only once in a year after the accounts are closed.
8. Detection of errors and frauds	It is very effective for early detection of errors and fraud.	Errors and frauds are left in the books till audit is conducted at the close of the year.

Interim Audit

Interim audit is conducted in between two annual audits with a view to find out the interim profit of the business to enable the organisation to declare an interim dividend to its shareholders. It is a kind of audit which is conducted between two periodical audits or balance sheet audits.

Advantages

i.   This type of audit is helpful to organisations for which publication of interim accounts is required.

ii. The final audit can be completed within the scheduled time, if interim audit has already been conducted by the organisation.

iii. Errors and frauds can be more quickly detected during the course of the interim audit.

iv. There is a moral check on the staff of the client as the accounts are checked after three or six months.

Disadvantages

i.   Figures may be altered in the accounts, which have already been audited.

ii. It will mean that the audit staff will have to prepare notes, when they finish the audit work.

iii. This audit implies additional work.

iv. In case of an interim audit, the interim trial balance has to be prepared and for this purpose, balancing of all existing accounts is required to be made at the middle of the year.

Partial Audit

In a partial audit, the work of the auditor is curtailed. The auditor is asked to check a few books, e.g., he may be asked to check the payment side of the cash book.

Partial audit is not permitted in case of limited companies (private or public) because according to the Companies Act, the duties of an auditor of a company cannot be curtailed. Again, in case of a very big proprietary firms, it may not be possible for the proprietor himself to disburse all payments and if he suspects misappropriation of cash, he may appoint an audit or to check only the cash book.

When an auditor is appointed to conduct partial audit, he must make it clear in his report that he has performed partial audit as per the instructions of the client.

Advantages

i.   It serves the specific interest of the client.

ii. There is much scope to render quick service, as the auditor has to deal with only one or two aspects of business transactions.

iii. Critical analysis of the books of account relating to a particular item or group of items is made possible.

iv. It may act as a moral check on the part of persons who intend to falsify accounts.

Disadvantages

i.   The conduct of this type of audit is strictly restricted under the Companies Act.

ii. The audit report does not reflect the financial position of the business as a whole.

iii. It cannot be widely used.

iv. This type of audit is conducted only for a particular purpose.

Occasional Audit

As the name indicates, this type of audit is conducted once a while, whenever the need arises and the client desires it to be carried out. This is possible only in case of proprietary concerns but in case of joint stock companies, banking and insurance companies, the audit has to be carried out once or twice a year according to the provisions of the Companies Act.

Advantages
i. The client can know its actual financial position on the date, when the books of accounts are audited.
ii. It brings some sort of satisfaction in the mind of the client that the audited accounts are accepted by all.
iii. Impartial view can be expressed through the procedure of audit.
iv. It can be profitably used in small concerns.

Disadvantages
i. The conduct of this audit brings some confusion about the authenticity of final audit in a big organisation.
ii. It is expensive.
iii. The auditor faces a lot of problems in conducting his audit work, as the client's staff is not habituated with the procedures of auditing.
iv. The books of accounts may not be available according to the requirement of audit procedures.

Standard Audit
Standard audit can be defined as a "complete check and analysis of certain items and contingent upon effective internal check, appropriate test checks on remaining items, the whole of work being in accordance with general auditing standards." From the above definition, it is clear that under this type of audit, certain items in the accounts are thoroughly checked and analysed and appropriate test checks are applied to other items, provided there is a good and effective internal check in operation.

Advantages
i. Development of new auditing standards in view of changing socio-economic condition can be made possible through scrutiny of auditing standards so far established.
ii. It controls the nature and extent of documents and evidences that are obtained through the procedure of an audit.
iii. It influences the audit programme.
iv. The destructive criticism often made by the general public that the management in collusion with auditor distorts the financial statements may be addressed through the application of standard audit procedures.

Disadvantages
i. It is very difficult to bring all organisations under the same accounting practices for the uniform application of standard audit.
ii. The application of a particular standard procedure to different organisations having different standards may invite chaos instead of development.
iii. Standards are always subject to change of circumstances, nature and environment of business.
iv. Finally, setting up standard narrows the development of standard.

Balance Sheet Audit
Balance sheet audit means limited audit in which all the balance sheet accounts are verified and tests imposed only on those profit and loss items that are directly related to the assets and liabilities such as repairs and maintenance, provision for depreciation, bad debts, etc. Accounts such as these are analysed, but otherwise

no detailed audit is conducted. In this type of audit, the audit is commenced from the balance sheet and then working back to the books of original entry and the related documents, etc.

This type of audit is more popular in United States than in England and other European countries. But this type of audit will be more widely used.

Advantages

i. It records the changing events of the period. The change in working capital can be reflected through balance sheet audit.

ii. This type of audit furnishes different information relating to over-capitalisation, under-capitalisation, over-trading and under-trading of the business.

iii. It establishes proper relationship between assets and liabilities of the business.

iv. It guides different parties interested in the affairs of the business in taking business decisions.

Disadvantages

i. It lacks in disclosing certain material information needed to evaluate different measuring bases.

ii. Balance sheet reflects the financial position of the business only at a give point of time. Events occurring after balance sheet date may affect materially the process of decision.

iii. Comparison between the two periods may be drawn, but the causes for the change of figures between the two periods are not stated.

iv. The information regarding the generation of profit or loss of the business is not stated in the balance sheet. This is required to make the balance sheet more informative and balance sheet audit more dynamic.

2.2.4   CLASSIFICATION ON THE BASIS OF AUDIT DIMENSION

The scope of an audit varies widely and depends on the purpose of an audit, the dimension of auditing work and the conditions of the audit requirement. On the basis of this dimensional aspect, auditing can be classified under the following types:

Management Audit

Management audit is a comprehensive critical review of all aspects of the management process. In fact, it is a tool of management control. It covers all areas of management like planning, organising, co-ordination and control. It assists at all levels of the management in the effective discharge of managerial functions.

A management audit is forward-looking, independent and systematic evaluation of the activities of the management at all levels for the improvement of the organisational profitability and attainment of other objectives of the organisation through improvements in the performance of the management function. In short, management audit is a guide, which helps in improving the efficiency of the management.

Cost Audit

Cost audit is an effective means of control in the hands of the management to have an idea about the working of the costing department of the organisation and to suggest ways and means for its smooth running. It is the detailed checking as well as the verification of the correctness of the costing techniques, systems and cost accounts.

Cost audit first time was introduced in India in the year 1965 with the introduction of clause (d) to Section 209 and 233B of Section 233 of the Companies Act. The need for such provision in the Act arose as the maintenance and proper use of scientific cost records is essential for companies that are engaged in the manufacturing and related activities.

Tax Audit

Tax audit refers to audit of incomes or expenses or specific claims of deductions or exemptions for the purpose of assessment of income tax. Tax audit is required in addition to financial audit, which does not fulfil the specific requirement of the tax authority.

Since the assessment year 1985–86, certain provisions under Section 44AB of the Income Tax Act was introduced for compulsory tax audit of accounts of certain persons. These persons shall get their accounts of the previous year audited by an accountant before the 'specific date' and obtain before that date the report of such audit in the prescribed form duly signed and verified by a qualified accountant.

Human Resource Audit

One of the defects of financial accounting is its failure to show the human resources in the balance sheet. However, it is a fact that external users may wish to know the degree of employees' morale, customer's satisfaction, product quality and the reputation of a business entity. So, disclosure of information regarding human resources in the annual report of the company may help a lot to the investors in framing an opinion whether to invest or not.

The auditor for the purpose of making audit of human resources, if included in the annual accounts, should carefully examine the basis of valuation of human resources. His examination should not relate to the process of valuation of the human resources but he should see that information upon which the calculations are based upon reliable and authentic methods. So, human resource audit is concerned about the human asset figure that appears in the balance sheet through checking, inspecting and appraising the various facts and figures, which are based on the estimated value of human resources.

System Audit

The purpose of the system audit is to design appropriate system of accounts suitable to the business and to obtain information, through the process of investigation, for improving the accounting method. In fact, accounting systems are required to be revised in order to ensure that it may provide the information desired by the executives as an aid to management decision.

So, system audit is concerned with that method of checking, which is directed to ascertain whether the accounting practices are up to date and economical and whether the existing practices are required to be changed so as to do the work better, quicker and at less cost under the present conditions.

Propriety Audit

Propriety audit is concerned with scrutiny of executive decisions bearing on the financial and profit and loss aspect of the organisation with special reference to public interest and commonly accepted customs and standards of conduct. While performing a propriety audit, the auditor would judge whether the standards of propriety have been maintained in making payments, incurring expenditure or entering into transactions.

Propriety audit ensures that the public money has not been utilised for the benefit of a particular person or section of a community and all transactions have been activated for the best interest of the organisation itself. Section 227 (1A) and CARO [Companies (Auditor's Report) Order], 2003 issued under Section 227(4A) of the Companies Act, 1956 also contain clauses dealing with the examination of transactions from the view point of propriety.

Performance or Efficiency Audit

The efficiency audit provides the means to appraise the performance of the enterprise and to diagnose the weakness of the enterprise. It aims to determine whether the resources of the business flow into remunerative or paying channels. It is concerned with the review of the organisational environment, measuring return on investment, cash flow performance etc. and comparing these with the standard.

The efficiency audit is based on the basic economic principles. The objectives of this type of audit are to evaluate and compare the optimum return with the amount of capital invested in the business and to ensure that investment techniques aim at giving optimum results. In short, efficiency audit is introduced to ensure the improvement of organisational efficiency.

Environmental Audit

Environmental audit is an excellent management tool for relating productivity to pollution. Environmental audit is the examination of the correctness of environmental accounts. In broader sense, environmental auditing is the examination of accounts of revenues and costs of environmental and natural resources, their estimate, depreciation and values recorded in the books of accounts.

In India, recognising the importance of environmental audit, its procedure was first notified under the Environment (Protection) Act, 1986 by the Ministry of Environment of Forests. Under this Act, every person carrying operations of an industry, operation or process requiring consent under Section 25 of the Water (Prevention & Control of Pollution) Act, 1974 or under Section 21 of the Air (Prevention & Control of Pollution) Act, 1981 or both or authorisation under the Hazardous Wastes (Management and Handling) Rule of 1989 issued under the Hazardous (Protection) Act, 1986 is required to submit an environmental audit report.

Social Audit

Business organisations are now regarded as a great social force. They are not expected to be only engaged in profit-earning activity and paying dividend to the shareholders but they have an important role to play in the social well-being. They have some responsibility to the society.

Social audit is aimed at an assessment of the performance of an entity towards the fulfilment of social obligations. The objective of social audit is to bring to light for public knowledge how far an organisation has discharged its responsibility to the society and to make an assessment of the social performance of an organisation. But audit of social accounts is not yet in practice and the term 'social audit' is still in a conceptual stage in India.

Cash Transaction Audit

Cash transaction audit is the oldest concept in auditing system. In the olden times, a person was appointed to check cash transactions only, i.e., whether the person responsible for recording cash receipts and payments on behalf of the business owner has done his job properly or not. Hence it was merely a cash audit.

So, when an audit is conducted of all items of cash book, it is known as cash audit. The auditor will check the receipt and payments made by cash with the vouchers and documents. It is useful in an organisation in which most of the transactions are made through cash. It is only a partial audit and at present the concept of auditing has a wider meaning.

Energy Audit

Energy audit is a relatively new branch of auditing. It is emerging as a consequence of heavily depleting physical energy resources in the world. The need for conservation of energy is most important parameter in the modern day world. Energy audit is aimed at determining whether right amount of energy, both organic and inorganic, is used by the enterprises and there occurs no avoidable loss or waste of energy due to human indifference. Conducting energy audit inevitably calls for technical input and an audit team with audit professionals and technical personnel is needed for the purpose.

Secretarial Audit

Secretarial audit is also a relatively new concept and is coming to be recognised with growing complexities in the corporate laws. Compliance with the provisions of various corporate laws is as important to be in the business. Any failure to comply with corporate laws may invite heavy penalty and/or even imprisonment.

It is therefore imperative for corporate entities to ensure compliance with the applicable legal requirements, which are numerous. A secretarial audit assures the corporate body that the legal requirements have been duly complied with and in time. If non-compliances are noticed by the audit, management will have time to rectify the situation with much lesser problems and costs.

◆ Suggested questions

A   Short-type questions:

1. What is management audit?
2. Distinguish between internal audit and statutory audit.
3. Write a short-note on the various classes of audits.
4. "Continuous audit is a double edged weapon"—Discuss.
5. What is interim audit? Why it is required?
6. Write short notes on:

    (a) Standard audit.

    (b) System audit.

    (c) Efficiency audit.

    (d) Social audit.

B   Essay-type questions:

1. What is statutory audit? Describe the points of differences between statutory audit and nonstatutory audit.
2. What is periodical audit? What are the advantages and disadvantages of periodical audit? Distinguish between continuous audit and periodical audit.
3. What is continuous audit? In which case is this audit applicable? State the advantages and disadvantages of continuous audit.
4. Discuss the advantages and disadvantages of balance sheet audit. Also state the auditor's position in relation to balance sheet audit.

Chapter 3

Techniques and Procedures of Auditing

3.1 INTRODUCTION

In finalising the audit programme and selecting the techniques and procedures to be applied to an audit, he must ensure that he fully understand the enterprise with which he is dealing. He must familiarise himself with its organisations and visit the locations in which they operate. He should comprehend the nature of the business and have a detailed knowledge of its products or services. He must ensure that he has fully grasped all the technicalities peculiar to the business. Only then he will be in a position fully to comprehend and identify the transactions which are being recorded in the accounting records, and in relation to which the internal controls will be operating.

The auditor should follow the appropriate audit procedure and adopt different techniques of auditing by maintaining the principles of auditing in conducting audit of an organisation in order:

i. To ascertain and record the accounting system and internal controls, assess the adequacy of the accounting system and evaluate the controls on which the auditor wishes to place reliance.

ii. To test the accounting records, and perform compliance tests on the operation of those internal controls on which the auditor wishes to place reliance.

iii. To compare the financial statements with the accounting records and perform substantive tests to see that they are in agreement.

iv. To carry out a review of the financial statements.

v. To report on the financial statements as required by the terms of auditor's appointment and in compliance with any relevant statutory obligation.

On the basis of his assessment of the accounting system and evaluation of the internal controls, the auditor will draw up an audit programme specifically designed for that particular audit.

3.2 PREPARATORY STEPS BEFORE COMMENCEMENT OF NEW AUDIT

Effective execution of any audit work requires appropriate planning and a well-designed audit programme. For effective audit planning and for designing appropriate audit programme, the auditor should prepare himself before the commencement of his audit work. For this purpose, the auditor should take the following steps:

1. Receiving Appointment Letter

The auditor is usually appointed by the shareholders in the annual general meeting and shall hold office till the conclusion of the next annual general meeting. The auditor should receive the appointment letter before starting his audit work as he has to conduct his audit work on the basis of terms of references as given in the appointment letter.

2. Communication with the Existing Auditor

Before accepting the work of a new audit, in the case of a continuing business, it is established professional etiquette for the proposed auditor to communicate with the previous auditor to see whether he has any objections to raise. This is also an official requirement as per the Institute of Chartered Accountants Act, 1949 and has to be adhered to by the practicing chartered accountants.

3. Acceptance of Appointment

If the auditor is satisfied with the reasons for not appointing the previous auditor, he can then accept the appointment. The auditor should confirm his acceptance to the concerned organisation through a letter of acceptance.

4. Ascertaining the Scope of Audit

After accepting his appointment, he should ascertain the precise nature and scope of his audit work. In case of statutory audit, the scope and the nature of audit work can be ascertained by referring to the statute. In case of other types of audit, the auditor should discuss with the client about his area of auditing work.

5. Knowledge About the Organisation

Before the auditor can determine his basic approach to an audit, he must ensure that he fully understood the enterprise. He must comprehend the nature of the business and have a detailed knowledge of its activities. He must familiarise himself with the organisation and visit the location at which it operates. This will enable him to understand the nature of transactions which are recorded in the books of accounts.

6. Knowledge of the Accounting System

The auditor should obtain a list of all books maintained by the organisation for recording its accounting transactions along with the information relating to the existing accounting system. He should also acquire full information about the internal control system of the organisation. In fact, the extent of his work is greatly influenced by the reliability of internal control system and appropriateness of accounting system adopted.

7. Complete List of Principal Officers

The auditor should also obtain a list of the principal officers of the organisation. He should also acquire knowledge about the area and extent of authority of each one of them. This will help the auditor to have appropriate clarification from the concerned officer.

8. Knowledge of Technical Details

The auditor must ensure himself that he has fully grasped all the technicalities peculiar to the business. Only then he will be in a position to identify the transactions of the accounting records and relate the accounting system with the internal control system adopted.

9. Observation of the Previous Auditor's Report

The auditor should go through the previous auditor's report as well as the final accounts of the previous year. This will help him to understand the nature of accounts, important areas for which detailed checking are required and the techniques to be used to conduct his audit work effectively.

10. Instructions to the Client

After completing the above-mentioned steps, the auditor should issue clear instructions to his client that the accounts should be finalised and kept ready for audit and the necessary schedules required to support the final accounts be prepared and made available to the auditor.

3.3 AUDIT ACTIVITIES

While making the five critical decisions in each of the five audit stages, auditors undertake a structured set of activities that correspond with the concepts of human information processing theory as they relate to decision making. In an auditing environment, these activities may be categorized as follows:

a.   Planning Activities

An auditor's planning activities correspond to hypothesis generation activities in human information processing theory and include strategic, tactical and operational planning activities. Audit planning activities include the identification of the criteria to be used in making each critical decision.

b.   Evidence Gathering Activities

An auditor's evidence gathering activities correspond to information search activities in human information processing theory. The activities include all the activities performed by auditors that have as their objective the gathering of audit evidence (e.g., analytical procedures, inspection, confirmation, vouching, recalculation, physical examination, observation, inquiry).

c.   Evidence Evaluation Activities

An auditor's evidence evaluation activities correspond to information evaluation activities in human information processing theory. Evidence evaluation activities include those activities performed by auditors that relate to (a) the estimation and evaluation of the sufficiency of quantity and appropriateness of quality of the evidence gathered, (b) the evaluation of exceptions and their implications and (c) the evaluation of audit risk components.

d.   Decision-Making Activities

An auditor's decision-making activities correspond to the activity of choice in human information processing theory. There is essentially only one decision-making activity and that is simply the activity of choosing a particular course of action. Thus, the auditor's choice is closely followed by an action of some kind.

e.   Other Activities

Other activities performed by auditors include delegation, supervision and review, which are continuous throughout the audit engagement.

3.4 AUDIT ENGAGEMENT LETTER

3.4.1 CONCEPT

The auditor and the client should agree on the terms of the engagement. In the interests of both the client and the auditor, the auditor should send an engagement letter, preferably before the commencement of the engagement, to help avoid any misunderstandings with respect to the engagement.

The purpose of the letter of engagement from an auditor to a client is to define the scope of his appointment. The letter should make it quite clear what has been agreed on as the terms of the engagement and which responsibilities are to be borne by the client.

3.4.2 FORM AND CONTENT

The form and content of audit engagement letter varies from client to client. The main contents of this letter are the following:

i.   An emphasis that the duties of accountant and auditor are different.

ii.   An emphasis that the main purpose of an audit is not the discovery of defalcations and irregularities.

iii. The scope of the engagement including any special work the auditor has agreed to do as part of the audit.

iv. An outline of the audit approach may also be included.

v. Details of other services to be provided, for example, accounting work and taxation advice.

vi. Details of the basis on which fees will be calculated.

According to Standards on Auditing-210 (SA-210) on 'Terms on Audit Engagements', the audit engagement letter would generally include the following:

- The objective of the audit of financial statements.
- Management's responsibility for the financial statements.
- Management's responsibility for selection and consistent application of appropriate accounting policies.
- Management responsibility for preparation of the financial statements on a going concern basis of accounting.
- Management's responsibility for the maintenance of adequate accounting records and internal controls for safeguarding the assets of the company and for preventing and detecting fraud or other irregularities.
- The scope of the audit, including reference to the applicable legislation, regulations and the pronouncements of the Institute of Chartered Accountants of India.
- The fact that having regard to the test nature of an audit, persuasive rather than conclusive nature of audit evidence together with inherent limitations of any accounting and internal control system, there is any unavoidable risk that even some material misstatements, resulting from fraud and to the lesser extent error, if either exists, may remain undetected.
- Unrestricted access to whatever records, documentation and other information requested in connection with the audit.
- The fact that the audit process may be subjected to a peer review under the Chartered Accountants Act.

3.4.3 REVISION OF ENGAGEMENT LETTERS

In case of recurring audit, the auditor should consider whether circumstances require the terms of the engagement to be revised and whether there is a need to remind the client of the existing terms of the engagement.

Where the terms of engagement are changed, the auditor and the client should agree on the new terms. However, the auditor should not agree to a change of engagement where there is no reasonable justification for making the changes in the engagement letter.

If the auditor is unable to agree to a change of the engagement and is not permitted to continue the original engagement, the auditor should withdraw and consider whether there is any obligation, either contractual or otherwise, to report the circumstances necessitating the withdrawal to other parties, such as the board of directors or the shareholders.

3.5 PREPARATION BY THE AUDITOR

Modern techniques require a new approach to the practical aspects of the auditor's work. Detailed checking and vouching no longer constitute the main aspect of the operations involved; the ascertainment of the internal control system, the investigation of its working and the verification of assets and liabilities in order to ensure the presentation of the true and fair view, now prevail. The attitude that an audit was mainly useful for the discovery or prevention of fraud is no longer accepted. It is now more generally appreciated that an audit not only ensures the true and fair presentation of the affairs of the organisation, but also that it can be of real benefit in bringing about the institution and maintenance of efficient business methods.

So, in order to conduct the work of audit smoothly and efficiently, the auditor should take the following steps:

3.5.1 AUDIT PLANNING

Audit planning is necessary for efficient and effective conduct of an audit. It should be continuously followed throughout the course of audit assignment.

The main objectives of audit planning are:

i. to ensure that the auditing works are conducted efficiently and profitably and

ii. to ensure that high standards of audit works are maintained, so that the risk of litigation against the practice for negligence is minimised.

It is important that audit should be carefully planned to ensure that the correct number of staff of the appropriate level of seniority are available when they are required. In addition to that, in case of large audits, the work must be planned so that as much as possible is done on an interim basis during the year. This has the double advantage of employing staff effectively throughout the year and ensuring that the only audit work that is left to the year end is worked that cannot be performed earlier. To enable this planning to be carried out efficiently, the auditor will need to liaison with the chief financial officer/accountant of the organisation and ensure that the audit firm is fully aware of the exact proposed timing of the client's own accounting procedures.

In the light of the expected scope of the assignment, the auditor should prepare his audit plan after taking into consideration, the following factors:

i. The statutory requirement under the assignment.

ii. The terms and conditions of engagement.

iii. The nature of timings of reporting.

iv. The significant audit areas.

v. The applicable legal provisions.

vi. Reliability of accounting and internal control system.

vii. The existing accounting practices followed.

viii. The areas requiring special attentions.

3.5.2 AUDIT PROGRAMME

Before starting an audit, a programme of work is usually drawn up. This is known as the 'audit programme'. It is a detailed plan of work, prepared by the auditor, for carrying out an audit. It is comprised of a set of techniques and procedures which the auditor plans to apply to the given audit for forming an opinion about the statement of account of an organisation.

Professor Meigs defined audit programme as "a detailed plan of the auditing work to be performed, specifying the procedure to be followed in verification of each item in the financial statements and giving the estimated time required".

So, audit programme may be defined as a careful flexibly written layout of the work to be done by the auditor and his staff in the conduct of an audit. The preparation of audit programme involves the following considerations:

i. Area or extent of work

ii. Allocation of work

iii. Time duration for the completion of the work

iv. Responsibility of the persons, who have been assigned the work for its' timely completion

The specimen of an audit programme is given below:

AUDIT PROGRAMME

Name of the organisation: M/s *ZYX* -Ltd. for the year ended on 31.3.20xx

Particulars of work	Extent of work to be done	Actual works completed	Time taken to complete	Completed by (signature)
A. Cash Book: 1. Posting 2. Casting 3. Vouching	One month Full Three months	June Full July, November and March		
B. Debtors' Ledger: 1. Posting 2. Casting 3. Vouching	One month One month Two months	April March October and March		
C. Physical Verification: 1. Cash 2. Fixed Assets 3. Stock	as on 31.3.20xx as on 31.3.20xx as on 31.3.20xx	as on 31.3.20xx as on 31.3.20xx as on 31.3.20xx		

Purposes of Audit Programme

There is no denying the fact that audit programme not only serves as the plan of action to be taken for the completion of assigned audit work efficiently and effectively, but the progress of the audit work may also be ascertained by it. However, different purposes of audit programme are given below:

i. For the purpose of co-ordinating the procedures of audit.

ii. For the purpose of ascertaining the progress of audit-work.

iii. For the purpose of recording the work done during the process of auditing. Such records can act as an evidence of work done.

iv. For the purpose of assigning responsibilities to the audit staff for the completion of audit work within the time limit.

Types of Audit Programme

An audit programme can be of the following two types:

1. Predetermined Audit Programme

In this audit programme, all the procedures of audit must be outlined in general, even though all procedures may not be relevant in a particular type of audit. The purpose of this type of audit programme is to offer either procedural guideline or to serve as a checklist. For this reason, this predetermined audit programme has been considered as tailor-made audit programme.

2. Progressive Audit Programme

The progressive form of audit programme is known as 'skeleton' form of audit programme. It sets forth briefly general scope, character and limitations of audit work. This type of programme is suitable in those cases where the condition of the business changes year after year.

Advantages of Audit Programme

1. Assurance of Completion of Work

It ensures that all necessary work has been done and nothing has been omitted.

2. Information About Work-Progress

The auditor is in a position to know about the progress of the work done by his assistants.

3. Uniformity of Work

A uniformity of the work can be attained as the same programme will be followed at subsequent audits.

4. Simplification of Work Allocation

It simplifies the allocation of works to various grades of articled and audit assistants.

5. Guidance to the Staff

It is a kind of guidance to the audit assistants for the work he has to perform.

6. Defence Against Charge of Negligence

The auditor can defend himself in case of a charge of negligence on the basis of the audit programme.

7. Division of Responsibility

Work of the audit can be divided amongst the different juniors who will be held responsible for their work.

8. Final Review of Work

An audit programme facilitates the final review of work before the report is signed.

9. Helpful to the New Employees

For a new employee, the audit programme is a guide to his duty.

10. Basis of Future Programmes

It is a useful basis for planning the programme for the subsequent years.

Disadvantages of Audit Programme

1. Loss of Initiative

An efficient audit assistant loses his initiative, because he has to follow the programme which has been fixed in advance.

2. Want of Flexibility

Even if the audit programme is well drawn up, it may not cover everything that might come up during the course of audit.

3. Rigidity in Programme

Each business may have a separate problem of its own and hence a rigid programme cannot be laid down for each type of business.

4. Unsuitable for Small Concerns

Drawing up of an audit programme may be unnecessary for a small organisation.

5. No Scope of Changes

The audit programme may be followed mechanically year after year though some changes might have been introduced by the client.

6. Concealment of Incapacity of Staff

Inefficient audit assistants may also take advantage of the programme to conceal their incapacity.

The aforesaid shortcomings can be overcome by obtaining up-to-date information and encouraging audit assistants to inform the deviations from the standard and the audit programme and accordingly the principal may modify the programme.

3.5.3 AUDIT NOTE BOOK

An audit note book is usually a bound book in which a large variety of matters observed during the course of audit are recorded. It is thus a part of the record of the auditor available for reference later on, if required. The matters may be observed during the course of audit for which no satisfactory answer have been given by the client or those which require to be incorporated in the audit report. It is a kind of permanent record available to the auditor.

The audit note book may be in two parts:

i.   for keeping a record of general information as regards the audit as a whole, and

ii. for recording special points which have been observed during the course of audit of the accounts of different years.

Value of Audit Note Book

The audit note book is of great value to an auditor at the time of preparing the report to be submitted to the shareholders. In case of a charge of negligence is filed against the auditor, a note book may prove to be a good evidence.

From this note book, an auditor may know the exact volume of work performed by his assistants. It also helps for future reference and guidance. This can serve as guide also in framing the audit programme in future, in so far as the points recorded in the note book indicate the weaknesses in the system of the accounting of the client, which requires to be looked into.

Contents of Audit Note Book

Some of the important points which are noted down in an audit note book are given below:

i.   A list of books of accounts maintained by the clients.

ii.   The names of the principal officers, their powers, duties and responsibilities.

iii. The technical terms used in the business.

iv.   The points that require further explanations.

v.   The particulars of missing vouchers, the duplicate of which have to be obtained.

vi.   The mistakes and errors discovered.

vii. Total or balances of certain books of accounts, bank reconciliation statement, etc.

viii. Notes and queries which might be required at a subsequent audit.

ix.   The points which have to be incorporated in the audit report.

x.   Any matter which requires discussions with the senior officials or with the auditor.

xi.   Accounting method followed in the business.

xii. Date of commencement and completion of audit.

xiii. Provisions in the Articles and Memorandum of Association affecting the accounts and audit.

xiv. Abstracts from minutes, contracts etc. having a bearing upon accounts.

xv. Particulars of accounting and financial policies followed.

Advantages of Audit Note Book

i. From the audit note book, an auditor may know the exact volume of work performed by his assistants.

ii. It helps for future reference and guidance. This can serve as a guide in framing the audit programme in future.

iii. It facilitates the preparation of the audit report.

iv. In case of change of audit assistants, no difficulty is faced by the new assistant in continuing the incomplete work.

v. It ensures that the audit programme has been sincerely followed.

vi. It is reliable evidence in the eye of law, if an auditor has to defend himself.

vii. The responsibility of errors undetected can be fixed on the assistant concerned.

viii. The important matters relating to the audit work may be easily recalled.

3.5.4 AUDIT WORKING PAPERS

Audit working papers are the written records kept by the auditor of the evidence accumulated during the course of the audit, the methods and procedures followed and the conclusions reached. They should include all the information that the auditor considers necessary to adequately conduct his examination and provide support for his audit report.

In short, audit working papers contain essential facts about accounts that are under audit.

Contents of Audit Working Papers

Audit working papers should include a summary of all significant matters identified, which may require the exercise of judgement, together with the auditor's conclusion thereon. If difficult questions of principle or of judgement arise during the course of the audit, the auditor should record the relevant information received and summarise both the management view points and his conclusions.

Purpose of Working Papers

Working papers are actually the compilation of all evidences, which are collected by the auditor in course of his audit. They serve the following purposes:

i. They show the extent of adherence to accounting principles and auditing standards.

ii. They are useful as evidence against the charge of negligence.

iii. They assist the auditor in co-coordinating and organising the work of audit assistants.

iv. They ensure the possibility of quick preparation of audit report.

v. Through the working papers, the auditor can know the distribution and accomplishment of work.

vi. Measurement of the efficiency of the assistants can be done with the help of working papers.

vii. They can be used as permanent record for future references.

viii.   They can act as a means to give training to the audit assistants.

ix.   They provide a means to control the ongoing audit work.

x.   Working papers assist the auditor in forming an opinion on the financial statements.

Contents of Working Papers

Standards on Auditing-230 (SA-230) on Documentation issued by the Institute of Chartered Accountants of India makes the following suggestions regarding the form and contents of working papers:

i.   The working papers should record the audit plan, the nature, timing and extent of auditing procedures performed and the conclusions drawn from the evidence obtained.

ii.   The exact form and content of working papers are affected by various matters such as:
    (a)   the nature of the engagement,
    (b)   the form of the audit report,
    (c)   the nature and complexity of client's business,
    (d)   the nature and conditions of the client's records and degree of reliance on internal controls, and
    (e)   the need in particular circumstances for direction, supervision and review of work performed by assistants.

iii.   Working papers should be designed and properly organised to meet the circumstances of each audit and the auditor's need in respect thereof.

iv.   Working papers should be sufficiently complete and detailed for an auditor to obtain an overall understanding of the audit.

v.   All significant matters that require the judgement, together with the auditor's conclusion thereon, should be included in the auditor's working papers.

vi.   To improve audit efficiency, the auditor normally obtains and utilises schedules, analysis and other working papers prepared by the client such as analysis of important revenue accounts receivables etc.

vii.   In case of recurring audits, some working papers may be classified as permanent audit files as distinct from current audit files relating primarily to the audit of a single period.

Responsibility for Protection and Preservation of Working Papers

Whosoever is in possession of working papers should be responsible for their safe custody. These should in no case be shown to a third party except with the permission of the client. As the working papers are prepared in respect of the client's business, they should be treated as highly confidential and should be preserved in all circumstances and at all times.

After the audit report has been prepared and delivered to the client, these papers may be filed and preserved for a period of time sufficient to meet the needs of the auditor's practice and satisfy any pertinent legal or professional requirements of record retention.

Ownership of Working Papers

An important and pertinent question arises as to who is the owner of these working papers. The claim of the auditor is that it is he who has collected the information for the purpose of discharging his duties. Therefore he is entitled to the possession of these papers. On the other hand, it is the claim of the client that the auditor is his agent and hence he should surrender these papers to the clients.

In fact, this question of ownership in respect to the working papers arose in the case of *Sockockingley vs. Bright Graham & Co.* (1938) in England. The question was whether the auditor had a right to retain the working papers as if it were their own property even after the payment of the audit fees. The court gave judgement in favour of the auditors on the ground that they were independent contractors and not agents of the client.

According to the views of the Institute of Chartered Accountants of India (SA-230), working papers are the property of the auditor. The auditor may, at his discretion, make portions of or extracts from his working papers available to his clients. Further, according to this standard of auditing practices, an auditor should adopt reasonable procedures for custody and confidentiality of his working papers and should retain them for a period of time sufficient to meet the needs of his practice and satisfy any pertinent legal and professional requirements of record retention.

3.5.5 AUDIT FILES

The file used by the auditor for preserving the written statements of necessary matters relating to audit is called the audit file. It maintains different audit documents, such as audit notes, audit programme, audit working papers, and the like. The efficient audit filling system strengthens the integrity in the audit work.

The audit file is generally of two types:

(1) Permanent Audit File

In the case of recurring audits, some working paper files may be classified as permanent audit files, which are updated currently with information of continuing importance to succeeding audit.

A permanent audit file normally includes the following:

i. Information regarding the legal and organisational structure of the organisation. In case of company form of organisation, this includes the Memorandum and Articles of Association.

ii. Extracts or copies of important legal documents, agreements and minutes relevant to the audit.

iii. A record of the study and evaluation of the internal controls relating to the accounting system.

iv. Copies of audited financial statements for previous years.

v. Analysis of significant ratios and trends.

vi. Copies of management letters issued by the auditor, if any.

vii. Record of communication with the retiring auditor, if any, before acceptance of the appointment as auditor.

viii. Notes regarding significant accounting policies.

ix. Significant audit observations of earlier years.

(2) Temporary Audit File

In the case of single period audit, some working paper files may be classified as temporary audit file, which contain information relating primarily to the audit of a single period.

A temporary audit file usually includes the following:

i. Draft financial statements being audited.

ii. Schedules supporting the financial statements.

iii. Extracts from relevant minutes.

iv. Audit programme and time budget.

v. Internal control questionnaire and where applicable, flow charts and notes on the system of internal control.

vi. Confirmations obtained from banks and other relevant organisations regarding items in the financial statements.

vii. Details of queries raised during the audit, and the answers obtained to them.

viii. Copy of letter of representation.

3.5.6 AUDIT MANUAL

Audit manual may be defined as a 'written internal auditing document'. Thus it provides different information as to detailed auditing procedures, objects of auditing, standard of performance, time recording procedure, preparation of audit report etc. The audit manual is prepared for the general guidance of the auditors with the object of planning the procedure of audit.

Advantages

  i. Different information regarding polices of the organisation and procedure of audit is available in the manual.

 ii. Information relating to required steps to be followed for conducting different auditing work can be collected from the manual.

iii. Audit manual provides answers to the routine questions to the audit staff.

 iv. Efficient distribution of work among the audit staff can be made possible.

  v. Audit manual provides useful information to the new entrants to the profession.

Disadvantages

  i. Different audit procedures as contained in the manual become very mechanical.

 ii. Creative thinking on the part of the audit staff is discouraged.

iii. If the manuals are not kept up to date, it may, instead of providing useful guidance, misguide the working staff.

 iv. It discourages the individual initiative.

  v. The procedure of audit as given in the audit manual may sometime fail to co-ordinate the activities of audit staff during the course of audit.

3.5.7 AUDIT MEMORANDUM

An audit memorandum is a statement containing all useful information regarding the business of the client. It indicates the method of operation, policies with regard to different aspects of the business as well as all the conditions in respect of audit.

Audit memorandum is very useful in case of first time audit by the concerned auditor in an organisation. While conducting his auditing work, the auditor requires certain information, which may be directly related with the method of operation of the business. If the auditor is not informed about the method of operation as well the operational activities of the organisation, he will not be in a position to conduct his audit effectively. Hence audit memorandum is useful to the auditor while the auditor wants to relate the financial transactions with the business activities, with the condition of the business in which the transactions being activated.

Audit memorandum usually contains the following:

  i. About the business—its early history and growth.

 ii. Nature of ownership of the organisation.

iii. Location of its principal offices and factories.

 iv. Sources of factors of production—materials, labour etc.

  v. Details about its manufacturing operations.

 vi. Principal products produced by the concern.

vii. Market condition and nature of competition in the market.

viii. Organisational structure and hierarchy.

ix. Method of accounting and nature of books of accounts.

x. List of persons involved in management.

3.6 PRINCIPLES AND TECHNIQUES OF AUDITING

The principles of auditing refer to fundamental consideration that sustain the function of auditing and direct its activities. Auditing has evolved for satisfaction of a social need to make the accounting statements reliable. To achieve this broad functional objective, certain techniques and procedures have been developed over the years on the basis of certain concepts and principles that are considered to be the governing forces. Standards on Auditing-200 on 'Basic Principles Governing an Audit' describes the basic principles which govern the auditor's professional responsibilities and which should be complied with whenever an audit is carried out. It also states that "compliance with the basic principles require that application of auditing procedures and reporting practices appropriate to the particular circumstances".

Auditing techniques refer to the methods and means adopted by an auditor for collection and evaluation of audit evidence in different auditing situations. When the audit objective is to see that debtors' balances are correctly stated in the balance sheets, the auditor would introduce confirmation and scrutiny of subsequent years' accounts as the appropriate audit technique. The method of collection of evidence to verify accounts maintained under manual system will be different from that when accounts are computerised. In the former case, audit trial will be available and usual techniques like posting verification and casting verification would be appropriate. However, in the latter case, because of loss of audit trial and accuracy of the computer, these techniques are replaced by more intensive and extensive examination of the internal control. Also, the technique may vary according to the nature of proposition to be tested.

Thus auditing principles are of fundamental nature which underlies the conduct of the audit. These principles are not liable to change frequently while audit techniques may vary according to the nature of propositions to be tested. For instance, audit technique to test the existence of cash in hand will be different from the method to verify recoverability of sundry debtors. Further, audit techniques may vary from organisation to organisation depending upon the nature of the business but the principles of auditing will remain the same irrespective of the nature of the organisation.

3.6.1 IMPORTANT AUDIT TECHNIQUES

The technique or strategy followed in order to collect proper evidence in support of the transactions recorded in the books of accounts is termed as techniques of auditing.

The important techniques usually adopted by the auditors include the following:

i. Vouching (of expenses)

ii. Physical verification (of fixed and current assets)

iii. Reconciliation (of stock statement)

iv. Confirmation (of customers or bank balance)

v. Re-computation (of depreciation and other calculations)

vi. Scanning (of legal formalities)

vii. Scrutiny (of ledger balances)

viii. Inquiry (of propriety aspect).

3.7 PROCEDURES FOLLOWED IN COURSE OF AUDIT

There is no fixed rule regarding the procedures the auditor would follow in the course of audit. He would fix up the procedures after reviewing the situations on the basis of auditor's own knowledge, intelligence, efficiency and experience. But the generally accepted procedures followed by an auditor include the following:

3.7.1 AUDIT EVIDENCE

It is the auditor's duty to express a professional opinion on financial statements and it must always be a matter of judgement whether the auditor has sufficient evidence on which to base such an opinion. The auditor can never be absolutely certain that the financial statements show a true and fair view, the question is whether as an honest and careful auditor he has adequate evidence on which to base a reasonable opinion.

The term evidence includes "all influences on the mind of an auditor which affect his judgement about the truthfulness of the propositions, submitted to him for review".

Types of Audit Evidence

Professor R. K. Mautz in his work *Fundamentals of Auditing* has rightly observed that "the nature of financial statement assertions leads to the conclusion that the nature of the following kinds of evidences are indicative of the validity of financial statement assertions in varying degrees depending on the circumstances of the examination".

Thus Professor Mautz cited nine types of audit evidences, which are as follows:

i. Physical examination by the auditor of the thing represented in the accounts

ii. Statement by independent third parties:
   (a) Oral evidence
   (b) Written evidence

iii. Authoritative documents:
   (a) Prepared outside the enterprise under examination
   (b) Prepared inside the enterprise under examination

iv. Statements by officers and employees of the concern under examination:
   (a) Formal statement
   (b) Informal statement

v. Calculations performed by the auditors

vi. Satisfactory internal control procedures

vii. Subsequent actions by the concern under examination and by others

viii. Subsidiary or detail records with no significant indications of irregularity

ix. Interrelationship within the date examined.

As per SA-500, the reliability of audit evidence depends on its sources (internal or external) and on its nature (visual, documentary or oral). While the reliability of audit evidence is dependent on the circumstances under which it is obtained, the following generalizations may be useful in assessing the reliability of audit evidence:

➢ External evidence is usually more reliable than internal evidence.

➢ Internal evidence is more reliable when related internal control is satisfactory.

➢ Evidence in the form of documents and written representations is usually more reliable than oral representations.

➢ Evidence obtained by the auditor himself is more reliable than that obtained through the entity.

In short, audit evidence is information obtained and recorded by the auditor in arriving at the conclusions on which he bases his opinion on the financial statements. Main sources of audit evidence include the following:

i. Accounting system and underlying documentation of the enterprise.

ii. Tangible assets.

iii. Management and employees of the organisation.

iv. Customers, suppliers and other third parties who have dealing with, or knowledge of, the enterprise or its business.

Although the auditor would never be absolutely certain that the financial statements show a true and fair view, he needs to obtain sufficient evidence to form a reasonable basis for his opinion thereon.

Methods of Obtaining Audit Evidence

Standards on Auditing-500 (SA-500) on "audit evidence" describes the method of obtaining audit evidences. According to this statement, the auditor obtains evidence in performing compliance and substantive procedures by one or more of the following methods:

1. Inspection

Inspection consists of examining records, documents or tangible assets. Inspection of records and documents provides evidence of varying degree of reliability depending on their nature and source and the effectiveness of internal controls over their processing. Four major categories of documentary evidences, which provide different degrees of reliability to the auditor, are

i. documentary evidence originating from and held by third parties,

ii. documentary evidence originating from third parties and held by the entity,

iii. documentary evidence originating from the entity and held by third parties and

iv. documentary evidence originating from and held by the entity.

Inspection of tangible assets in one of the methods to obtain reliable evidence with respect to their existence but not necessarily as to their ownership or value.

2. Observation

Observation consists of witnessing a process or procedure being performed by others. For example, the auditor may observe the counting of inventories by client personnel or the performance of internal control procedures that leave no audit trial.

3. Inquiry and Confirmation

Inquiry consists of seeking appropriate information from knowledgeable persons inside and outside the entity. Inquiries may range from formal written inquiries addressed to third parties to informal oral inquiries addressed to persons inside the entity. Responses to inquiries may provide the auditor with information which he did not previously possess or may provide him with corroborative evidence.

Confirmation consists of the response to an inquiry to corroborate information contained in the accounting records. For example, the auditor requests confirmation of receivables by direct communication with the debtors.

Confirmation is an evidence gathering activity performed by the auditor, usually in the substantive testing stage of the audit. (It may be noted that the word 'confirmation' is also used to describe the physical evidence that relates to the performance of the confirmation activity; thus '20 confirmations were received from the client's debtors' is an evidence statement.)

Confirmation refers to the process of requesting and receiving information in writing and from a third party, attesting to the validity (i.e., the existence or occurrence) of an item, such as an asset, liability, transaction or economic event. (A confirmation may, in some circumstances, also provide evidence relating to the completeness or accuracy of an account balance or underlying class of transaction.)

A written response received directly by the auditor from a third party arising from a written request by the auditor directly to the third party generally provides reliable evidence as to the existence of an asset or liability (or the occurrence of a transaction or economic event). However, auditors consider the appropriateness of the authority of the person signing the confirmation, and where possible, the confirmee's integrity and competence.

As per SA-505, the auditor should determine whether the use of external confirmations is necessary to obtain sufficient appropriate audit evidence to support certain financial statement assertions. In making this determination, the auditor should consider materiality, the assessed level of inherent and control risk and the evidence from other planned audit procedures will reduce audit risk to an acceptably low level for the applicable financial statement assertions. The auditor should employ external confirmation procedures in consultation with the management.

External confirmations are frequently used in relation to account balances and their components, but need not be restricted to these items. For example, the auditor may request external confirmation of the terms of agreements or transactions an entity has with third parties. The confirmation request is designed to ask if any modifications have been made to the agreement, and if so, the relevant details thereof. Other examples of situations where external confirmations may be used include the following:

- Bank balances and other information from bankers.
- Accounts receivable balances.
- Stocks held by third parties.
- Property title deeds held by third parties.
- Investments purchased but delivery not taken.
- Loans from lenders.
- Accounts payable balances.
- Long outstanding share application money.

SA-505 also states that the auditor should consider whether there is any indication that external confirmations received may not be reliable. The reliability of the evidence obtained from external confirmation depends on the application of appropriate procedures by the auditor in designing the external confirmation request, performing the external confirmation procedures and evaluating the results of the external confirmation procedures.

While performing confirmation procedures, the auditor should maintain control over the process of selecting those to whom a request will be sent, the preparation and sending of confirmation requests and the response to those requests. The auditor should, however, ensure that it is the auditor who sends out the confirmation requests, that the requests are properly addressed and that it is requested that all replies and the undelivered confirmations are delivered directly to the auditor. The auditor considers whether replies have come from the purported senders.

When the auditor forms a conclusion that the confirmation process and alternative procedures have not provided sufficient appropriate audit evidence regarding an assertion, the auditor should undertake additional procedures to obtain sufficient appropriate audit evidence.

4. Computation

Computation consists of checking the arithmetical accuracy of source documents and accounting records or performing independent calculations.

Recalculation (or computation) is an evidence gathering activity that may be applied in all of the audit stages. However, it is particularly applicable to the substantive testing stage.

The activity of recalculation refers to the auditor performing mathematical calculations (such as additions and extensions) and reconciliation as well as the counting of items. Recalculation primarily provides evidence as to the accuracy (of valuation) of an account balance or underlying class of transaction.

In the substantive testing stage, recalculation by the auditor may provide highly reliable, but incomplete, evidence as to the accuracy (of valuation) of an account balance or underlying class of transaction. For example, the auditors (perhaps using CAATs) may check the calculations of quantity x unit cost in a client's inventory records. This provides highly reliable evidence as to the accuracy of valuation of the inventory, but it is incomplete evidence as for example, evidence is required as to the accuracy of the unit cost figures included in the records.

However, it is to be noted that the reliability of the evidence gathered depends of the competence and experience of the person making the recalculation.

5. Analytical Review

Analytical review consists of studying significant ratios and trends and investigating unusual fluctuations and items.

3.7.2 ANALYTICAL PROCEDURES

Concept

The term 'analytical procedure' refers to a collection of activities performed by auditors to gather evidence in four of the five audit stages (i.e., all except the control testing stage). When they are performed in the substantive testing stage, they are considered to be a 'substantive procedure'.

According to SA-520, 'analytical procedure' means the analysis of significant ratios and trends, including the resulting investigation of fluctuations and relationships that are inconsistent with other relevant information or which deviate from predicted amounts.

Analytical procedures involve a comparison of the value of an actual ratio/trend/account balance/ transaction etc. The objective of this comparison is to identify and investigate the reason for any unusual or unexpected relationship between the actual and expected values. Auditors estimate the expected value (of the ratio/trend/account balance/transaction etc.) before calculating the actual value in order to avoid the actual value biasing the auditor's estimate of the expected value. When the application of an analytical procedure does not identify any unusual or unexpected difference, then, by inference, the results provide evidence in support of management's assertions.

Components of the Procedures

Analytical procedures may be performed in the client acceptance/rejection stage in order to assist in obtaining a better understanding of the client's business; in the audit planning stage to identify possible problem areas; in the substantive testing stage as a means of gathering substance evidence in relation to one or more account balances or classes of transactions (i.e., as a substantive procedure); and in the opinion formation stage, as a means of gathering evidence as to the consistency of the financial statements with the auditor's knowledge of the business of the entity.

Analytical procedures include:

- *Reasonable tests*: In a reasonable test, the expected value is determined by reference to data partly or wholly independent of accounting information system, and for that reason, evidence obtained through the application of such a test may be more reliable than evidence gathered using other analytical procedures, e.g., the reasonableness of the recorded value of the total annual revenue of a freight company may be estimated by comparing the recorded value with the expected value, where the expected value is equal to the product of the total tonnes carried during the year and the average freight rate per tonne. The performing of a reasonableness test is sometimes referred to as 'predictive testing'.

- *Scanning*: An auditor may scan (or eyeball) account balances, listing of balances etc., with the objective of detecting any unusual or unexpected balances or transactions. In this instance, the expected value of account balances, transactions etc. is based on the auditor's knowledge of the business of the entity or perhaps intuitive knowledge.

- *Review*: An auditor may review reconciliation, compilations and aggregation of transactions and/or account balances, again with the object of detecting any unusual or unexpected balances or transactions. Again, expectations are based on the auditor's knowledge of the business of the entity.

- *Regression analysis*: In regression analysis, the expected or predicted value is determined using the statistical technique of regression.

- *Roll forward procedure*: Where substantive evidence of a detailed nature has been gathered in relation to a particular account balance at a point of time prior to balance date, analytical procedures called 'roll forward procedures' are used to determine the reasonableness of the value of the account balance as at balance date. For example, if customer balance comprising the account balance 'trade account receivable' were confirmed as at the end of October and balance date was the end of December, then the auditor will perform roll forward procedures to determine the reasonableness of trade accounts receivable as at balance date.

- *Ratio analysis*: The computation and comparison of the actual value of a ratio with the expected value. The expected value may be based, for example, on
  - ➤ prior period values,
  - ➤ values in other divisions of the entity,
  - ➤ industry average,
  - ➤ forecast values, and
  - ➤ non-financial information, such as general economic conditions, technological changes in the client's industry and new products from competitors.

  Once again, the objective of this analytical procedure is to detect any unusual or unexpected value for the ratio. Examples of ratios used in ratio analysis include:
  - ➤ Days sales in receivables
  - ➤ Days sales in inventory
  - ➤ Gross profit percentage
  - ➤ Inventory turnover.

- *Common size analysis*: Common size analysis is a type of cross-sectional analysis used for comparing the percentage components of balance sheets and income statements of one entity, or a division of an entity (expected value), with comparable data from one or more other entities/divisions (actual or recorded value). This analysis may be used for either (i) the comparisons of a (prospective) client's data with the industry average and/or an industry competitor or (ii) for the comparison of income statements of different divisions of the same entity.

Analytical procedures generally provide less reliable substantive evidence than the other category of substantive procedures/test (tests of detail). The substantive evidence gathered using analytical procedures is thus generally used to corroborate other substantive evidence gathered, rather than used as a sole source of evidence.

Example of Use of Analytical Techniques

Pantaloons Fashion Shops Ltd. owns a chain of high fashion shops in metro cities. Each shop is operated by a separate subsidiary company. All subsidiaries buy from the parent company. The auditor of the Kolkata Pantaloon shop is reviewing the accounts for the year ending 31 March 2007 before starting the audit.

The accounts of the shop reveal the following:

[Figures in Rs.]

PARTICULARS	2005–06	2006–07	2007–08 (BUDGETED)
Sales	12,00,000	12,76,000	12,80,000
Cost of Sales	8,00,000	9,18,000	8,50,000
Gross Profit	4,00,000	3,58,000	4,30,000
Salaries and Wages	1,56,000	1,42,000	1,40,000
Other Establishment Expenses	1,40,000	1,50,000	1,48,000
Net Profit	1,04,000	66,000	1,42,000
Stock in trade	1,16,000	1,06,000	1,24,000
Sundry Creditors	1,42,000	1,58,000	1,48,000

External data available to Mr. Sircar, the auditor includes the following:

- Rate of inflation @ 5%.
- A management institute survey of the businesses in Kolkata in which city the shop is situated indicates an 8% growth in real terms.
- The rate of gross profit earned by other shops in the group was 30% and average stock was 45 days worth. Sundry creditors in three other shops averaged 13% of the turnover.
- iv. Salaries and wages in the other shops averaged 15% of the turnover.

From all this data, Mr. Sircar could

- i. compute estimated turnover for the year 2006–07 as 12,00,000 × 1.05 × 1.08 = Rs. 13,60,800. The actual turnover is significantly less. The difference must be enquired into.
- ii. determine that gross profit from the turnover of the current year should be 12,76,000 × 33.33% = Rs. 4,25,290. But actual gross profit is only Rs. 3,58,000, i.e., only 28% of the turnover.
- iii. identify that stock should be about 45 days worth: Rs. 9,18,000 × 45/365 = Rs. 1,13,178. Actual stock is lower but not materially so.
- iv. calculate that sundry creditors should be Rs. 9,18,000 × 0.13 = Rs. 1,19,340. But the actual figure is much more the expected figure.
- v. salaries and wages perhaps ought to be Rs. 12,76,000 × 0.15 = Rs. 1,91,400. If the direction of causation was reversed, turnover should be 1,42,000 × 100/15 = Rs. 9,47,000. Salaries and wages do agree with the budget and should be confirmable by considering the numbers on the staff.
- vi. Other expenses should perhaps have risen by 5%, but they should be reviewed after disaggregation.

Observations

i.   Stocks are in line with expectations, but not the sundry creditors.

ii. Globally other overhead is out of line and requires disaggregation.

iii. Sales are lower than expected. Causes may be misappropriation of stock or cash. Close monitoring is to be ensured.

iv. Gross profit is way out of line. This does not appear to be cut-off errors as stock seems to be about right and sundry creditors are not far away from the expected figure. Debtors are negligible in this type of retail business. It seems that misappropriation of stock or cash has occurred. Full checking is required. It may be of course that the management have other explanations—burglary losses, excessive shop lifting, price competition, sale of old stock at low prices etc.

So, the auditor should apply analytical procedures at the planning stage to assist in understanding the business and in identifying areas of potential risk. Also, the auditor should apply analytical procedures at or near the end of the audit when forming an overall conclusion as to whether the financial statements as a whole are consistent with the auditor's knowledge of the business.

Evidence Evaluation Activities

The audit evidence tends to be persuasive rather than absolute and the auditors tend to seek evidence from different sources or of a different nature to support the same assertions. The auditors seek to provide reasonable but not absolute assurance that the financial statements are free from misstatement. Auditors do not normally examine all the information available but reach their conclusions about financial statement assertions using a variety of means including sampling.

Evidence evaluation activities in auditing correspond to information evaluation activities in human information processing theory. Evidence evaluation activities are those activities performed by auditors that relate to the evaluation of audit evidence gathered. The evaluation of evidence requires skill and care, and is a task usually performed by experienced auditors who apply a degree of professional skepticism and consider the concept of substance and form.

Evaluation activities incorporate the activities of estimation as well as evaluation. Auditors estimate or evaluation based on the following points:

- Whether the audit evidence gathered is of sufficient quantity and appropriate quality to make a decision based on that evidence before making the actual decision. In other words, auditors estimate whether the evidence is relevant and sufficiently reliable.

- Audit risk factors during each audit stage. In particular, auditors evaluate
  - ➤ the acceptable and achievable level of audit risk at the financial statement level, in the client acceptance/retention stage,
  - ➤ inherent risk, control risk and acceptable level of detection risk, at the account balance level, in the audit planning stage,
  - ➤ control risk during the control testing stage to compare with the control risk evaluated during the audit planning stage,
  - ➤ audit risk, at the account balance level, for comparison with the acceptable level of audit risk, during the substantive testing stage,
  - ➤ audit risk, at the financial statement level, for comparison with the acceptable level of audit risk, during the opinion formulation stage.

- Exceptions found during the final three audit stages (an evaluation activity), namely, control deviations in the control testing stage and misstatements in the substantive and opinion formulation stages.

Basic Techniques for Collecting Audit Evidence

There are nine techniques through which audit evidence can be collected. These are the following:

   i. Physical examination and counting.

  ii. *Confirmation*: This should be in writing. External sources are preferable to internal sources.

 iii. Examination of original documents: Original documents should be compared with the entries in the books. This technique is basically called vouching.

  iv. Re-computation: It includes additions, calculations, balance extractions etc.

   v. Retracing bookkeeping procedures: Checking postings.

  vi. Scanning: This is somewhat indefinite but is widely used, especially in seeking the unusual or the unlikely transactions.

 vii. Inquiry: Asking questions. This is a necessary and valid technique. However, auditors acquire a habit of always seeking confirmations of oral answers.

viii. Correlation: Seeking internal consistency in records and accounts.

  ix. Observation: Seeing for oneself is the best possible confirmation especially in connection with internal control systems.

Varieties of Evidence

The evidence an auditor collects can be divided into the following categories:

   i. Observation

  ii. Testimony from independent third parties, e.g., bank letters, circulars to debtors.

 iii. Authoritative documents prepared outside the firm, e.g., title deeds, share and loan certificates etc.

  iv. Authoritative documents prepared inside the firm, e.g., minutes, copy invoices etc.

   v. Testimony from directors and officers of the company. This may be formal, for example, the letter of representation, or informal, for example in replies to ICQ. (Internal Control Questionnaires)

  vi. Satisfactory internal control. For many items this is the most useful evidence.

 vii. Calculations performed by the auditor. Evidence of the correctness of many figures can be obtained this way.

viii. Subsequent events. The audit is usually performed well after the year end and many assertions can be verified by reference to subsequent events.

  ix. Relationship evidence. Evidence confirming the truth about one item may tend to confirm the truth about another. For example, evidence confirming the correctness of investment income also confirms some aspects of the item 'investments'.

   x. Agreement with expectations. Verification can be assisted by the computation and comparison of ratios and absolute magnitudes with those achieved (a) in the past; (b) by other companies; and (c) budgeted. Conversely, inconsistencies and unusual or unexpected items will alert the auditor.

  xi. External events. The client is not isolated from the world and the auditor should use his knowledge of current events in assessing a company's accounts. For example, consider revolution and the value of overseas subsidiaries.

Reliability
The reliability of audit evidence can be assessed to some extent on the following presumptions:

i. Documentary evidence is more reliable than oral evidence.

ii. Evidence from outside the enterprise is more reliable than that secured solely from within the enterprise.

iii. Evidence obtained by the auditor by such means as analysis and physical inspection is more reliable than evidence obtained from others. Auditors always say 'show me' not 'tell me'.

iv. Original documents are more reliable than photocopies or facsimiles.

Limitations
The quality and quantity of evidence needs is constrained by the following:

i. Absolute proof is impossible.

ii. Some assertions are not material.

iii. Time is limited. Accounts must be produced within a time scale and the auditor may have to make do with less than perfection to comply with the time scale.

iv. Money is limited. The ideal evidence may be too expensive to obtain.

v. Sensitivity. Some items are of greater importance than others.

3.7.3 ROUTINE CHECKING
Routine checking is a total process of accounting control, which includes

i. examination of the totalling and balancing of the books of prime entry,

ii. examination of the posting from the primary books to the ledger accounts,

iii. examination of totalling and balancing of the ledger accounts and of the trial balance prepared with those balances and

iv. overall examination of writing up the transactions properly.

In short, the routine checking is concerned with ascertaining the arithmetical accuracy of casting, posting and carry forwards. For the purpose of confirming the arithmetical accuracy and detecting frauds and errors of very simple nature, this method is adopted as basic to all types of audit work. The scope of application of routine checking depends upon the nature and size of the organisation as well as the effectiveness of the internal check and control system.

Advantages
i. It is the simplest form of audit work.

ii. Detection of errors and frauds of simple nature can be very easily detected.

iii. The books of accounts can be thoroughly checked.

iv. It is the basis of checking the final account as it helps in checking castings and postings.

v. Arithmetical accuracy of all the transactions can be confirmed by this method.

vi. It offers an opportunity to train the new entrants to the profession.

Disadvantages
i. It is not generally considered as an important part of audit work where self-balancing system is maintained.

ii. As the audit staff are engaged in same type of work, the possibility of becoming monotonous may grow in this system.

iii. Negligence of work and taking the advantage of internal check system are frequent.

iv. It fails to detect errors and frauds arising from the fraudulent manipulation in accounting principles.

3.7.4 TEST CHECKING

The term 'test checking' stands for the method of auditing, where instead of a complete examination of all the transactions recorded in the books of accounts, only some of the transactions are selected and verified. The underlying intention is to test some of the transactions to form an opinion for the whole. According to Professor Meig, "test checking means to select and examine a representative sample from a large number of similar items".

The justification of test checking lies on theory of probability which states, in effect that a sample selected from a series of items will tend to show the same characteristics present in the full series of items, which is commonly referred to as "population" or "universe".

Objectives of Test Checking

Accounts of large organisations usually include an enormous number of transactions. But the auditor is not in a position to check each and every transaction within the limited time and due to the constraint of resources available to him. So, he has to depend on selective verification of the transactions. The selection of transactions will be made in such a way that the auditor will verify a small but representative number of transactions and he can draw conclusions about the transactions as a whole. So, the basic objective of test checking is to draw a valid conclusion by undertaking examination of some transactions from the large number of transactions and thereby save time and cost.

Advantages

i. It is one of the best techniques of auditing through which cost of audit can be reduced.

ii. It can ensure the speed of audit work.

iii. It can easily locate the deficient areas and thus helps to come to the conclusion as to the acceptability of financial records.

iv. It is a labour saving device.

v. It acts as a guide to the auditor to arrive at a conclusion regarding the true and fair view of the state of affairs of the business.

Disadvantages

i. It will prove inefficient where internal check and control system are not operating or found ineffective.

ii. It is not suitable for small concerns.

iii. It will bound to show incorrect result if the samples are not proper representative of the population.

iv. It does not offer any consistency in selecting the percentage of check that will be adopted by all concerns.

Precautions to be Taken Before Taking Test Checking Technique

i. The auditor should review the existing internal control in order to ascertain its effectiveness.

ii. The transactions to be selected for test checking must be homogenous.

iii. The transactions to be test checked must form an adequate sample.

iv. As per as possible, the transactions to be selected for test checking should be on the basis of random number tables.

v. The results of the test checks themselves should be examined, particularly the nature of errors.

Transactions Not Suitable for the Adoption of Test Checking

If the number of transactions in any area is sufficiently large, the auditors usually adopt test check technique. However, as a practical measure, usually the following types of transactions and records are kept outside the purview of test checking:

i. In industries where the activities are based on seasonal fluctuations, the auditor cannot adopt test checking on an annual basis.

ii. Exceptional transactions or the transactions of a non-recurring nature are also not suitable for adoption of test checking.

iii. Some transactions have legal implication, i.e., has to be recorded on the basis of legal provisions. Such transactions cannot be test checked.

iv. Areas involving computation and calculations should not be subject to test checking.

v. There should not be test checking for opening as well as closing entries.

vi. Bank reconciliation statement cannot be checked by adopting this technique.

vii. Presentation and disclosure of information in the balance sheet and the profit and loss account should not be subjected to test checking.

3.7.5 AUDITING IN DEPTH

Auditing in depth is a technique that assists the auditor in conducting test checking and adoption of such a system becomes essential in large organisations, where detailed examination of all the records is not possible. It is a method of auditing under which a few selective transactions are subjected to a thorough scrutiny for arriving at the accuracy of the data.

This technique involves the selection of a sample of transactions from one area of accounting and tracing them from the beginning to the conclusion. This system is undertaken to examine the effectiveness of the internal control and internal check system. In order to conduct the work of auditing in depth of a specific transaction, the auditor has to examine thoroughly the different stages of the transaction.

For example, in respect of goods purchased, the auditing in depth technique will be applied through the following stages:

i. Examine the requisition note from the stores, ensuring that it has been signed by the appropriate official.

ii. Examine the copy of the order placed by the purchasing department, ensuring that it was properly executed on the official form, complied with all the client's regulations and was authorised by the appropriate official.

iii. Examine the delivery note from the supplier and compare it with the copy of the order.

iv. Examine the goods inward note made out when the goods were received, noting if it has been properly signed, if it indicates that the correct goods have been received and if their quantity and condition have been checked.

v. Check the entries in the store records.

vi.   Check in the accounts department that the invoice received from the supplier has been matched with the copy of the order and the copy of the goods received note before being processed, and that the calculations have been checked.

vii.   Check the appropriate entries in the accounting records, and

viii. Compare the returned cheque with the invoice and supplier's statement, if any.

From the above example, it can be seen that the auditor would trace the transaction right through the system. He would not merely satisfy himself that the entries in the records were correct, but would ensure that the appropriate internal controls relating to authorisation of transactions, the checking of one document against another and physical inspection of goods has been properly operated at the appropriate times. He would also ensure that a proper system was in force to claim credits in respect of short deliveries or deliveries of defective goods.

Where the examination of successive stages in the depth test produces satisfactory results, it is accepted practice that the auditor may progressively reduce the number of items to be examined at subsequent stages. However, if the tests reveal an unacceptable number of errors, it will be necessary for the auditor to increase the number of items examined in order to discover whether the original sample was representative.

Advantages

i.   Precision in course of audit work can be achieved.

ii.   It guards against the fraudulent manipulation of accounts.

iii.   It does not offer any monotony in work to the auditor. Because the auditor will have to deal in all the time with new ideas and techniques.

iv.   It saves the cost of audit.

v.   The experience in auditing in depth can be widely used in preparing audit plan.

Disadvantages

i.   As the concept is linked with selective verification, its application may be fruitless if the selection of item is wrong.

ii.   Instead of saving cost and time, this technique entails loss of time and extra cost because of unskilled handling of audit affairs.

iii.   Proper selection of transactions for conducting auditing in depth is too much risky. If the items are not properly selected, it will not at all serve its purpose.

iv.   This technique cannot be applied to small organisations.

v.   It has been observed that the auditor relies too heavily upon intuition. Here, he uses no objective method of measuring the adequacy of samples.

3.7.6 WALK-THROUGH TESTS

Auditors need to have an understanding of a client's accounting system and control environment. From this initial understanding, it is possible to plan the audit and determine the audit approach. The audit approach may be to rely on substantive tests alone, or in some areas, to rely partly on internal control evidence as well as substantive tests. The problem is how to gain an understanding of the accounting system and associated control environment. One way is to use walk through tests.

Walk through tests are defined as tracing one or more transactions through the accounting system and observing the application of relevant aspects of the internal control system. For example, the auditor might look at the sales system of a whole seller and trace a sale from its initiation through the sales figure in the profit and loss account. This will involve looking at customer's orders, how the orders are documented and recorded, credit control approval, how the goods are selected and packed, raising of an advice note and/or delivery note, invoicing procedures, recording the invoice in the books of accounts and so on. At each stage the controls applied are examined.

If the preliminary understanding of the systems and control environment leads the auditor to plan the audit to include some internal control reliance, then the system needs to be investigated in more depth than the knowledge provided by walk-through tests.

Work through tests will also be applied in the following areas:

i.   In any situation where the auditor has not obtained his description of the system from a personal investigation of the system by questioning operating staff and documents and records.

ii. At the final audit when the auditor needs to review the system from the date of the interim completion to the year ends. He must first determine if the system has changed and walk through tests will achieve this.

3.7.7 Rotational Tests

Rotational tests are of two kinds:

i.   *Rotation of audit emphasis*: The auditor performs a systems audit on all areas of the client's business every year, but each year he selects one area (wages, sales, stock control, purchase etc.) for special in-depth testing.

ii. *Visit rotation*: When the client's organisation has numerous branches, factories, locations etc., it may be impractical to visit them all each year. In such cases, the auditor visits them in rotation so that while each will not be visited every year, all will be visited over a period of years.

There is an opinion that each yearly audit is independent of all others and adequate evidence must be found in all areas each year. However, auditor normally serves for many years and rotational testing makes sense in terms of efficiency and effectiveness. However, it is vital that rotational tests are carried out randomly so that client staffs do not know which areas or locations will be selected in any one year.

3.7.8 Cut-Off Examination

Cut-off procedures are the procedures designed to ensure that at the year-end trading transactions are entered in the period to which they relate. In other words, the term 'Cut-off' refers to the procedure adopted to ensure the separation of transactions as at the end of one accounting year from those at the commencement of the next following year, especially for items which may overlap, e.g., sales, purchase, stock etc.

Significance of Cut-Off in Auditing

The cut-off procedure is very significant in auditing to ensure that the revenue and expenditure of one year do not get recorded in the following year as that will distort the true and fair view of the accounts. The auditor must either establish that there are satisfactory internal controls in respect of cut-off and carry out compliance tests to ensure that these controls are functioning properly or carry out appropriate substantive tests. An obvious way in which accounts can be manipulated is for purchase invoices in respect of goods purchased shortly before the year end to be held over and entered in the following accounting period, the goods will be included in stock, but the purchases will not be included in the accounts as either a liability or a charge. Similarly, the profits and assets can be inflated by including goods that have been sold, but not yet despatched, in both stock and sales. Tests should be carried out between the purchase invoices, goods inward records and store records on the one hand, and the sales invoices, goods outward records and store records on the other, to ensure that there is consistency in treatment.

Cut-off manipulation was an important feature in which the auditors of Thomas Gerrard & Son Ltd. (1967) were held to have been negligent. The auditors' negligence arose primarily from their failure to follow up the alterations of the purchase invoices.

3.7.9 PHYSICAL EXAMINATION

Auditors use the term 'physical examination' to describe a special type of evidence gathering activity usually performed in the substantive testing stage of the audit engagement. (Physical examination is different to inspection and observation.) Physical examination refers to the examination by the auditor of a physical asset of the entity, such as machinery, equipment and inventory.

When evidence of completeness of an asset is required, the auditor gathers evidence that the asset physically examined has been included in the accounting records. For example, if evidence of the completeness of inventory was required, the auditor physically examines a quantity of inventory items and then ensures those items have been included in the accounting records.

When evidence of validity (existence) of an asset already included in the accounting records is required, the auditor physically examines that asset. For example, if evidence of the validity (existence) of the recorded quantity of inventory was required, the auditor selects a number of inventory items that has been recorded, and then ensures that quantity of items actually exists by physically examining the items.

In the substantive testing stage, physical examination provides complete and highly reliable evidence as to the validity (existence) of physical assets and incomplete, although highly reliable evidence of the completeness of the physical assets. This assumes that the person making the physical examination is competent and appropriately experienced.

3.7.10 STATISTICAL SAMPLING

Auditors have long considered it sufficient in given circumstances not to check all the items within any section of the work, but to test them to satisfy themselves whether they may consider the whole group as being satisfactory for their purposes. This is based upon the assumption that, subject to special circumstances such as beginning or end of period test, the number tested are sufficiently indicative of the accuracy or otherwise of the whole group.

Statistical sampling is only the extension of this common-sense point of view by the application of the mathematical theory broadly stated that, provided a sufficiently large and representative sample is taken from a large population, the sample will reveal the same characteristics of the whole group within measurable limits.

The use of these methods in practice does not require a detailed mathematical or statistical knowledge of the formulae on which the actual tests are based. Sets of tables are available which, on having decided the degree of confidence the auditor wishes to place in the result and the accuracy he desires, he can consult, and the amount of the tests to be carried out is specified.

Procedures for Application of Statistical Sampling

When statistical sampling is to be applied to a certain section of the audit, the procedures to be undertaken are the following:

  i. The nature of the unit and the field or population should be carefully defined, as any indefinite items wrongly included will vitiate the usefulness of the test.

  ii. The precise nature of the attributes to be tested should be defined, such as errors or authentication signatures, or if the sample is in respect of variables the data must be examined to determine the basic figures to be applied.

iii. The population should be broadly examined to ascertain whether any stratification will be necessary.

iv. The level of confidence and precision limits should be fixed in accordance with the auditor's judgement.

v. In accordance with the auditor's judgement as above, the sampling tables should be consulted, giving the sample size in the case of attributes, and where variables are concerned, a preliminary sample may be necessary.

vi. Random digit tables should be consulted showing the items to be selected for examination.

vii. The test should be evaluated comparing the result obtained with the predetermined acceptance or rejection levels.

viii. Where the sample is accepted, the auditor must ensure that the results are properly recorded so that it is called upon to prove that he has applied due care, skill and diligence to the work, he may be able to show his confidence to have been rightly placed.

Concept of Audit Sampling

Audit sampling means drawing conclusions about an entire set of data by testing a representative sample of items. The set of data, which may be a set of account balances (e.g. debtors, creditors, fixed assets) or transactions (e.g. all wage payments, all credit notes), is called the population. The individual items making up the population are called sampling units.

As given in SA-530, 'audit sampling' means the application of audit procedures to less than 100% of the items within an account balance or class of transactions to enable the auditor to obtain and evaluate audit evidence about some characteristics of the items selected in order to assist in forming a conclusion concerning the population.

When using either statistical or non-statistical sampling methods, the auditor should design and select an audit sample, perform audit procedures thereon, and evaluate sample results so as to provide sufficient appropriate audit evidence.

Reasons for Applying Sampling Technique

The auditor, in considering a particular population has to consider how to obtain assurance about it. Sampling may be the solution. A complete check of all the transactions and balances of a business is no longer required of an auditor. The reasons for this are as follows:

i. *Economic*: The cost in terms of expensive audit resources would be prohibitive.

ii. *Time*: The complete check would take so long that account would be ancient history before users saw them.

iii. *Practical*: Users of accounts do not expect or require 100% accuracy. Materiality is very important in accounting as well as in auditing.

iv. *Psychological*: A complete check would so bore the audit staff that their work would become ineffective and errors would be missed.

v. *Fruitfulness*: A complete check would not add much to the worth of figures if, as would be normal, few errors were discovered. The emphasis in auditing should be on the completeness of record and the true and fair view.

Factors that may be taken into account in considering whether or not to sample include the following:

i. *Materiality*: Some items of expenses may be so small that no conceivable error may affect the true and fair view of the accounts as a whole.

ii. *Number of items in the population*: If the number of items in the population are few (e.g., land and buildings), a 100% check may be economical.

iii. *Reliability of other items of evidence*: Analytical review (e.g., wages relate closely to number of employees, budgets, previous years etc.) or proof in total (VAT calculations). If other evidence is very strong, then a detailed check of a population may be unnecessary.

iv. *Cost and time*: Cost and time considerations can be relevant in selecting between evidence seeking methods.

v. A combination of evidence seeking methods is often the optimal solution.

Limitations of Application

However, there are certain exceptions. In some cases, a 100% check is necessary and sampling is not advisable. Some of the exceptional areas, where application of sampling technique is to be avoided include the following:

i. Unusual or exceptional items.

ii. Categories with special importance where materiality does not apply (for example, Director's remuneration).

iii. Categories which are few in numbers but of great importance (for example, land and buildings).

iv. Any area where the auditor is put upon enquiry.

v. High-risk areas.

But the auditors should carry out procedures designed to obtain sufficient appropriate audit evidence to determine with reasonable confidence whether the financial statements are free from material misstatement. Two words in the last sentence are relevant here—reasonable and material. It is not necessary that auditors should ensure that financial statements are absolutely 100% accurate. Sampling does not provide absolute proof of 100% accuracy but it can provide reasonable assurance that some elements of the financial statements are free from material misstatement.

Approaches to Sampling Technique

There are two approaches to sampling in auditing. These are:

i. Judgemental sampling

ii. Statistical sampling

Judgemental Sampling

This means selecting a sample of appropriate size on the basis of the auditor's judgement. This approach of sampling is also called as 'seat of pants' approach.

This approach has some advantages, which include the following:

i. No special knowledge of statistics is required.

ii. The auditor can bring his judgement and expertise into play. Some auditors seem to have a sixth sense.

iii. No time is spent on playing with mathematics. All the audit time is spent on auditing.

iv. The approach has been followed by the auditors for many years. It is well understood and refined by experience.

However, judgemental sampling approach is suffering from certain limitations. These limitations are as follows:

i. It is unscientific.

ii. There is no real logic to the selection of the sample or its size.

iii. No quantitative results are obtained.

iv. Personal bias in the selection of samples is unavoidable.

v. It is wasteful; usually sample sizes are too large.

Statistical Sampling

Drawing inference about a large volume of data by an examination of sample is a highly developed part of the discipline of statistics. It seems only common sense for the auditor to draw upon this body of knowledge in his own work. In practice, a high level of mathematical competence is required if valid conclusions are to be drawn from sample evidence. However, most firms that use statistical sampling have drawn up complex plans that can be operated by staff without statistical training. These involve the use of tables, graphs or computer methods.

The advantages of using statistical sampling are the following:

i. It is scientific.

ii. It is defensible.

iii. It provides precise mathematical statements about probabilities of being correct.

iv. It is efficient; overlarge sample sizes are not taken.

v. It can be used by lower grade staff that would be unable to apply the judgement needed by judgement sampling.

There are some disadvantages:

i. As a technique, it is not always fully understood so that false conclusions may be drawn from the results.

ii. Time is spent playing with mathematics, which might better be spent on auditing.

iii. Audit judgement takes second place to precise mathematics.

iv. It is inflexible.

v. Often several attributes of transactions or documents are tested at the same time. Statistics does not easily incorporate this.

Sampling Methods

There are several methods available to an auditor for selecting items. These include the following:

i. *Simple random sampling*: In this method, all items in the population are given a number. Numbers are selected by a means that gives every number an equal chance of being selected. This is done by using random number tables or computer-generated random numbers.

ii. *Systematic random sampling*: This method involves making a random start and then taking every *n*-th item thereafter. This is a commonly use method, which saves the work of computing random numbers. However, the sample may not be representative as the population may have some serial properties.

iii. *Stratified sampling*: In this method, the population is divided into sub-populations and is useful when parts of the population have higher than normal risk (for example, foreign customers, costly items). Usually, high-value items form a small part of the population and are 100% checked and the remainder is sampled.

iv. *Cluster sampling*: This method is useful when data is maintained in clusters or groups as wage records are kept in weeks and sales invoices in months. The idea is to select a cluster randomly and then to examine all the items in the cluster chosen. The problem with this method is that this sample may not be representative.

v. *Multi-stage sampling*: This method is appropriate when data is stored in two or more levels. For example stock in a retail chain of shops. The first step is to randomly select a sample of shops and the second stage is to randomly select stock items from the selected shops.

vi. *Block sampling*: Under this method, one block of items are selected at random. For example, all sales invoices for the month of July are selected for checking. This common sampling method has none of the desired features and is not usually recommended.

vii. *Value-based sampling*: This method uses the currency unit value rather than the items as the sampling population. It is now very popular and also termed as monetary unit sampling.

viii. *Haphazard sampling*: It means simply choosing items subjectively but avoiding bias. This method is acceptable for non-statistical sampling, but is insufficiently rigorous for statistical sampling.

Having carried out, on each sample item, those audit procedures that are appropriate to the particular audit objective, the auditor should

i. analyse any errors detected in the sample;

ii. project the errors found in the sample to the population; and

iii. reassess the sampling risk

On the basis of the above evaluation of the sampling results, the auditor needs to consider whether errors in the population might exceed the tolerable limit and in that case the auditor has either to change the method of selecting the sample of the technique of auditing itself.

3.7.11 Surprise Checking

'Surprise checking' means audit verification on a non-routine and surprise basis. Usually the routine checking plan of the auditor as well as its timing is known to the client. As a result, the client's staff to cover up incompleteness in the books and records before the visit by the auditor. However, surprise check as a part of normal audit procedure, significantly enhances the effectiveness of an audit. For carrying out surprise check, the auditor visits the client's office without prior intimation and verifies certain specific matters, the regularity of which is vital for audit. For example, the correctness of cash balances in hand is immensely important because of the nature of this asset. It is the general experience that irregularities and fraud are facilitated when books and records are not maintained systematically and regularly. Many important frauds and errors that are not detected from continuous check may be detected through the process of surprise checking.

Purposes of Surprise Checking

In any area of audit verification, the process of surprise checking is applicable. However, following are the specific area, where the process of surprise checking can be effectively applied:

i. For the verification of books of accounts and records, which are maintained in the branch offices.

ii. For the verification of cash, stock and similar type of assets, which are kept at other places.

iii. For checking of cash balance on a non-routine basis.

iv. For checking of investments on a non-routine basis.

v. For the verification of the regularity of the maintenance of books of accounts, statutory registers and other important documents.

vi. For the physical verification of stock and stores on a non-routine basis.

vii. For verification of the operation of any specific internal control procedures.

3.7.12 AUDIT FLOW CHART

A graphical presentation of different stages of a document, flow of goods or cash, with the aid of various symbolic marks, for the purpose of operation and control of audit organisation may be termed as 'audit flow chart'. In other words, it can be described as a map of inter-related operations.

It is arranged specially for indicating the sequence and also the types of operation as a part of total unit. Narrative description is replaced by the use of different symbols. The symbols are standardised in a greater way and the different interconnecting lines indicate the flow direction, which is either horizontal or vertical. The reason for the adoption of this chart is due to its advantages of making easy to 'visualise the relationship between different parts of the integrated system' of the organisation. The need for proper study and evaluation of internal control system has long been felt. The efficient preparation and introduction of the flow chart in a wide basis may fulfill the necessity.

Advantages

  i.   It acts as an effective tool to study internal control system of the organisation. Thus the weaknesses in the internal controls may be revealed by the examination of the flow chart.

  ii. Identification and location of various responsibility areas of the organisation can be made possible from this chart.

  iii. It gives a bird's eye view on the happenings of the business operations and areas where more control need be emphasised.

  iv. It can depict a situation relating to accounting and auditing system in a concise and simple way.

  v.   It is an important tool through which the training of audit staffs can be facilitated.

  vi. This chart can be introduced by the audit managers as a control device for their audit operation.

Disadvantages

  i.   It consumes time in preparing this chart.

  ii. It is not possible to have same pattern of flow chart that will be suitable to all types of organisations.

  iii. All the activities or operations of an organisation in all cases cannot be possible to be accumulated in a flow chart.

  iv. It is very difficult to form a judgement in selecting the level of sub-division that may be proper reflection of actual position.

3.7.13 TEST OF CONTROL

Test of control is performed to obtain audit evidence about the effectiveness of

  i.   the design of the accounting and internal control systems, that is, whether they are suitably designed to prevent or detect and correct material misstatements and

  ii. the operation of the internal controls throughout the period.

Tests of control include tests of the elements of the control environment where strengths in the control environment are used by auditors to reduce control risk.

As per SA-400 tests of control may include

➢ inspection of documents supporting transactions and other events to gain audit evidence that internal control are operated properly, for example, verifying that a transaction has been authorised,

➢ inquiries about, and observation of, internal controls, which leaves no audit trials, for example, determining who actually performs each function and not merely who are supposed to perform it,

➢ re-performance of internal controls, for example, reconciliation of bank accounts, to ensure they were correctly performed by the organisation, and

➢ testing of internal control operating on specific computerised applications or over the overall information technology function, for example, access or programme change controls.

The auditor should obtain audit evidence through tests of control to support any assessment of control risk, which is less than high. The lower the assessment of control risk, the more evidence the auditor should obtain that accounting and internal control systems are suitably designed and operating effectively.

3.7.14 INTERNAL CONTROL QUESTIONNAIRES

Internal control questionnaires now form an important part of any efficiently conducted audit. By their use, any system of internal control may be investigated and its weaknesses revealed. It is usual to have sets of standardised questionnaires, which may be applied subject to modification on any type of audit.

The procedure employed is to use the standard questionnaire relevant to the various sections of an organisation on the first occasion. These are completed by staff on the job and are thereafter examined by the manager in charge. Points of lesser importance may be dealt with and questions inapplicable to the job eliminated. In conjunction with the questionnaire, an audit programme for the job may be prepared. This does not signify that the audit cannot be commenced until the questionnaire has been dealt with or a standard form of programme will have been already in use.

Such questionnaires have already been proved to save much time in audit planning and do much to ensure that no aspect of the work is overlooked from the point of view of the audit. On the first occasion, a greater amount of work will be involved than on subsequent audits, as it is necessary to investigate the whole system of control, thereafter checks may be made to ensure that the system is being adhered to where changes in the system are deemed necessary, the auditor should request notification, but in any case he should be able to discover any such alterations, and no doubt the questionnaire will need bringing up to date from time to time.

3.7.15 AUDIT TESTS

Audit tests are of two types.

Compliance Test

A compliance test is a test, which seeks to provide audit evidence that internal control procedures are being applied as prescribed.

Example

i. Checking for authorisation on a credit note. This should confirm that all credit notes are suitably authorised before being issued.

ii. Checking for the casting stamp on a purchase invoice. This should confirm that all invoices are cast before being paid.

Substantive Test

A substantive test is a test of a transaction or balance which seeks to provide audit evidence as to the completeness, accuracy and validity of the information contained in the accounting records or financial statements.

Example

i.   Circularisation of debtors to confirm the accuracy of the balance on the sales ledger.

ii. Matching a purchase invoice with the original order and goods received note to confirm that the purchase in bonafide.

Compliance Procedures

Compliance procedures or tests are done to obtain audit evidence about the effective operation of the accounting and control systems, that is, that properly designed controls identified in the preliminary assessment of control risk exist in fact and have operated throughout the relevant period. Compliance tests are sometimes called tests of control.

The first stage in the auditor's assessment of the reliability of a system is a preliminary review of the effectiveness of the system by using an internal control evaluation questionnaire, which contains key questions. If the system appears to be defective or weak, then the auditor may need to abandon the systems approach and apply substantive tests. If the system is effective, then the next stage is for the auditor to obtain evidence that the system is applied as in his description at all times. This evidence is obtained by examining a sample of the transactions to determine if each has been treated as required by the system, i.e., to see if the system has been complied with.

Two points must be made about compliance tests:

i.   It is the application of the system that is being tested not the transaction although the testing is through the medium of the transactions.

ii. If discovery is made that the system was not complied with in a particular way, then
     (a) the auditor may need to revise his system description and re-appraise its effectiveness and
     (b) he will need to determine if the failure of compliance was an isolated instance or was symptomatic.

It may be that a larger sample may be taken.

Example

Suppose a system provided that all credit notes issued by the client had to be approved by the sales manager and that a space was provided on each credit note for his initials. Then the auditor would inspect a sample of the credit notes to determine if all of them had been initialled. In practice other internal controls, e.g., checking of calculations, would be tested on the same credit notes.

Substantive Procedures

Substantive procedures (or substantive tests) are activities performed by the auditor during the substantive testing stage of the audit that gather evidence as to the completeness, validity and/ or accuracy of account balances and underlying classes of transactions.

Management impliedly assert that account balances and underlying classes of transactions do not contain any material misstatements; in other words, they are materially complete, valid and accurate. Auditors gather evidence about these assertions by undertaking activities referred to as substantive procedures.

In short, substantive procedures are tests to obtain audit evidence to detect material misstatement in the financial statements. In fact, all audit works come within the compass of substantive testing. However, it is usually used to mean all tests other than compliance tests. A substantive test is any test that seeks direct evidence of the correct treatment of a transaction, a balance, an asset, a liability or any item in the books or the accounts.

They are generally of two types:

i.   Analytical procedures and

ii. other substantive procedures, such as test of details of transactions and balances, reviews of minutes of directors' meetings and enquiry.

For example, an auditor may

- physically examine inventory on balance date as evidenced that inventory shown in the accounting records actually exists (validity assertion);

- arrange for suppliers to confirm in writing the details of the amount owing at balance date as evidence that accounts payable is complete (complete assertion); and

- make inquiries of management about the collectibility of customers' accounts as evidence that trade debtors is accurate as to its valuation.

Evidence that an account balance or class of transaction is not complete, valid or accurate is evidence of a substantive misstatement.

There are two categories of substantive procedures—analytical procedures and test of details. Analytical procedures generally provide less reliable evidence than the tests of detail. It is also to be noted that analytical procedures are applied in several different audit stages, whereas tests of detail are only applied in the substantive testing stage.

Example

i.   *Of a transaction*: the sale of a part of machinery will require the auditor to examine the copy invoice, the authorisation, the entry in the asset register and other books, the accounting treatment and some evidence that the price obtained was reasonable.

ii. *Of a balance*: direct confirmation of the balance in deposit account obtained from the bank.

iii. *Completeness of information*: obtaining confirmation from a client's legal adviser that all potential payments from current litigation had been considered.

iv. *Accuracy of information*: obtaining from each director a confirmation that an accurate statement of remuneration and expenses had been obtained.

v.   *Validity of information*: validity means based on evidence that can be supported.

vi. *Analytical review*: evidence of the correctness of cut-off by examining the gross profit ratio.

Difference Between Compliance Procedure and Substantive Procedure

A compliance procedure is a test procedure that seeks to provide evidence that the internal control system is being applied as prescribed. The auditor thus needs to carry out compliance tests to assess the efficiency of the internal control system. He cannot rely on the system unless he has obtained satisfactory results to compliance tests.

A substantive test on the other hand is one designed to provide evidence as to the accuracy of the amount or account balance. The auditor must carry out substantive tests on all aspects of the financial statements as compliance tests do not provide sufficient, relevant and reliable evidence on which to base his opinion. Items such as stock valuation or provision for doubtful debts are not subject to internal control and are very judgemental. The auditor must substantially test such items specifically rather than testing a system.

3.8   REPRESENTATION BY MANAGEMENT

Representation by management means the confirmation by the management, either written or oral, about the items shown in the financial statements of the concerned organisation. In other words, representation by management constitutes acknowledgement by the management about its responsibility for the preparation and presentation of financial information.

The management of an organisation is responsible for the preparation and presentation of financial information through financial statements. It is obvious that management would be required to make several representations on various matters relating to financial statements during the course of audit. The management may make these representations either in orally or in writing to the auditors. A written representation may either take the form of a letter from the management or letter by the auditors outlining auditor's understanding and confirmation of the same. For example, if the management confirms through a letter to the auditors that they have recorded all known liabilities in the financial statements, such confirmation is called management representation.

3.8.1 REPRESENTATION BY MANAGEMENT AS AUDIT EVIDENCE

SA-580 requires that the auditor may rely upon the management's representation, preferably in writing, as a sort of information or evidence to consider and if the representations relate to matters that are material to financial information. Further, the auditor should:

i.   consider whether the individual making the representations are expected to be well informed on the matter,

ii. seek corroborate evidence from sources inside or outside the organisation, and

iii. evaluate whether the representations made by the management appear reasonable and consistent with other audit evidence obtained, including other representations.

However, it should be noted that representation by management is not substitute for normal audit procedure. For example, a representation by the management as to the existence, ownership and cost of the machineries located at a distant place is not substitute for adopting audit procedures regarding verification and valuation of machineries.

3.8.2 DOCUMENTATION OF REPRESENTATION BY MANAGEMENT

The auditor should keep the following documents as his working papers:

i.   Written representation of the management.

ii. Auditor's understanding of management representation duly acknowledged by the management.

iii. Authenticated copies of relevant minutes of meeting of the board of directors or similar body.

If the management is not willing to give in writing the representation, the auditor should prepare himself a letter in writing setting out his understanding of management representation that have been made during the course of audit verbally and sent it to the management with a request to acknowledge and confirm that his understanding of representation is correct.

If management refuses to acknowledge or confirm the letter sent by the auditor, this would constitute the limitation of the scope of his examination. In such a case, the auditor should consider the effect of such refusal on his report.

3.8.3 LETTER OF REPRESENTATION

The purposes of the letter of representation are that it is a reminder to management that they are responsible for the preparation of the accounts and for the truth and fairness of the information contained therein. It is also a contributory form of audit evidence but it in no way relieves the auditor from checking any of the information in the accounts.

It is also a formal record of all representations made to the auditor during the course of audit. The main contents of the letter of representation are as follows:

i.   A statement that all relevant information and explanations have been made available to the auditor.

ii. A statement that the accounting treatment of all items is consistent with previous periods except as disclosed.

iii.   Details of all significant accounting policies adopted.

iv.   A statement that the organisation has good title to all assets included in the balance sheet.

v.   A statement that all known material liabilities and all significant post balance sheet events have been dealt with in the accounts.

vi.   A statement that the accounts comply with the relevant provisions of the prevailing acts and rules governing the organisation.

The basic objective of a letter of representation is to provide a formal record of presentations made to and relied upon by the auditor. It also ensures that there can be no misunderstanding between the management of the organisation and the auditor as to the representations which were made during the course of the audit.

The basic elements of a management representation letter as prescribed in SA-580 include the following:

1. *Addressee*

A management representation letter should be addressed to the auditor containing the relevant information and be appropriately dated and signed.

2. *Date*

A management representation letter should normally be dated the same date as the auditor's report on the financial information or a date prior thereto.

3. *Signature*

It should ordinarily be signed by the members of the management who have primary responsibility for the entity and its financial aspects, e.g., managing director, finance director.

4. *Refusal*

If management refuses to provide representations on any matter that the auditor considers necessary, this will constitute a limitation on the scope of his examination.

5. *Confirmation*

If case management is not willing to give in writing the representations made by it during the course the course of audit, the auditor should himself prepare a letter in writing setting out his understanding of management's representations that have been made to him during the course of audit and send it to management with a request to acknowledge and confirm that his understanding of the representations is correct.

The auditor should document in his working papers evidence of management's representations.

3.9 DELEGATION, SUPERVISION AND REVIEW OF AUDIT WORK

Except for the smallest audit engagements, it is not possible for an auditor to perform the entire audit by themselves. This is because the audit would take to long to complete and/or the cost of performing the audit would be prohibitive. This means that it is usually necessary for the auditor to delegate significant work (or authority to delegate further work) to other staff members within the audit firm. Delegation is only possible if there is appropriate supervision and review of the work performed. The person that supervises and reviews works performed by others is a person who is at least as equally experienced and competent as the person to whom the work/authority has been delegated and is usually the person that delegated the work/authority.

3.9.1 DELEGATION

An auditor only delegates work/authority to persons with the appropriate experience and competence. This applies to all levels of organisations within the audit firm. Thus a senior staff member to whom work/authority has been delegated only further delegates work/authority to other staff members that have the appropriate experience and competence.

An auditor/staff member delegating work/authority ensures that the person to whom the work/authority has been delegated completely understands the nature of the work that the person is required to perform as well as the limits of any delegated authority.

3.9.2 SUPERVISION

Auditors and audit staff members supervise the work delegated by them to others so as to minimise the risk of a lessoning of the standard of care. The more complex the nature of the work delegated and less experienced and competent the staff member to whom the work has been delegated, then the greater the degree of supervision.

Auditors supervise work while the delegatee is performing it. This contrasts with the review of work which auditors carry out after the delegatee has performed the work.

The purpose of supervision is to provide the supervisor with a degree of assurance that the work of the delegatee is being performed in accordance with the instructions given and with the appropriate standard of care.

3.9.3 REVIEW

Work performed by the auditor and his or her audit staffs is reviewed. Work performed by the auditor (the engagement partner) is reviewed by a person not personally involved with the client (the review partner and/ or personnel from quality control). The person that delegated the work to those staff members usually reviews work performed by the auditor's staff member.

The purpose of this quality review is to ensure that the work was performed in accordance with the instructions given, with the appropriate standard of care and in accordance with any delegated authority. In relation to work performed in the control testing, substantive testing and opinion formulation stages, the reviewer ensures that audit procedures performed conform to the audit programmes, that audit procedures required to be performed have been properly performed, that the evidence obtained has been properly documented and that conclusions reached as consistent with the evidence obtained.

3.9.4 CONTROL OF QUALITY OF AUDIT WORK

The audit firm should implement quality control policies and procedures designed to ensure that all audits are conducted in accordance with Auditing and Assurance Standards.

As per SA-220, the objectives of quality control policies and procedures to be adopted by an audit firm will ordinarily incorporate the following:

i. *Professional requirements*: To maintain the audit quality, the personnel in the audit firm involved in the conduct of audit are to adhere to the principles of independence, integrity, objectivity, confidentiality and professional approach.

ii. *Skills and competence*: Technical knowledge and professional competence are very much required to enable the personnel to perform their duties effectively, efficiently and with competence in order to maintain the quality of audit work.

iii. *Assignment*: Effective assignment of work ensures the quality of audit work. The right person should be assigned with the right type of job, i.e., audit work is to be assigned to personnel who have the degree of technical training and proficiency required in the circumstances.

iv. *Delegation*: In order to ensure that the work performed meets appropriate standards of quality, there should be sufficient direction, supervision and review of work at all levels.

v.   *Consultation*: Expert opinion from within or outside the audit firm can be taken to maintain the quality of audit work. So, if required, consultation is to occur with those who have appropriate authorities.

vi.   *Acceptance and retention*: In taking decision regarding acceptance and retention of existing as well as new clients, the ability of the firm to serve the client properly and the independence aspects of the firm are to be considered. For this purpose, an evaluation of prospective clients and a review on an ongoing process of existing clients is to be conducted.

vii.   *Monitoring*: Continuous monitoring of the adequacy and operational effectiveness of the quality control policies and procedures adopted by the firm are to be made to maintain the quality of audit work throughout.

The general quality control policies and procedures of the firm should be communicated to its personnel in a manner that provides reasonable assurance that the policies and procedures are understood and implemented.

3.10   PROFESSIONAL SCEPTICISM

Professional scepticism in auditing implies an attitude that includes a questioning mind and a critical assessment of audit evidence without being obsessively suspicious or sceptical. Such an attitude results, for example, in the auditor asking more questions than usual and more probing questions, critically analysing these answers and then studiously comparing this analysis with other evidence gathered.

Auditors adopt an attitude of professional scepticism when they evaluate audit evidence. When the auditor adopts such an attitude, the auditor does not accept evidenced gathered at its face value; rather the auditor evaluates the evidence bearing in mind the possibility that, for example,

*   the evidence may be misleading,
*   the evidence may be incomplete or
*   the person providing the evidence may be either incompetent or motivated to provide evidence that is misleading or incomplete.

The lower the acceptable level of audit risk or the greater the risk of material misstatement, the greater the application of an attitude of professional scepticism.

Auditors usually consider evidence gathered through inquiry to provide evidence that is less than reliable as the competence and integrity of the person responding may not be capable of being ascertained with any degree of certainty and/or the inquiree may be motivated to be less than completely honest. This is a prime example of where auditors adopt an attitude of professional scepticism.

3.11   AUDIT RISK AND MATERIALITY

All items should be subject to substantive tests but the extent of such tests depends on the materiality of the item and the inherent risk of misstatement attached to the item. As an example of materiality, consider petty cash which, even if grossly wrong, may be unlikely to affect the view given by the financial statements. As an example of inherent risk, consider the evaluation of the value of work in progress in a construction company. The valuation may be critical to the financial statements yet it may be very difficult to establish precisely.

The auditor may expect to be able to rely upon their preliminary assessment of control risk to reduce the extent of their substantive procedures. In such cases, the auditor should make a preliminary assessment of control risk for material financial statement assertions and should then plan and perform compliance tests to support that assessment. For example, the preliminary walk through tests might indicate good controls over debt collections in an enterprise. The auditor may then assess the control risk attached to the assertion that all debts, that should have been collected, have been collected. Compliance tests should then be planned and performed to support that assessment. If those tests do support the assessment, then the extent of substantive tests can be reduced.

3.11.1 CONCEPT OF MATERIALITY

An auditor is not required to have evidence that all items in a set of accounts are 100% correct. His duty is to give opinion on the truth and fairness of the accounts. Errors can exist in the accounts and yet the accounts can still give a true and fair view. The maximum error that any particular magnitude can contain without marring the true and fair view is the tolerable error. Tolerable error is auditing materiality.

As per SA-320 on 'audit materiality', information is material if its misstatements could influence the economic decisions of users taken on the basis of the financial information. Materiality depends on the size and nature of the item, judged in the particular circumstances of its misstatement.

In his audit planning, the auditor needs to determine the amount of tolerable error in any given population and to carry out tests to provide evidence that the actual errors in the population are less than the tolerable error. For example, stock can be a large amount in a set of accounts. Stock is computed by counting and weighing, by multiplying quantity by price and by summing individual values. Errors can occur at any of these stages. Applied prices may be incorrect. The effect of incorrect prices may be to compute a stock figure that is above or below the correct stock figure by an amount that is above the tolerable limit.

3.11.2 AUDIT RISK

Audit risk is a term which has grown in importance in recent years. Audit risk means the chance of damage of audit firm as a result of giving an audit opinion that is wrong in some particular. So, the term applies to the risk that the auditor will draw wrong opinion or an invalid conclusion from his audit procedures. A wrong audit opinion means for example saying that the accounts show a true and fair view when in fact they do not.

Audit risk has several components:

i. *Inherent risk*: Inherent risk is the risk attached to any particular population because of factors such as the following:
    ➤ The type of industry—a new manufacturing hi-tech industry is more prone to errors of all sorts than a stable business like a brewery.
    ➤ Previous experience indicates that significant errors have occurred.
    ➤ Some population is always prone to error, e.g., stock calculation, work in progress valuation.

ii. *Control risk*: That is the risk that internal controls will not detect and prevent material errors. If this risk is large then the auditor eschew compliance tests altogether and apply only substantive tests.

iii. *Detection risk*: This is the risk that the auditor's substantive procedures and analytical review will not detect material errors.

The assurance that an auditor seeks from sampling procedures is related to the audit risk that he perceives. The sample sizes required will be related to the audit risk that he perceives. The sample sizes required will be related to materiality and to audit risk.

3.11.3 RELATIONSHIP BETWEEN MATERIALITY AND AUDIT RISK

As given in SA-320, there is an inverse relationship between materiality and the degree of audit risk, that is, the higher the materiality level, the lower the audit risk and vice versa. The auditor takes the inverse relationship between materiality and audit risk into account when determining the nature, timing and extent of audit procedures. For example, if, after planning for specific audit procedure, the auditor determines that the acceptable materiality level is lower, audit risk is increased.

The auditor would compensate for this by either:

i. reducing the assessed degree of control risk, where this is possible and supporting the reduced degree by carrying out extended or additional tests of control; or

ii. reducing detection risk by modifying the nature, timing and extent of planned substantive procedures.

3.12 FINAL REVIEW

The auditor must plan his audit to ensure all significant matters are considered. If he reviews the management and statutory accounts before planning the audit, he can incorporate all potential problem areas. Identification of such areas will come from looking at the trends of the accounts and comparing them with the budget. After completing the audit as planned and before writing the audit report, the auditor is required to make a final review of the activities he has done.

The objective of the review carried out at the conclusion of the audit is quite different from the initial review. The final review is required to assist in forming an opinion on the truth and fairness of the financial statements and their compliance with the Companies Act.

The final review will probably be carried out with the aid of a checklist covering the following points:

i. *Analytical review of the figures, including ratio analysis.* This may reveal evidence not previously found during the audit which may affect the view shown by the accounts. The auditor is concerned that this view is in accordance with his knowledge of the client and that a reasonable person would draw valid and consistent conclusions from the financial statements.

ii. All disclosure requirements as per the Companies Act and Auditing and Assurance Standards have been met, including accounting policies.

iii. All statutory and other reporting requirements of the enterprise have been met.

iv. Finally, that taken as a whole, the financial statements show a true and fair view of the enterprise's results for the period and its financial position at the balance sheet date.

The points which the auditor will consider in carrying out the final review of the financial statements include the following:

• Whether the financial statements have been prepared using acceptable and appropriate accounting policies which have been consistently applied.

• Whether the financial statements comply with statutory and other reporting requirements and other regulations such as Auditing and Assurance Standards.

• Whether the view presented by the financial statements is consistent with the auditor's own knowledge of the business.

• Whether the financial statements present information in a form readily understandable by those reading them.

In considering the above points, the auditor will pay particular attention to the results of the analytical review procedures that he carries out. These procedures involve in particular the following:

i. The computation and analysis of significant ratios and trends.

ii. The comparison of figures in the financial statements with previous years and other relevant available data.

iii. The investigation of any material variations that arise.

Throughout the final review, the auditor needs to take account of the materiality of the matters under consideration and the results of the other audit work he has carried out. A review is not, of itself a sufficient basis for the expression of an audit opinion.

3.13 CASE STUDIES

CASE STUDY 1: ON AUDIT EVIDENCE

Capital Electronics Departmental Stores sell a high proportion of their merchandise on hire purchase. The system of dealing with HP sales is highly organized and well controlled. The HP debtors ledger is kept on a specially designed microcomputer system. The HP debtors of the company as on 31.3.2007 appear in the accounts at 4.6 lakhs out of gross assets 20.5 lakhs.

Discussion

a. What assertions are the directors implying in stating the HP debtors at 4.6 lakhs?
b. What possible misstatements could occur?
c. What varieties of evidence may be collected regarding this current asset?
d. What basic techniques for collecting evidence can be applied to the item?

CASE STUDY 2: ON RELATED PARTY TRANSACTIONS

You are the auditors of Apollo Services Ltd. And you have recently been reading a report on a similar company that criticized the auditors for failing to comment on the existence of the material related party transactions.

Discussion

a. What do you mean by this term 'related party transactions'?
b. What steps do you consider should be incorporated into your audit work to minimize the risk of similar criticism being levelled at your firm?
c. Illustrate your comment with examples of related parties and types of transactions.

◆ Suggested questions

A   Short-type questions:

1. 'Test check is based on presumption'—What is that presumption?
2. What is audit memorandum?
3. What is audit manual?
4. Discuss the importance of surprise check.
5. Distinguish between principles of auditing and techniques of auditing.

B   Essay-type questions:

1. What are the considerations to be kept in mind by an auditor before commencement of an audit?
2. What is audit programme? Discuss the advantages and disadvantages of conducting an audit according to a predetermined audit programme. How can these disadvantages be overcome?
3. How an audit programme is prepared? State the objectives of audit programme. What are the steps to be followed in drawing an audit programme?
4. What are audit files? What are the contents of audit files? What are the advantages of audit files?
5. What is audit note book? Of what purpose does it serve? What are the contents of audit note book?

6. What is audit working paper? What are its objectives? Discuss the essential characteristics of a good working paper. Who can claim the ownership of those papers?

7. What is routine checking? What types of work are included in routine checking? What are the objectives of routine checking? Describe the advantages and disadvantages of routine checking. Discuss the duties of an auditor in this regard.

8. What is test checking? In what circumstances test checking is advisable? What factors are to be considered before resorting to test checking? What are the advantages and disadvantages of test checking? Discuss the duty of the auditor in this regard.

9. What is auditing in depth? Discuss the advantages and disadvantages of this audit technique.

10. Discuss briefly the methods of obtaining audit evidence. In this context, state what do you mean by 'compliance test' and 'substantive test'.

11. What do you mean by techniques of auditing? Discuss the various techniques adopted by an auditor in the course of his audit work.

Chapter 4

Internal Control, Internal Check and Internal Audit

4.1 INTRODUCTION

Before the auditor can determine his basic approach to an audit, he must ensure that he fully understands the organisation with which he is dealing. He must familiarise himself with its organisational structure and comprehend the nature of the business. He must also ensure that he has fully grasped all the technicalities peculiar to the business. Only then he will be in a position fully to comprehend and identify the transactions, which are being recorded in the accounting books and in relation to which the internal controls will be operating.

Formerly, business systems were usually installed with the object of getting work done by the cheapest and quickest methods available, but while these objects have not been lost sight of, it has been realised that establishment of the piecemeal methods of uncoordinated work process is ultimately neither cheap nor efficient. Overall planning is necessary to establish a flow of work through the whole business, enabling it to run smoothly and efficiently and with the added requirement that its assets shall be safeguarded at the same time.

This overall planning and its practical operation is included under the title of internal control, which is established by the management and although the auditor in his role as an auditor has no right to require any particular method of control to be operated, but he is virtually concerned with it, as the efficiency or otherwise of the internal control will greatly influence the auditor's method of working.

4.2 INTERNAL CONTROL

4.2.1 DEFINITION

Internal control refers to the various methods and procedures adopted for the control of production, distribution and the whole system (financial and non-financial) of the enterprise.

In other words, internal control system—the whole system of controls, financial or otherwise, established by the management in order to carry on the business of the enterprise in an orderly and efficient manner, ensure adherence to management policies, safeguard the assets and secure as far as possible the completeness and accuracy of the records.

The special report on internal control of the American Institute of the Certified Public Accountants and its statements on auditing procedures contain the following definition of internal control: "Internal control comprises the plan of organisation and all the coordinated methods and measures adopted within a business to safeguard its assets, check the accuracy and reliability of its accounting data, promote operations efficiency and encourage employees to prescribed managerial policies."

In the opinion of W. W. Bigg, "internal control is best regarded as indicating the whole system of controls, financial or otherwise, established by the management in the conduct of a business including internal check, internal audit and other forms of control."

So, on the basis of above definitions, it may be stated that a system of internal control provides a measure for the management to obtain information, protection and control, which are quite important for the successful working of a business organisation.

4.2.2 Basic Elements of Internal Control

An effective system of internal control should have the following basic elements:

Financial and Other Organisational Plans

This may take the form of a manual suitably classified by flow charts. It should specify the various duties and responsibilities of both management and staff, stating what powers of authorisation reside in various members. This is important as in the event of staff absence or otherwise, the correct flow of work and the internal control system could be vitiated by the wrong implementation of procedures by staff either innocently or wilfully.

Competent Personnel

Personnel are the most important element of any internal control system. If the employees are competent and efficient in their assigned work, internal control system can be operated effectively even if some of the other elements of internal control system are absent.

Division of Work

The procedure of division of work properly among the employees of the organisation is important. Each and every work of the organisation should be divided in different stages and should be allocated to the employees in accordance with their quality and skill.

Separation of Operational Responsibility from Record Keeping

If each department of an organisation is being assigned to prepare its own records and reports, there may be a tendency to manipulate results for showing better performance. So, in order to ensure reliable records and information, record-keeping function is separated from the operational responsibility of the concerned department.

Separation of the Custody of Assets from Accounting

To protect against misuse of assets and their misappropriation, it is required that the custody of assets and their accounting should be done by separate persons. When a particular person performs both the functions, there is a chance of utilising the organisation's assets for his personal interest and adjusting the records to relieve himself from the responsibility of the asset.

Authorisation

Under the internal control system, all the activities must be authorised by a proper authority. The individual or group, which can grant either specific or general authority for transactions, should hold a position commensurate with the nature and significance of the transactions and the policy for such authority should be established by top management.

Managerial Supervision and Review

The internal control system should be implemented and maintained in conformity with the environmental changes of the concern. With adapting any specific control system permanently, how far the procedures of flexible controls have been followed in real practice should be observed and re-examined.

4.2.3 OBJECTIVES OF INTERNAL CONTROL

Internal control is of fundamental importance to the auditor, because before he can plan the tests he intends to carry out in his audit programme, he must decide the extent to which he intends to rely on the system of internal control. But before depending upon the internal control system of the organisation, the auditor should ensure that the following objectives of internal control as per SA- 400 are achieved by the organisation:

Proper Authorisation
Transactions are executed with management's general and specific authorisation.

Prompt Recording of Transactions
All the transactions are promptly recorded in the correct amount in the appropriate accounts and in the accounting period in which executed so as to permit preparation of financial information within a framework of recognised accounting policies and to maintain accountability of assets.

Restricted Access to Assets
Access to assets is permitted only in accordance with management's authorisation.

Actions Against Deviations
The recorded accountability for assets is compared with the existing assets at reasonable intervals and appropriate action is taken with regard to any differences.

Advantages
The various advantages that may be derived from internal control system are summarised as below:

1. Identification of Defects

Under internal control system, the total activities are segregated in such a way that the work preformed by one employee is automatically checked by another employee. So, if there is any defect in the system, it is easily detected.

2. Flexibility

In this system, year-wise comparative analysis is done. So, if there is any change in the mode of operation, the changes in the system could easily be accommodated. So, the opportunity for flexibility is available.

3. Savings in Time

If the internal control system is in operation in an organisation, there is no need for the preparation of separate audit programmes for each and every audit engagement. Thus it saves time to a great extent.

4. Lesser Risk of Omission

Under this system, the total work is sub-divided into a number of activities and each employee is assigned each type of activity. So, there is least chance of oversight or omission of any issue.

5. Provision for Training Facility

Due to lack of adequate experience, the auditor may face difficulty in establishing a close relationship between audit programme and the internal control system. This system itself provides training facilities to auditors to overcome this difficulty.

Disadvantages
It is also important to appreciate the following inherent limitations of internal control system:

1. Chances of Human Error

The possibility of human error due to carelessness, mistakes of judgment or the misunderstanding of instructions may make the system ineffective.

2. Costly

The management's usual requirement is that a control procedure should be cost-effective. But in many cases, the cost of internal control procedure is not proportionate to the potential loss due to fraud and error.

3. Ignorance of Unusual Activity

It is the fact that most of the internal control techniques are directed towards anticipated types of transactions and not on unusual transactions.

4. Collusion

There may be the possibility of circumvention of controls through collusion with parties outside the organisation or with employees of the organisation.

5. Abuses of Responsibility

It may happen that a person responsible for exercising control abuses that responsibility.

6. Rigidity

There is the possibility that the system may become inadequate due to changes in the conditions and compliance with procedures may deteriorate.

4.2.4 EVALUATION OF INTERNAL CONTROL

The evaluation of internal controls is fundamental to an audit. It is on the basis of this evaluation the auditor will:

   i.   determine the nature and extent of his audit procedure, i.e., draws up his audit programme, and

   ii. draft his letters of weaknesses, drawing the attention of management to inform them about the weaknesses of the system.

Because of its importance, evaluation must be clearly distinguished from the process of ascertaining and recording the system.

Before taking up the work of audit in an organisation, the auditor should ascertain the authenticity of the internal control system existing in the organisation. He will evaluate the control system in order to determine whether he would depend on the internal control system or not and if so, to what extent he would depend on the system.

The auditor himself will determine the process or procedure applying his own knowledge and judgment in the context of nature and size of the organisation under audit.

The auditor, while evaluating the system of internal control, should consider the following matters:

   i.   Whether the basic principles of internal control, which is prevailing in the organisation, have been properly followed;

   ii. Whether the procedure which are prescribed from theoretical point of view have been properly implemented, and

   iii. After definite interval of time, whether any changes are made in the system of internal control in the context of changed circumstances of the organisation.

On the basis of evaluation on the effectiveness of the internal audit system, the external auditor will decide the extent of degree of his reliance on the functioning of the internal audit system.

4.2.5 INTERNAL CONTROL AND THE AUDITOR

The Institute of Chartered Accountants of India in its Standards on Auditing (SA-400) has stated: "The duty of safeguarding the assets of a company is primarily that of the management and the auditor is entitled to rely upon the safeguards and internal controls instituted by the management, although he will of course take into account any deficiencies he may find therein, while drafting his programme."

So far as the auditor is concerned, the examination and evaluation of internal control system is an indispensable part of the overall audit programme. The auditor needs reasonable assurance that the accounting system is adequate and that all the accounting information that should be recorded has been recorded. Internal control normally contributes to ensuring recording of such information. The auditor should gain an understanding of the accounting system and related internal controls and should study and evaluate the operations of these internal controls upon which he wishes to rely in determining the nature, timing and extent of other audit procedures.

He can formulate his entire audit programme only after he has had a satisfactory understanding of the internal control systems and their actual operation. According to the American Institute of Certified Public Accountants, the auditor is required to make a proper review of the existing internal control and on the basis of such a review, the auditor is to determine the resultant extent of the tests to which auditing procedures are to be restricted.

A proper understanding of the internal control system in its control and working also enables an auditor to decide upon the appropriate audit procedure to be applied in different areas covered by the audit programme. In a situation where the internal controls are considered weak in some areas, the auditor might choose an audit procedure on test that otherwise might not be required; might extend certain tests to cover a large number of transactions or other items than he otherwise would examine; and at times may perform additional tests to bring him the necessary satisfaction.

From the above, it can be concluded that the extent and nature of the audit programme is substantially influenced by the internal control system in operation. In deciding upon a plan of selective checking, the existence and operation of internal control system is of great significance.

4.2.6 INTERNAL CONTROL CHECKLIST

Checklists are 'aides-memoire' to the auditor to ensure all important aspects of the accounts have been considered. Checklists can also be used in assessing the internal control systems when they would list the crucial questions the auditor must ask. Checklists should be completed, signed and placed on the current working papers files as an evidence that the matters included have been covered.

In fact, checklist is a series of instructions and/or questions which the auditor must follow and answer. When he completes the instructions, he initials the space against the instruction. Answers to the checklist instructions are usually Yes, No or Not Applicable.

A few examples of checklist instructions are given below:

i. Are books of serially numbered cash sales slips used by sales assistants?

ii. Is there a proper system controlling the issue and return of the books of cash sales slips?

iii. Are sales assistants forbidden to receive cash?

iv. Is a copy of the cash sale slip given to
 (a) the cashier?
 (b) the customer?

v. Are the details of prices and calculations shown on the cash sale slips subject to independent checking?

vi. Does the customer, before receiving the goods, take the cash sale slip to the cashier and pay for the goods?

vii. Do sales assistants only deliver goods to the customer against the receipted cash sale slip?

viii. Are there regular collections of cash from the cashiers during business hours?

ix. Is all cash received banked intact on day of receipt? If not, give details of the system.

x. Is the total of the cash banked reconciled by a responsible official, other than the chief cashier, with
(a) cashier's records?
(b) the sales records?

4.2.7 INTERNAL CONTROL QUESTIONNAIRE

An internal control questionnaire is basically a comprehensive list of questions, covering every aspect of the client's system, the answers to which will enable the auditor to assess the internal controls in operation. To facilitate the assessment, the questions are asked in a form whereby the answer 'yes' is satisfactory, whereas the answers 'no' appear to indicate a weakness.

Basic Characteristics of Internal Control Questionnaire

i. The internal control questionnaires will be drafted as far as possible in a form whereby the questions can simply be answered 'yes/no/not applicable'.

ii. Though the internal control questionnaires are normally in a standardised pre-printed form for particular types of enterprises, their application to individual clients in a skilled matter requires the attention of senior staff.

iii. The internal control questionnaires will require reviewing and updating at regular intervals and on the basis of changing situations, amendments are required to be made to the system.

iv. Staff responsible for the completion or review of internal control questionnaires should be required to sign and date them. This both fixes responsibility and indicates the date on which answers to questions were obtained.

v. 'No' answers will require attention at the subsequent evaluation stage. They will also frequently require cross-reference to systems notes and a letter of weaknesses, as well as to the internal control evaluation.

Typical Questions to be Found in an Internal Control Questionnaire

(a) In Respect of Stocks and Work-In-Progress

i. Are stocks kept in proper storage accommodation which protects them against
(a) deterioration?
(b) access by unauthorised persons?
(c) other risks (e.g., fire)?

ii. Is there an adequate system in operation in respect of goods received to ensure that they are
(a) checked as to quantity and quality?
(b) properly recorded in the records?

iii. Are all stocks issues from stores made only against properly authorised requisitions?

iv. By whom can requisitions be authorised?

v. Are bin cards or equivalent records maintained at the stores?

vi. Are perpetual inventory records maintained in respect of both quantity and value for
(a) raw materials?
(b) components?

       (c) finished goods?

       (d) consumable stores?

vii.   Are store records maintained by persons independent of

       (a) the storekeepers?

       (b) the persons responsible for actually checking the physical stocks?

viii. Are the physical stock quantities regularly counted and reconciled with the stores records by persons independent of the storekeepers? State approximate frequency of reconciliation.

ix.   Are all material discrepancies revealed independently investigated?

x.   Are stores records amended to agree with actual quantities?

xi.   Are there proper arrangements in operation for writing down stocks that are

       (a) defective?

       (b) obsolete?

       (c) slow-moving?

xii. Is the costing system fully integrated with the financial accounting records?

xiii. Is there a sound system in operation for charging direct costs to work-in-progress accounts?

xiv. Does the system clearly distinguish between fixed and variable overheads?

xv. Does the treatment of overheads comply with the requirements of generally accepted accounting principles?

xvi. Does the system ensure that excess costs are written off and not included in work-in-progress?

xvii. Has adequate insurance been taken out in respect of

       (a) theft?

       (b) fire?

       (c) other risks (e.g., flood)?

(b) *In Respect of Fixed Assets*

i.   Are registers of fixed assets maintained, showing adequate details of all material assets?

ii.   Are regular physical inspection made to ensure the continued existence and to confirm, the condition of assets, by responsible officials other than those who

       (a) maintains registers of fixed assets or

       (b) has custody of fixed assets.

iii. Is there a proper system for distinguishing between capital and revenue expenditure?

iv. By whom is capital expenditure authorised? Give details of who may authorise capital expenditure and the precise limits of their authority.

v.   Is the authorisation of capital expenditure properly recorded?

vi. By whom is the sale or scrapping of fixed assets authorised? Give details of who may authorise the sale or scrapping of fixed assets and the precise limits of their authority.

vii. Is the authorisation of the sale or scrapping of fixed assets properly recorded?

viii. When fixed assets are sold or scrapped, are there controls in force to ensure that

       (a) appropriate entries are made in the accounting records and registers and

       (b) receipts for sale are properly accounted for.

ix.   Are the rates of depreciation for the major classes of fixed assets adequate?

x.   Do the rates of depreciation take due account of obsolescence?

xi. Is the system adequate to ensure the correct calculation of depreciation in respect of individual assets?

xii. Are the balances on the asset register regularly reconciled with the accounting records?

Note: It is difficult to draft a standardised questionnaire of different items of internal control, because there are a number of methods of controlling the business internally. However, the above illustrative questionnaires have been given to give an idea about the internal control questionnaire.

4.2.8 INTERNAL CONTROL AND COMPUTERISED ENVIRONMENT

The overall objective and scope of an audit does not change in a computer information system environment. However, the use of a computer changes the processing, storage, retrieval and communication of financial information and may affect the accounting and internal control system employed by the entity. The auditor should consider the effect of a computer information system environment on the audit. In planning the portions of the audit, which may be affected by the computer information system environment, the auditor should obtain an understanding of the significance and complexity of the computer information system activities and the availability of the data for use in the audit.

As per SA-401, when the computer information systems are significant, the auditor should also obtain an understanding of the computer information system environment and whether it may influence the assessment of inherent risk and control risks. The nature of the risks and the internal control characteristics in computer information system environments include the following:

Lack of Transaction Trials

Some computer information systems are designed so that a complete transaction trial that is useful for audit purposes might exist for only a short period of time or only in computer-readable form. Where a computer application system performs a large number of processing steps, there may not be a complete trial. Accordingly, errors embedded in an application's programme logic may be difficult to detect on a timely basis by manual procedures.

Uniform Processing of Transactions

Computer processing uniformly processes like transactions with the same processing instructions. Thus, the clerical errors ordinarily associated with manual processing are virtually eliminated. Conversely, programming errors will ordinarily result in all transactions being processed incorrectly.

Lack of Segregation of Functions

Many control procedures that would ordinarily performed by separate individuals in manual systems may become concentrated in a computer information system environment. Thus, an individual who has access to computer programmes, processing or data may be in a position to perform incompatible functions.

Potential for Errors and Irregularities

The potential for human error in the development, maintenance and execution of computer information systems may be greater than in manual systems, partially because of the level of detail inherent in these activities. Also, the potential for individuals to gain unauthorised access to data or to alter data without visible evidence may be greater in computer information systems than in manual systems.

Both the risks and the controls introduced as a result of these characteristics of computer information systems have a potential impact on the auditor's assessment of risk and the nature, timing and extent of audit procedures. SA-401 also states that the inherent risks and control risks in a computer information system environment may have both a pervasive effect and an account specific effect on the likelihood of material misstatements as:

> the risks may result from deficiencies in pervasive computer information systems activities such as programme development and maintenance, system software support, operations, physical security and control over access to special-privilege utility programmes (these deficiencies would tend to have a pervasive impact on all application systems that are processed on the computer),

> the risk may increase the potential for errors or fraudulent activities in specific applications, in specific databases or master files or in specific processing activities (for example, errors are not uncommon in systems that perform complex logic or calculations or that must deal with many different exception conditions. Systems that control cash disbursements or other liquid assets are susceptible to fraudulent actions by users or by computer information system personnel).

4.2.9 INTERNAL CONTROL AND CORPORATE GOVERNANCE

The listing agreement was amended recently and the following amendment was incorporated in Clause 49, popularly known as corporate governance clause:

The CEO, i.e., the Managing Director or Manager appointed in terms of Companies Act, 1956 and CFO, i.e., the whole time Finance Director or any person heading the finance function discharging the finance function shall certify to the Board that:

They accept the responsibility for establishing and managing internal controls and that they have evaluated the effectiveness of the internal control systems of the company and they have disclosed to the auditors and audit committee the deficiencies in the design and operation of internal controls, if any, of which they are aware and the steps they have taken or proposes to take to rectify these deficiencies.

They have to indicate to the auditors and Audit committee:

i. Significant changes in internal control during the year;

ii. Significant changes in accounting policies during the year and that the same have been disclosed in the notes of the financial statements; and

iii. Instances of significant fraud of which they have become aware and the involvement therein, if any, of the management or an employee having a significant role in the company's internal control system.

4.2.10 INTERNAL CONTROL IN SPECIFIC AREAS OF BUSINESS

This section is divided into the areas of activity usually found in a business. At the beginning of each area, the objectives of internal control in the area are stated and some measures to achieve the objectives are discussed.

Internal Control in General

Objectives

To carry on the business in an orderly and efficient manner, to ensure adherence to management policies, safeguard its assets, and secure the accuracy and reliability of the records.

Measures

i. An appropriate and integrated system of accounts and records.

ii. Internal controls over those accounts and record.

iii. Financial supervision and control by management, including budgetary control, management accounting reports, and interim accounts.

iv. Safeguarding and if necessary duplicating records.

v. Engaging, training, allocating to specific duties staffs who are capable of fulfilling their responsibilities.

vi. Rotation of duties and cover for absences.

Cash Sales and Collections

Objectives

i. To ensure that all cash, to which the enterprise is entitled, is received.

ii. To ensure that all such cash is properly accounted for and entered in the records.

iii. To ensure that all such cash is promptly and intact deposited.

Measures

i. Prescribing and limiting the number of persons who are authorised to receive cash, e.g. sales assistants, cashiers, etc.

ii. Establishing a means of evidencing cash receipts, e.g., pre-numbered duplicate receipt forms, cash registers with sealed till rolls. The duplicate receipt form books should be securely held and issue controlled.

iii. Ensuring that customers are aware that they must receive a receipt form or ensuring that the amount entered in the cash register is clearly visible to the customer.

iv. Appointment of officers with responsibility for emptying cash registers at prescribed intervals, and agreeing the amount present with till roll totals or internal registers. Such collections should be evidenced in writing and be initialled by the assistant and the supervisor.

v. Immediate and intact banking. Payments out should be from funds drawn from the bank on an imprest system.

vi. Investigation of shorts and excess.

vii. Independent comparison of agreed till roll totals with subsequent banking records.

viii. Rotation of duties and cover for holidays (which should be compulsory) and sickness.

ix. Collections by salesmen should be banked intact daily. There should be independent comparison of the amounts banked with records of the salesmen.

x. Persons handling cash should not have access to other cash funds or to bought or sales ledger records.

Payment into Bank

Objectives

i. To ensure that all cash and cheques received is deposited into bank intact.

ii. To ensure that all cash and cheques received are banked without delay at prescribed intervals, preferably daily.

iii. To ensure that all cash and cheques received are accounted for and recorded accordingly.

Measures

i. Cash and cheques should be deposited into bank intact.

ii. Cash and cheques should be deposited into bank without delay.

iii. The bank paying-in-slip should be prepared by an official with no access to cash collection points or bought or sales ledger.

iv. Banking should be made with security in mind, e.g., for large cash deposits, security guards should be used.

v. There should be independent comparison of paying-in-slips with collection records, post lists and sales ledger records.

Cash Balances

Objectives

i. To prevent misappropriation of cash.

ii. To prevent unauthorised cash payments.

Measures

i. Establishment of cash floats of specified amounts and locations.

ii. Appointment of officials responsible for each cash transaction.

iii. Arrangement of security measures including use of safes and restriction of access.

iv. Use of imprest system with rules on reimbursement only against authorised vouchers.

v. Strict rules on the authorising of cash payments.

vi. Independent cash counts on a regular and a surprise basis.

vii. Insurance arrangements e.g. for cash balances and fidelity guarantee.

viii. Special rules for IOUs. Preferably these should not be permitted.

Cheques Payments

Objectives

To prevent unauthorised payments being made from bank accounts.

Measures

i. Control over custody and issue of unused cheque books. A register should be kept if necessary.

ii. Appointment of an official to be responsible for the preparation of cheques or traders credits.

iii. Rules should be established for the presentation of supporting documents before cheques can be made out. Such supporting documents may include goods receipts note, orders, and invoices etc.

iv. All such documents should be stamped 'paid by cheque no..........' with date.

v. All cheques should be signed by at least two persons, with no person being permitted to sign if he is a payee.

vi. No cheques should be made out to bearer except for the collection of wages or reimbursement of cash funds.

vii. All cheques should be strictly crossed.

viii. The signing of blank cheques must be prohibited.

ix. Special rules for authorising and checking direct debits and standing orders.

x. Separation of duties: custody, recording and initiation of cheque payments.

Purchases and Trade Creditors

Objectives

i. To ensure that goods and services are only ordered in the required quantity, are of quality and at the best terms available after appropriate requisition and approval.

ii. To ensure that goods and services received are inspected and only acceptable items are accepted.

iii. To ensure that all invoices are checked against authorised orders and receipts of the subject matter in good condition.

iv. To ensure that all goods and services invoiced are properly recorded in the books.

Measures

i. There should be procedures for the requisitioning of goods and services only by specified personnel on specified forms with space for acknowledgement of performance.

ii. Order forms should be pre-numbered and kept in safe custody. Issue of blank order form books should be controlled and recorded.

iii. All goods received should be recorded on goods received notes or in a special book.

iv. All goods should be inspected for condition and agreement with order and counted on receipt. The inspection should be acknowledged.

v. At intervals, a listing of unfulfilled orders should be made and investigated.

vi. Invoices should be checked for arithmetical accuracy, pricing, correct treatment of VAT and trade discount and agreement with order.

vii. Total of entries in the invoice register or day book should be regularly checked.

viii. Responsibility for purchase ledger entries should be vested in personnel separate from personnel responsible for ordering, receipts of goods and the invoice register.

ix. The purchase ledger should be subject to frequent reconciliation in total by or be checked by an independent senior official.

x. Ledger account balances should be regularly compared with the supplier's statements of account.

xi. Cut-off procedures at the year-end are essential.

xii. A proper coding system is required for purchase of goods and services so that correct nominal accounts are debited.

Sales and Debtors

Objectives

i. To ensure that all customers' orders are promptly executed.

ii. To ensure that sales on credit are made only to bona fide goods credit risks.

iii. To ensure that all sales on credit are invoiced, that authorised prices are charged and that before issue all invoices are completed and checked as regards price, trade discounts and VAT.

iv. To ensure that all invoices raised are entered in the books.

v. To ensure that all customers' claims are fully investigated before credit notes are issued.

vi. To ensure that every effort is made to collect all debts.

Measures

i. Incoming orders should be recorded, and if necessary, acknowledged, on pre-numbered forms. Orders should be matched with invoices and lists prepared at intervals of outstanding orders for management action. Sequence checks should be made regularly by a senior official.

ii. Credit control: There should be procedures laid down for verifying the credit worthiness of all persons or enterprises requesting goods on credit. A credit limit should be established.

iii. Selling prices should be prescribed. Policies should be laid down on credit term, trade and cash discounts and special prices.

iv. Invoicing should be carried out by a separate department. Invoices should be pre-numbered and the custody and issue of unused invoice blocks controlled and recorded.

v. All invoices should be independently checked for agreement with customer order, with the goods despatched records, for pricing, discounts, VAT and other details. All actions should be acknowledged by signature or initials.

vi. Accounting for sales and debtors should be segregated by employing separate staff for cash, invoice register, sales ledger entries and statement preparation.

vii. Sales invoices should be pre-listed before entry into the invoice register or day book and the pre-list total independently compared with the total of the register.

viii. Customers claims should be recorded and investigated. Similar controls should be applied to credit notes. At the end of the year, all unclear claims should be carefully investigated and assessed.

ix. A control account should be regularly and independently prepared.

x. All balances must be reviewed regularly by an independent official to identify and investigate overdue accounts, debtors paying by instalments, and accounts where payments do not match with the invoices.

xi. Bad debts should only be written off after due investigation and acknowledged authorisation by senior management.

xii. At the year-end, an aged analysis of debtors should be prepared to evaluate the need for a doubtful debt provision.

4.3 INTERNAL CHECK

4.3.1 DEFINITION

The internal check is an arrangement of the duties of the staff members of the accounting functions in such a way that the work performed by a person is automatically checked by another.

In the opinion of Spicer and Pegler, "A system of internal check is an arrangement of staff duties, whereby no one person is allowed to carry through and to record every aspects of a transaction, so that without collusion between two or more persons, fraud is activated and at the same time the possibilities of errors are reduced to the minimum."

Internal check has been defined by the Institute of Chartered Accountants of England and Wales as "the checks on day to day transactions which operate continuously as part of the routine system, where the work of one person is proved independently or in complementary to the work of another, the object being the prevention or early detection of errors or frauds".

On the basis of the above definitions, it may be concluded that "internal check is a system where the work is divided amongst the employees in such a manner that not a single individual is allowed to carry on the whole function from the beginning to the end and the work of an individual is being automatically checked by another".

4.3.2 GENERAL CONSIDERATIONS IN FRAMING A SYSTEM OF INTERNAL CHECK

Work Assignment
No single person should be given the total part of a particular work. All dealings and acts of every employee should, in the ordinary course, come under the review of another.

Rotation of Employees
The duties of members of the staff should be changed from time to time without any previous notice, so that the same officer or subordinate does not, without a break, perform the same function for a considerable length of time.

Compulsory Leave
Every member of the staff should be encouraged to go on leave at least once in a year. Experience has shown that frauds successfully concealed by the employees are often detected when they are on leave.

Separation of Inter-Related Jobs
Persons having physical custody of assets must not be permitted to have access to the books of accounts.

Uses of Mechanical Devices
To prevent loss or misappropriation of cash, mechanical devices such as the automatic cash register should be employed.

Periodical Review
The financial and administrative power should be distributed very judiciously among different officers and in such a manner that the powers actually exercised should be reviewed periodically.

Responsibility
The responsibility of each individual must be properly defined and fixed. The work of the business should be allocated amongst various staff members in such manner that their duties and responsibilities are clearly and judiciously divided.

Safeguards
For stock taking at the end of the year, trading activities should, if possible, be suspended. The task of stock taking and evaluation should be done by staff belonging to several sections of the organisation. It may prove dangerous to depend exclusively on the stock section staff for these tasks since they may be tempted to under-state and/or overstate of the value of the stock.

Supervision
A strict supervision should be exercised to ensure that the prescribed internal checks and procedures are fully operative.

Reliance
No staff members of the business should be relied upon too much. The system must provide for an automatic checking of the work of every employee by another employee.

operation and for this where detailed checking is not necessary, in that case to what extent the auditor would depend on internal check is a matter of debate.

If through review, the auditor thinks that the system of internal check is adequate and free from errors, he can depend on the system and instead of detailed checking; he can resort to test checking. But if he observes any weakness in the system, he shall not depend on internal check and conduct his work extensively and in detail.

So, the auditor is expected to apply proper judgment with reasonable care and skill to appraise the system. Thus, he has to determine to what extent he would spend on internal check system. Hence, it is clear that the internal check system does not reduce the liability of the auditor.

4.3.5 GENERAL PRINCIPLES OF INTERNAL CHECK FOR A FEW TRANSACTIONS

Aspects like cash sales, cash receipts, cash payments, payments of wages, credit purchases, credit sales, stores and material wastage form important parts in the procedure and conduct of an audit. These matters are important in the sense that fraudulent manipulations or frauds and errors in those areas are bound to prevail unless there exists an efficient system of internal check. So, the principles of internal checks in the stated areas are given below. It should be noted in this context that the application of the principles in actual practice depends upon the nature and size of the organisation and as well as in relation to the concept of materiality.

Internal Check System with Regard to Purchase

Purchases are of two types—cash purchase and credit purchase. The internal check as regards cash purchase is quite simple in comparison with credit purchase. The internal check as regards cash and credit purchases are set forth as below:

(a) Purchase Requisition

No purchase should be made without purchase requisition slip issued by the store department. The procedure for issuing purchase requisitions should be specified. The details about the quantity, quality and the time by which the goods must be supplied be clearly mentioned in the requisition slip.

(b) Enquiry for Purchase

In order to purchase the required item, the purchase department makes an enquiry about the terms and conditions of purchases from different suppliers. For this purpose, tenders are generally invited and usually tenders having the lowest price should be accepted.

Purchase Order

The purchase manager or any other authorised officer of the organisation should be entrusted with the sole authority to issue purchase order. One original and other three copies of the order should be prepared. The original purchase order is to be sent to the supplier. The first copy should be sent to the store department, second copy to the accounts department and the last copy are to be retained by the purchase department reference.

Receipts of Goods

The goods received from the supplier are to be checked as per the copy of the purchase order and the challan of the suppliers. Goods receipt register is to be maintained for the purpose of recording of the receipts of goods after proper inspection regarding quantity and quality of the goods either at the store department or centralised godown of the organisation. All invoices received from the supplier are to be entered in the Purchase Day Book after proper scrutiny.

Making the Payment

Purchase department should thoroughly check the invoices and send the same to the accounts department. The accounts department should compare the invoice with the purchase order and should also

---

4.3.3 OBJECTIVES OF INTERNAL CHECK

The objectives of internal check system can be set forth as follows:

Assigning Responsibility

To allocate the duties and responsibilities of every employee in such a manner that they may be identified and held responsible for a particular error or fraud.

Minimising Error or Fraud

To minimise the possibility of any error or fraud done by any staff member.

Detecting Errors or Frauds

To detect errors or frauds easily due to independent checking of work done by one employee by another employee.

Reducing Clerical Mistakes

To minimise the possibility of omission of any transaction from being recorded in the books of accounts.

Enhancing Work Efficiency

To enhance the efficiency of the staff, as the management of duties is based on the principle of division of labour.

Obtaining Confirmation

To obtain confirmation of facts and entries, physical and financial, by the presentation and necessary maintenance of records.

Reducing Burden of Work

To reduce the burden of the work of independent auditor by introducing the internal check system in a scientific way.

Exercising Moral Pressure

To exercise moral pressure on the employees by introducing continuous review process of the total system.

Ensuring Reliability

To facilitate business control by ensuring the reliability of accounting records and books.

Obtaining Supervision Advantages

To obtain the advantages of supervising the various assets, inflow and outflow of cash and goods of the business.

Advantages of Internal Check

The advantages that can be derived from internal check can be discussed from different points of view:

From Business Point of View

(i) Proper Allocation of Work

Rational allocation of work among the different staff members of the organisation brings precision in work.

(ii) Control Device

The distribution of work under this system is such that it acts as a control device against unscrupulous employees. The chances of fraudulent manipulation are thus minimised due to the existence of this check.

(iii) Speedy Work

As the individual staff member is engaged in the same type of jobs for a considerable period of time, it results efficient performance of the activities and high speed of work.

(iv) Increase in Efficiency and Skill

A good system of internal check increases the efficiency of work among the staff as due to its proper planning for assigning right job to the right person.

(v) Easy Preparation of Final Accounts

Since no individual worker is allowed to handle a job completely and the work is divided among the employees in a proper manner, the books of accounts can be kept up to date and as a result, the final accounts can be prepared easily.

(vi) Creation of Moral Check

Knowledge of subsequent checking of each employee, works by other acts as a great check to commission of errors and frauds.

From the Viewpoint of the Owners

(i) Reliability on Accounts

If there is a good system of internal check, the owner of the organisation may rely upon the genuineness and accuracy of the accounts.

(ii) Orientation of Accounting

As the responsibility of each staff is clearly defined and fixed, it develops a system of accounting, which is known as responsibility accounting.

(iii) Economical Operation

Although it seems that the introduction of well-integrated system of internal check is costly, but in actual practice, it is observed that the staff patterns are so arranged that the existing staff be properly filled in different operating area involving no extra cost.

From the Viewpoint of the Auditor

(i) Facilitation of Audit Work

Sound and efficient internal check system may facilitate to a greater extent, the work of the auditor by relying on 'test check'.

(ii) Attention to Other Important Matters

As the auditor gets confidence on the internal check system, he can avoid the basic routine checking work to some extent and can give attention to other important matters.

Shortcoming of Internal Check System

Dependence on each other proves fatal in the quick disposal of the work. If one person is absent, the day-to-day work will be seriously disrupted. This is the main shortcoming of the internal check system.

Following are some more shortcomings of internal check system:

1. Monotony

Involvement in the same kind of work may result in monotonous attitude on the part of the person who is engaged in the same type of job.

2. Carelessness

The possibility of some of the responsible and high officials being complacement increases as they believe, though not always right, that under a sound system of internal check nothing can go wrong.

3. Collusion

The real purpose of the internal check is bound to fail if collusion among the staff exists in disguise.

4. Limited Application

The application of this system is limited only in big organisations. Its application in small organisations may result in loss of time and unnecessary expenditure.

5. Dependence

Statutory auditors in almost all the cases rely on the internal check system. Accordingly they apply test chec and therefore, do not apply thorough check.

6. Possibility of Disorder

In the absence of a properly organised system of internal check, there will be chaos and disorder in the w ing of a business.

Safeguard Against the Shortcomings of Internal Check

The advantages of the internal check system out weigh its disadvantages. Hence the wide acceptab the system in the conduct of an audit is appreciated. The stated defects of the system, however, overcome if the management is careful in its effective implementation. The payment of proper ince staffs may to a great extent remove the carelessness of the staff. The monotony of a job may be a inter-departmental transfer of the employees. Regarding the collusion, it can be stated that the wh is bound to fail if the morality of the employees deteriorates. General punishments like fine, ter service etc. may temporarily check collusion, but without upgrading the morality of the staff, it is to stop collusion permanently.

4.3.4 INTERNAL CHECK AND THE AUDITOR

The basic responsibility of the auditor is to certify the fairness and authenticity of the accou ness. To achieve this objective, the auditor is expected to discharge his duties in such a way the actual state of affairs of the business. It is true that an efficient system of internal che auditor's work easy and convenient. He may be relieved of detailed checking of the transac extent an auditor should depend on the system of internal check in solely a matter of h Though the auditor conducts the examination of the accounts independently, yet he has to system of the business because it becomes practically impossible for the auditor to cond of accounts thoroughly after the close of the financial accounts.

Where the system of the internal check is not in operation, it is desirable that detailed checking of transactions irrespective of the type of organisation and the v Because in order to save his time, if he adopts the method of test checking of few tr and frauds are detected later on, the auditor will be held responsible. But where the in

check the calculations. Only responsible official should draw cheque for the payment of invoice, which are to be marked as 'paid' after payment. All payments are to be made against "A/c payee cheque".

Internal Check System with Regard to Sales

Sales are the most important source of income in a business organisation. In case of most of the business organisations, it is the only source of income. Therefore, the system of internal check to be adopted for sales should be extremely effective. The system of internal check regarding sales should take care of the following aspects:

(a) Independent Sales Department

There should be a separate and independent sales department, which should function as a composite of several sub-departments. Sales manager or a senior competent officer should be in charge of the department.

(b) Receipts of Orders

On receipt of the order, it should be numbered and preserved is Orders Received Book with full details of the order. A confirmatory written order should be obtained against verbal orders. The Despatch Department should be given a copy of the order with necessary particulars.

(c) Packing of Goods

Packing of the goods should be made by the Despatch Department as per the copy of the sales order, and accordingly a separate statement showing the goods packed should be prepared by the department.

(d) Preparation of Invoices

The statement of goods as prepared by the Despatch Department should be checked with the customers' orders and then the invoice will be prepared in triplicate.

(e) Checking of Invoices

A responsible official should check the invoice, particularly the rates charged and the calculations made. He should also see that the terms and conditions in the order have been duly followed and there is no scope for complaint by the customer. He should then put his initial on the invoice.

(f) Despatching the Goods

With the help of the copy of invoices, entries should be made in the Sales Day Book. On despatch of the goods, records should be made in the Goods Outward Book. Two copies of the invoice may be sent to customer who will return one of them after signing it.

Internal Check System with Regard to Cash Receipts

The risk of misappropriation of cash needs no emphasis. The chances of fraud are numerous in cash transactions. In order to reduce the chances of fraud in cash transactions, the internal check system as regards to cash receipts should be very effective and takes into consideration the following principles of internal check for cash transactions:

(a) Separation of Duties

The cashier should have no access to the ledgers and other books of original entry except the rough cash book that is required for spot recording of cash receipts.

(b) Control Over Receipts Book

The printed receipts book, serially numbered, should be used as and when cash are collected and the same should be countersigned by the responsible manager. The unused receipt book should be kept in safe custody.

(c) Handling of Incoming Remittances

Incoming correspondences including all remittances should be opened by the cashier in the presence of responsible officer of the concern. All receipts of cheques should be marked, by means of a rubber stamp as 'A/c payee only'.

(d) Depositing Cash into Bank

All collections, both cash and cheque, should be deposited into bank daily. The counterfoil portion of the paying-in-slip should be filled by the clerk and the portion that is to be retained by the bank should be filled in by the cashier.

(e) Reconciling Bank Statement

Bank reconciliation statement should be prepared at regular intervals by the cashier to know the actual position of bank balances.

(f) Correction of the Cash Book

Any spoiled slip should be marked cancelled and should not be turned out and be removed from the receipt book. For the purpose of altering words or figures, overwriting should be discouraged and fresh writing with proper initial is encouraged.

Internal Check System with Regard to Cash Payments

The principles of internal check as regards payments of cash can be set forth as follows:

(a) Payments Through Cheques

Generally all payments should be made by account payee cheque.

(b) Separation of Duties

The person in charge of making payments should have no connection with the receipts of cash.

(c) Proper Authorisation

It is to be seen that all cheques have been duly signed by the authorised person and no payments exceeding the amount of Rs. 20,000 should be made without 'A/c payee cheque'. It is according to the provision of sec 40A(3) of the Income Tax Act, 1961 that any sum exceeding Rs. 20,000 to be paid by a crossed cheque; otherwise the expenses will not be allowed as deductions in computing business income.

(d) Safety Measures for Unused Cheques

All the unused cheques should be kept in proper safe custody.

(e) Control Over Payment Vouchers

Arrangements should be made to ensure that the vouchers supporting payments could not be presented for payment twice. Such vouchers should be stamped as 'paid' before the cheques are signed.

(f) Confirmation with the Creditors

An official should check up the statement received from creditors and verify with the invoices and ledger accounts. Only after proper verification, the cheques should be drawn in favour of the creditors. Confirmation of accounts with the creditors should also be made through direct correspondence.

(g) Cash Discount

To ensure the availability of cash discounts, monthly or periodic payments should be made on the fixed dates.

(h) Reconciliation of Bank Balance

Bank Reconciliation statements should be prepared to reconcile bank and cash balances from time to time by some authorities other than the cashier.

4.4 INTERNAL AUDIT

4.4.1 DEFINITION

Internal audit means the independent appraisal of activity within an organisation for the review of accounting, financial and other business practices. It consists of a continuous and critical review of financial and operating activities by a staff of auditors functioning as a part of the management and reporting to management and not to the shareholders.

According to W.B. Meigs, "internal auditing consists of a continuous and critical review of financial and operating activities by a staff of auditors functioning as full time salaried employee".

According to the Institute of Internal Auditors in the United States, "internal auditing is an independent appraisal function established within an organisation to examine and evaluate its activities as a service to the organisation".

As per SA-610, "Internal Audit is a separate part of internal control system. The objective of internal audit is to determine whether other internal control systems are well designed and properly operated. Internal auditor is appointed by the management and is part of overall organisation system of internal control."

So, internal audit can be defined as "an independent appraisal function established by the management of an organisation for the review of internal control system as a service to the organisation. It objectively examines, evaluates and reports on the adequacy of internal control as a contribution to the proper, economic, efficient and effective use of resources".

In fact, internal audit is a special type of control. It deals primarily with accounting and financial matters. The work of the internal auditor is more or less same as that of an external auditor. The internal auditor has to make an effort to find out the weaknesses of the internal control system in operation and to suggest necessary improvements.

4.4.2 BASIC PRINCIPLES OF ESTABLISHING INTERNAL AUDITING IN A BUSINESS CONCERN

Independent Status
The internal audit department should have an independent status in the organisation. The internal auditor must have sufficiently high status in the organisation. He may be required to report directly to the Board of Directors.

Scope of Audit
The scope of internal audit department must be specified in a comprehensive manner to the extent practicable. In fact, the department must have authority to investigate from financial angle every phase of organisational activity.

Clear Objectives
It must have an unambiguous and clear understanding of the objectives on each assignment given to it from time to time.

Formation of the Department
The management should take care in selecting the staff of the internal audit department. The size and qualification of the staff of the internal audit department should be commensurate with the size of the business organisation.

Time-Bound Programme
The programme of the internal auditor should be time bound with the provision for periodic reporting.

Internal Audit Report
The copy of the report of the internal auditor should be made available to the statutory auditor.

Follow-Up Action
There must be a specific procedure to follow up the report submitted by the internal audit department.

Performance of Executive Actions
The internal audit department should not be involved in performance of executive actions.

4.4.3 SCOPE AND OBJECTIVES OF INTERNAL AUDIT
The primary objective of internal audit lies in helping management attain maximum efficiency by providing an important source of review of operations and records for the assistance of all levels of management.

As per SA-610, following are the objectives on internal audit:

➢ Review of accounting system and related internal control

➢ Examination of financial and operating system

➢ Examination of effectiveness and efficiency of financial control

➢ Physical examination and verification

Thus, internal audit carries out a thorough examination of the accounting transactions as well as that of the system according to which these have been recorded with a view to reassuring the management that the accounts are being properly maintained and the system contains adequate safeguards to check any leakage of revenue or misappropriation of property and the operations have been carried out in conformity with the plans of the management.

So, the objectives of an internal audit can be stated as follows:

Accuracy in Accounts
To verify the accuracy and authenticity of the financial accounting and other records presented to the management.

Adoption of Standard Accounting Practices
To ascertain that the standard accounting practices, as have been decided to be followed by the organisation, are being adhered to.

Proper Authority on Assets
To establish that there is a proper authority for every acquisition, retirement and disposal of assets.

Confirmation of Liabilities
To confirm that liabilities have been incurred only for the legitimate activities of the organisation.

Analysis of Internal Check System
To analyse and improve the system of internal check to see whether it is working properly and effectively and whether the system is economical.

Prevention and Detection of Fraud
To implement such techniques in the conduct of the internal audit so that it can detect and prevent frauds in the accounts.

Provision for New Ideas
To provide a channel whereby new ideas can be brought to the attention of the management.

Review of the Operation of Internal Control System
To review the operation of the overall internal control system and to bring material departures and non-compliance to the notice of the appropriate level of management.

Special Investigation
To provide scope and make avenues for special investigations for the management.

Review of Organisational Activities
To review the operations carried out in the organisation to assure the management that they are being carried out in compliance with the management objectives, policies and plans.

4.4.4 ESSENTIAL ELEMENTS OF INTERNAL AUDIT
The essential elements of internal audit are the following:

Independence
Internal auditing is carried on by independent personnel. Internal auditors are employees of the firm and thus independence is not always easy to achieve.

Staffing
The internal audit unit should be adequately staffed in terms of numbers, grades and experience.

Relationships
Internal auditors should foster constructive working relationships and mutual understanding with management, with external auditors, with any review agencies and where appropriate with an audit committee. Mutual understanding is the goal.

Due Care
An internal auditor should behave much as an external auditor in terms of skill, care and judgment. He should be up to date technically and have personal standards of knowledge, honesty, probity and integrity much as an external auditor.

Specific Audit Planning
On the basis of the objectives of the organisation and the objective of the internal audit of the organisation, the internal auditors should prepare the audit programme in order to cover the specified tasks assigned by the management.

Systems Control
The internal auditor must verify the operations of the system in much the same way as an external auditor, i.e., by investigation, recording, identification of controls and compliance testing of the controls.

Evidence
The internal auditor has similar standards for evidence as an external auditor. He will evaluate audit evidence in terms of sufficiency, relevance and reliability.

Reporting

The internal auditors must produce timely, accurate and comprehensive reports to management on a regular basis.

Advantages

1. Prevention of Errors and Frauds

It helps in the prevention of errors and frauds including misappropriation of cash and goods.

2. Early Detection of Errors and Frauds

It makes early detection of errors and frauds possible.

3. Continuous Review of Internal Control System

It undertakes continuous review of the internal control system, and as a result, it is capable of reporting irregularities for enabling corrective action in time.

4. Assurance Regarding Accuracy of Books and Accounts

It checks books, records and accounts to ensure correct recording and their maintenance up to date.

5. Preparation of Interim Accounts

It facilitates the preparation of interim accounts.

6. Early Completion of Annual Audit

It is of great use in early completion of annual statutory audit.

7. Periodic Physical Verification

It carries out periodic physical verification of assets like cash, stock, investments and items of fixed assets.

8. Assistance to the Statutory Auditor

It can render direct assistance to the statutory auditor by undertaking detailed checking of the accounting data and leave him free to concentrate on more important issues of principle, presentation and policy on accounting.

Disadvantages

1. Extra Cost

Internal audit system is not possible to be adopted by small organisations because the cost of running an internal audit department is very high.

2. Biased Opinion

Internal audit department employees are the paid staff of the organisation. In most of the cases, they have to work according to the directions of the management. So it is not expected that they will provide unbiased opinion about the financial statements.

3. Possibility of Becoming Ineffective

If the employees of the internal audit department are not efficient or if the internal audit is not conducted effectively, it will provide no assistance to the management.

4. Possibility of Distortion

If the management is interested to distort financial figures and if it is supported by internal audit department, the users of the financial statements will be totally misguided.

5. Inefficient Staff Members

As there is no prescribed qualification for the appointment of internal auditors, less qualified persons can get appointment in the department. They will not be able to discharge their duties properly.

4.4.5 AREA OF INTERNAL AUDIT

As per SA-610, the scope and objective of internal audit vary widely and are dependent upon the size and structure of the organisation and the requirements of its management.

Normally, however, internal audit operates in one or more of the following areas:

Review of Accounting System and Related Internal Control

The establishment of an adequate accounting system and related controls is the responsibility of management, which demands proper attention on a continuous basis. The internal audit function is often assigned specific responsibility by management for reviewing the accounting system and related accounting controls, monitoring their operation and suggesting improvements thereto.

Examination for Management of Financial and Operating Information

This may include review of the means used to identify, measure, classify and report such information and specific inquiry into individual items including detailed testing of transactions, balances and procedures.

Examination of the Effectiveness of Operations

Generally, the external auditor is interested in the results of such audit work only when it has an important bearing on the reliability of the financial records.

Physical Verification

The internal audit generally includes examination and verification of physical existence and condition of the tangible assets of the entity.

4.4.6 DISTINCTION BETWEEN INTERNAL AUDIT AND EXTERNAL AUDIT

On accounting matters, the internal and the external auditors operate mainly in the same field and they have a common interest in ascertaining that there is an effective system of internal control to prevent or detect errors and frauds and to ensure that it is operating satisfactorily and that an adequate accounting system exists to provide the information necessary for preparing true and fair financial statements. There are, however, some fundamental differences between the work of an internal auditor and that of an external auditor.

These are as follows:

Appointment

The internal auditor is appointed by the management, generally the directors are responsible for the appointment.

The external or the statutory auditor is appointed according to the concerned statute. Generally, in case of company form of organisation, the auditors are appointed by the shareholders in the annual general meeting.

Scope

The extent of the work undertaken by the internal auditor is determined by the management.

The area of the work to be undertaken by the external auditor arises from the responsibilities placed on him by the governing statute.

Approach

The internal auditor's approach is with a view to ensuring that the accounting system is efficient so that the accounting information presented to management throughout the period is accurate and discloses material facts.

The external auditor's approach, however, is governed by his duty to satisfy himself that the accounts to be presented to the shareholders show a true and fair view of the profit or loss for the financial period and of the state of the company's affairs at the end of that period.

Responsibility

The internal auditor's responsibility is to the management. It follows that the internal auditor, being a servant of the company, does not have the independence of status.

The external auditor is responsible directly to the shareholders. Unlike the internal auditors, he is a representative of the shareholders and has independence of status.

Objective

The objective of internal audit is to ensure that already laid down policies, procedures and other internal control functions are functioning as designed, whereas the objective of the external auditor is to express opinion on financial statements whether those statements are showing true and fair view.

Independence

External auditor is more independent in reporting than an internal auditor.

Notwithstanding these important differences, the work of both the internal auditor and the external auditor on accounting matters is carried out largely by similar means, such as:

i.   examination of the system of internal check, for both soundness in principle and effectiveness in operation,

ii. examination and checking of accounting records and statements,

iii. verification of assets and liabilities, and

iv. observation, inquiry, the making of statistical comparisons and such other measures as may be judged necessary.

The wide experience of the external auditor may be of assistance to the internal auditor, while on the other hand. the latter's intimate acquaintance with the business concern may be of help to the external auditor. Co-operation in planning of the respective auditors may save unnecessary work, although the external auditor must always satisfy himself as to the work carried out by the internal auditor.

4.4.7 RELIANCE UPON THE WORK OF AN INTERNAL AUDITOR

Standards on Auditing (SA-610) describe the scope of reliance by the external auditor upon the work of an internal auditor. The purpose of this statement is to provide guidance as to the procedures, which should be applied by the external auditor in assessing the work of the internal auditor for the purpose of placing reliance upon that work. This statement states that while the external auditor has sole responsibility of his report, however, much of the work of the internal auditor may be useful to him in his examination of the financial statements. The responsibility of the external auditor is not reduced by any means because of the reliance placed on the wok of the internal auditor.

As per SA-610, the external auditor can use the work of the internal auditor after evaluation of the internal audit function. The external auditor should document his evaluation and conclusion in this respect while evaluating the work of internal audit function to determine the extent to which he can place reliance upon, the following aspects to be considered:

➢   Whether internal audit is undertaken by an outside agency or by an integral audit department within the entity itself.

➢   Scope of internal audit and management action and internal audit report.

➤ Technical compliance of the internal auditors, i.e., whether the internal auditors have required experience and professional qualification.

➤ Due professional care by the internal auditor, i.e., whether internal audit work appears to be properly planned, supervised, documented and existence of adequate audit manuals.

According to this statement, the following observations are made:

i. The role of the internal audit function within an entity is determined by management and its prime objective differs from that of the external auditor, who is appointed to report independently on financial information.

ii. The external auditor should, as part of his audit, evaluate the internal audit function to the extent he considers that it will be relevant in determining the nature, timing and extent of his compliance and substantive procedures. Depending upon such evaluation, the external auditor may be able to adopt less extensive procedures than would otherwise be required.

iii. By its very nature, the internal audit function cannot be expected to have the same degree of independence as is essential when the external auditor expresses his opinion on the financial information. The report of the external auditor is his sole responsibility, and that responsibility is not by any means reduced because of the reliance he places on the internal auditor's work.

Where the internal audit is carried out, it is for the external auditor to decide, whether and to what extent, consistent with his statutory responsibilities, he can rely on the work of the internal auditor in order to reduce the extent of his own examination of details. His decision in this matter will depend upon his judgment on the facts of each case, having regard in particular to the following:

i. The extent and efficiency of the internal audit, i.e., in order to assess these matters, the external auditor should examine the internal audit programmes, working papers and reports and should make such tests as he thinks fit of the work done by the internal auditor.

ii. The experience and qualifications of the internal auditor and his staff member and the character of their reports as also the action taken by the management on the basis of the report.

iii. The authority vested in the internal auditor and the level of management to which he is directly responsible.

However, the statutory auditor cannot in any circumstances divest himself of the responsibilities laid on him by the statute. In other words, if the external auditor has curtailed the extent of his checking, putting reliance the work of the internal auditor, the responsibility for any deficiency in that financial statements that may remain undetected will be of the external (statutory) auditor, and he cannot plead that he has relied on the work done by the internal auditor.

4.4.8 EVALUATION OF INTERNAL AUDIT FUNCTION

The external auditor should carry out an evaluation process of the internal audit functions of the organisation as a part of his audit activities. In order to determine the scope of work and the extent of reliability upon the work of an internal auditor, this evaluation is required to be conducted by the external auditor. At the time of evaluation by the external auditor for the assessment of reliability of internal audit functions, following aspects are required to be covered as given in SA-610:

Status of the Auditor
Before ascertaining the degree of reliance upon the work of internal auditor, it is required to be known whether the internal audit is being conducted by an outside agency or by the departmental team. It is also required to assess the level in the organisation to whom the report is to be furnished and whether the internal auditor is not restricted to communicate freely with the external auditor.

Scope and Area of Function

It is also required to evaluate the nature and area of work of the internal auditor and also the depth of coverage of his functions. To place more reliance on the work of the internal auditor, it is also to be ensured that the management considers and where appropriate act upon the recommendations of the internal auditor.

Professional Competence

Internal auditor should have adequate professional qualification and proficiency in conducting internal audit function. So, technical competence and experience of the persons conducting internal audit function also required to be assessed before determining the extent of reliance on the internal auditor.

Due Diligence and Care

Due diligence and professional care from the end of internal auditors should be ensured. It should be ascertained that the internal audit appears to be properly planned, duly supervised, regularly reviewed and effectively documented. Due professional care will be established by the internal auditors with the help of proper internal audit manual, standards of auditing practices and working papers.

Where, following the general evaluation described above, the external auditor intends to rely upon specific internal audit work as a basis for modifying the nature, timing and extent of his procedures, he should review the internal auditor's work taking into account the following factors as provided in SA-610:

i. The scope of work and related audit programmes are adequate for the external auditor's purpose.

ii. The work was properly planned and the work of assistants was properly supervised, reviewed and documented.

iii. Sufficient appropriate audit evidence was obtained to afford a reasonable basis for the conclusion reached.

iv. Conclusions reached are appropriate in the circumstances and any reports prepared are consistent with the results of the work performed.

v. Any exceptions or unusual matters disclosed by the internal auditor's procedures have been properly resolved.

The external auditor should document his evaluation and conclusion of all the above factors.

4.5 AUDITOR'S INDEPENDENCE

We mean by the term 'auditor's independence' that the judgment of the auditor is not subordinated to the wishes or directions of any person who might have engaged him or to his own self-interest.

It is not possible to define the term 'independence' in a precise manner. Basically, it is a condition of mind and personal in character. However, professional conduct of the auditors supports auditor's independence. Auditors, by their function of reporting on financial statements, lend creditability to those statements. Parties interested in such statements put implicit faith and trust on those statements based on the opinion of the auditor. So, for the auditors, independence has a special meaning and significance. Unbiased audit can be carried out only when the auditor is able to resist all pulls and pressures. The auditor should not only be independent, but also must appear to be so; otherwise his report would be suspect and lack credibility.

4.5.1 ADVANTAGES OF INDEPENDENT AUDIT

The principal advantage of an independent audit lies in the society being able to get an informed, objective and unbiased opinion on the financial statements of an organisation, which is used in making significant economic decisions by interested segments of the society, i.e., shareholders, creditors, bankers etc. It is to be noted that only the auditor is in a position to examine the accounts and transactions of an organisation with a view to form an opinion. His report is, therefore, the only real safeguard available to the various parties interested in the financial affairs of the organisation.

4.5.2 PROVISIONS FOR SAFEGUARDING INDEPENDENT AUDITORS

Several provisions have been included in the Companies Act with the objective of securing independence of the auditor. In general, these provisions endow the auditor with certain statutory rights, define certain relationship that may entail a compromise in maintaining independence, requiring that normally auditor would be appointed in the general meeting by the shareholders and making the removal of auditor difficult by laying down procedures under the Companies Act. The rights of the auditor are statutorily defined in several sections and they cannot be curtailed or limited by the management or even by the shareholders. The management has no authority to terminate the appointment of any auditor. The auditor when appointed shall be entitled to hold office till the conclusion of the next annual general meeting. Though mid-term removal of the auditor is not ruled out, it can be accomplished only by the shareholders in the general meeting and with previous approval of the Central Government. It is also worth mentioning that the duties cast on the auditor cannot be diluted by any agreement between the organisation and the auditor. There can be thus no temptation for the auditor to do less than what the law requires.

4.5.3 IMPORTANT ASPECTS OF AUDITOR'S INDEPENDENCE

Auditor's independence is an important factor in establishing the creditability of the audit opinion. Auditor's independence refers to the independence of the auditor from parties, other than shareholders, that have an interest in the financial statements of an organisation and in particular independence of the auditor from the management of the organisation.

There are two aspects to independence: independence in fact and independence in appearance. Independence in fact refers to the actual independence of the auditor. It is concerned with the state of mind of the auditor and how the auditor acts in a specific situation. It is difficult, and in many cases not possible, to determine whether an auditor has acted independently, because it involves knowing what has gone on in the mind of the auditor.

The other aspect of independence is independence in appearance. This is how other people might view the independence of the auditor. It is necessary for auditors to not only act independently, but also be seen to be independent, because independence in appearance reduces the opportunity for an auditor to act otherwise than independently.

Auditor's independence as it relates to independence in appearance may be addressed in statutory law, professional standards and audit firm policy. For example, statutes, standards and/or individual audit firm policy may address independence by

- prohibiting owners of accounting firms (e.g., proprietors and partners) and their staff from holding shares in, lending to or otherwise having a beneficial interest, either directly or indirectly, in audit clients,
- prohibiting owners and their staff from receiving any benefits from client organisations, other than through the receiving of audit fees. This includes a prohibition of owners and their staff from
  - ➢ borrowing money from the audit client,
  - ➢ accepting commissions for new business referred by the audit firm to the audit client, and
  - ➢ accepting discounts given to audit staff members normally only available to the client's staff.
- prohibiting owners and their staff members from holding any office, including the office of director, in client organisations,

- preparation and maintenance of a list of clients and associated companies that is made available to all owners and staff of the audit firm,

- annual signing by all owners and staff of an independent statement, stating that they are familiar with the firm's independence policy, they hold no prohibitive investments and they hold no prohibitive relationships, and

- prohibiting the undertaking of consulting work (such as taxation and corporate advising work) for existing audit clients.

Some accounting firms establish so-called 'Chinese walls' with respect to audit and management consulting services provided to the one client. Other firms may limit the value of consulting work for an audit client to an amount not exceeding the audit fee. However, there is increasing concern that these strategies do not fully address the problem of independence. The arguments by some members of the auditing profession that the knowledge gained through the undertaking of such consulting work by audit firms enables the auditor to perform a more effective audit is somewhat specious, as the consulting work performed for an audit client is (or should be) performed by employees within the audit firm who have no auditing responsibilities for the client.

- Rotating audit staff, including the auditor (commonly referred to, in a partnership of auditors, as the engagement partner) say for every five years. A primary objective of the rotation would be to guard against the possibility of the auditor and his/her staff becoming to close to senior management, with a consequent impairment of the auditor's independence. Along similar lines is the fixed term audit engagements, in which one audit firm would retain the audit engagement for a fixed period, say five years. Undoubtedly, such policies would increase the cost of an audit engagement.

- Not accepting entities as a client in which partners (or former partners) of the auditor are members of the governing body of the client. This would, for example, require an auditor, to relinquish the audit of a company, which engaged a former partner as a director. In practice, such a policy may result in audit clients not offering, or former audit partners not accepting such positions.

- Not accepting audit engagements, which would result in the fees earned from that audit engagement being greater than, say 5%, of the total income of the audit firm. Such a law, standard or policy requires a degree of flexibility in relation to the establishment of a new auditing firm, which may only have three or four audit clients.

- Having another appropriate qualified and experienced person within the firm (commonly referred to a review partner) review the work performed by the engagement partner.

4.6 DISTINCTION BETWEEN INTERNAL CHECK, INTERNAL AUDIT AND INTERNAL CONTROL

Internal check has been defined by the Institute of Chartered Accounts in England and Wales as the "checks on day-to-day transactions which operate continuously as part of the routine system whereby the work of one person is proved independently or complementary to the work of another, the object being the prevention or earlier detection of error or fraud" . The internal check in accounting system implies the organisation of the system of bookkeeping and arrangement of staff duties in such a manner that no one person can completely carry through a transaction and record every aspect thereof.

Internal audit has been defined by the Institute of Internal Auditors in the United States recently as an "independent, objective assurance and consulting activity designed to add value and improve an organisations operations. It helps an organisation accomplish its objectives by bringing a systematic disciplined approach to evaluate and improve the effectiveness of risk management, control and governance process".

Traditionally internal auditing was considered to be restricted to the examination of the books of accounts of the organisation with a view to ascertaining whether they correctly record the transaction. In fact, a good internal control system should have internal audit as an integral part. The modern concept of internal auditing as given in the aforesaid definition shows that internal auditing has moved significantly ahead by shouldering greater responsibilities to become one of the important management control devices.

It can be seen from the above definitions of both internal check and internal audit that they are parts of overall control system. Internal check operates as a built in device as far as staff organisation and job allocation aspects of the control system are concerned. On the other hand, the adequacy and operations of internal control on a regular basis is to be reviewed by the management through internal audit system to ensure that all significant controls are operating effectively. Thus, internal check is merely an arrangement of bookkeeping and clerical duties, but internal audit involves evaluating the quality and operation of the various controls.

4.7 CASE STUDIES

CASE STUDY 1

Fast Move Ltd. is a listed company in the food processing industry. They have 10 factory sites and 2,500 workers. They have grown very rapidly in recent years under the direction of Siddhartha, who is a very dynamic person. He tries to operate on the lowest possible costs and sees internal control as himself and his factory managers. The company has recently moved into the production of mass-produced South Indian foods and gambled that they will grab a large market share. They have an audit committee (not liked by Siddhartha) but no internal audit department.

Discussion

a. What advantages might accrue to the company if the company sets up an internal audit department?
b. How might the auditors approach the audit?
c. What specific duties are imposed on the auditor regarding internal control and internal audit?

CASE STUDY 2

Skylark Real Estate Ltd. is a company offering estate agency services to the public through a network of branches all over the country. The company has some 300 staff in all. The board consists of six people, a part-time chairman, a chief executive, two other full time executives and two representatives of the owners. The company is jointly owned by a foreign bank and the City Property Group. The company has an internal audit department consisting of Sanjeev who is a young chartered accountant and Rajeev who is an accounting expert. They have also a secretary, Ritwika. They report their activities monthly in detail to the board and to the audit committees of the foreign bank and the City Property Group.

Discussion

a. What work would the internal audit department do?
b. In what ways may the external auditors place reliance on their work?
c. Draw up a checklist, which the external auditor could use to assess the internal auditors as potentially being capable of producing work on which the external auditors may rely.

◆ Suggested questions

A   Short-type questions:

1. Distinguish between internal control system and internal check system.
2. What is internal control questionnaire?

3. Should the statutory auditor examine the accounts already checked by the internal auditor?

4. To what extent the internal auditor is responsible for the internal control?

5. How does the internal check system affect the work of an external auditor?

6. What precautions are to be taken in the application of internal check system?

7. State briefly what are the matters now to be included in the Auditor's Report in respect of the internal audit system of a large manufacturing company?

8. What are the objectives of internal audit?

B   Essay-type questions:

1. What do you mean by the term 'internal control'? What are the important features of a good system of internal control?

2. What is internal audit? Distinguish between internal control and internal audit? "The modern concept of internal audit envisages scope of internal audit much beyond financial audit"—explain.

3. (a) Distinguish between internal audit and statutory audit. (b) Can the statutory auditor rely upon the internal audit in carrying out his function as a statutory auditor?

4. Suggest a set of rules you would recommend for the internal control over the purchases of raw materials and stores of a large manufacturing company.

5. Draft a form of questionnaire, which you would use for determining the effectiveness of the client's internal control over payrolls.

6. (a) Distinguish briefly internal control, internal check and internal audit. (b) Discuss the general considerations in framing a system of internal control in respect of purchase of goods.

7. Comment on the following statements:

    (a) "The statutory auditor is entitled to rely on the internal auditor".

    (b) "The statutory auditor should test internal control system before relying on the same".

8. (a) Discuss the objectives of Internal control system. (b) Discuss the advantages and limitations of internal control system.

9. "In a good system of internal check, the work of one is checked indirectly by the work of another"—Explain and discuss this statement with examples.

10. What system of internal check would you recommend for a manufacturing company to prevent fraud in connection with credit purchase of raw materials?

Chapter 5

Vouching

5.1 MEANING OF VOUCHING

The examination of documentary evidence in support of transactions contained in the books of accounts is referred to as vouching. It is the technique followed in an audit for establishig authenticity of the transactions recorded in the primary books of accounts.

It essentially consists of verifying the record of transactions contained in the books of accounts with the relevant documentary evidence and the authority on the basis of which the entries were made. It also consists of examining in the process whether the amount mentioned in the voucher has been posted to an appropriate account, which would disclose the nature of the transaction on its inclusion in the final statements of account.

According to Taylor and Perry, "Vouching is the examination of the evidence offered in substantiation of entries in the books, including in such examination the proof so far as possible, that no entries have been omitted from the books".

According to Joseph Lancaster, "Vouching is a device used to prove that various transactions for the period are fairly, truly and sincerely reflected in the books of accounts".

So, from the above definitions, it can be said that, "vouching is a technique of auditing which checks the accuracy of entries made in the books of accounts with the help of available documentary evidences".

5.2 OBJECTIVES OF VOUCHING

Vouching is concerned with examining documentary evidence to ascertain the authenticity of entries in the books of accounts. It is a technique used by the auditor to judge the truth of entries appearing in the books of accounts.

Success of an audit depends on the efficiency with which vouching has been conducted. The following are the objectives for which vouching techniques are adopted by the auditor:

i. To check that all transactions recorded in the books of accounts are supported by documentary evidence.

ii. To verify that no fraud or error has been committed while recording the transactions.

iii. To see that each and every transaction recorded has been adequately authorised by a responsible person.

iv. To ensure that the distinction has been made between capital and revenue items while recording the transactions.

v. To have a greater precision in reporting the financial information as true and fair.

vi. To ensure the reliability of the figures presented in the books of account.

vii.   To confirm that no transaction has been recorded in the books of accounts, which are not related to the organisation under audit.

viii. To ensure the accuracy in totaling, carrying forward and recording of an amount in the accounts.

5.3   IMPORTANCE OF VOUCHING

The audit normally takes place long after the transactions have taken place, and the auditor, not being in picture at the time, cannot have the benefit of direct experience of the transactions. Necessarily, he has to depend on evidence and the voucher constitutes the necessary evidence of the transaction. The auditor's basic duty is to examine the accounts, not merely to see its arithmetical accuracy but also to see its substantial accuracy and then to make a report there on. This substantial accuracy of the accounts and emerging financial statements can be known principally by examination of vouchers, which are the primary documents relating to the transactions. If the primary document is wrong or irregular, the whole accounting statement would, in turn, become wrong and irregular. The auditor's role is to see whether or not the financial statements are wrong or irregular, and for this, vouching is simply essential. The importance of vouching was also highlighted in the case of *Armitage vs. Brewer & Knott* (1930) in which it was held that vouching is an important part of auditor's duty. If he shows any negligence in exercising care while vouching the books of accounts, his clients can claim damages.

The success of an audit will depend on the efficiency with which vouching has been applied during the process of auditing. Various frauds can be detected only if vouching is conducted in an intelligent manner. Wherever an auditor suspects a fraud, he should also check the sources of documentary evidence. Sometimes fictitious bills of expenses and purchases may be obtained. Payments against these bills may be misappropriated. This type of fraud can be detected by the intelligent vouching only.

Thus it is clear from the aforesaid discussion that vouching perhaps constitutes the backbone of auditing. If vouching is conducted faithfully and effectively, it will help in establishing reliability of profit and loss account and balance sheet. So, vouching can be considered as the essence of auditing.

5.4   VOUCHING AND VERIFICATION

Vouching may be defined as the examination by the auditor of all documentary evidence, which is available to support the genuineness of transactions entered in the books of accounts. Vouching is a substantive auditing procedure designed to obtain evidence as to the completeness, accuracy and validity of the data produced by the accounting system. While obtaining evidence through vouching, the auditor aims to obtain reasonable assurance in respect of following assertions in regard to transactions recorded in the books of account that:

i.   transaction is recorded in the proper accounts and revenue or expense properly allocated to the accounting period;

ii.   a transaction pertains to entity and took place during the relevant period;

iii. all transactions that have actually occurred have been recorded; and

iv.   transactions have been classified and disclosed in accordance with recognised accounting policies and practices.

Thus, it is through vouching that the auditor comes to know the genuineness of transactions recorded in the books of account.

On the other hand, the term verification usually applies to the process of auditing that examines, by appropriate manner, whether assets and liabilities are properly stated in the balance sheet. The term 'verification' may also apply to items of profit and loss account for checking of the account balances and their presentation.

Verification in the context of balance sheet items involves an inquiry into the ownership, valuation, existence and presentation of assets and liabilities.

Regarding assets, the auditor while verifying whether the assets are owned by the client also looks into whether any charge has been created on those assets and whether the same has been appropriately disclosed. In case of liabilities, the auditor would like to see that these are actually owed by the organisation.

Thus it is clear from the above that vouching deals with the examination of transactions at their point of origin while verification usually deals with the balances contained in the Balance Sheet and Profit and Loss Account.

5.5 VOUCHING AND ROUTINE CHECKING

Routine checking is a total process of accounting control which includes:

  i.   examination of the totalling and balancing of the books of prime entry;

 ii.   examination of the posting from primary books to the ledger accounts;

iii.   examination of totalling and balancing of the ledger accounts and of the preparation of trial balance made with those balances; and

 iv.   overall examination of writing up the transactions properly.

In short, the routine checking is concerned with the ascertainment of the arithmetical accuracy of casting, posting and carry forward of balances.

Confusion sometimes arises that the concept of vouching and routine checking are similar and complementary to each other. But this is not true in actual practice. Broadly speaking, vouching includes routine checking and it is considered as a part of it. Vouching includes routine checking, checking of all totals, subtotals, carry forwards, posting and checking of all ledger accounts. The scope of routine checking is confined with the books of accounts but in case of vouching, the auditor has to go beyond the books of account in order to trace out the source of transaction.

5.6 CONCEPT OF VOUCHER

There is no denying the fact that without voucher, vouching cannot be conducted. Vouchers are considered as an integral part of vouching. Voucher is documentary evidence, both internal and external, which is used to support the entries made in the books of accounts of a business.

A transaction is supposed to be recorded in the books of accounts only when the documentary evidence is available to support the transaction. It may be a receipt, counterfoil of a receipt, resolution passed in a meeting, cash memo, pay-in-slips, purchase invoices, minutes of a meeting etc. All such documentary evidences are known as voucher.

Voucher can be of two types—

  i.   Primary vouchers, and

 ii.   Collateral vouchers.

  i.   **Primary vouchers**: When written evidence is available in original, it is known as primary vouchers.

       For example: purchase invoices, counterfoil of cash receipt etc.

 ii.   **Collateral vouchers**: In certain cases, evidence in original are not available. Copies of such evidences are made available for the purpose of audit. These vouchers or documents are known as collateral vouchers.

       For example: Copies of resolution passed at a meeting, Xerox copy of demand drafts etc.

On the basis of sources of documents, vouchers can again be of two types—

  i.   Internal vouchers and
  ii. External vouchers.

  i.   **Internal vouchers:** Vouchers originating within the organisation are known as internal vouchers.

       For example: Sales invoices, Minute Book of Board Meetings, Material requisition slip etc.

  ii. **External vouchers:** Vouchers originating from the outside sources are known as external vouchers.

       For example: Mortgage Deed, Bank Statement etc.

5.7 INTERNAL AND EXTERNAL EVIDENCE

The evidence that a voucher provides may be of various natures and can be of the following two types—

  i.   **Internal Evidence:** It is one that has been created and used within the client's organisation and its' never going to outside party. Examples are duplicate sales invoices, employees time reports, purchase requisitions, minute books etc. These documents are parts of the records of the concern and have been prepared in the normal course.

  ii. **External Evidence:** It is one which emanates from outside the client's organisation. A document issued by a person with whom some business transactions had been entered into or who paid or was advanced an amount constitutes such evidence. For example, payee's receipt, lease agreement, bank statement etc. Sometimes, in certain transactions external evidence is obtained directly by the auditors e.g. confirmation of balances from debtors and creditors.

The auditor should attempt to obtain as much external evidence as possible, since such evidence is generally more reliable than internal evidence. External evidence should be preferred, since the likelihood of its being fabricated is much less because it requires collusion with an outsider. However, when external evidences are not available or appropriate, the auditor is obliged to accept internal evidence. Every evidence whether internal or external, should be subjected to appropriate scrutiny and corroboration should be obtained, whenever possible. A lack of corroboration will require the auditor to investigate further to arrive at the fact.

5.8 GENERAL PRINCIPLES OF VOUCHING

In conducting vouching appropriately and effectively, the auditor should follow certain principles, which are stated as below—

  i.   While vouching a transaction, the auditor must verify the authenticity of the transaction, accuracy of amount recorded and proper classification of accounts.

  ii.   The voucher, which has already been checked by the auditor should be cancelled or tick marked with a special sign, so that it may not be used again for fictitious transactions.

  iii. It should be seen that every voucher is authorised by an officer responsible for this purpose.

  iv.   If there is any alteration in the vouchers, it must be supported by the concerned officer's initials.

  v.   While vouching transactions, the auditor should keep in mind that the distinction is made between capital and revenue items.

  vi.   It should be seen that the date of the voucher falls within the accounting period.

  vii. It should also be ensured that the voucher is made out in the client's name.

viii. The voucher should include all the relevant documents which would be expected to have been received or brought into existence on the transactions having been entered into, i.e., the voucher is complete in all aspects.

ix. The account in which the amount of the voucher is adjusted is the one that would clearly disclose the character of the receipt or payment posted thereto on its inclusion in the final accounts.

x. All the vouchers should be numbered serially and dated.

xi. The amount in the receipt must be shown in words and figures. If the two differs, then it should be investigated.

xii. If any voucher is missing, the concerned official should be asked to give proper explanation. If no satisfactory explanation is received, it should be further investigated.

5.9 TEEMING AND LADING: A CHALLENGE TO VOUCHING

Teeming and Lading is a method adopted to misappropriate cash. The misappropriation of cash is activated by making a false entry relating to a transaction, which in turn is cancelled by a further entry and so on until such fraud is discovered. This method is also known as "Delayed Accounting of Money Received" as it is a method of concealment of a shortage by delaying the recording of cash receipts.

Example: Suppose, debts due from Mr. X is Rs. 50,000, from Mr. Y Rs. 1,00,000 and from Mr. Z Rs. 1,50,000. Now, say an amount of Rs. 50,000 is being received from Mr. X in discharge of his debt in the first week of January, but no entry is made in the cash book by the cashier, who misappropriates the cash. Say, in the next month, when cash is received from Mr. Y amounting to Rs. 1,00,000, the cashier records Rs. 50,000 in the name of Mr. X and the remaining Rs. 50,000 in the name of Mr. Y. Again, in the next month, when Mr. Z pays his debt of Rs. 1,50,000, the cashier records Rs. 50,000 in the name of Mr. Y and Rs. 1,00,000 in the name of Mr. Z. Rs. 50,000 is to be shown in the balance sheet as amount due from Mr. Z. Thus, after a certain period of time, the amount due from Mr. Z has been written off as bad debt and the money received has been thus misappropriated. However, if it is detected by the auditor, immediately the cashier passes a false entry recording the receipts from Mr. Z by paying an amount of Rs. 50,000 out of his own pocket and thus the cashier utilizes the money of the business for a certain period of time without any authority.

So, this type of fraud is a real challenge to the auditor. By adopting appropriate techniques of vouching, the auditor should detect this type of fraud and prevent misappropriation of cash. For the purpose, the auditor should take the following steps as a part of vouching technique:

i. He should verify the debtor's ledger, particularly those debtors who are making part payments of their dues.

ii. He may collect the balance confirmation certificate from debtors, whose accounts have been shown as due.

iii. Before the commencement of the work of vouching, he should evaluate the efficiency of the internal check system regarding the receipts of cash from the customers of the organisation.

iv. He should have a clear idea about the discount facility provided to the customers and the amount of bad debts to be written off.

v. If he suspects any fraud having already been committed, he should verify those transactions which have been shown in the cash book as deposited into bank and also checks the bank reconciliation statement.

vi. He should send the statement of accounts to the customers, whose accounts have been shown as due with a request that if a customer finds any discrepancy in the statement of account, he should contact the auditor without any delay.

5.10 VOUCHING OF DIFFERENT TYPES OF TRANSACTIONS

Vouching of Capital Expenditure

Capital expenditure means the expenditure relating to purchase of fixed assets. In order to vouch these types of transactions, it is to be seen the authenticity of the transaction, that it is properly authorised by authority and the amount of transaction is duly capitalized.

Land & Building

(a) Documents to be Checked

(i) Title deed (ii) Mortgage Deed in case of mortgaged property (iii) Broker's Note (iv) Contract (v) Receipts (vi) Architect's certificate (vii) Fixed Asset Register (viii) Minutes of the Directors' Meeting.

(b) Duty of the Auditor

i.   The Land & Building may be freehold or leasehold. If it is freehold, it should be verified with the owner's title. But if it is leasehold, the lease deed should be examined.

ii. If the property is purchased directly from the vendor and if any contract is made with the vendor, that contract should have to be checked.

iii. It also requires to be examined whether the ownership title of the property in favour of the client is legal or not.

iv. The various incidental charges are required to be incurred for the purchase of land and buildings, e.g., registration expenses of the property. These expenses should be verified with proper documents and receipts and the auditor should also confirm that these expenses have been duly capitalized.

v.   If any building is constructed for the purpose of the business, the contract made with the building contractor should be examined and in order to confirm the cost of construction, the certificate from the architect should be examined.

Assets Acquired under Hire Purchase System

(a) Documents to be Checked

(i) Board's Minute Book, (ii) Hire purchase agreement, (iii) Fixed Assets Register, (iv) Receipts from the vendor, (v) Bank Statement.

(b) Duty of the Auditor

i.   The Minutes Book of the Board Meeting should be checked in order to confirm that the purchase of assets on hire purchase system has been approved by the Board.

ii. The hire purchase agreement should be checked carefully and the description of the assets, cost of the assets, hire purchase charges, and terms of payment and rate of interest should be noted.

iii. It should be ensured that the concerned assets have been included in the related asset account at its cash value. It should also be checked that installments due have been paid according to the terms of the hire purchase agreement.

iv. It should be checked that the hire purchase charges applicable to the period from the commencement of the agreement to the end of the financial year have been charged against current profits.

v.   It should also be confirmed that the asset acquired on hire purchase basis have been included at its cash value in the balance sheet and depreciation has been calculated on the cash value from the date of the purchase. The amount due to the hire purchase vendor in respect of the capital outstanding has either been shown as a deduction from the asset concerned or as a separate amount under current liabilities.

Trade Mark and Copyright

(a) Documents to be Checked

(i) Schedule of Trade Marks and copyright, (ii) Assignment Deed or Agreement, (iii) Contracts.

(b) Duty of the Auditor

i. A Schedule of Trade Marks and Copyright duly signed by the responsible officer should be obtained and the same should be scrutinized. It should be confirmed that all of them are shown in the Balance Sheet.

ii. The Written Agreement in case of assignment of copyright and the Assignment Deed in case of transfer of Trade Marks should be examined.

iii. Existence of copyright should be verified by reference to contract between the client and the other party.

iv. It should be seen that the value has been determined properly and the cost incurred for the purpose of obtaining the Trade Marks and Copyrights have been capitalized.

v. It should also be ascertained that the legal life of the Trade Marks and Copyright have not yet expired.

vi. It should also be ensured that the amount paid for both the intangibles and assets is properly amortized having regard to appropriate legal and commercial consideration.

Vouching of Investments

(a) Documents to be Checked

(i) Broker's Purchase Note, (ii) Letter of allotment and calls, (iii) Share certificate or Debenture certificate, (iv) Bank Pass Book, (v) Receipts and (vi) Director's Meeting Minute Book.

(b) Duty of the Auditor

i. The auditor should examine whether investment has been made in accordance with the governing laws. Generally the organisation has its own rules regarding investment of money outside the business. It is required to be verified whether these rules have been complied with or not. Apart from this, it has to be seen that the governing provisions of the Companies Act regarding investment has been followed or not.

ii. Investments are generally purchased through brokers. If the shares etc. are purchased through brokers, the price paid should be verified with broker's bill and the receipt.

iii. If the investments are purchased through banks, the Bank Pass Book should be checked.

iv. On the basis of Director's Meeting Minute Book, the auditor should be confirmed about the approval of the Board for the purchase of investments.

v. The auditor should verify the title of the investment through register to confirm that the investments purchased have been transferred in the name of the company.

vi. If the investment is purchased at cum-dividend, it should be examined whether the purchase price has been shown properly under capital and revenue and the dividend receivable during the period has been accounted for or not.

Vouching of Borrowing from Banks

(a) Documents to be Checked

(i) Certificate from bank for securities deposited, (ii) Minute of the Board Meeting, (iii) Bank Statement, (iv) Letter of Loan Sanction, (v) Bank Pass Book.

(b) Duty of the Auditor

i. Borrowing from bank may be either in the form of overdraft limits or cash credit. The auditor should confirm about the type of the loan from the letter of loan sanctioned from the bank.

ii. Reconciliation of the balances in the overdraft or cash credit with that shown in the pass book should be done and it should be confirmed that the last mentioned balance by obtaining a certificate from the bank showing the balance in the accounts as at the end of the year.

iii. A certificate from the bank showing particulars of securities deposited with the bank as security for the loan should be obtained. It should be confirmed that the same has been correctly disclosed and duly registered with Registrar of Companies and recorded in the Register of Charges.

iv. The auditor should verify the authority under which the loan has been raised. In the case of a company, only the Board of Directors is authorised to raise a loan or borrow from a bank.

v. He should also confirm in the case of a company that the restrictions contained in Section 223 of the Companies Act as regards the maximum amount of loan that the company can raise have not been contravened.

vi. It should also be ascertained the purpose for which the loan has been raised and the manner in which it has been utilized and that this has not prejudicially affected the concern.

Vouching of Trading Transactions

Credit Purchases

(a) Documents to be Checked

(i) Purchase invoices, (ii) Copies of orders placed, (iii) Goods received note, (iv) Copies of challans from supplier, (v) Goods inward register, (vi) Stock records.

(b) Duty of the Auditor

i. The main objective of vouching of credit purchases is to see that all purchase invoices are entered in the purchase book and the goods entered in the purchases books are actually received by the client and the client pays for only those goods which are delivered by the supplier.

ii. The auditor should examine the internal check system in force and should see that only credit purchases of goods are recorded in the purchase book.

iii. It should be confirmed that the purchase of goods is sanctioned by a responsible official and only those goods are purchased in which the organisation deals with.

iv. The goods purchased should be actually received by the client. For the purpose, the goods inward register, stock records and challans from the supplier should be verified.

v. The auditor should be more careful while vouching the purchases made in the first month and the last month of the accounting period, because sometimes the purchases of the last year may be included in the purchase of first month of the current year or purchases of the last month of the current year may be recorded in the next year. As a result, the profit and loss account of the current year will not present true and fair position of the operating results.

Credit Sales

(a) Documents to be Checked

(i) Sales invoices, (ii) Challans, (iii) Sales register/Goods outward register, (iv) Stock records, (v) Purchase order from customers.

(b) Duty of the Auditor

i. The main objective of vouching of credit sales is to see that all sales invoices are entered in the sales book and the goods sold entered in the sales book are actually disposed off by the client and the client receives for only those goods which are supplied to the customers.

ii. The auditor should examine the internal check system in force and should see that only credit sales of goods are recorded in the sales book.

iii. The sales register should be examined with copies of sales invoices. The sale of capital goods shall not be recorded in the sales book.

iv. The sales tax etc. collected through sales invoices must be recorded under separate accounts.

v. It should be verified that all sales invoices are prepared on the basis of challans and then sales invoices are entered in sales book and from there, posted to the respective customer account. No sales invoice should be left unrecorded.

vi. Trade discount allowed to the customers should be checked. No separate entry for discount should be passed in the books.

vii. The statement of account should be verified by obtaining confirmation from the customers.

viii. The auditor should be more careful while vouching the sales made in the first month and the last month of the accounting period, because sometimes the sales of the last year may be included in the sales of the first month of the current year and sales of the last month of the current year may be recorded in the next year. As a result, the profit and loss account of the current year will not present true and fair position of the operating results.

Consignment Sale

(a) Documents to be Checked

(i) Consignment Day Book, (ii) Account Sales, (iii) Agreement between the consignor (client) and the consignee, (iv) Balance confirmation certificate from the consignee, (v) Pro-forma invoices, (vi) Goods outward book.

(b) Duty of the Auditor

i. It should be ascertained that credit has been taken only for the profit on the goods sold through the consignee before the year end. No profit should be taken for the profit on goods remaining in the hands of the consignee.

ii. Where it is desired to show the result of each consignment, the goods sent on consignment, through consignment day book, should be debited to the consignment account. The auditor should check debits in each of consignment account by reference to the pro-forma invoice, consignment day book, goods outward book, transport documents of the goods, acknowledgement of the goods by the consignee and the Account Sales.

iii. Credits in the consignment account should be verified with the help of the Account Sales received from the consignee.

iv. The agreement between the consignor and the consignee should be verified to check the commission and other expenses which are credited to consignee account.

v. It should be ensured that the stock lying with the consignee at the year end should be taken in the balance sheet at cost on a consistent basis and credited to consignment account to arrive at the result of the consignment transactions.

vi. Confirmation of the balance in the account of the consignee from the consignee should be obtained.

vii.   Sometimes' the goods are consigned not at cost but at an inflated price. The auditor should see that the necessary adjustments to remove the loading are made at the end of the year.

viii. It is possible that the goods consigned are treated as ordinary sales. The auditor should see that necessary adjustments are made at the year end in respect of the unsold goods, commission and the expenses incurred by the consignee. The consignee should not be shown as a debtor for unsold goods and in valuation of stock, these goods should be included in stock at cost worked out on a consistent basis.

Goods on Sale or Return

(a) Documents to be Checked

(i) Receipt of approval from customer, (ii) Sales invoices, (iii) Stock Records, (iv) Goods Inward Book, (v) Goods Outward Book.

(b) Duty of the Auditor

i.   The auditor should see that whether a separate record has been maintained for goods sold on approval basis,

ii.   He should ensure that the goods sent has not been included in sales unless the customer has intimated his approval or the stipulated time limit for such approval has expired.

iii. The auditor should also check the internal control system in respect of sales on approval basis. Usually, on the receipt of approval from customers or expiry of time limit, sales invoices are prepared, a copy of which is sent to the customer.

iv.   It should also required to be ensured that necessary arrangements have been made to get back the goods, if within the stipulated time, the customer informs about the return of the goods.

v.   He should also verify whether the goods sent on sale or return basis has been taken in the closing stock as stock with customer, if no intimation has received from the customer or still the time limit has not expired.

vi.   He should also get a statement from customer that the goods are lying with him on approval basis.

Vouching of Cash Book

Collection from Debtors

(a) Documents to be Checked

(i) Sales invoices (ii) Receipts issued to customers (iii) Statement of customers' accounts (iv) Existing and past discount chart (v) Correspondence with the customers.

(b) Duty of the Auditor

i.   The auditor should first of all check the existing internal control system in respect of cash collection, particularly collection from customers. When cash is received from customers, a cash memo is issued; a counterfoil or carbon copy of such cash memo is retained by the receiving clerk. The auditor should verify the amount received from customers from that counterfoils or carbon copies issued.

ii.   He should also ensure that amount received from customers has been entered in the cash book on the day it is received.

iii. He should also ensure that all these receipts are serially numbered. If any receipt is found to be missing, he should ask the clarification from the concerned officials.

iv.   It should be seen that the discount allowed to customers is authorised by a responsible officer. In addition to that, the terms and conditions of discount should be properly ascertained and the discount rates should be compared with the rates prevailing in the market.

v. In case of suspicion, the auditor can contact the customers directly with the approval of the client to verify the receipt of cash from them.

Interest and Dividend Received on Investments

(a) Documents to be Checked

(i) Bank statement (ii) Dividend warrant (iii) Schedule of Securities (iv) Agreement with party

(b) Duty of the Auditor

i. While vouching dividends, the auditor should check dividend warrant counterfoils and covering letters received along with cheque.

ii. If the dividend and interest is collected through bank, the auditor should verify the amount from the bank statement. In case of warrant received and amount not yet collected by the bank, the auditor should ensure that it has been shown as cheque yet to be collected.

iii. While vouching interest, the auditor should check the fixed interest bearing security statement. Interest on bank deposit should be checked from the bank pass book. But if interest is on the loan given to a party, it can be checked from the agreement made with the concerned party.

iv. The auditor should ensure that all interest received and accrued have been accounted for in the books and properly shown in the balance sheet.

v. If interest or dividend is received for the pre-acquisition period, the auditor should see whether proper adjustment has been made with the cost of investment for this pre-acquisition dividend or interest.

Bad Debts Recovered

(a) Documents to be Checked

(i) Notification from the court/bankruptcy trustee (ii) Letter from Collection Agency (iii) Letters from debtors (iv) Schedule of Bad Debts (v) Bank pass book.

(b) Duty of the Auditor

i. The auditor should ascertain the total amount lying as bad debt. In some cases, the court distributes the amount recovered from the insolvent person to his creditors in proportion of their claims. In this respect, total amount of debt, treated as bad from the party concerned plays a very important role.

ii. The auditor should ensure that all the bad debt recovery has been properly recorded in the books of account.

iii. Credit Manager's files are also to be checked properly for the purpose of ascertaining the actual amount recovered.

iv. The auditor should also ensure that the amount collected on account of bad debt recovery has been deposited into the bank promptly.

v. The amount recovered should also be counterchecked from the counterfoils or carbon copies of the receipt issued to the debtors. The auditor should also ensure that all these receipts are serially numbered.

Insurance Claim Received

(a) Documents to be Checked

(i) Counterfoil of the receipt (ii) Insurance policy (iii) Statement of claim submitted (iv) Copy of the survey report (v) Correspondence with the insurance company.

(b) Duty of the Auditor

i. The auditor should check the counterfoil of the acknowledgement of receipt issued by the client to know the actual amount recovered from the Insurance Company.

ii. The auditor should examine the statement of the claim submitted by the client along with the insurance policy to ensure that the claim has been submitted according to the provisions in the insurance policy.

iii. All the correspondences with the insurer on final determination of claim and payment thereof should be examined along with the copy of survey report.

iv. The accounting treatment of the amount received should be seen in order to ensure that revenue is credited with the appropriate amount and that in respect of claim against an asset, the profit and loss account is debited with the shortfall of the claim admitted against the book value.

v. The auditor should also see that entries in the profit and loss account has been appropriately described, if the claim was lodged in a previous year but no entries were then passed.

Cash Sales

(a) Documents to be Checked

(i) Sales invoices (ii) Cash Sales Summary (iii) Copies of cash memo

(b) Duty of the Auditor

i. The system of internal check should be examined with the objectives of finding out the defects therein, if any, whereby cash sales could be misappropriated,

ii. The practice followed in the matter of issuing cash memos should be ascertained. Cash sales are usually verified with carbon copies of cash sales,

iii. One of the important matters to which attention of the auditor should be paid in the process is that the dates on the cash memos should tally with those on which cash collected in respect thereof has been entered in the cash book,

iv. The computation of sales should be ascertained by the auditor in order to verify whether the price of goods sold has been calculated correctly,

v. If a cash memo has been cancelled, its original copy should be inspected for as it could be that the amount thereof has been misappropriated,

vi. If cash collections are made through automatic cash registers, the daily totals entered in the cash book should be checked with the till rolls.

Income from House Property

(a) Documents to be Checked

(i) Bills issued to tenants (ii) Tenancy agreement (iii) Rent receipts (iv) Statement of rent received (v) Rent reconciliation statement,

(b) Duty of the Auditor

i. The auditor should examine the rent received from house properties with the counterfoils of the rent receipts in order to ascertain the amount of rent and the period for which it is paid.

ii. He should check the copies of bills issued to the tenants by reference to the agreement with the tenant and charges paid by the client on behalf of tenants e.g. electricity charges.

iii. He should verify the statement of rent received prepared tenant-wise or property wise, if any, and check it with the Rent Register, if any maintained for the tenants.

iv. He should also vouch the entries for rent received in advance or accrued rent in order to see that proper adjustment entries are passed for the amount of rent pertaining to the accounting year concerned.

v. Reconciliation between the amount of rent received and the amount of rent receivable should be done by the auditor and if there is any difference, it should be enquired into. In this context, adjustment against, if any deposit should also be checked.

vi. The auditor should obtain a certificate from the responsible officer in respect of any vacant property during the year.

Remuneration Paid to Directors

(a) Documents to be Checked

(i) Resolutions of the general meeting (ii) Articles of Association (iii) Agreement with the directors (iv) Director's Attendance Register (v) Receipts issued by the directors.

(b) Duty of the Auditor

i. The auditor should check the terms and conditions of appointment of directors first by referring to the minutes of the general meeting.

ii. He should also examine the Articles of Association in order to ascertain the mode of payment.

iii. The agreement with the directors should also be checked to know the amount to be paid to the directors for attending board meetings and for other works by way of commission or otherwise. In this respect, the auditor should also check the director's attendance in the board meetings as available in the Attendance Register.

iv. It should be ensured that all the legal formalities as per the provisions of Sections 198, 309, 349 and 350 and Schedule XIII of the Companies Act, where applicable, have been duly complied with.

v. Computation of the net profits and the commission payable to directors in terms of clause 4A of Part II of Schedule VI to the Companies Act should be checked thoroughly.

vi. The amount paid to the directors as their .remuneration should also be checked with receipts issued by the directors for this purpose.

Travelling Expenses

(a) Documents to be Checked

(i) Travelling Rules of the organisation (ii) Approved Tour Programmes (iii) Tour Report (iv) Board Meetings Minutes (v) R. B. I. Permission Letter (vi) Air, railways tickets etc.

(b) Duty of the Auditor

i. Before conducting vouching work of travelling expenses, the auditor should know the rules in the organisation on admissibility and rates of travelling expenses and daily allowances,

ii. The auditor should ensure himself first whether the travelling expenses have been incurred only on those tour programmes which are approved by the competent authority,

iii. The auditor then should thoroughly check the travelling expenses bills submitted by the employees along with the supporting vouchers as may be appropriate,

iv. The auditor then should also confirm himself that the statement of business done or tour report has been submitted by the employees and reviewed by the proper authority,

v. In case of foreign trip, the board's resolution should be seen to ensure that the trip has been sanctioned. The auditor should also ensure that necessary permission has been obtained from the Reserve Bank of India for foreign exchange transactions in connection with foreign trip,

vi. It should also be checked by the auditor that advances, if any, taken by the employees of this purpose have been properly accounted for.

Cash Purchases

(a) Documents to be Checked

(i) Cash memo (ii) Cash bill (iii) Goods Inward Book (iv) Payment order (v) Original receipts from the payee.

(b) Duty of the Auditor

i. Cash purchase is an important area where the defalcation and misappropriation of cash can be made possible. For this reason, it should be carefully examined by the auditor whether proper authorisation is there for such purchase from the appropriate authority.

ii. In case of emergency, cash purchase of goods may be made. So, the auditor should evaluate the situation under which cash purchase is made to ascertain the emergence of such purchase.

iii. Usually purchases of stores and stationery items are made on cash basis. So the auditor should ensure that there is adequate internal control system which will help in controlling manipulation of cash purchases.

iv. It should be seen that the goods purchased are actually received by the store keeper. For this purpose, cash memos can be compared with the entries in Goods Inward Book to verify the actual goods received.

v. The auditor can also check the discount facilities provided by the suppliers and ensure himself that only net amount after deducting discount availed have been entered in the books.

Salaries and Wages Paid

(a) Documents to be Checked

(i) Salary bills (ii) Wage sheets or Pay roll (iii) Counterfoil of cheques (iv) Appointment letters (v) Service agreement (vi) Employment registers.

(b) Duty of the Auditor

i. For the purpose of vouching salaries and wages, the auditor is required to go through the internal procedure and to get confirmed that they are not altered since the last audit.

ii. The additions, calculations and castings of the salary bills and wage sheets should be properly checked by the auditor.

iii. The total amount paid for salaries and wages should be compared with the entries in the cash book. For this purpose, the auditor should compare the total of wage sheet and salary bill with the amount of cheque withdrawn. If there is any excess amount withdrawn, the auditor should ensure that they are deposited into the bank immediately.

iv. It should be the duty of the auditor to ensure that the unclaimed salaries and wages have been deposited into bank or the concerned cheque has been cancelled.

v. The auditor has to see whether the wage sheet and salary bill is duly certified by a responsible officer and to check the employment register for the purpose of finding out dummy employees and workers.

vi. He should further check attendance records, salary bill and wage sheets of earlier months and appointment letter of new employees. If there is an abnormal increase in the wages and salaries of a month over the previous month, he should inquire into the reasons for such increase.

Payment of Sales Tax

(a) Documents to be Checked

(i) Periodical sales return (ii) Treasury challans (iii) Sales tax assessment order (iv) Reconciliation statement (v) Certificate from registered dealers.

(b) Duty of the Auditor

i. The auditor should see the receipted challans of the Reserve Bank of India or State Bank of India in support of the payment vouchers and should ensure that the amount of tax deposited agrees with the amount of tax payable as per the return submitted,

ii. He should also check sales tax register with the copies of invoices and confirm that proper sales tax has been charged, collected and deposited,

iii. He should check the calculations made in the returns and ascertain that the total liability as per returns agrees with the sales-tax collected and thus ensure that the sales tax payable and liability of each year are properly recorded,

iv. He should obtain the certificates from registered dealers to ascertain that the sales-tax returns agree with the sales-tax collected by them for the period as shown in different invoices,

v. Finally, the auditor should find out the total tax-liability and ensure himself that proper provision has been made in the accounts for the tax liability.

Research and Development Expenditure

(a) Documents to be Checked

(i) Minutes of the Board Meeting (ii) Memorandum and Articles of Association of the client (iii) Annual Budget (iv) Receipts and other relevant papers from the third parties.

(b) Duty of the Auditor

i. The nature of research and development work has to be ascertained first by the auditor to ensure himself that it is related with the normal activities of the undertaking.

ii. The auditor should also ascertain whether the concerned research activity is authorised by the Board and has relevance to the objectives of the company and ensure that no expense unrelated to the research and development programme is allowed to be debited to this account.

iii. The auditor should check the accounting entries passed for this purpose. He should confirm that if the research expenses are paid for developing products or for inventing a new product, they are treated as deferred revenue expenditure to be written off over a period of three to five years, if successful. In case, it is established that the research effort is not going to succeed, the entire expenses incurred should be written off to the profit and loss account.

iv. He should also ensure that if any plant and machinery have been purchased specially for the purpose of research activity, the cost thereof, less the residual value is appropriately debited to the Research and Development Account over the years of research.

v. The auditor should see that the tax benefit arising out of the research and development expenses is taken into account in creating tax provision.

vi. Finally, he should ascertain the accounting policy of the concern regarding treatment of research and development expenditure.

Travelling Salesman's Commission

(a) Documents to be Checked

(i) Agreement with the salesman (ii) Receipts issued by salesman (iii) Statement of sales (iv) Appointment letters of the salesman (v) Commission statement.

(b) Duty of the Auditor

i. The auditor should see the appointment letter given to the salesman or the agreement with the salesman in order to know the rate of commission entitlement and other terms and conditions of his assignment.

ii. An examination of the statement submitted by the salesman regarding sales should be made and checked with the sales records in order to find out the amount of sales effected by the salesman. This is required as usually, sales commission is paid on the basis of sales effected through a salesman.

iii. The auditor should also check the statement of commission submitted by the salesman in order to check the accuracy of calculation of commission payable to the salesman.

iv. It should be ensured by the auditor that the commission is paid only on sales booked and executed within the year and the payment of commission should be vouched with the receipts signed by the salesman.

v. The auditor should also check whether provision has been made in the accounts for commission due but not paid to the salesman.

Freight, Carriage and Custom Duty

(a) Documents to be Checked

(i) Freight note (ii) Transport receipts (iii) Rate schedule of transport charges (iv) Rate of custom duty (v) Custom duty payment challans (vi) Correspondence with transporters and customs authorities.

(b) Duty of the Auditor

i. The auditor should ascertain the nature of expenses first i.e., whether they relate to the purchase of raw-materials or purchase of assets or sale of goods as the accounting treatment of these expenses depend on the purpose for which they have been incurred.

ii. He should ensure that all the expenses incurred in this connection are properly authorised.

iii. He should ascertain the possibility of duty drawback or refund of custom duty, if any, and see whether adequate adjustments have been made in the books of account for this purpose.

iv. The auditor should also refer to the terms and conditions of purchases and sales to know whether the expenses incurred in this connection are recoverable from the third party.

v. He should also check the adequacy of transit insurance to cover the risk of loss due to goods lost in transit.

vi. The auditor should also examine all the relevant documents and ensure that all the payments made in this connection have been fully accounted for.

Preliminary Expenses

(a) Documents to be Checked

(i) Board's Minute Book (ii) Receipts for the registration fees paid (iii) Bills and receipts issued by the printers (iv) Prospectus (v) Statutory report (vi) Other supporting papers and vouchers.

(b) Duty of the Auditor

i. The auditor should ascertain first as to whether the expenses capitalized as preliminary expenses are actually connected with the formation of the company.

ii. The expenses incurred for the formation of the business should be approved by the Board of Directors in their meeting. It is the duty of the auditor to see whether the expenses incurred has got due approval from the authority.

iii. The auditor should also justify the expenses from the angle of propriety aspect of the business. He should check the rightness of the amount of expenses.

iv. The accounting policy of the concern regarding writing off of preliminary expenses should also be evaluated in order to justify the appropriateness of the policy adopted.

v. In some cases, the approval from the shareholders is also required to be obtained for incurring expenses on account of preliminary expenses. The auditor should confirm that the required approval has been obtained from the shareholders in this regard.

vi. The concern is also entitled to get exemption for the preliminary expenses incurred in computing business income under the Indian Income tax Act. The auditor should see whether this aspect is properly dealt with or not.

Royalty Payable to a Foreign Collaborator

(a) Documents to be Checked

(i) Collaboration agreement (ii) Statement of royalty payable (iii) Permission from Reserve Bank of India (iv) Receipts from the foreign collaborator, (v) Other supporting papers and vouchers.

(b) Duty of the Auditor

i. The auditor should go through the agreement with the foreign collaborator to note the rate of royalty, method of calculation of royalty, mode of payments etc.

ii. He should also examine the statement showing detailed calculation of royalty payable and verify whether it has been calculated according to the agreement along with the checking of payment vouchers.

iii. He should confirm that adequate and necessary provision has been made for the royalty accrued but not yet paid to the foreign collaborator during the year.

iv. He should ensure himself that necessary permission has been obtained from the Reserve Bank of India for making payments outside the country, if royalty is required to be payable in foreign currency.

v. The auditor should also examine that the recovery of short-working facility is duly availed off.

vi. The amount of royalty paid or payable during the year should be compared with that of last year and reasons for variation, if significant, should be inquired into.

Custom Duty Paid on Import of Machinery

(a) Documents to be Checked

(i) Accounts submitted by the clearing agents (ii) Deposit Account with Custom Authorities (iii) Receipts issued by Customs Authorities for payments made (iv) Statement of duty payable (v) Other supporting papers and vouchers.

(b) Duty of the Auditor

i. The auditor should ensure himself that the custom duty paid in connection with the import of machinery only and the machinery is purchased for the use of the business concerned.

ii. He should verify the amount of custom duty with reference to bill of entry duly stamped by custom authority.

iii. If the machinery is imported through clearing agents, the auditor should also refer the accounts submitted by the clearing agent in order to ensure total charges including custom duty on account of import of machinery.

iv. The payment of custom duty should be checked with the receipts received from the custom authority.

v. The auditor should check the accounting aspect of custom duty paid against import of machinery, *i.e.*, whether it has been capitalized by debiting machinery account.

Insurance Premium Paid

(a) Documents to be Checked

(i) Insurance policy (ii) Insurance premium receipts (iii) Cover note issued by the Insurance Company (iv) Correspondence with the Insurance Company (v) Other supporting papers and vouchers

(b) Duty of the Auditor

i. For the purpose of vouching insurance premium paid on different policies first of all the adequacy of the insurance should be examined very carefully. It should be the duty of an auditor to review the insurance policy periodically in order to ascertain the under-insurance in each of the policies undertaken.

ii. The auditor should check the payment of insurance premium from the receipts obtained from the insurance companies.

iii. It should be ensured by the auditor that premiums are not in arrears and the prepaid insurance has been properly adjusted against subsequent premium payable.

iv. If the insurance premium paid against risk of fire etc. on any property, the auditor should confirm that the property belongs to the concern. However, if the premium is paid against key-man insurance policy, the auditor should evaluate the necessity of such insurance coverage.

v. Finally, the auditor should check the entries passed for the premium paid to ensure that proper distinction has been made between" fire and other natural hazards insurance with key-man insurance.

Author's Note

In this chapter, a number of transactions are considered for vouching purposes, but it is not possible to consider every possible type of transactions that could be subject of an examination-question. From the transactions discussed in this chapter, it is expected that the students should be able to answer any type of transactions in the examination by following the approach adopted for vouching different transactions in this chapter.

◆ Suggested questions

A   **Short-type questions:**

1. Write the objectives of vouching.
2. What do you mean by vouchers? What are its' different types?
3. Distinguish between Vouching and Routine checking.
4. Explain the following statement—
   (a) 'Vouching is the essence of auditing'.
   (b) 'In vouching payments, the auditor does not merely seek proof that money has been paid away'.

5. What do you mean by Teeming and Lading'? What is the duty of an auditor in this respect?

6. State what information you would require and what documentary evidence you would see while vouching Director's Remuneration.

B   **Essay-type questions:**

1. How do you vouch the following—

    (a) Custom duty paid on import of machinery.

    (b) Income from House Property.

    (c) Royalty Payable to a foreign collaborator.

    (d) Travelling Expenses.

    (e) Interest and Dividend Received.

    (f) Directors' fees paid.

    (g) Preliminary Expenses.

    (h) Insurance Premium paid.

2. How would you as an auditor examine the following—

    (a) Goods sent on sale or return.

    (b) Goods sent on consignment.

    (c) Payment of Interest on Share Capital.

    (d) Shares issued at a discount.

3. State what information you would require and what documentary evidence you would see while vouching the following—

    (a) Freight, Carriage and Custom duty.

    (b) Commission paid to sole-selling agent.

    (c) Credit purchase.

    (d) Book Debts Realised.

4. What is Vouching? Discuss the features of vouching? State the important considerations before conducting vouching.

5. While auditing the accounts of a trading concern, how would you examine that all liabilities incurred before the close of the year in respect of wages, freight and travellers commission have been included in the accounts?

6. Discuss the principal considerations involved in the examination of Debtors' and Suppliers' Ledger.

7. What are the special steps to be taken by the auditor in vouching the following transactions—

    (a) Sales made during the last few days of the year.

    (b) Goods sent to debtors free of charge by way of quantitative discount.

8. How will you deal with the following as an auditor?

    (a) Bonus to employees which was hitherto being charged to profit and loss account on accrual basis is now being accounted for on cash basis.

    (b) There is a significant fall in market price of some investments held for a long time by the concern.

    (c) Outstanding liabilities for expenses show a considerable fall as compared to last year.

Chapter 6

Verification and Valuation of Assets and Liabilities

6.1   INTRODUCTION

One of the most important duties of an auditor in connection with the audit of the accounts of a concern is to verify the assets and liabilities appearing in the Balance Sheet. He has not only to examine the arithmetical accuracy of the transactions in the books of accounts by vouching only, but he has also to see that the assets as recorded in the Balance Sheet actually exist.

If the auditor fails to verify the assets, he will be held liable as was decided in the case of *London Oil Storage Co. Ltd. vs. Seear, Hasluck & Co.* (1904). It was held in that case that "the auditor should verify the existence of the assets stated in the balance sheet; otherwise he will be liable for any damage suffered by the client".

6.2   MEANING OF VERIFICATION OF ASSETS

Verification means the proof of existence or confirmation of assets and liabilities on the date of Balance Sheet. Verification usually indicates verification of assets of any organisation, which can be done by the examination of value, ownership, existence and possession of any asset. According to Spicer and Pegler, "Verification of assets implies an enquiry into the value, ownership and title, existence and possession and the presence of any charge on the assets".

So, verification is a process, which includes:

   i.   valuation of assets at its proper value,

  ii.   ownership and title of the assets,

 iii.   confirmation about the existence of the assets, and

  iv.   satisfaction about the condition that they are free from any charge or mortgage.

6.3   MEANING OF VALUATION OF ASSETS

Valuation of assets means the examination of the accuracy and propriety of the valuation of those assets, which are shown in the Balance Sheet of any concern at the end of the financial year.

So, valuation is an operation, which includes:

   i.   obtaining all the necessary information regarding valuation,

  ii.   analysing all the figures available,

 iii.   confirming the fact that the valuation is being determined on the basis of generally accepted conventions and accounting principles,

iv. ensuring the consistency of the methods followed for the valuation from year to year, and

v. obtaining an opinion regarding the accuracy of valuation.

6.4 DIFFERENCE BETWEEN VERIFICATION AND VALUATION

Valuation of assets is a part and parcel of verification. Without proper valuation of assets, verification is not possible.

Verification includes, apart from valuation, the examination of ownership right, the existence of the asset in the business and its freeness from any sort of charge or mortgage.

6.5 IMPORTANCE OF VERIFICATION OF ASSETS

The auditor's duty is not complete when he has vouched the entries appearing in the books. The substantiation of an entry under the date on which it is made does not prove the existence of the related asset at the date of the Balance Sheet, nor is the value of such asset necessary the same as on the date of the original entry. The auditor has the further duty of substantiating the existence and value of such items as at the date of the Balance Sheet. This work can be performed through proper verification of assets.

If the Balance Sheet contains an asset, which, in fact, does not exist or which is stated at a value different from what in considered reasonable, both the balance sheet and the profit and loss account would be incorrect. For instance, when the balance of Sundry Debtors include debts amounting to Rs. 5000, which are irrecoverable and no provision has been created against such bad debts, then the amount of profit, the value of assets and the value of proprietor's fund would be shown in excess by that amount.

Auditor's duty under the Companies Act has been extended by the promulgation of the Companies (Auditors Report) Order 1988, issued under Section 227 (4A) of the Companies Act. This order requires the auditor to state in his report some additional matters, which include matters like verification of fixed assets and stock. On these accounts, it is essential that assets should be verified with utmost care.

6.6 IMPORTANCE OF VALUATION OF ASSETS

Principally, the auditor is required to verify the original cost of asset and to confirm, as far as practicable, that such a valuation is fair and reasonable. As regards the manner in which the original cost should be ascertained, there are well-defined modes of valuation that are expected to be followed.

Assets are valued either on a 'going concern' or a 'break up value' basis. Under going concern method, it is necessary to find out and calculate the cost of acquisition of the concerned assets and the rate of depreciation required to be provided. Break up value basis is considered, when the company is being wound up. In this method, assets are valued at their realizable value. So, value of an asset is being determined differently in different ways.

It is thus evident that the auditor is expected to apply his knowledge and skill considering the value of each asset with a view to confirm that it is true and fair, having regard to the principles on which assets are generally valued. In the words of Lancaster, "An auditor is not a valuer and cannot be expected to act as such. All that he can do is to verify the original cost and to ascertain as far as possible that the current values are fair and reasonable and are in accordance with the accepted commercial principles".

So, valuation forms an important part of every audit. This is because the fairness of the Balance Sheet depends much upon how correctly the valuation of various assets and liabilities has been made. The auditor has to see that the assets and liabilities appearing in the Balance Sheet have been exhibiting their proper value.

6.7 GENERAL PRINCIPLES FOR VERIFICATION OF ASSETS

The following are the general principles which are required to be considered by the auditor in conducting verification and valuation of assets in an organisation:

Acquisition of Individual Asset
The cost of asset acquired should be verified with their purchase agreements or ownership rights and the receipts of the seller in respect of the price paid. It should be verified that expenditure on assets newly acquired and that on the renewal and replacement of old assets has been correctly recorded consistent with the method that has been generally followed in the past.

Acquisition of Group of Assets
Where an organisation has taken over the assets of a going concern, the agreement of purchase should be inspected and that the amount paid for them should also be ascertained.

Sale of Assets
When an asset is sold, its sale proceeds should be vouched with respect to the reference to the agreement, containing the terms and conditions of sale, counterfoil of the receipt issued to the purchaser or any other evidence which may be available.

If the sale of a fixed asset has resulted in capital profit, it should be transferred to capital reserve. However, the profit limited to the original cost or a loss should be transferred to the profit and loss account.

Depreciation
It is now obligatory for a company to provide for depreciation out of profits in accordance with the provisions under sub-section (1) of Section 205 of Companies Act, before any profit can be distributed as dividend. The law requires that depreciation should be provided in any one of the ways specified in Section 205 (2).

The value of certain assets (viz. plant and machinery) is also affected by an accident or by obsolescence. Any asset that has been discarded, after such a happening, should be shown in the Balance Sheet only at realisable value.

Physical Verification of Fixed Asset
The existence of fixed assets, where practicable, should be verified by physical inspection or by comparing the particulars of assets as entered in the schedule attached to the Balance Sheet, with the Asset Register and also reconciling their total value with the general ledger balances.

Inspection of Current Assets and Investments
Wherever possible, all the securities and documents of title, cash, negotiable instruments etc. representing the assets should be inspected at the close of the last day of the accounting period. If this is not practicable and the examination is undertaken at a latter date, a careful scrutiny of transactions subsequent to the date of the Balance Sheet must be made to ensure that the changes in their balances that have subsequently taken place are bonafide and are supported by adequate evidence.

Charges on Asset
It should be ascertained that no unauthorised charge has been created against an asset and all the charges are duly registered and disclosed.

Where shares or securities are lodged with a bank to secure a loan or an overdraft, a certificate should be obtained from the bank showing the nature of the charges, if any.

Assets with Third Parties

Where assets, for example, government securities, share and debentures, stock sent on consignment, goods sent on sale or approval basis etc. are in the custody of a third party other than a bank, these must be inspected.

6.8 PROBLEMS OF VERIFICATION

Without proper verification of assets and liabilities, it is not possible for the auditor to certify the Balance Sheet as it exhibits a true and fair view of the state of affairs of the business. It will never be possible on the part of the auditor to perform the function in his own responsibility and in accordance with his own knowledge and expertise.

For example, if the auditor is required to verify the stock-in-trade at the end of the accounting period, it will take weeks and months to complete this work. Not only that, the auditor will have to take help of experts in this field. In addition to that, there are certain assets, which have no physical existence in appearance, namely goodwill, patent, copyright, trade marks etc. In these cases, the auditor has to conduct verification on the basis of available documents.

In Kingston Cotton Mills Ltd. Case (1896), it was held that, "it is no part of an auditor's duty to take stock. No one contends that it is. He must rely on others for the details of stock-in-trade". So there was no breach of duty on the part of the auditor. An auditor is not supposed to take stock himself and in the absence of suspicious circumstances, he can accept a stock certificate by a trusted official of the company.

6.9 PROBLEMS OF VALUATION

The various problems which an auditor faces while conducting valuation of assets and liabilities are stated below:

Character of the Assets

In some cases, it is not possible to identify the character of the asset for the purpose of valuation as whether it is fixed asset or current asset. The mode of valuation process of fixed asset is different from the mode of valuation process of current assets, e.g., investments.

Use of Assets

In some situations, the same asset is available for sale and again is used in the organisation. The valuation process also depends on the nature of use of the concerned assets, e.g., stock of furniture.

Estimated Life

The life of the fixed assets is not certain. The valuation of these assets is made on the basis of estimated life of the assets. However, the determination of estimated life is not an easy task.

Eventual Problems

It is not possible for the auditor to take into consideration the events occurring after Balance Sheet date, which have the effect on valuation of assets.

Lack of Information

The auditor may not be in possession all the relevant information, which is required to be considered by the auditor in the determination of the value of assets.

6.10 WINDOW DRESSING—A CHALLENGE TO VERIFICATION

Window dressing may be defined as an artificial practice to show the current ratio position favourable. When window dressing technique is adopted in accounting statement presentations, the financial position is shown in such a way that it seems to be better than the actual position. It is more of misrepresentation than fraud.

Window dressing may be practiced in any one of the following ways:

i. Deferring purchases, i.e., purchase of a year may be shown as of next year.

ii. Extensive drive is made for the collection of book debts to show the book balance favourable.

iii. Incomes for the next year are recorded in advance in the accounts of the current year.

iv. Borrowed capital can be shown as long-term debt capital.

v. Provision of inadequate amount of depreciation and bad debts.

vi. Charging revenue expenditure as capital expenditure.

vii. Over and/or under-valuation of assets and liabilities.

viii. Inflating the profits by entering non-existent items of purchase returns and sales return.

ix. Utilising secret reserves during the depression period without making the fact known to the shareholders.

The auditor should carefully verify the existence of the assets and liabilities. He should see that no attempts have been made by the client to adopt window dressing. It may sometimes happen that the client may show a particular asset in paper only which, in fact, does not exist physically. Window dressing is a challenge to the work of verification, which should have to be faced by the auditor through conducting of effective verification work.

6.11 VERIFICATION AND VALUATION OF ASSETS

Verification of asset is an important audit technique. Conventionally, the scope of this technique is limited to inspection of assets and collection of information about the assets.

Through verification, the auditor should confirm himself:

i. that the assets are in existence on the date of the Balance Sheet,

ii. that the concerned asset has been acquired for the use in the business,

iii. that the asset has been purchased under a proper authority,

iv. that the concern has the right of ownership of the asset,

v. that the asset is free from any charge not disclosed in the Balance Sheet,

vi. that the assets is correctly valued, and

vii. that the asset is correctly presented in the Balance Sheet.

Verification of assets is primarily the responsibility of the management. They are expected to have a much greater knowledge of the assets of the business as regards their condition, location etc. than that which an outsider might be able to acquire on their inspection. They are competent to determine the values of the assets at which they should be included in the Balance Sheet. The auditor is only expected to apply his skill and expertise considering the value of each asset with a view to confirm that they are truly and fairly disclosed in the Balance Sheet.

For the purpose of applying verification techniques, we may divide the assets into the following four categories:

i. Intangible assets, viz. goodwill, patent, trade mark, copyright etc.

ii. Fixed assets, viz. land & building, plant & machinery, furniture & fixtures, motor vehicles etc.

iii. Current assets, viz. stock-in-trade, sundry debtors, prepaid expenses and accrued incomes, cash and bank balances etc.

iv. Fictitious assets, viz. preliminary expenses, discount on issue of shares or debentures etc.

6.12 VERIFICATION AND VALUATION OF INTANGIBLE ASSETS

6.12.1 GOODWILL

Goodwill is considered as an intangible fixed asset. The value that is shown in the Balance Sheet does not appear to be its present value, because the present value of goodwill depends upon a number of factors like financial position of the business, earning capacity at present and its future trend etc. But in actual practice, it is not valued at cost.

Valuation of Goodwill

There are several methods of valuation of goodwill. However, goodwill should not be recognised in the accounts unless it is purchased. Regarding valuation of goodwill, an appropriate method is to be adopted to write the cost down out of the available profits and in this way, it should be ensured that the capital of the business is represented by tangible assets only.

Auditor's Duty Regarding Valuation

i. The auditor should confirm himself that goodwill appearing in the Balance Sheet has not been shown in excess of its cost price.

ii. The auditor should see that the goodwill is never appreciated in the books of a company.

Verification of Goodwill

Goodwill is the excess of the price paid for a business as a whole over the book value or the computed value or the agreed value of all tangible assets purchased. It is not possible to be verified physically; hence verification of goodwill means proper checking of accounting entries passed for goodwill.

Auditor's Duty Regarding Verification

i. The goodwill as recorded in the books of account should be properly examined and the same is to be verified with the Balance Sheet.

ii. If goodwill is created on account of purchasing a running business, the auditor should verify it with the contract made between the client and the vendor.

iii. Sometimes, management intends to capitalise the current expenditure, which is usually high. The auditor should raise objection to this practice.

iv. In case of goodwill once written off, but later on brought back in order to write off the debit balance of profit and loss account or any capital loss, the auditor should investigate the reasons for this and may refer to the resolutions adopted at the Directors Meeting and the approval of the shareholders.

v.   The auditor should ensure that as required by Accounting Standard-10 for fixed assets, goodwill has been recorded in the books only when some consideration in money or moneys has been paid for.

6.12.2 PATENT

A patent is an official document, which secures to an investor exclusive right to make, use and sell his invention.

Valuation of Patent
The patent is valued at cost less depreciation. Cost is the acquisition cost, which may be purchase cost or invention cost. Also the cost of registration of patent should be included in the valuation, while the renewal fees should be charged off to revenue. Since patent suffers depreciation through effluxion of time, it is preferable to adopt fixed installment method of charging depreciation based on its legal life.

Auditor's Duty Regarding Valuation
i.   The patent should be examined to see that the company concerned is registered as the owner of the patent.

ii. It should be seen that the patent is valued at cost less depreciation. If it is found that the commercial life of the patent is shorter than its legal life, the depreciation should be spread over its commercial life only.

Verification of Patent
Actual patent should be physically verified by the auditor and it should be seen that it has been duly registered. In case of joint registration of the patent with an individual, who might have developed the patented article, it should be seen that a registered assignment by the individual in favour of the company has been made.

Auditor's Duty Regarding Verification
i.   The auditor should check the Patent Register in order to verify that it has been properly included therein.

ii. The auditor should also ensure that the legal life of the patent has not yet been expired.

iii. The latest renewal certificate of the patent should also be verified by the auditor.

iv. The patent may also be subject to litigation about its little. A certificate from the solicitors of the company should be obtained to ensure that it is free from encumbrances.

6.12.3 COPYRIGHT

A copyright is the exclusive legal right to produce or reproduce some kind of literary work. It is the legal protection provided to an author by which the reproduction of his work by others is restricted.

Valuation of Copyright
Generally, the value of the copyright is not fixed, as copyright loses its value with the passage of time. In the Balance Sheet, it is shown at cost less amounts written off from time to time.

Auditor's Duty Regarding Valuation
i.   The auditor should see that the value of copyright is determined on proper basis including the period of copyrights.

ii. It should be ensured that if any copyright does not command sale of any books, the same should be written off in that year.

iii. It should be confirmed that the legal life of the copyright has not expired.

iv. The auditor should see that the copyright having no commercial value has been completely written off.

Verification of Copyright

In verifying copyright, the auditor should inspect the agreement between the author and the publisher. If there are many copyrights with the business of the client, the auditor should ask for a schedule thereof from the client and verify them from the schedules.

6.12.4 TRADE MARKS

A trade mark is a distinctive mark attached to the goods offered for sale in the market so as to distinguish the same from similar goods available in the market and also to identify them with a particular trader.

Valuation of Trade Marks

The trade mark is a symbol of the organisation's prestige. The value of trade mark may be justified by reference to its renewal fees. If the trade mark is purchased, the price paid for it is to be considered as the value of the trade mark.

Auditor's Duty Regarding Valuation

i.   The auditor should see that trade marks are properly valued and shown in the Balance Sheet.

ii. If the trade mark has been purchased, the auditor should also verify the payment made to the seller against the acquisition of trade mark.

iii. The auditor should ensure that all expenses incurred in the acquisition of the trade mark has been treated as capital expenditure, any renewal fees paid has been treated as revenue expenditure.

Verification of Trade Marks

Trade marks can be verified by examining the assignment deed duly endorsed by the office of the register of trade mark. If trade marks are purchased, the assignment of interest or the assignment deed should be inspected.

Auditor's Duty Regarding Verification

i.   The auditor should see that they are registered in the name of the client and is the property of the client.

ii. He should also see that proper distinction between capital and revenue expenditure is maintained. All research expense in this connection should also be capitalised.

iii. In case the trade marks have been purchased from others, the auditor should check the expenditure incurred in connection with their acquisition, e.g., registration fees, payments made to vendor, etc.

6.13 VERIFICATION AND VALUATION OF FIXED ASSETS

6.13.1 LAND AND BUILDINGS

Almost all the business or commercial undertakings have land and buildings of their own. For the purposes of verification and valuation of land and buildings, it can be classified into two types:

i.   Freehold property.

ii. Leasehold property.

Freehold Property

(a) Verification

i. The auditor should inspect the title deed and see that they appear to be in order. He should obtain a certificate from the legal advisor of the client confirming the validity of the title to the property.

ii. He should also verify that the conveyance deed has been duly registered as required by the Indian Registration Act and the particulars to be endorsed thereon have been duly endorsed.

iii. If the property is mortgaged, the title deed would be in the possession of the mortgagee. A certificate to this effect should be obtained.

iv. In the case of property built or created by the client himself, the auditor should ensure that proper capitalisation of materials, labour and overhead is done.

(b) Valuation

i. The original cost and any improvement thereon should be checked with original deed and receipt. It is also to be seen that all expenses incurred on registration, brokerage or other legal fees have been duly capitalised.

ii. The cost of buildings should be depreciated at appropriate value, depending upon the quality of their structure and the use made of them.

iii. The auditor should check the expenditure on repairs so as to exclude that expenditure from capital cost.

iv. In respect of property built by the client, contractor's bill and other relevant accounts should be referred.

Leasehold Property

(a) Verification

i. The auditor should inspect the lease or assignment thereof to ascertain the amount of premium, if any, paid for securing the lease and its terms and conditions.

ii. The auditor should also ensure whether the lease has been duly registered.

iii. He should also verify that all conditions prescribed by the lease are being duly complied with.

iv. He should confirm himself any writing off of any legal expenses incurred to acquire the lease.

(b) Valuation

i. The value of the leasehold property should be checked from the lease deed. Any addition or expansion thereon should be examined by reference to the contractor's bills and other supporting papers.

ii. The auditor should ensure that the provision for any claim that might arise under the dilapidation clause on the expiry of the lease has been made.

iii. He should see that the cost as well as legal expenses incurred to acquire the lease is being written off at an appropriate rate over the unexpected term of the lease.

iv. He should also check the accounting of leasehold property to ensure himself that it is maintained separately.

6.13.2 BUILDING

(a) Verification

i. The auditor should examine the title deed of buildings to see whether the client holds the title on the Balance Sheet date. If the building has been mortgaged, the title deed will be in the possession of the mortgagee from whom a certificate should be obtained.

ii.   He should see the appropriate lease deed, if the building is leasehold, to ascertain the cost, amortization, etc.

iii. He should also ensure that all conditions in the lease deed have been fulfilled by the client.

iv.   The auditor should see the relevant particulars of buildings have been entered in the fixed assets register maintained by the client.

(b) Valuation

i.   The auditor should verify the original cost of the building by reference to the deed of conveyance. If the building is constructed by the client, he should verify the original cost by reference to the contractor's bill.

ii.   He should also verify that appropriate depreciation has been provided against the building. In case, no depreciation is provided on the building, a note to this effect should be given in the profit and loss account.

iii. He should see that the buildings have been valued at cost less depreciation. In case of a company, the requirements of Schedule VI have to be complied with.

iv.   If any revaluation has taken place, the auditor should verify the basis of revaluation and ensure that the disclosure of the same has been made.

6.13.3   PLANT AND MACHINERY

(a) Verification

i.   The auditor should call for the plant register or detailed break up schedule of plant and machinery. For the balance appearing in the Balance Sheet, he should identify the specific items and check the details thereof.

ii.   In the case of a company, the management is duly bound to physically verify the plant and machinery and the auditor should ask for the related working papers for his examination.

iii. The additions and disposals during the year should be verified by reference to the purchase invoices and other appropriate documents.

iv.   The auditor should verify some of the important items of plant and machinery on test check basis.

(b) Valuation

i.   The cost price of any plant or machinery plus any cost of installation will be vouched with supplier's invoices and other supporting documents.

ii.   The auditor should see that proper depreciation has been provided during the year.

iii. He should check as to whether any of the items has been disposed off or sold during the year. If so, he should satisfy that it was properly authorised and the sale proceeds credited to plant and machinery account. Any capital profit made should be transferred to capital reserve.

iv.   The auditor should also verify that the plant and machinery has been properly shown under fixed assets in the Balance Sheet.

6.13.4   FURNITURE AND FIXTURES

(a) Verification

i.   The auditor should ascertain whether a register is maintained for furniture and fixtures detailing the nature of the item, its acquisition cost, location, code number etc.

ii. He should also verify whether the furniture and fixtures bear on them the code numbers allotted.

iii. He should inquire whether physical verification of the furniture and fixtures has been carried out by the management and if so, he should examine the working papers.

iv. The auditor should verify physically some of the important items of furniture and fixtures on test check basis.

(b) Valuation

i. The auditor should satisfy that the furniture and fixtures have been properly depreciated and value written off for damaged or unserviceable items.

ii. He should see that the cost of furniture and fixture has been properly ascertained and recorded in the books of accounts.

iii. He should inquire whether any of the items have been disposed off or sold during the year. If so, he should check that it was properly authorised and the sale proceeds credited to furniture and fixture account. Any capital profit made therein should be transferred to capital reserve.

iv. The auditor should also verify that furniture and fixtures have been properly shown under fixed assets in the Balance Sheet.

6.13.5 MOTOR VEHICLES

(a) Verification

i. The auditor may call for a schedule of motor vehicles and compare it with the Motor Vehicles Register maintained by the organisation.

ii. He should also examine the registration document for each vehicle. He should compare the registration number and description given in the registration document with the particulars shown in the ledger account or Motor Vehicle Register.

iii. If the vehicle is registered in the name of a person other than the client, the auditor should inspect the letter confirming the arrangement and ascertain that there is no charge on the vehicle in favour of such person.

iv. The auditor should also check the insurance premium receipts to ensure that the vehicles are fully insured against accidents, theft, etc.

(b) Valuation

i. The motor vehicles are to be valued at cost less depreciation.

ii. The cost price of any motor vehicle will be vouched with supplier's invoices and other supporting documents. However, he should see that expenditures on repair have been charged to profit and loss account and not added to its cost.

iii. The auditor should verify the adequacy of the depreciation. It is a common practice for the motor vehicles to be written off over the mileage they are expected to run.

iv. He should also verify that the motor vehicles have been properly shown under fixed assets in the Balance Sheet.

6.13.6 ASSETS ACQUIRED UNDER HIRE PURCHASE SYSTEM

(a) Verification

i. The existence of the assets acquired can be confirmed by physical verification of the assets by the auditor or by reviewing the working papers of physical verification of fixed assets done by the management.

ii. The company is not the owner of the asset till the last installment under hire purchase agreement has been paid. However, the possession right of the asset can be verified by reference to the hire purchase agreement.

iii. A default in payment of the hire purchase installment entitles the hire vendor to take back the possession of the asset. So, the hire purchase agreement has to be examined to ascertain the nature of encumbrances.

iv. The auditor should also see that the asset purchased is included in the fixed asset register.

(b) Valuation

i. Fixed assets are generally valued at cost less depreciation. So, the auditor will have to examine the hire purchase agreement and the price list to ascertain the cash cost of the asset.

ii. Depreciation should be deducted and the auditor should ensure that the rate normally charged by the company on same or similar assets has been applied on a consistent basis.

iii. The auditor should confirm the proper recording of assets acquired under hire purchase agreement. The interest element in the installments should be charged to revenue.

iv. The assets purchased on hire purchase agreement may also be shown at the capital value of installments paid to date. In that case also, the depreciation at the normal rate for the full period on the cash value will have to be charged.

6.14 AUDIT OF DEPRECIATION

Accounting Standard-6 issued by the Institute of Chartered Accountants of India on 'Depreciation Accounting' defines depreciation as follows:

> Depreciation is a measure of the wearing out, consumption or other loss of value of depreciable assets arising from use, effluxion of time, obsolescence through technology and market change. Depreciation is calculated so as to allocate a fair proportion of the depreciable amount in each accounting period during the expected useful life of the asset. Depreciation includes amortization of assets whose usefulness is predetermined.

6.14.1 LEGAL NECESSITY OF A PROVISION FOR DEPRECIATION

On account of the provision under Section 205 that no dividend shall be declared except out of profit arrived at after providing for depreciation in accordance with the provisions of the Act, it becomes obligatory for every company distributing dividend to make a provision for depreciation.

Sub-section (2) of Section 205 prescribes different methods that may be adopted for computing the amount of depreciation. These are summarized below:

Method as per Income Tax Act

The charge on account of depreciation may be calculated in the manner required by Section 350, i.e., at the rates prescribed for different assets by the Income Tax Act, 1961 and the rules framed there under in respect of depreciation.

Amount to be Depreciated

It may he calculated at a rate arrived at by dividing 95% of the original cost of the asset to the company by the number of years at the end of which 95% of its original cost has been provided for as depreciation.

Other Methods as Approved by Government of India

The provision for depreciation may be made on any other method approved by the Central Government, which has the effect of writing off by way of depreciation 95% of the original cost to the company of each depreciable asset at the expiry of the specified period.

Where No Rate Is Available

If a company possesses a depreciable asset for which no rate for depreciation has been prescribed by the Income Tax Act, 1961 or the rules framed there under, the amount of depreciation should be computed on such basis as the Central Government may approve, either by any general order published in the Official Gazette or any special order in particular case.

6.14.2 PROVISION FOR DEPRECIATION FOR PAST YEARS

The provisions as contained in Section 205 (1) prescribes that if a company has not provided for depreciation for any previous financial year or years ending after 28.12.1961 [the date when the Companies (Amendment) Act came into force], it shall, before declaring or paying dividend, provide for such depreciation:

i. either out of that financial years' profit, or

ii. out of the profits of any other previous financial year or years. There are, however, two exceptions to this rule:

    (a) the profits of financial year or years ended before 2viii.1ii.1960 may be distributed even though in arriving at these profits, no depreciation in respect of past years had been provided.

    (b) A company may be permitted by the Central Government, if it is thought necessary, to pay dividend for any financial year without first providing for depreciation for that year or for any earlier years. The Central Government, would, however, exempt a company only if it finds that such a distribution is necessary in the public interest [Section 205 (1)iii.].

6.14.3 DEPRECIATION ON LOW VALUE ITEMS

The Department of Company Affairs, Ministry of Law, Justice and Company Affairs, Government of India, issued a notification during December 1993, which has been inserted as Notes No. 8 in Schedule XIV to the Companies Act, 1956 that:

Notwithstanding anything contained in the schedule, depreciation on assets, whose actual cost does not exceed Rs. 5,000 shall be provided @100%. However, in respect of the fixed assets acquired prior to December, 1993 alternative basis of computation of depreciation is permitted.

But Note 4 to the Schedule XIV requires that, where during any financial year any addition has been made to any asset, the depreciation on such asset should be calculated on a pro-rata basis from the date of such additions. As Note 8 to Schedule XIV prescribes the rate of depreciation of 100%, pro-rata depreciation should be charged on addition of the said low-value items of fixed assets also. However, the company can write off fully low-value items on the consideration of materiality. Where such an accounting policy is followed by a company, the same should be properly disclosed in the accounts.

6.14.4 DEPRECIATION ON WASTING ASSETS

In terms of the decision in the case *Lee vs. Neuchatel Asphalte Co. Ltd.* (1889), there does not appear any necessity to provide depreciation on wasting assets like mines, quarries, etc. In the present day context, however, it is highly doubtful whether the principle applied in this case holds good.

Wasting assets are exhausted by being in use and necessarily this involves depletion of the capital employed on such assets. It is, therefore, necessary with a view to maintain the capital employed, a charge for such depletion for ascertaining a true and fair view of the financial statements. Also according to the opinion of the Company Law Board, depreciation on wasting assets is a necessary charge for arriving at the true and fair picture of the Profit and Loss Account and the Balance Sheet.

6.14.5 CHANGE IN THE METHOD OF DEPRECIATION

According to Section 205 (2) and 350 of the Companies Act 1956, two methods of charging depreciation, namely, straight-line method and reducing balance method have been proposed. However, a company is also allowed to follow any other method of charging depreciation duly approved by the Central Government. Whatever method of depreciation is followed by a company, it should be followed consistently. Consistency in the method is necessary to ensure comparability of the results of the operations of the enterprise from period to period. It is to be noted that Companies Act, 1956 does not restrain a company to change the method of depreciation.

However, Accounting Standard-6 issued by the Institute of Chartered Accountants of India has suggested the change in the method of depreciation only when:

i. the change is required by the statute or for compliance with an accounting standard or

ii. the change in the method of depreciation will ensure more appropriate presentation of financial statements.

If the change in the method of depreciation has to be effected due to any of the above reasons, following procedures should be observed:

i. The change in the method should be implemented with retrospective effect. In other words, depreciation should be recalculated in accordance with the new method from the date of the asset coming into use.

ii. The adjustment for excess or short depreciation should be treated as prior period and extraordinary item and should be reflected in income statement accordingly.

iii. The change in the method of depreciation should be treated as change in accounting policy and should be disclosed accordingly.

6.14.6 AUDITOR'S DUTY AS REGARDS DEPRECIATION

Apart from fixed assets in respect of which depreciation must be provided, it also has to be provided on semi-permanent assets, e.g., patents, trade marks etc. Since the auditor is not in a position to estimate the working life of a majority of them, for fixing the deprecation of these items, he has to rely on the opinion of persons who have a technical knowledge of such assets. He must, however, satisfy himself that an honest attempt has been made to estimate the working life of each asset, that the total provision for depreciation is adequate and that the method adopted for determining that amount to be written off is properly disclosed in the Profit and Loss Account and the Balance Sheet.

In part III of Schedule VI of the Companies Act, it is provided that any amount written off as depreciation is to be regarded as a provision, but that any amount so written off, which is in excess of the amount, to which in the opinion of the directors is reasonably necessary for the purpose, to be regarded as a 'reserve'. The amount should be shown as a reserve under the head 'Reserve and Surplus' on the liabilities side of the Balance Sheet. It is the duty of the auditor to ensure that the above provisions are being followed in maintaining depreciation accounting.

So, the duties of an auditor in connection with depreciation can be stated as follows:

i. The auditor will see which method of depreciation, i.e., whether straight-line method or reducing balance method as stipulated in Schedule XIV to the Companies (Amendment) Act 1988 is being followed by the company.

ii. The auditor will check that depreciation has been provided at the rates not less than the rates specified in Schedule XIV to the Companies (Amendment) Act 198viii.

iii. He will see that if any other method of depreciation is in use, it has got the approval of the Central Government.

iv. He will also see that the method of depreciation and the rate of depreciation, which are not in accordance with Schedule XIV, have been duly disclosed.

v. The auditor will ensure that if an asset is sold, discarded, demolished or destroyed, the excess of written down value over its sale proceeds or its scrap value have been written off in the financial year in which it is sold, discarded, demolished or destroyed.

vi. The auditor should ensure that the provision for depreciation on additions, deletions etc. during the accounting year have been made on pro rata basis.

vii He will see that extra shift depreciation for double shift or triple shift, working has been computed in respect of plant and machineries in proportion of the number of days the company worked double shift or triple shift, as the case may be, bears to the total number of normal working days during the year.

viii. The auditor should see that dividend has been declared only out of profits arrived at after provision for depreciation.

ix. He will see that the amount of depreciation written off has been clearly disclosed in the profit and loss account.

x. He should see that the accounting policy of the company has clearly stated the method of depreciation in use.

xi. The auditor should satisfy himself that adequate amount of depreciation has been provided. If he is not satisfied with the adequacy of amount of depreciation, he will persuade the management to make further provision for depreciation.

xii. He will see the same method of charging depreciation is being followed year after year. If there is any change in the method of depreciation, he will ascertain the reason and satisfy himself with its justification.

xiii. He will see that excess depreciation provided so far has been transferred to reserve and shown under the head 'Reserves and Surplus' on the liabilities side of the Balance Sheet.

xiv. The auditor should check that the following information has been disclosed in the financial statements:
   (a) the historical cost or other amount substituted for historical cost of each class of depreciable assets;
   (b) total depreciation for the period for each class of assets; and
   (c) the related accumulated depreciation.

6.15 VERIFICATION AND VALUATION OF INVESTMENTS

In carrying out an audit of investments, the auditor should aim at collecting sufficient audit evidence in order to assure himself about the existence, ownership, valuation and possession of investment in favour of the client.

The following aspects are important in this respect:

Existence

The auditor should verify that investments shown in the Balance Sheet really exist on the date of the Balance Sheet.

Ownership
The auditor should assure himself that investments shown in the Balance Sheet are owned by the enterprise.

Accounting Records
He should check the transactions of acquisitions, disposal etc. of the investments during the accounting period in order to verify as to whether they are properly recorded in the books of accounts.

Valuation
He should confirm that investments are stated in the Balance Sheet at appropriate amount in accordance with the recognised accounting principles.

Disclosure
He should also confirm that investments are properly classified and disclosed in the financial statements in accordance with the recognised accounting principles and relevant statutory requirements.

Internal Control
The auditor should evaluate the internal control procedures relating to investments in order to determine the nature, timing and extent of the procedural aspects.

Almost all the business and commercial undertakings have investments of different types of their own. In case of finance and investment companies, the amount of investment constitutes a major part of the total assets of these companies. For the purpose of verification and valuation, investments can be broadly classified into the following two types:

   i.   Quoted investments.

   ii.   Unquoted investments.

6.15.1 QUOTED INVESTMENTS

(a) Verification

   i.   The auditor should physically inspect the investments. It should be physically verified at the last date of the accounting year. If the investments are not in the possession of the company, a certificate should be obtained from the concerned party concerned that is holding the investment.

   ii.   The auditor should assure himself that the title of the investments is in the name of the client only.

   iii.   The purchase and sale of investments should be verified with reference to the broker's contract note, bill of costs etc.

   iv.   If the amount of purchases or sales of investments are substantial, the auditor should check the price with reference to stock exchange quotations.

   v.   The auditor should also examine the relevant provisions of Section 227 (1(A)) and see that a company not being an investment or banking company, whether so much of the assets of the company as represented by shares and debentures have been sold at a price less than that at which they were purchased by the company.

   vi.   He should also confirm that the relevant provisions of the CARO, 2003 have been duly complied with in this regard.

(b) Valuation

   i.   The auditor should satisfy himself that the investments have been valued and disclosed in the financial statements in accordance with the recognised accounting policies and practices and relevant statutory requirements.

ii. He should examine whether in computing the cost of investments, expenditure incurred on account of transfer fees, stamp duty etc. is included in the cost of investment.

The auditor may ascertain that the market values of investments are in accordance with the authentic market reports or stock exchange quotations. To judge the overall reasonableness of the amount invested, the auditor may relate the amount with the preceeding year's figure and calculate relevant ratios.

6.15.2 UNQUOTED INVESTMENTS

(a) Verification
i. The auditor should ascertain the power of the enterprise to make investments by examining the Memorandum of Association in case of investment by a company to ensure that the investments are not ultra-vires the company.

ii. He should also ascertain that all the legal formalities relating to purchase of investments have been duly complied with.

iii. Where investments are in large numbers, the auditor should obtain the schedule of securities certified by a senior officer of the company. The statement must include the name of the investment, the book value, the market price, date of purchase etc.

iv. The auditor must verify the whole of the investment at one time. Investments are of a negotiable character and their verification at the same time removes the danger of their substitution for others.

(b) Valuation
i. The unquoted shares held as investments should ordinarily be valued at cost. However, if on study of the latest annual accounts of the companies, the shares of which are held as investment and the dividend records of such companies, it appears that there has occurred a permanent and material fall in the value of investments, a proper provision against such fall in values should be made. The auditor should confirm this compliance.

ii. Unquoted shares and debentures should be shown in the Balance Sheet under the main head 'Investments' on the asset side, indicating the mode of valuation and the aggregate amount of the unquoted shares and debentures should also be stated.

iii. The auditor should confirm that equity and preference shares are shown separately as also fully paid up and partly paid shares being distinguished.

iv. If the shares or debentures are held in the subsidiary of the company, the auditor should assure that the above should be shown under the sub-heading 'Investment in Subsidiaries'.

6.16 VERIFICATION AND VALUATION OF CURRENT ASSETS

6.16.1 STOCK-IN-TRADE

Introduction
The valuation of stock is frequently the main factor in determining the results shown by the accounts. Apart from the effect for the Balance Sheet, incorrect stock would affect the profit of the year that has closed as well as that of next year.

Auditor's Duty
The valuation of the closing stock, therefore, is an important step essential for the determination of the profits of the year and also for truly disclosing the financial position of the organisation at the end of the year. It is

the duty of the auditor, being intimately connected with these aspects of financial statements, to verify the existence of the stock-in-trade possessed by the organisation at the end of the year and to ascertain that the same has been valued correctly on a consistent basis.

The precise duties in regard to verification of stock-in-trade are not defined. Under the circumstances, these have to be deduced from an interpretation of the general responsibilities of auditors in regard to the statements of accounts verified by them, especially in regard to stock-in-trade.

Case Decisions

Justice Lindley, while delivering his famous judgement in the case of *Kingston Cotton Mills Ltd.* (1896) observed: "It is no part of the auditor's duty to take stock. No one contends that it is so. He must rely on other people for details of the stock-in-trade in hand. In the case of a cotton mill, he must rely on some skilled person for the material necessary to enable him to enter the stock-in-trade at its proper value in the balance sheet."

In the same case, Justice Lopes observed: "An auditor is not bound to be a detective or as was said to approach his work with a foregone conclusion that there is something wrong. He is a watch dog, but not a blood hound. He is justified in believing tried servants of the company in whom confidence is placed by the company. He is entitled to assume that they are honest to rely upon their representations, provided he takes reasonable care."

In another judgement in the case of *Westminster Road Construction & Engineering Co. Ltd.* (1932), it was held that an auditor must make the fullest use of all materials available to him and although he is not a stock-taker and not a valuer of work-in-progress, he will be guilty of negligence, if he fails to take notice of all available evidence from which it could be reasonably deduced that the work-in-progress was overvalued.

The decisions thus appear to have settled following the three principles for the general guidance of the auditor:

i. That it is no part of the auditor's duty to take stock.

ii. That for the purpose, he can rely upon statements and reports made available to him in regard to the valuation of stock so long as there is no circumstance, which may arouse his suspicion, and he is satisfied.

iii. That an auditor would be failing in his duty if he does not take reasonable care in verifying the statement of stock according to the information in his possession and the expert knowledge expected of him in regard to methods of verification and stock control.

Provisions of the Companies Act

The recent changes in the Companies Act have also considerably advanced the responsibilities of auditors in this regard. Section 209 of the Act requires a company to maintain proper books of accounts. Such books of accounts must include books kept to record transactions in stock-in-trade.

The Companies (Amendment) Act of 1956 empowers the Central Government under Section 227 (4A) to require companies engaged in production, processing, manufacturing or mining activities to maintain books as would and furnish particulars in relation to utilisation of material or labour or other items of cost as may be prescribed.

Furthermore, by Section 541 (2), proper books of accounts have been defined to include statement of annual stock-taking and of all the goods purchased and sold.

Accounting Presentation

Part II of Schedule VI to the Companies Act prescribes that the figures of opening and closing balances of stock and work in progress be disclosed in the profit and loss account. Part I of the same schedule requires that the mode of valuation of stock be shown on the Balance Sheet. The recent amendment to Schedule VI includes requiring particulars of materials purchased, opening and closing stock-in-trade and also of turnover made during a particular accounting period.

Steps for Verification

The steps for verification of year end stock includes the following:

i.   Review the procedure and arrangements for the maintenance of stock records.

ii. Secure the original rough stock sheet, if available.

iii. Check all additions and test fair proportions of extensions.

iv. Ascertain the basis and method of valuation adopted and confirms that the same has been followed consistently.

v.   Verify the cost of raw materials and stores by reference to purchase invoices.

vi. Confirm that stock has been valued at 'lower of cost or market price' principle.

vii. Ascertain that the goods not belonging to the client have not been included in stock-in-trade.

viii. Examine the stock sheets to ascertain that they only contain goods normally dealt in by the business.

ix. Find out whether there has been a complete physical stock-taking.

x.   See that the stock sheets have been signed by the responsible person.

6.16.2 WORK-IN-PROGRESS

As per the 'Guidance Note on Audit of Inventories' (Guidance Note-2) issued by the Institute of Chartered Accountants of India, in general, the audit procedures regarding verification of work-in-progress are similar to those used for stock-in-trade, i.e., stock of raw materials as well as of finished goods. However, the auditor should pay attention to the following matters due to the difference in nature of work-in-progress as compared to the stock of finished goods and stock of raw materials:

i.   The auditor has to carefully assess the degree of completion of the work-in-progress for assessing the appropriateness of its valuation.

ii. He should examine the cost records and obtain expert opinion where necessary.

iii. He should also obtain a certificate from the production engineer to confirm the correctness of the cost records.

iv. The elements of cost and the method of pricing of the various elements may be compared with that of the last year and if there is a material deviation, the reasons for the same may be investigated.

v.   In certain cases, physical verification of work-in-progress may not be possible due to the nature of the product and the manufacturing process involved. In such cases, the auditor should give greater emphasis on ascertaining the reliability of the system of control of work-in-progress.

vi. It may also be useful for the auditor to examine the subsequent records of production.

6.16.3 SUNDRY DEBTORS

(a) Verification

i.   Existence of book debts can be verified by examining the books of accounts and satisfying that the entries therein are supported by proper sales documents.

ii. Balance of book debts should be sent to the debtors for their confirmation, which will also establish the existence of the book debts.

iii. The examination of debtor's ledgers with related sales documents and correspondence with debtors will confirm the ownership of book debts.

iv. The auditor should also inquire whether any dispute is there on any of the balance included in sundry debtors. In this case, the documents regarding dispute should be examined.

(b) Valuation

i. Usually the balances shown in the debtor's ledger are supported by sales documents represent the value of book debts.

ii. The auditor should call for the lists of book debts and debts written off and arrive at the conclusion about adequacy of write off and provision for doubtful debts.

iii. The confirmation of balances by debtors will help establish the valuation of book debts.

iv. It should be ensured by the auditor that sundry debtors are valued only at realisable value.

6.16.4 Bills Receivable

(a) Verification

i. The auditor should examine the Bills Receivable Book and prepare a schedule of all those bills receivable that have not yet matured before the date of the preparation of the Balance Sheet.

ii. Where the number of bills is large and they are kept with the bankers for collection, the auditor should obtain a detailed certificate from the bank to ascertain the clear position about the bills.

iii. For bills that are discounted or endorsed but remain outstanding at the time of audit, any contingent liability in respect of such bills should be maintained as a footnote of the Balance Sheet.

iv. The bills that have been dishonoured before the due date of the Balance Sheet should not be included in the Balance Sheet as 'bills receivable in hand' as they are no longer assets.

(b) Valuation

i. The auditor should see that the bills are properly drawn, stamped and duly accepted and they are not overdue. In case of the renewal of any bills, the auditor should examine the new bill with the old bill.

ii. Sometimes, the bills might have matured and honoured subsequent to the date of the Balance Sheet, but prior to the date of the audit. The auditor should check the cash received as shown in the cash book of the next year.

iii. If the bills have been retired before the date of the Balance Sheet, the proceeds thereof should be checked by reference to the cash book.

iv. For the bills discounted prior to the date of maturity and the date of maturity is to fall after the date of Balance Sheet, the discount on such bills must be properly apportioned between periods covered by two separate financial years.

6.16.5 Cash at Bank

(a) Verification

i. The auditor should compare the balances as shown in the pass book with the balances as shown in the cash book.

ii. The auditor should prepare a bank reconciliation statement or should check the statement prepared by the client in order to ascertain the correct bank balance.

iii. He should obtain a balance confirmation certificate from the bank at the close of the year.

iv. He should also obtain separate certificate for Fixed Deposit Account, Current Account and Savings Bank Account from different banks to confirm total deposits in different banks.

(b) Valuation

i. In order to ascertain the current position with regard to cheques issued but not yet presented or cheques deposited but not collected, the auditor should confirm through cash book and pass book figures.

ii. Where amounts are deposited in foreign banks under exchange control regulations, the fact to be disclosed.

iii. Where amounts are kept in different reserve account in the banks, in order to avail deductions under Indian Income Tax Act, the fact should also be disclosed.

iv. The auditor should also ensure that the bank balances are properly disclosed in the Balance Sheet according to Schedule VI of the Companies Act.

6.16.6 CASH IN HAND

(a) Verification

i. The most common practice in verifying cash balance is to obtain a certificate from the accountant about the actual cash balance in hand on the date of the Balance Sheet.

ii. The auditor should verify the cash in hand by actually counting it on the close of the business on the date of the Balance Sheet.

iii. In certain cases, the client maintains an unduly large balance of cash in hand consistently. In those cases, the auditor should make a surprise check to ascertain whether the actual cash in hand agrees with the balances as shown by the books.

iv. As far as cash in transit is concerned, the auditor should verify this balance with the help of proper documentary evidences and correspondence.

(b) Valuation

i. If the cash-in-hand is not in agreement with the balance as shown in the books, it is the duty of the auditor to call for an explanation.

ii. Often postage and other stamps are taken with the cash in the Balance Sheet. The auditor should confirm the balance of postage and stamps by physical counting only.

iii. He should also check the system of making payments and safety arrangements provided for the protection of cash balance.

iv. In case of cash maintained at the local branches and the auditor is unable to pay a visit to the branch, he may ask the branch manager to deposit the balance of cash in the bank on the Balance Sheet date.

6.16.7 PREPAID EXPENSES

(a) Verification

i. The auditor should verify the receipts for pre-payments, i.e., expenses paid during the period for future financial periods.

ii. The amount of pre-paid expenses should be shown in the asset side of the Balance Sheet under current assets. The auditor should assure that it has been shown properly in the Balance Sheet.

iii. Prepaid expenses for the last accounting period should be properly adjusted. The auditor should see the expenses paid in the last year pertaining to the current accounting year have been properly adjusted.

iv. The auditor should also check the adjustments made in the next year, if possible, against the prepaid expenses made during the year.

(b) Valuation

i. The auditor should check the calculations for ascertaining the portion of expenses belonging to the next period by reference to the contract or other documents.

ii. In respect of rent, rates and taxes, the auditor should check the payment vouchers and satisfy that allocation to carry forward has been made on time basis.

iii. In respect of insurance premium, the auditor should also satisfy himself that the carry forward allocation has been made on the basis of the terms of policy and the premium paid.

iv. In case of pre-paid sales commission, where salesman are allowed to take payments out of future earnings, the auditor should examine the statement of sales to determine the commission earned.

6.17 VERIFICATION AND VALUATION OF FICTITIOUS ASSETS

6.17.1 PRELIMINARY EXPENSES

The expenses incurred for the formation and commencement of a company are usually grouped under the heading 'Preliminary Expenses'. These include stamp duties, registration fees, legal costs, cost of printing, etc.
   In order to verify preliminary expenses, the auditor should take into consideration the following matters:

i. It should be confirmed by the auditor that no expenses other than those which are related to the formation of a company are included under this head.

ii. The auditor should examine the contracts relating to preliminary expenses. If preliminary expenses incurred by the promoters have been reimbursed to them by the company, the resolution of the Board and the power in the Articles of Association to make such payment should be seen.

iii. The auditor can cross check the amount of preliminary expenses with that disclosed in the prospectus, statutory report and the Balance Sheet.

iv. Being a fictitious asset, it should be written off as early as possible and the auditor should verify that the balance of preliminary expenses, which has not been written off, is shown in the Balance Sheet under the heading 'Miscellaneous Expenditure'.

v. Underwriting commission and brokerage in shares and debentures should not be included under the head 'preliminary expenses'. The auditor should also confirm this aspect.

vi. The bills and statements supporting each item of preliminary expenses should be checked.

vii. The auditor should also assure that proper deduction has been availed against taxable income under the Income Tax Act, 196i.

6.17.2 DISCOUNT ON ISSUE OF SHARES OR DEBENTURES

This refers to the expenditure or losses essentially of a revenue nature, which instead of being charged off as and when incurred, is accumulated in an account and the balance in the account is written off over a period of years during which its benefit is expected to accrue to the business.

In order to verify the discount on issue of shares or debentures, the auditor should pay attention to the following matters:

i. The auditor should confirm that it continues to appear as an asset on the right side of the Balance Sheet as long as the discount is not written off.

ii. If during the year, any amount has been added thereto, the auditor should ask for the justification for the same.

iii. Being a fictitious asset, it should be written off as early as possible. The auditor should also confirm this aspect.

iv. The auditor should see that the discount on issue of shares or debentures has been shown separately under the heading 'Discount on Issue of Shares or Debentures'.

v. In issuing shares or debentures at a discount, whether the governing provisions relating to issue of shares and debentures have been duly complied with or not should also be checked by the auditor.

6.18 VERIFICATION AND VALUATION OF CONTINGENT ASSETS

The contingent assets are those which may arise on the happening of an uncertain event. As a general practice, contingent assets are not recorded in the Balance Sheet because that would imply taking credit for revenue which has not accrued. But it is logical as the contingent liabilities are shown in the Balance Sheet, the contingent assets should also be shown. The Companies Act does not require disclosure of contingent assets in the Balance Sheet. However, if contingent assets have a significant value, it may be advisable to disclose such assets in a note to the Balance Sheet.

As regards valuation of contingent assets, it may be noted that ordinarily no valuation would be required. However, if such assets are disclosed by way of a note, a proper valuation based on the related contract would be made. Where full realisation of such assets is doubtful even on the face of contingency occurring, it would be safer to value the assets on a realisable basis.

6.19 VERIFICATION AND VALUATION OF LIABILITIES

The verification of liabilities is of equal importance as that of an asset. The auditor has to satisfy himself that all liabilities whether existing or contingent have been properly determined and disclosed in the Balance Sheet. In case liabilities are overstated or understated, the Balance Sheet shall not represent a fair view of the state of affairs of the company. Therefore, the auditor should ensure that:

i. liabilities shown in the Balance Sheet are actually payable;

ii. all liabilities are properly recorded in the books;

iii. the recorded liabilities are payable for the legitimate operations of the business; and

iv. the nature and extent of contingent liabilities has been disclosed in the Balance Sheet by way of a foot note.

For the purpose of applying verification technique, we may divide the liabilities into the following three categories:

i. Fixed or long-term liabilities, viz. share capital, debentures, long terms loan from bank and other financial institutions etc.

ii. Current liabilities, viz. sundry creditors, bills payable, bank overdraft etc.

iii. Contingent liabilities, viz. disputed liability of income tax, suits pending for damages etc.

6.20 VERIFICATION AND VALUATION OF FIXED OR LONG-TERM LIABILITIES

6.20.1 DEBENTURES

(a) Verification

i. The auditor should go through the Memorandum of Association and Articles of Association of the company in order to determine the extent of borrowing power of the company and also to ascertain the limitation upon the borrowing power, if any.

ii. A prospectus must have been issued and filed with the Registrar of Companies. The auditor should verify the prospectus to ensure that the terms of the prospectus have been complied with.

iii. Balances from the Register of Debenture holders will have to be extracted and the total amount received from Debenture holders to be tallied with the total of Debenture Account in the general ledger.

iv. The auditor should also examine a copy of the debenture bond to ascertain the terms and conditions on which the debentures have been issued, the particulars of assets charged as security and the method of redemption.

v. If the debentures are mortgaged debentures, the debentures trust deed should be studied by the auditor and it should be seen that the terms and conditions of the trust deed have been fully observed by the company.

(b) Presentation

i. Debentures have to be shown under the head 'Secured Loans'.

ii. The debentures subscribed by the directors and managers should be shown separately.

iii. Interest accrued and due on debentures but not paid should be included along with debentures, but interest accrued but not due has to be shown under 'current liabilities'.

iv. The nature of security provided should also be disclosed.

v. The terms and conditions of the redemption or conversion of the debentures should be stated with the earliest date of redemption or conversion.

6.20.2 SECURED LONG-TERM LOANS

A company can obtain loans from banks and other financial institutions on the basis of security provided. For the purpose of verification of long-term loans, it can be classified under two broad categories:

i. Loans against security of fixed assets.

ii. Loan against security of stock.

Loans Against Security of Fixed Assets

i. The auditor should examine the Memorandum and the Articles of Association to see whether the company is empowered to borrow money against fixed assets.

ii. He should scrutinize the loan account in the ledger and the documents relating to the fixed assets.

iii. He should also examine the mortgage deed and find out whether the mortgage is properly executed.

iv. He should enquire whether the lender has a right to lend money against such security.

v. The auditor should also obtain confirmation from the lender for the amount of loan.

vi. He should see whether principal amount of the loan is being repaid as stipulated and whether interest on loan are paid regularly as per the terms of loans as prescribed in CARO.

Loans Against Security of Stock

i. The auditor should inspect the receipts of the go-down keeper, if the loan has been taken against the go-down keeper's receipts.

ii. If the stocks are at dock or in bonded warehouse, the dock warrant or the warehouse certificate duly endorsed in favour of the lender should also be examined,

iii. The auditor should see that the rent for the warehouse has been paid by the client regularly. If it has not been paid, adequate provision should has to be maintained for the purpose.

iv. He should also obtain a certificate from the lender showing particulars of securities deposited and confirm that the same has been correctly disclosed and duly registered with Registrar of Companies and recorded in the Register of Charges.

v. The auditor should verify the authority under which the loan has been raised. In the case of a company, only the Board of Directors is empowered to raise a loan or borrow from a bank.

vi. He should also confirm that the restraint as contained in Section 293 of the Companies Act as regards the maximum amount of loan that a company can raise has not been contravened.

6.21 VERIFICATION AND VALUATION OF CURRENT LIABILITIES

6.21.1 SUNDRY CREDITORS

i. The auditor will verify creditors more or less on similar lines as in the case of sundry debtors. He should take a statement of balance of the trade creditors duly signed by the authorised official and these balances should be verified with the purchase ledger balances.

ii. He may also obtain confirmatory statements from the creditors.

iii. He should also examine the invoices as sent by the suppliers. He should carry out test checking of purchases made during the year, particularly those made at the close of the year.

iv. If debts have not been paid for a long time, he should enquire into the situation in detail. Sometimes, it is seen that instead of paying to the creditors, the amount might have been misappropriated by the officials.

v. If the client maintains provision in respect of discount on creditors, he should check the same with reference to the creditors account.

vi. The purchase ledger should also be checked by the auditor with the books of original entry, invoices, credit notes etc.

vii. For any purchase returns, he should examine the 'Return Outward Book' and verify them with the help of credit notes as sent by the suppliers.

viii. The auditor should pay special attention to the entries made either in the beginning or at the end of the year to check the fictitious entries in this respect.

6.21.2 BILLS PAYABLE

i. The auditor should get a statement of bills payable and compare it with the Bills Payable Book and Bills Payable Account.

ii. For the bills, which have been met after the date of the Balance Sheet but before the date of audit, he should examine the Cash Book and Bank Pass Book.

iii. The bills payable already paid should be checked from the cash book and the auditor should examine the returned bills payable.

iv. He should also ensure that the bills which have been paid are not recorded as outstanding.

v. He should get confirmation in respect of amounts due on the bills accepted by the client that are held by them.

vi. He should reconcile the total of the bills payable outstanding at the end of the year with the balance in the Bills Payable Account.

6.21.3 BANK OVERDRAFT

i. The auditor should examine the overdraft agreement with the bank in order to ascertain the terms and conditions of overdraft and the maximum limit thereon.

ii. The Memorandum of Association in case of a company should be examined to ascertain the borrowing powers of the company and any limitations thereon.

iii. The auditor should verify the minutes of the Board Meeting to assure that the bank overdraft borrowing is being authorised by the board.

iv. If the client is a company and if the overdraft is against any security, the auditor should see whether the charge created was registered with the Registrar of Companies, if required.

v. The auditor should also obtain the confirmation certificate from the bank in respect of amount of overdraft at the close of the year.

vi. The auditor should also check whether interest on overdraft has been duly accounted for.

vii. The auditor should also confirm that the amount overdrawn is within the maximum limit sanctioned by the bank,

viii. It is to be seen whether any security was offered for the overdraft in terms of agreement, depending on which the overdraft is to be classified as secured or unsecured.

6.21.4 PROVISION FOR TAXATION

i. The auditor should ascertain the tax liability and check the computation of the assessable profit and loss account. Thus, adjustments affecting taxable profit must be carefully scrutinised.

ii. He should also go through past completed assessment in order to know what sort of adjustments were actually made in the past.

iii. He should also check the amount of advance tax paid and the calculations thereof. Advance tax is required to be verified in order to provide the liability of future taxation.

iv. If income tax return has already been filed before the date of audit, the auditor should also check the copy of the income tax return.

v. The auditor should ensure the amount of overall provision on the date of the Balance Sheet adequate having regard to the figure of provision of the year, the advance tax paid, past provision made and assessment orders in respect thereof received up to the date of audit, pending appeals and refunds, if any.

vi. He should also obtain a certificate from the tax practitioner regarding the amount of tax payable.

6.21.5 Outstanding Liabilities for Expenses

i.   The auditor should ask for the list of outstanding expenses from the client classified on the basis of nature of expenses.

ii. He should verify the supporting documents evidencing the outstanding expenses.

iii. He should also verify the basis of estimation of outstanding expenses, if they are provided on an estimated basis.

iv. He should check the next year cash book in order to see that the usual outstanding expenses have been paid off by the time of audit.

v.   He should also ensure that no outstanding expenses have been paid, which has not been provided in the account. If paid, he should check the adjustment entries passed for this purpose.

vi. He should compare the list of outstanding expenses of the current year with that of the previous year to identify any major deviations.

vii. The auditor should also ensure that no usual outstanding expenses have been left out to be provided.

viii. He should also confirm that outstanding expenses have been shown under current liabilities in the Balance Sheet.

6.22 VERIFICATION AND VALUATION OF CONTINGENT LIABILITIES

A contingent liability is not an actual liability, but which will become a liability on the happening of an event in future. It may be converted into actual liability on an uncertain event in the future. W. B. Meigs defines contingent liability as "the potential obligations which may in future develop into actual liability or may dissolve without necessitating any outlay". Simply stated contingent liability is not an actual liability but will become a liability on the happening of an event in the future. The examples of contingent liabilities are:

i.   discounting of bills receivables,

ii. pending suits for damages or compensation,

iii. disputed liability on account of income tax, and

iv. guarantee given by the bank on behalf of the company.

As per Part I of Schedule VI to the Companies Act, 1956 a footnote may be added to the Balance Sheet to indicate the amount of contingent liability.

While going through the books of accounts, correspondence, minute books, bank statements and other relevant documents, the auditor may identify the existence of contingent liabilities of the concern. The auditor's duty in this respect would be:

i.   inspect the minutes book of the company to identify all contingent liabilities existing at the end of the year,

ii. scrutinize the lawyers' bill to ascertain unreported contingent liabilities,

iii. examine correspondence with the bank in respect of bill discounted but not yet matured,

iv. examine bank letters to ascertain guarantees given on behalf of other companies or individuals,

v.   scrutinise correspondence with suppliers, customers, lawyers etc. to ascertain the existence of contingent liabilities,

vi. check the investments in the shares made by the client to identify the liabilities on partly paid up shares,

vii. find out the arrears of preference dividend on cumulative preference shares, and

viii. obtain a certificate from the management that the known contingent liabilities have been included in the accounts and they have been properly disclosed.

6.23   CASE STUDIES

CASE STUDY ON STOCK TAKING 1

Albert David Supplies Ltd. have a large warehouse in Pune from which they supply their customers with over 1,000 chemicals and medicines purchased from numerous suppliers both in India and abroad. They do not maintain a continuous inventory of their stocks. At the year end, Tuesday, 31 March 2007, they wish to assess the stock physically.

Discussion

a. Draw up full stock taking instructions for the stocktaking.
b. How should the stock be valued according to AS-2?
c How should the auditor seek evidence for the physical stock?

CASE STUDY ON STOCK TAKING 2

Your client is a whole sale merchant of electrical goods with a head office in Mumbai and four branches in Kanpur, Nagpur, Chennai and Kolkata. The client has total annual sales of Rs. 10 lakhs and total stocks of Rs. 2 lakhs. The stocks are located as follows:

Head office, Rs. 75,000; Kanpur branch, Rs. 45,000; Nagpur branch, Rs. 30,000; Chennai branch, Rs. 22,000; and Kolkata branch, Rs. 28,000.

Your client is planning yearly stock-taking.

Discussion

a. List five things which your client should do to ensure an accurate stocktaking.
b. List four things you should do in planning your audit attendance at the stocktaking.

◆ Suggested questions

A   **Short-type questions**

1. What is verification of assets and liabilities?
2. Distinguish between verification and valuation.
3. Discuss the importance of verification and valuation of assets.
4. What is intangible asset? Give five examples of intangible assets.
5. What do you mean by fictitious assets? Give example.
6. What is meant by contingent liability? Discuss the auditor's duty in this regard.
7. What is goodwill? As an auditor, how would you ascertain that an amount paid for goodwill is justified?
8. Do you think that verification of assets and liabilities is necessary when vouching has been done properly?
9. "Verification forms an important part of the whole system of audit". Explain.

10. "Intangible Assets are not always Fictitious Assets". Illustrate.

11. Discuss the problems in the valuation and verification of assets.

12. "Verification includes valuation". Comment.

13. How and in what way does verification of assets and liabilities differ from vouching?

14. What do you mean by 'window-dressing' of the Balance Sheet? State the duties of an auditor in this respect.

15. "Information and means of information are by no-means equivalent terms". Comment.

B   **Essay-type questions**

1. "An auditor is not a valuer, though he is intimately connected with values". Discuss referring to the relevant case decisions.

2. "It has been stated that the valuation of investment for the Balance Sheet purpose depends largely upon the object for which investments are held". Discuss the statement.

3. How do you verify the following items:

   (a) Raw material stock

   (b) Land

   (c) Preliminary expenses

   (d) Investment

   (e) Work-in-progress

   (f) Copyright

   (g) Machine purchased on H. P. System

   (h) Patterns and designs

   (i) Freehold properties

   (j) Loans and advances

   (k) Debtors

   (l) Secured loan.

4. How will you as an auditor deal with the following:

   (a) Cash

   (b) Provision for taxation

   (c) Leasehold properties

   (d) Unpaid dividends

   (e) Goods in transit

   (f) Disposal of plant

5. What are the special points to which an auditor should direct his attention for ascertaining the adequacy of provision for bad and doubtful debts in the context of proper valuation of sundry debtors?

6. "Physical presence of the auditor at the time of year end verification of stock is though not always possible, it is recommended that he should at least be present as an observer". Signify the importance of this statement and list out the important aspects which the auditor should look into to ensure an effective physical verification programme.

7. (a) What are the general considerations for evaluation and verification of assets? (b) State your views on the following: (i) Events occurring after the Balance Sheet date and (ii) prior period and extraordinary items.

Chapter 7

Company Audit

7.1 INTRODUCTION

A company is said to be an artificial person created by law having a separate legal entity distinct from its shareholders. It cannot be directly managed by its owners, i.e., shareholders, because they are very large in number having small holding and also scattered over a wide area. As such, the management and control of the affairs of the company is done by other persons generally known as directors. Hence, it becomes essential for a company to appoint an independent and qualified person, i.e., an auditor, to verily and certify the truth and fairness of the financial statements.

7.2 PRELIMINARIES BEFORE COMMENCEMENT OF COMPANY AUDIT

Before commencing the actual audit work of a company, the auditor should go through the following preliminaries:

Ensuring That His Appointment Is In Order

Before accepting the offer for appointment as auditor in a company, the auditor should ensure himself that his appointment is made according to the provisions of Sections 224 and 225 of the Companies Act and whether all the formalities being maintained by the company before giving him the appointment as auditor.

The auditor will go through the following:

i. He should see whether his appointment has been made according to Section 224 (1B) of the Companies Act. For this purpose he will obtain a copy of resolution adopted at board meeting or the shareholders meeting as the case may be.

ii. If he is appointed in place of a retiring auditor, he will enquire whether due notice was served to the retiring auditor. He will get informed from retiring auditor about the circumstances under which he has retired and whether he should accept the appointment. This is a professional requirement as per Chartered Accountants Act, 1949.

iii. He should, within thirty days of receipt of appointment letter, inform the Registrar in writing that he has accepted or refused to accept the appointment.

iv. If he is appointed to fill the casual vacancy caused by the death of the previous auditor, he will get the copy of the minutes of the board meeting in this regard and also get the confirmation of death of the previous auditor.

v. He will see that if the company has failed to appoint or re-appoint any auditor in the annual general meeting, the Central Government has appointed him to fill the vacancy.

vi. If he is appointed due to the resignation of the previous auditor he must see that he has been appointed in a general meeting of shareholders. The board of directors will have no right to appoint him under such circumstances.

vii. He will verify whether his remuneration has been fixed according to the provisions of the Companies Act.

Inspection of Statutory Books and Documents

(a) Documents

Before the auditor commences the work of audit, he should examine the following documents:

  i. Memorandum of Association

   The auditor will go through the following points:
   - To see whether the activities of the company are consistent with the 'objective clause'.
   - To check whether the amount of share capital is within the limit of authorised capital.
   - To observe whether there is any amendment to memorandum and if so, whether legal formalities have been complied with.

 ii. Articles of Association

   The auditor will go through the following points:
   - The issue of share capital and its subdivisions.
   - The payment of underwriting commission and brokerage on shares.
   - The amount of minimum subscription.
   - Date and amount of call.
   - Appointments, duties and powers of auditors in addition to statutory powers and duties.
   - Appointment and remuneration of directors.

   The above are the list of few examples, which are available in the Articles of Association. The Articles may contain several other items and the auditor should go through each item very carefully. If he does not go through the Articles and consequently fails to audit properly, he will be held liable as was held in the case of *Leeds Estate Building and Investment Society Ltd. vs. Shepherd* (1887).

iii. Prospectus:

   In case of newly started company and company that has preferred to go in for public issue, the auditor will examine the prospectus to see the matters like whether shares can be issued at a discount; the amount payable on application, allotment and calls, underwriting commission and brokerage etc.

 iv. Certificate of Incorporation and Certificate of Commencement:

   These certificates are required to be examined to see whether the company has been duly incorporated and it has started its business, in case of public limited company, after getting commencement of certificate.

(b) Books and Registers

The following is the list of books and registers required to be maintained by the companies:

  i. Register of Members (Section 150)

 ii. Index of Members (Section 151)

iii. Register and Index of Debenture Holders (Section 152)

 iv. Register of Mortgage and Charges (Section 143)

  v. Register of Investments [Section 49 (7)]

 vi. Foreign Register (Section 157 and 158)

vii. Register of contracts with companies and firms in which the directors are interested (Section 297, 299 and 301)

viii. Register of directors, managing director, manager and secretary (Section 303)

ix. Register of director's shareholdings (Section 307)

x. Register of Loans [Section 370 (1c)]

xi. Minute Books (Section 193).

Inspection of Contracts
The auditor should inspect and examine the contracts, which have been entered into by a company with others, for example,

i. contracts with the vendors of any property,

ii. contracts with the brokers and underwriters for their commission, and

iii. contracts with the promoters for the preliminary expenses, etc.

Study of Previous Year's Balance Sheet and Auditor's Report
The auditor should inspect the previous year's Balance Sheet to verify the opening balances of the current year. Moreover, according to the Companies Act, the corresponding figures of the previous year have to be given in the Balance Sheet of the current year. The auditor should also study the audit report of the previous year(s) in order to identify the problem areas of the company.

Study of Internal Control System in Operation
The study and evaluation of the internal control system in operation is important, because it serves as a basis for reliance thereon. It helps the auditor in determining the extent of the test to which auditing procedures can be restricted.

7.3 AUDIT OF SHARE CAPITAL TRANSACTIONS

Share capital may be defined as the capital raised by a company by the issue of shares. Section 86 of the Companies Act provides that the share capital of a company limited by shares shall be of two kinds only, namely,

i. Preference Share Capital

ii. Equity Share Capital.

The audit of share capital is necessary on incorporation as well as when further shares are issued.

7.3.1 AUDIT PROCEDURE
Audit of Shares Issued for Cash
While conducting audit of share capital transactions, the auditor has:

i. to ensure that the requirements as laid down in Sections 69 and 149, in this connection have been duly complied with,

ii. to see that the issue of shares is properly authorised and that there is no over issue beyond the limit as prescribed in the memorandum,

iii. to see that the provision relating to rights of shareholders are duly complied with, and

iv. to ensure that generally accepted accounting principles are followed while preparing the accounts.

While auditing the amount of share capital, the auditor will have to follow the procedures as given below:

(a) Application Stage

i. He should check the original applications and compare the entries in the Application and Allotment Book with the help of these applications.

ii. He should compare entries in the Application and Allotment Book with those in the Cash Book and the Bank Statement.

iii. He should ensure that the amount received on application is not less than 5% of the nominal value of shares [Section 69 (3)].

iv. He should ensure that the applications money was deposited into a scheduled bank until the certificate to commence business is obtained or they are returned in accordance with the provisions of Section 69 (5).

v. He should vouch the amount refunded to unsuccessful applications with copies of letters of regret sent to them.

vi. He should check the totals in the Application and Allotment Book and see that appropriate journal entries have been passed accordingly.

(b) Allotment Stage

i. The auditor should examine the Director's minutes book to verify approvals for allotment.

ii. He should check copies of letters of allotment and letters of regret with entries in the Application and Allotment Book.

iii. The money received on allotment should be vouched by comparing the entries in the Applications and Allotment Book with the Cash Book or Bank Statement.

iv. He should check the postings in the Share Register for the amount received on application and allotment with the totals in the Application and Allotment Book.

v. He should see that the total of shares issued does not exceed the total authorised capital according to the memorandum.

vi. He should see that the totals have been correctly made and that the proper entry has been passed for this purpose.

(c) Call Stage

i. The auditor should examine the Director's minutes book for verifying approval for call money.

ii. He should check the entries in the Calls Book from the copies of call letters.

iii. In order to verify the amount of calls in arrear, he should compare the total amount due on calls as per registers and the actual money received as per cash book or statement of bank account.

iv. He should also verify the calls in advance received by the company.

v. He should check the postings from the calls book and the cash book into the share register.

vi. He should see that the appropriate entries have been passed in the books accordingly.

(d) Other Aspects

i. The auditor should see that the shares issued by the company are within the amount of authorised capital of the company.

ii. The allotment of shares has been made in conformity with the conditions as stipulated in the prospectus.

iii. If the shares are issued through underwriters, the auditor should see the contracts with the underwriters to ascertain whether the terms and conditions have been complied in full by the underwriters. In this respect, he should also see that the commission given to the underwriters does not exceed the statutory limit.

Audit of Shares Issued for Consideration Other than Cash

Shares may be issued for consideration other than cash under the following circumstances:

i. Issue of shares against purchase consideration to the vendor for the business taken over by the company.

ii. Issue of shares against services rendered to the underwriters, promoters or any other special service rendering agencies by way of payment of their remuneration or for any expenses incurred by them.

iii. Issue of shares to the existing shareholders as bonus shares.

In order to issue shares for consideration other than cash, the auditor should follow the procedures as follows:

Issue of Shares to Vendors/Promoters

(a) Examination of Contract

The auditor should examine the contract entered into by the company with the vendors/promoters to know the amount of purchase consideration and the mode of payment. For the purchase consideration settlement, the mode of payment would be according to the prospectus. So, the auditor should also examine the prospectus to see the mode of payment.

(b) Checking of Director's Minutes Book

The decision regarding issue of shares to the vendors/promoters is taken at the board meeting. The resolution passed by the directors for allotment of shares to vendors/promoters should be confirmed from the minutes book.

(c) Filing of Contracts with the Registrar

Such contracts are required to be filed with the Registrar of Companies within 30 days from the date of allotment.

(d) Allotment of Shares to the Nominees

If shares have been allotted to the nominees of the vendors/promoters, the auditor should examine the vendor's/promoter's authority given to them in their favour.

Issue of Shares to Underwriters

(a) Examination of the Contract

The auditor should examine the contract with the underwriters. The auditor is required to know the terms and conditions of the contract between the company and the underwriters.

(b) Examination of the Prospectus

The auditor should also examine the prospectus of the company to see the mode of payment. The auditor should verify whether the right for the payment of commission in the form of shares has been mentioned in the prospectus or not.

(c) Director's Minutes Book

He should examine the resolution of the directors by reference to the Director's minutes book.

(d) Examination of the Articles of Association

He may confirm the amount of underwriting commission from the Articles of Association. In fact, in the Articles of Association, the maximum limits of underwriting commission that can be given to the underwriters and the mode of payment and procedure to be followed are mentioned.

Issue of Bonus Shares

(a) Examination of the Articles of Association

The auditor should examine the Articles of Association to ascertain whether the Articles permit capitalisation of profit and also whether the company had a sufficient number of unissued shares for allotment as bonus shares.

(b) Assurance About the Compliance of SEBI Guidelines

The auditor should ensure himself that SEBI Guidelines (Chapter XV of the SEBI [D & IP] Guidelines, 2000) relating to issue of bonus shares have been complied with.

(c) Checking of Allotment Book

The auditor should trace the allotment of shares as per particulars contained in the Allotment Book or Sheets into the Register of Members.

(d) Confirmation About the Fulfillment of Legal Requirements

The auditor should confirm that all statutory requirements relevant to the issue of shares have been complied with. The company has to file the particulars of the bonus shares allotted with the Registrar together with a copy of the resolution on the basis of which allotment of bonus shares has been made.

(e) Inspection of the Minutes Book of Shareholders' Meeting

The auditor should inspect the minute books of the shareholders' meeting for the resolution authorising declaration of the bonus and Director's minutes of meeting for the resolution appropriating profits for being applied in payment of shares to be allotted to shareholders as bonus shares.

(f) Checking of Accounting Entries

The auditor should also check the accounting entries passed for issue of bonus shares and confirm that they are in conformity with the legal requirements and basic accounting principles.

Issue of Sweat Equity Shares

As per explanation to Section 79A of the Companies (Amendment) Act, 1999, the term 'sweat equity shares' mean the equity shares issued by the company to its employees or directors at a discount or for consideration other than cash for providing know how or making available right in the nature of intellectual property rights or value additions, by whatever name called.

The auditor should cover the following aspects while checking the issue of sweat equity share transactions:

(a) Authorised by a Special Resolution

The issue of sweat equity shares is authorised by a special resolution passed by the company in the general meeting.

(b) Details About Shares Issue Be Specified

The resolution specifies the number of shares, current market price, consideration, if any, and the class or classes of directors or employees to whom such equity shares are to be issued.

(c) Minimum Time Gap for Issue

The minimum time gap for issue of shares is not less than one year has, at the date of the issue, elapsed since the date on which the company was entitled to commence business.

(d) SEBI Guidelines

The sweat equity shares of a company, whose equity shares are listed on a recognised stock exchange, are issued in accordance with the regulations by the SEBI.

(e) Issue Out of Already Issued Type Shares

The sweat equity shares issued by the company should be of a class of shares already issued by the company.

Shares Issued at a Discount

According to Section 79 of the Companies Act, a company can issue shares at a discount subject to the fulfillment of the following conditions:

i.   The issue should be authorised by an ordinary resolution of the company and sanctioned by the Central Government.

ii. No such resolutions shall be sanctioned by the Company Law Board in cases the maximum rate for discount exceeds 10%, unless the Board is of the opinion that a higher rate of discount is justified by the special circumstances of the case.

iii. The issue should be made within 2 months of the sanction by the Company Law Board, but not earlier than one year after the date of commencement of business.

iv. The shares should be of a class already issued by the company.

Auditor's Duty

i.   The auditor should confirm that alt the conditions of Section 79 have been duly complied with.

ii. He should also see that the amount of discount, not yet written off, is shown separately in the Balance Sheet under the head 'Miscellaneous Expenditure'.

iii. The auditor should check that the appropriate entries have been passed in the books of accounts.

Shares Issued at a Premium

According to Section 78 of the Companies Act, a company can issue shares at a premium subject to the fulfillment of the following conditions:

i.   Where a company issues shares at a premium, whether for cash or otherwise, a sum equal to the aggregate amount or value of the premium on those shares shall be transferred to an account, to be called the 'Securities Premium Account' as per Section 78 (1) of the Companies Act.

ii. The securities premium account may be applied by the company:
    (a) in paying up unissued shares of the company to be issued to members of the company as fully paid bonus shares,
    (b) in writing off the preliminary expenses of the company,
    (c) in writing off the expenses of, or the commission paid or discount allowed on any issue of shares or debentures of the company, and
    (d) in providing for the premium payable on the redemption of any redeemable preference shares or of any debentures of the company [Section 78 (2)].

Auditor's Duty

i.   The auditor should examine the prospectus, the Articles of Association and the minutes book of the Directors to ascertain whether they permit the issue of shares at a premium and if so, at what rate.

ii. He should check the amount of premium received.

iii. He should also check that the share premium received has been taken, to the 'Securities Premium Account' and shown on the liabilities side of the Balance Sheet under the head "Reserves and Surplus".

iv. He should see that the 'Securities Premium Account' if utilised, has been utilised for the purposes as specified in Section 78.

Calls in Arrears

Calls in arrears refer to that portion of the share capital, which has been called up, but not yet paid by the shareholders. When a shareholder fails to pay the amount due on allotment and/or calls, the Allotment Account and/or Calls Account will show debit balance equal to the total unpaid amount of each installment. Generally such amount is transferred to a special account called 'Calls in Arrear' Account.

The balance of 'calls in arrear account' at the end is shown in the Balance Sheet as a deduction from respective Share Capital Account. Interest on calls in arrear may be collected by the directors from the shareholders if the Articles of Association so provide. If the company has adopted 'Table A', then it can charge interest @ 5% p.a. from the due date to the actual date of collection of call money.

Auditor's Duty

i.   The amount due from shareholders in respect of calls in arrears should be verified by reference to the Share Register.

ii. If any calls are due from directors, that should be shown separately in the balance sheet.

iii. Often the Articles provide that interest be charged on calls in arrears; the adjustment of interest in such a case should be verified.

iv. The auditors should also check that the appropriate entries have been passed in the books of accounts and ensure himself that calls in arrear are properly shown in the balance sheet.

Calls in Advance

A company, if permitted by the Articles may accept from members either the whole or part of the amount remaining unpaid on any shares held by him as calls in advance. But the amount so received cannot be treated as a part of the capital for the purpose of any voting rights until the same becomes presently payable and duly appropriated (Section 92 of the Companies Act).

A company, if so authorised by the Articles may pay dividend in proportion to the amount paid upon each share, where a larger amount is paid up on some shares than that on other (Section 93 of the Companies Act).

Interest may be paid on calls in advance if Articles of Association so provide. If the company has adopted 'Table A', then it is required to pay interest @ 6% p.a. from the date of receipt to the due date (Article 18 of Table A). Such interest is a charge against profit. However, such interest can be paid out of capital, when profits are not available for such payment.

Auditor's Duty

i.   The auditor should see that the provisions regarding payment of calls in advance exist in the Articles.

ii. He should see that calls in advance have not been treated as part of the share capital and it is shown separately in the Balance Sheet.

iii. He should ensure that the payment of interest on calls in advance does not exceed the percentage stated in the Articles.

iv. He should vouch the receipt of such amount and the payment of interest there on by inspecting the relevant entries in the cash book or pass book.

Forfeiture of Shares

If a shareholder fails to pay the calls made on him, the directors may have the power of forfeiting the shares held by him. The directors are empowered, subject to the fulfillment of certain conditions, may remove his name from the Register of Members and to treat the amount already paid by him forfeited to the company.

But it should be noted that shares could be forfeited only if the Articles authorise the directors to do so. Forfeiture shall be void, if it is contrary to the provisions of the Articles. Forfeiture of shares can ordinarily be made only for non-payment of calls, but the Articles may provide for forfeiture on grounds other than nonpayment of calls.

Conditions to be Fulfilled before Forfeiting Shares

1. Notice to the Shareholder

Before forfeiting any shares, the defaulting member must be served with a notice requiring him to pay the unpaid amount of call together with interest. The notice must mention the day on or before which the payment is to be made and also mention that in the event of non-payment, the shares will be liable to forfeiture.

2. Resolution of the Board

If the requirements of the above notice are not complied with, the shares may be forfeited by a resolution of the directors.

Auditor's Duty

i. The auditor should ascertain that the articles authorise the Board of Directors to forfeit the shares and that the power has been exercised by the Board in the best interest of the company.

ii. He should verify the amount of call that was outstanding in respect of each of the share forfeited.

iii. He should also ascertain that the procedure in the Articles has been followed, viz. the notice given (14 days, according to Table A) to the defaulting shareholders, warning them that in the event of non-payment by a specified date, the shares shall be forfeited.

iv. The auditor should verify the entries recorded in the books of accounts consequent upon forfeiture of shares to confirm that the premium, if any, received on the issue of shares has not be transferred to the Forfeited Shares Account.

Re-Issue of Forfeited Shares

A forfeited share is merely a share available to the company for sale and remains vested in the company for that purpose only. Re-issue of forfeited shares is not allotment of shares but only a sale. When shares are re-issued, return of the forfeited shares need not be filed under Section 75 (1) of the Companies Act, 1956.

The share, after forfeiture in the hands of the company, is subject to an obligation to dispose it off. In practice, forfeited shares are disposed off by auction. These shares can be re-issued at any price so long as the total amount received for those shares is not less than the amount in arrear on those shares.

Auditor's Duty

i. The auditor should ascertain that the Board of Directors has the authority under the Articles to re-issue forfeited shares.

ii. He should refer to the resolution of the Board of Director, re-allotting forfeited shares.

iii. He should vouch the amount collected from person to whom the shares have been allotted and also check the entries recorded for this purpose.

iv. The auditor should see that the total amount received on the shares, including that received prior to forfeiture, is not less than the par value of shares.

v. He should also verify the surplus resulting on the re-issue of shares credited to the Capital Reserve Account.

Issue of Right Shares

According to Section 81 of the Companies Act, 1956 the new shares that are offered in the first instance to the existing equity shareholders of the company are known as 'right shares', because they are so offered to the existing shareholders as a matter of their right.

Where at any time after the expiry of two years from the formation of a company or at any time after the expiry of one year from the allotment of share of the company made for the first time after its formation, whichever is earlier, the company proposes to issue further shares, then such further shares shall be offered to the existing equity shareholders of the company, in proportions, as nearly as possible to their present holding of shares. The existing shareholders shall have to exercise their right within 15 days or such further time as may be mentioned. Thereafter they may accept such offer, may decline to accept or may transfer their right to their nominees.

Auditor's Duty

i. The auditor should ensure that the provisions of Section 81 have been duly complied with.

ii. He should satisfy that appropriate resolution was passed either by the Board or the general meeting depending upon the circumstances of the issue.

iii. He should see that consideration money was duly received.

iv. He should also check to ensure that the guidelines issued by SEBI have been duly followed.

v. He should examine the filing of the return of allotment with the Registrar.

vi. He should satisfy that the allotment was made on pro rata basis.

Buying Back of Equity Shares

The Companies (Amendment) Act 1999 contains provisions regarding buying back of own securities by a company. The word 'security' includes both equity and preference share. But preference share can also be redeemed perhaps the provision is intended to equity share only.

As per Section 77A of the Companies Act

i. A company may purchase its own shares or other specified securities out of:
   (a) its free reserves
   (b) the securities premium account, or
   (c) the proceeds of any earlier issue other than from issue of shares made specifying for buy-back purposes.

ii.   No company shall purchase its own shares or other specified securities, unless:
   (a)   the buy-back is authorised by its articles,
   (b)   a special resolution has been passed in general meeting of the company authorising the buy-back,
   (c)   the buy-back is or less than 25% of the total paid up capital (both equity and preference) and free reserves of the company,
   (d)   the debt–equity ratio is not more than 2:1 after buy-back,
   (e)   all the shares or other specified securities are fully paid up,
   (f)   the buy-back of the shares or other specified securities listed on any recognised stock exchange is in accordance with the regulations made by SEBI, and
   (g)   the buy-back in respect of shares or other specified securities other than those in point vi. is in accordance with the guidelines as may be prescribed.

iii.   Every buy-back shall be completed within 12 months from the date of passing the special resolution or a resolution passed by the Board.

iv.   A solvency certificate to be filed before making buy-back.

v.   A company shall after completion of the buy-back file with the Registrar and the SEBI, a return containing such particulars relating to the buy-back within 30 days of such completion.

As per Section 77AA of the Companies Act

In case of shares are bought back out of free reserves, then a sum equal to the nominal value of shares bought back shall be transferred to a reserve account to be called the 'Capital Redemption Reserve Account' and details of such transfer shall be disclosed in the balance sheet. This account, as per SEBI Guidelines, shall be allowed to be used for issue of fully paid bonus shares.

As per Section 77B of the Companies Act

No company shall, directly or indirectly, purchase its own shares or other specified securities:

i.   through any subsidiary company including its own subsidiary companies; or

ii.   through any investment company or group of investment companies; or

iii.   if a default, in repayment of deposit or interest thereon, redemption of debentures or preference shares or payment of dividend or repayment of a term loan or interest thereon to any financial institution or bank, is subsisting, and

iv.   in case it has not complied with provisions of Section 159, Section 207 and Section 211.

Auditor's Duty

i.   The auditor should ensure that the provisions of Section 77A have been complied with.

ii.   He should vouch that amount of consideration was duly paid.

iii.   He should satisfy that appropriate resolution was passed in general meeting of the company authorising the buying-back option.

iv.   He should also ensure that the guidelines issued by SEBI have been duly followed.

v.   He should examine the filing of the return after completion of the buy-back with the Registrar and the SEBI.

vi.   The auditor should also verify that the proper accounting entries have been passed immediately after the buy-back.

Employees Stock Option Scheme (ESOPS)

'Employees Stock Option' means the option given to the whole-time directors, officers and employees of a company to purchase or subscribe at a future date, the securities offered by the company at a pre-determined price. Section 2 (15A) of the Companies Amendment Act, 2000 has allowed the companies to offer stock option scheme to their employees subject to SEBI Guidelines, 2000 in this regard.

SEBI Guidelines on ESOPS

i.   Issue of stock options at a discount to the market price would be regarded as another form of employee compensation and would be treated as such in the financial statement of the company regardless of the quantum of discount.

ii. The issue of ESOPS would be subject to approval of shareholders through a special resolution.

iii. In cases of employees being offered more than 1% of shares, a specific disclosure and approval would be necessary in the annual general meeting.

iv. A minimum period of one year between grant of options and its vesting must be prescribed. After one year, the period during which the option can be exercised would be determined by the company.

v.   The operation of the ESOP Scheme would have to be under the superintendence and direction of a Compensation Committee of Board of Directors in which there would be a majority of independent directors.

vi. ESOP would be open to all permanent employees and to the directors of the company but not to the promoters and large shareholders. With the specific approval of the shareholders, the scheme would be allowed to cover the employees of a subsidiary or a holding company.

vii. Directors report shall contain the following disclosures:
(a) The total number of shares covered by the ESOP as approved by the shareholders;
(b) The pricing formula;
(c) Options granted, options vested, options exercised, options forfeited, extinguishments or modification of options, money realised by exercise of options, total number of options in force, employee-wise details of options granted to senior managerial personnel and to any other employee who receive a grant in any one year of options amounting to 5% or more of options granted during that year.
(d) Fully diluted earnings per share (EPS) computed in accordance with international accounting standards.

Auditor's Duty

i.   The auditor will see whether the company has strictly adhered to the above conditions as stipulated in SEBI Guidelines in connection with ESOP.

ii. He will vouch the receipt of cash against issue of shares under option exercised by checking the entries in the cash book and bank statements.

iii. He will judge the reasonableness of the price at which options were given.

iv. He will see that paid up capital have not exceeded the authorised capital due to exercise of option.

v.   He should ensure that discount on issue under option has been treated as employee compensation and has been charged to the profit and loss account.

vi. The auditor will see that the fact of ESOP has been adequately disclosed in the balance sheet.

Issue and Redemption of Preference Shares

Issue of Preference Shares

A company limited by shares, if authorised by its Articles, may issue preference shares, which are liable to be redeemed at the option of the company before or on a predetermined date. However, after the commencement of the Companies (Amendment) Act, 1996 no company limited by shares shall issue any preference share that is irredeemable or is redeemable after the expiry of a period of 20 years from the date of its issue.

Auditor's Duty

i. The auditor should see that the issue of redeemable preference shares is properly authorised by the Articles.

ii. He should vouch the issue and check the necessary records made to the books of account in this connection.

iii. So long as the shares are not redeemed, the terms of redemption, if any, must be stated in the balance sheet along with the earliest date of redemption.

iv. He should vouch the receipts of issue price from the Cash Book and the Share Registers.

Redemption of Preference Shares

Section 80 of the Companies Act describes the conditions to be fulfilled for the purpose of redemption of preference shares. The conditions are:

i. The shares to be redeemed are fully paid up.

ii. The shares are to be redeemed out of profit available for distribution as dividend or out of proceeds of a fresh issue made for the purpose of redemption.

iii. The premium on redemption, if any, is to be provided for either out of the Securities Premium Account or out of divisible profits of the company, and

iv. If the shares are to be redeemed out of profits, otherwise available for dividend, an amount equal to the nominal amount of shares to be redeemed has to be transferred to the Capital Redemption Reserve Account.

Auditor's Duty

i. The auditor should see that the redemption of preference shares is in accordance with the provision of Section 80 of the Companies Act.

ii. In case the shares are redeemed out of fresh issue, the auditor should verify the Articles and the minutes of the director's meeting.

iii. In case the shares are redeemed out of divisible profits, he should see that the nominal value of shares redeemed has been transferred to the Capital Redemption Reserve Account.

iv. The auditor should also ensure that the Capital Redemption Reserve Account is treated as part of capital and not applied except for paying up un-issued share capital of the company to be issued to members as fully paid up bonus shares.

7.4 AUDIT OF DEBENTURES

Debentures are considered as one of the important sources of external fund to a company. A company may issue debentures to raise funds, provided it is empowered to do so. Memorandum and Articles of Association assigns powers to the company in this regard. Debentures are not considered a part of the capital of the company. Debenture holders are merely the creditors of the company. They have the right to receive interest at a fixed percentage irrespective of the quantum of profit earned by the company in a particular period.

7.4.1 AUDIT PROCEDURE

Issue of Debentures

Debentures may be issued at par or at a premium or at a discount. When the debentures are issued at a premium, the amount of premium collected should be credited to Premium on Debenture Account. Subsequently, this balance is transferred to Capital Reserve Account, as it is a Capital Profit. Where the debentures are issued at a discount, the amount of discount allowed should be debited to Discount on Issue of Debenture Account. The balance in this account will appear in the Balance Sheet untill written off.

Auditor's Duty

i.   The auditor should verify that the prospectus had been duly filed with the Registrar before the date of allotment of debentures.

ii. He should check the allotment of debentures by reference to the Director's minutes book.

iii. He should also check the amount collected in the Cash Book with the counterfoils of receipts issued to the applicants and also cross check the amount into the Application and Allotment Book.

iv. The auditor should verify the entries on the counterfoils of debentures issued with the Debentures Register.

v.   He should examine the Debenture Trust Deed and note the conditions contained therein as to issue and repayment.

vi. If the debentures are covered by a mortgage of charge, it should be verified that the charge has been correctly recorded in the Register of Mortgage and Charges and it has also been registered with the Registrar of Companies.

vii. Where debentures have been issued as fully paid up to vendors as a part of the purchase consideration, the contract in this regard should be checked.

viii. Compliance with SEBI Guidelines should also be seen.

Redemption of Debentures

A company can issue redeemable as well as irredeemable debentures. If debentures are redeemable, it can be done either any of the following three ways:

i.   By way of periodical drawing

ii. By way of payment on fixed date

iii. By payment whenever the company desires to do so

Auditor's Duty

i.   The auditor should inspect the Debentures or the Trust Deed, for the terms and conditions of the redemption of debentures.

ii. The auditor should also refer to the Article of Association.

iii. He should see the Directors' minutes book authorising the redemption of debentures.

iv. He should also vouch the redemption with the help of Debenture Bonds cancelled and the Cash Book.

v.   The auditor should also examine thoroughly the accounting treatment given to the redemption.

Interest on Debentures

A predetermined fixed rate of interest is payable on debentures irrespective of the fact that the company has been able to earn any profit or not. Debenture holders are the creditors of the company, and not the owners. They have no voting rights and cannot influence the management for the affairs of the company, but their claim of interest rank ahead of the claims of the shareholders.

Auditor's Duty

i.   The repayment of interest should be vouched by the auditor with the acknowledgement of the debenture holders, endorsed warrants and in case of bearer debentures with the coupons surrendered.

ii. The auditor should reconcile the total amount paid with the total amount due and payable with the amount of interest outstanding for payment.

iii. Interest on debentures is payable, whether or not any profit is made. Therefore, a provision should be made unless it has been specially agreed with the debenture holders that interest in such a case would be waived by them. The auditor should also consider this aspect.

iv. The auditor should also consider the disclosure part of the interest on debentures. He should ensure that the interest paid on debenture, like that on other fixed loans, must be disclosed as a separate item in the profit and loss account.

Re-Issue of Redeemed Debentures

A company may issue debentures previously redeemed, either by re-issuing the debentures or issuing others in their place. But re-issue is not possible, if the Articles or a contract or resolution, recorded at a general meeting, or terms of issue or some other act of the company expressly or impliedly manifest the intention that, on redemption, the debentures shall be cancelled.

However, the re-issue of redeemed debentures or the issue of others in their place is treated as a new issue for the purpose of stamp duty and the rights and privileges attaching to the debentures that re-issued shall be the same as if the debentures had never been redeemed.

On these considerations, it is necessary for the auditor to verify the re-issue of debentures in the same manner as those issued for the first time.

Auditor's Duty

The auditor will verify the following:

i.   Whether the Articles permit such re-issue.

ii. Whether the terms and conditions of debenture impose any restriction on re-issue of debentures after they have been redeemed.

iii. Whether the company has passed any resolution in the general meeting for re-issue of redeemed debenture.

iv. Whether Section 121 of the Companies Act, which empowers the holders of re-issued debentures same rights and priorities as the original holders, have been complied with.

v.   Whether particulars of re-issued debentures have been clearly shown in the balance sheet.

vi. Whether fresh stamp duty has been paid on re-issued debentures.

Issue of Debentures as Collateral Security

Debentures may be issued to creditors, bankers or any other person, without receiving any cash thereon. It acts as a collateral security and becomes real debentures in the event of the default of the loan. Usually the nominal value of such debentures is more than that of the amount of loan.

Auditor's Duty

i. The auditor should see that such debentures do not appear on the liabilities side of the balance sheet, but are shown by way of a note under the heading loan.

ii. The auditor should ensure that necessary entries made in the Register of Mortgages and that the necessary papers are filed with the Registrar of Companies.

iii. He should also examine the loan agreement and confirm that it has been approved by the Board.

iv. He should also check whether the debentures are automatically cancelled as soon as the loan is repaid.

7.5 SPECIFIC PROVISION AS REGARDS ACCOUNTS IN THE COMPANIES ACT

The provisions in the matter of books of accounts, which a company is required to maintain are contained in Section 209 of the Companies Act, 1956. They are briefly summarised below:

Books to be Maintained

Every company shall keep at its registered office proper books of account, with respect to:

i. all sums of money received and expended by the company and the matters in respect of which the receipt and expenditure takes place,

ii. all sales and purchases of goods by the company,

iii. the assets and liabilities of the company, and

iv. in the case of a company pertaining to any class of companies engaged in production, processing, manufacturing or mining activities, such particular relating to utilisation of material and labour or to other items of cost as may be prescribed in such class of companies as required by the Central Government to include such particulars: Section-209 (1).

Place of Preservation of Books

All the books are usually required to be kept at the registered office in India. All or any of the above stated books of account might be kept at such other place instead of registered office in India as the Board of Directors may decide. The company must file with the Registrar a notice in writing giving the full address of the other place [Section 209 (1)].

Books of Branch Offices

Where a company has a branch office, whether in or outside India, the company shall be deemed to have complied with the aforementioned provisions if the company maintains proper books of account relating to transactions affected at the branch office and also arranges to obtain from the branch proper summarised returns, at intervals of not more than three months, for being kept at the registered office or at the other place [Section-209 (2)].

Method of Accounts

For the purpose of sub-section (1) and (2), proper books of account shall not be deemed to be kept with respect to the matters specified therein:

i. if they are not kept such books as are necessary to give a true and fair view of the state of affairs of the company or branch office, as the case may be, and to explain its transactions and

ii. if such books are not kept on accrual basis and according to the double entry system of accounting [Section-209 (3)].

Inspection of Books of Accounts

The books of accounts and other books and papers shall be kept open for inspection by any director during business hours [Section 209 (4)].

Period of Preservation

The books of accounts of every company relating to a period of not less than eight years immediately proceeding the current year together with vouchers relevant to the entry in such books of accounts shall be preserved in good order. In case of a company incorporated less than eight years before the current year, the books of account for the entire period proceeding the current year shall be preserved [Section-209 (4A)].

Penalty

If the managing director or manager and in the absence of any of them, any director of the company fails to take reasonable steps to secure compliance with the requirements of law aforementioned or by a willful act causes any default by the company, he shall be punishable for each offence with imprisonment for a term, which may extend to six months, or a fine, which may extend to Rs. 10,000 or both [Section 209 (5)].

7.6   SPECIAL REQUIREMENTS OF COMPANY AUDIT

The company audit is compulsory in nature and governed basically by the provisions of the Companies Act. While conducting audit in a company form of organisation, the auditor should take into consideration certain requirements of company audit as dictated by the provisions of the Companies Act.

The special requirements to be kept in mind by the auditor while conducting company audit are described below:

Verification of the Constitution and Power

A company can function within the limits prescribed by the documents on the basis of which it has been registered. It raises its capital from the public on certain conditions. On this account, it is essential that the auditor, prior to starting the audit of a company, shall examine the following:

(a) Memorandum of Association

It is a charter containing particulars of business activities that the company can undertake and the powers it can exercise in regard thereto. If a company enters into a transaction, which is ultra vires, the shareholders may restrain the management from charging the loss, if any, has been suffered thereon, to the company. If the auditor fails to detect and report the transactions, which are ultra vires the company, he would be guilty of negligence.

(b) Articles of Association

These are rules and regulations for the internal management of the company and they define the rights of different classes of shareholders, conditions under which calls can be made, the maximum and the minimum number of directors, their qualifications, disqualifications and removal etc. The terms and conditions of these provisions have relevance to the examination of transactions that the auditor is required to carry out. He should, therefore, study the Articles and include extracts from them in his permanent audit file. The auditor, who fails to take note of the provisions in the Articles in the verification of statements of accounts, would be guilty of professional negligence.

(c) Prospectus

It is a formal document which a public company must issue before it makes the allotment of shares under Section 56. It must contain all the terms and conditions on which subscription to the shares are sought to be obtained from the public. In case the company fails to carry out any of these undertakings, or if any statement made by it ultimately is proved to be false, the shareholder has the right to claim refund of the amount paid by him. The auditor should, therefore, study carefully all the conditions and stipulations made in the prospectus and in case any of them has not been carried out to draw the attention of shareholders thereto.

Knowledge About Authority Structure of the Company

With a view to carrying out the audit effectively, it is necessary that the auditor should know the authority structure of the company. Under Section 291 of the Act, the Board of Directors of a company are entitled to exercise all such powers and to do all such acts and things, as the company is authorised to do.

Section 292 specifies five types of decisions that can be taken by the Board of Directors only in Board's meetings.

These include:

   i.   making calls on partly paid shares,

   ii.   issue of debentures,

  iii.   borrowing money otherwise than on debentures,

  iv.   investing the fund of the company, and

   v.   making loans.

Apart from the above, the Board also carries out a number of other functions. Such functions include:

   i.   Adopting of accounts before the same to be submitted to the auditor for their report (Section 215).

   ii.   Appointment of the first auditors and filing of casual vacancy (Section 224).

  iii.   Investment in shares of companies within the limits (Section 372A).

  iv.   Entering into contracts with persons who are directors of the company or related to or associated with the directors as specified in Section 297 of the Companies Act.

However, the Board shall not exercise any power or do any act or thing, which is directed or required by any legislation or by the memorandum or articles of the company, to be exercised or done by the company, in a general meeting.

Following are some of the matters, which only the shareholders can sanction in a general meeting:

   i.   Appointment and fixation of remuneration of auditors in the annual general meeting (Section 224).

   ii.   Declaration of dividend (Regulation 85, Table A).

  iii.   Appointment of relative of directors to an office or place of profit in the company (Section 314).

  iv.   Sale, lease or a disposal of the whole of the company's undertakings or a substantial part of it and donations above a certain limit [Section 293 (1)].

Some matters which require the sanction of the Central Government, for example, sanctioning loans to directors by a company other than a banking or a finance company cannot be exercised by the Board of Directors or the shareholders.

7.7   COMPANY AUDITOR

An auditor is a person who is appointed to conduct an independent examination of books, accounts and supporting vouchers to report on the reliability and fairness of profit and loss account and balance sheet. He is a professional, having specialised knowledge and expertise in all branches of accounting.

In order to ensure that the person conducting the audit of accounts of company has sufficient knowledge in accounting, the Companies Act requires him to be a chartered accountant within the meaning of the Chartered Accountants Act, 1949. Apart from being well versed in accounting, the auditor should be honest, tactful, methodological, cautious and careful. Lord Justice Lindley in his famous case London and General Bank (1895) held that "an auditor must be honest, i.e., he must not certify what he does not believe to be true and he must take reasonable care and skill before he believes what he certifies is true". Learned Judge Lopes in Kingston Cotton Mill case remarked: "an auditor need not be over-cautious or always suspicious. He is a watchdog but not a bloodhound. He is justifying in believing the tried servants of the company and entitled to rely upon their representation provided he takes reasonable care".

7.7.1 Appointment of Auditors

The provisions regarding appointment of the auditors are contained in Section 224 of the Companies Act.

First Auditor

Section 224 (5) provides for the appointment of first auditors by the Board of Directors within one month of the date of registration of the company. The auditor or auditors so appointed shall hold office till the conclusion of the first annual general meeting.

But the company may at a general meeting remove such an auditor and appoint another in his place, on a nomination being made by any member of the company, notice being given to the members of the company, not less than 14 days before the date of the meeting.

If the first auditor is not appointed by the directors, within one month of registration, the company in general meeting may appoint the first auditor. The auditor of a company is normally appointed by the shareholders by passing a resolution at the annual general meeting. Once appointed, he holds office from the conclusion of that meeting to the conclusion of the next annual general meeting.

An auditor once appointed may be reappointed in the next annual general meeting or a new auditor may be appointed in his place. It is obligatory on the part of a company to annually make such an appointment, as well as to give, within seven days of the appointment, intimation to every auditor so appointed or reappointed.

Subsequent Auditors

Subsequent auditors of a company are appointed every year by the shareholders in annual general meeting by passing an ordinary resolution. According to Section 224 (1), "Every Company shall, at each annual general meeting, appoint an auditor to hold office". Section 224 (1A) requires the auditor so appointed to communicate his acceptance or refusal to the Registrar of Companies within the period of 30 days of the receipt of appointment order from the company intimating his appointment.

If the auditor so appointed does not accept the appointment, the vacancy can neither be treated as casual vacancy nor a vacancy by resignation. The Research Committee of the Institute of Chartered Accountants of India has clearly expressed this opinion on the strength of the provisions of the Companies Act, which vest the general power with shareholders and the delegation of powers to the Board of Directors is not permitted. Therefore, another general meeting has to be convened to appoint new auditor.

Appointment by Central Government

According to Section 224 (3), where at an annual general meeting, no auditors are appointed or re-appointed, the Central Government may appoint a person to fill the vacancy. Within seven days of the power of the Central Government becoming exercisable, the company shall give notice of that fact to the Central Government. Failure to give such notice will make the company in default with a fine, which may extend to Rs. 5,000.

Appointment Against a Casual Vacancy

If due to death, insanity or insolvency etc, a casual vacancy of the auditor arises, the Board of Directors can fill the same under Section 224 (6). The auditor appointed against such a vacancy will hold office till the conclusion of the next annual general meeting.

Appointment by Special Resolution

The Companies (Amendment) Act, 1974 introduced Section 224A, which provides that in the case of a company in which 25% or more of the subscribed share capital is held whether individually or collectively by:

i. a public financial institution or a government company or any state government or

ii. any financial or other institution established by any provincial or state Act in which a state government holds not less than 51% of the subscribed share capital or

iii. a nationalised bank or an insurance company carrying on general insurance business

the appointment of the auditor shall be made by a special resolution.

If the company fails to pass a special resolution, it shall be deemed that no auditor has been appointed by the company at its annual general meeting and the Central Government will be empowered to make an appointment.

Appointment of Auditors of Government or Certain Other Companies

Section 619 provides that the auditor of a government company shall be appointed or reappointed by the Central Government on the advice of the Comptroller and Auditor General of India.

The Amendment Act also introduced another section, i.e., Section 619B, which extends the provision of Section 619, to a company in which the Central Government or state government or any government company or any government corporation hold either single or jointly not less than 51% of the paid up share capital.

The professional auditor should keep these provisions in mind while accepting an appointment as the auditor of a company since the onus of complying with the provisions of Section 619B lies with the concerned companies. All the same, it would be necessary on the part of the auditors appointed or re-appointed under Section 224 of the Act to ensure, before accepting the appointment/re-appointment, that the company concerned is in fact outside the ambit of Section 619B of the Act.

7.7.2 TENURE OF APPOINTMENT

Section 224 (1) of the Companies Act provides that an auditor is appointed from the conclusion of one annual general meeting until the conclusion of next annual general meeting. But, if the annual general meeting is not held within the period prescribed by Section 166, the auditor will continue in office till the annual general meeting is actually held and concluded. So, if an annual general meeting is adjourned, his tenure will extend till the conclusion of the adjourned meeting.

7.7.3 RE-APPOINTMENT OF RETIRING AUDITOR

According to the provisions of Section 224 (2), retiring auditor, by whatsoever authority appointed, shall be automatically re-appointed by passing an ordinary resolution except in the following circumstances:

i. Where he is not qualified for re-appointment.

ii. Where he has given to the company a notice in writing of his unwillingness to be re-appointed.

iii. Where a resolution has been passed at the meeting, appointing somebody else instead of him or providing expressly that he shall not be re-appointed.

iv. Where a notice has been given of an intended resolution to appoint some person in the place of retiring auditor, and by reason of death, incapacity or disqualification of that person, the resolution cannot be proceeded with.

The re-appointment will not be automatic. Also, the non-reappointment of the retiring auditor in the annual general meeting is not removal of the auditor. It will be considered simply as retirement.

The auditor will also not been re-appointed in the following two special cases:

i. Where he holds the audit of specified number of companies or more than that on the day of appointment in terms of Section 224 (1B) of the Companies Act.

ii. Where 25% or more of the subscribed capital of the company is held by public financial institution(s), government companies etc. or a combination of them, unless the retiring auditor is appointed by a special resolution.

The rights of retiring auditor are as follows:

i. He has the right to receive the notice of the resolution.

ii. He has the right to make a written presentation to the company and requests its notification to members of the company.

iii. The auditor has the right to get his representation circulated among the members.

iv. He has the right to get his representation read out at the meeting, if it has not been sent to the members because of delay or default on the part of the company.

7.7.4 CEILING ON NUMBER OF AUDITS

The Companies (Amendment) Act, 1974 added two new sub-sections 224 (1B) and 224 (1C) on ceiling on number of audits. The objective of these sections is to prevent concentration of audits in few hands. These sections was further amended in 1988 and finally revised in the year 2000.

According to Section 224 (1B), an individual cannot be the auditor of more than 20 companies at a time. Further, out of these 20 companies, not more than 10 should be companies having a paid-up share capital of Rs. 25 lakhs or more. In case of a partnership firm of auditors, the ceiling is 20 companies per partner of the firm and if a partner is also a partner in any other firm, the overall ceiling in relation to such a partner will be 20.

Example

In a firm of Chartered Accountants, say, there are three partners— X, Y and Z. The overall ceiling of the firm will be $3 \times 20 = 60$ company audit, out of which not more than $3 \times 10 = 30$ companies may have paid up share capital of Rs. 25 lakhs or more.

Again, say X is also a partner of another firm of Chartered Accountants. In that case, in these two firms, total number of company audit he can undertake as a partner of the firms is limited to 20 only subject to the ceiling of 10 large company audits, i.e., companies having a paid-up share capital of Rs. 25 lakhs or more. It is his responsibility to allocate these 20 company audits between these two firms.

Section 224 (1B) has been amended by the Companies (Amendment) Act, 1988 to disallow the appointment of person, who are in full time employment elsewhere, as company auditor. Even in case of partnership, such a partner shall be excluded from counting the number of audits per partner.

According to the amendments in the Companies Act in 2000, the above provisions are applicable in case of public limited companies only. So, private limited companies are excluded in computing the ceiling of number of audits.

However, the Institute of Chartered Accountants of India has issued a notification [No. 1- CA (7)/53/2001] in the Gazette of India dated May 19, 2001 to include private companies also within the ceiling of 30 companies. According to the notification, "a member of the Institute in practice shall be deemed to be guilty of professional misconduct, if he holds at any time appointment of more than specified number of audit assignment of the companies including private companies".

7.7.5 REMUNERATION OF AUDITOR

i.   In case of an auditor appointed by the Board of Directors or the Central Government, his remuneration may be fixed by the Board of Directors or the Central Government as the case may be.

ii. In all other respect, it must be fixed by the company in general meeting or in such manner as the company in general meeting may determine.

'Remuneration' includes any sum paid by the company in respect of the auditor's expenses in carrying out his duties. Obviously, the general meeting can disperse without deciding the amount of the remuneration of the auditor. However, it must provide the manner in which the remuneration can be determined. If an auditor renders services other than the audit work, he will be entitled to get additional remuneration for such work. A special disclosure of all amount paid to the auditor in whatever capacity is required to be made in the Profit and Loss Account as:

i.   as auditor

ii. as adviser, or in any other capacity in respect of
     a. taxation matters, b. company law matters, c. management services, and

iii. In any other manner.

The aforesaid manner of disclosure is required by Part II of Schedule VI to the Act.

Where the auditor is re-appointed in the next annual general meeting, the amount fixed for the previous year continues to be the remuneration of the auditor unless specific changes are made.

7.7.6 QUALIFICATION OF AN AUDITOR

Section 226 of the Companies Act prescribes the qualification and disqualification of Company Auditors. According to Section 226 (1), "a person shall not be qualified as auditor of a company unless he is a Chartered Accountant within the meaning of the Chartered Accountants Act, 1949".

It further provides that a firm whereof all the partners practicing in India are qualified for appointment as auditors may be appointed by firm's name to be the auditor of the company. In this connection, it may be noted that under the Chartered Accountants Act, 1949 only a chartered accountant having a certificate of practice can be engaged in the public practice of the profession of accountancy. Therefore, only a practicing chartered accountant can be appointed as an auditor of a company.

In addition to above, a person, holding a certificate under the law in force in the whole or any portion of a Part B State immediately before the commencement of the Part B States (Laws) Act, 1953 or of the Jammu and Kashmir (Extension of Laws) Act, 1956 as the case may be, entitling him to act as an auditor of the companies in the territories which, immediately before 1 November 1956 were comprised in that state or any portion thereof, shall also be entitled to be appointed to act as an auditor of companies registered anywhere in India.

Thus, the auditor of a company must either be:

i.   a practicing chartered accountant; or

ii. the holder of a certificate in erstwhile Part B States entitling him to act as an auditor of companies.

7.7.7 DISQUALIFICATION OF AN AUDITOR

Section 226 (3) provides the criteria or conditions for disqualification of auditors. According to it, none of the following shall be qualified for appointment as an auditor of a company:

i.   A body corporate;

ii. An officer or employee of the company;

iii. A partner or an employee of an officer or employee of the company;

iv. A person who is indebted to the company for an amount exceeding Rs. 1,000 or who has given any guarantee or provided any security in connection with the indebtness of any third person; and

v. A person holding any security of the auditee company when such security carries voting right.

A person shall not be qualified for appointment as an auditor of a company if he is, by virtue of Section 226 (3), disqualified for appointment as an auditor of any other company, which is that company's subsidiary or holding company or a subsidiary of that company's holding company.

If the auditor ceases to be a member of the Institute of Chartered Accountants of India or adjudged as having unsound mind or is an undischarged insolvent, he attracts disqualification.

If after his appointment, an auditor becomes disqualified subject to any of the points listed above, he shall be deemed to have vacated his office as such.

7.7.8 REMOVAL OF AUDITORS

An appointed auditor may be removed from his office either in accordance with the provisions of the Companies Act or as per restrictions imposed by the Chartered Accountants Act.

Removal as per the Companies Act

The removal of the auditor in accordance with the provisions of the Companies Act depends upon the option of the concerned company. He may be removed before the expiry of his term or after the expiry of his term. The service of the first auditor appointed by the Board and supposed to hold office till the conclusion of the first annual general meeting can be terminated beforehand by way of passing a resolution in a general meeting. However, the removal of any subsequent auditor before the expiry of his term is difficult in the sense that it requires the approval of the Central Government as per Section 227 (7). So, the Central Government has to be convinced about the unsuitability of the existing auditor to continue as auditor.

The Companies Act lays down clear procedures about the removal of auditors in Sections 224 and Section 225.

Removal Before the Expiry of the Term

i. Under Section 224 (5) (a), it is provided that the company can remove in a general meeting the first auditor appointed by the Board of Directors.

ii. Under Section 224 (7), it is provided that except the first auditor, auditors appointed as per Section 224 could be removed before the expiry of the term in a general meeting, only after obtaining previous approval of the Central Government.

Removal After the Expiry of the Term

The auditor can be removed after the expiry of his term of office, as per the procedures laid down in Section 225. According to the section, for removal of a retiring auditor or appointing another auditor in his place, the following procedures must be observed:

i. Special notice must be given by a member of the intended resolution to be passed at an annual general meeting.

ii. On receipt of such a notice, the company shall forward a copy thereof to the retiring auditor.

iii. The retiring auditor then may make written representation to the company not exceeding a reasonable length and request their notification to the members of the company.

The company shall, unless the representations are received by it too late to do so

i. state the fact of the representation in any notice of the resolution given to members of the company and

ii. send a copy of the representation to every members of the company to whom notice of the meeting is sent.

If a copy of the representation is not sent as aforesaid, because they are received too late or because of the company's default, the auditor may require that the representation shall be read out at the meeting. However, these are not required, if the Company Law Board is satisfied that the above rights are abused by the auditor.

Removal as per Chartered Accountants Act

An auditor may also be removed from his office due to his professional misconduct. Following are some of the important clauses of the Chartered Accountants Act, 1949, which mention the professional misconduct for which a Chartered Accountant may be removed from his office:

i. If a Chartered Accountant accepts the position as an auditor previously held by another Chartered Accountant without first communicating him in writing.

ii. If a Chartered Accountant is grossly negligent in the conduct of his professional duties.

iii. If a Chartered Accountant is engaged in any business or occupation other than the profession of accountancy unless permitted by the council of the Institute.

iv. If a Chartered Accountant contravenes any of the provisions of the Act and regulation made there under etc.

7.7.9 STATUS OF THE COMPANY AUDITOR

The auditor of a company can be considered a servant of the company, an agent of the shareholders as well as an officer of the company.

A Servant of the Company

Like any other employee or director of a company, an auditor also renders his services to the company. The employees get remuneration from the company for their services. The auditor is receiving remuneration from the company (not termed as audit fees) for the services rendered by him for the company. Hence, like employees of the company, the auditor may also be considered as a servant of the company.

But if payment to auditor by the company makes him a servant of the company, it will create lot of confusion. Then the doctor who is paid by the patient is to be treated as servant of the client. So, it would not be logical to treat the auditor as servant of the company.

An Agent of the Company

Except in certain special situations where an auditor is appointed by the Directors or the Central Government, an auditor is normally appointed by the shareholders. Not only that, the auditor checks the accounts on behalf of the shareholders and he has to submit his report to the shareholders. It therefore appears that an auditor is an agent of the shareholders.

Lord Cranworth in the course of his judgment in the case *Spackman vs. Evans* also said: "The auditor may be the agent of the shareholders, so far as it relates to the audit of the accounts. For the purpose of the audit, the auditors will bind the shareholders".

However, according to the Law of Agency, "he who does through another does by himself". It means that any act of the agent will be purported to be the act of the principal. But this relationship does not exist between the shareholders and the auditors. Again, under the same law, the knowledge of an agent regarding a matter is also taken as the knowledge of the principal. So far as company auditor is concerned, he is not supposed to intimate the shareholders any information other than the actual results and financial position through financial statements. Therefore, a company auditor cannot be treated as an agent of the shareholders. He can best be described as the representative of the shareholders under certain circumstances.

An Officer of the Company

An auditor is an officer of the company under Section 2 (30) of the Companies Act for the purpose of the following sections:

  i.   Section 477: Powers to summon persons suspected of having property of the company.

 ii.   Section 477: Power to order public examination of promoters, directors, officers, etc.

iii.   Section 539: Penalty for falsification of books.

 iv.   Section 543: Power of the court to assess damages against delinquent directors, officers etc. in course of winding up procedure.

  v.   Section 545: Prosecution of delinquent officers and members of the company.

 vi.   Section 621: Offences against Act to be cognizable only on complaint by Registrar, Shareholder or Government.

vii.   Section 625: Payment of compensation in cases of frivolous or vexatious prosecution.

viii. Section 633: Power of the court to grant relief in certain cases.

Except for the above sections, an auditor shall not be considered as an officer under the Companies Act, 1956. In addition to that there are many legal decisions where a company auditor has been termed as an officer of the company. In London and General Bank case, it was held by Justice Lindley that it seems impossible to deny that for some purposes and to some extent, an auditor is an officer of the company. It was also held in the famous Kingston Cotton Mills Co. Ltd. case that the auditors are officers of the company.

But an officer is bound by the service rules of the company and is required to work as per the directions given to him. But independence in the work of an auditor is a well-established principle. He needs to be independent of management in order to make his report reliable to the shareholders and other interested parties like bankers, creditors, etc. Therefore, the auditor must work according to his own judgment and independent thought even though that may not suit the desire of management. So, to treat the auditor as an officer of the company is contrary to the basic philosophy of audit.

The position of an auditor is, therefore, a bit controversial. Sometimes he may appear to be an agent of the shareholders and sometimes he may be considered an officer of the company. But an auditor is an independent person rendering professional services to the company in return of fees. He can neither be an agent of the shareholders nor be an officer of the company, nor is he a servant of the company.

7.7.10 Auditor's Rights, Duties and Liabilities

The auditor of a company has statutory rights, duties and liabilities under the Companies Act.

Rights of a Company Auditor

An auditor of a company is required to report on the truth and fairness of the financial statement of the company. To perform his duties effectively, he requires some rights and powers. In case of sole proprietor or partnership firm, the rights and duties of an auditor are determined by the agreement entered into by him with the sole proprietor of the partnership firm as the case may be. But the Companies Act, 1956, has specifically laid down the rights and duties of a statutory auditor of a joint stock company. These rights and duties are absolute and cannot be curtailed in any way. Any resolution or provision in the Articles in this regard will be null and void. It was held in the case of *Newton vs. Birmingham Small Arms Co. Ltd.* that any resolution precluding the auditor from of any information to which he is entitled to as per Companies Act is inconsistent with the Act.

The Companies Act provides the following rights to the auditor to enable him to discharge his duties properly:

Right of Access to Books and Vouchers

Section 227 (1) of the Companies Act, 1956 provides that the auditor of a company shall have the right of access, at all times, to the books and vouchers of the company whether kept at the head office or elsewhere. This right of the auditor is the fundamental basis on which the auditor can proceed to examine and inspect the records of the company for the purpose of making his report.

Right to Obtain Information and Explanations

Section 227 (1) also entitles the auditor to require from the officer of the company such information and explanations as the auditor may think necessary for the performance of his duties. Corresponding to the right to ask for information and explanations, Section 221 of the Act also makes it obligatory for the concerned officers of the company to furnish without delay the relevant information to the auditor.

Right to Visit Branch Offices and Access to Branch Accounts

Section 228 (2) of the Companies Act gives specific rights to the company auditor where the accounts of any branch office are audited by another person. The company auditor has the right to visit branch office, if he deems it necessary to do so for the performance of his duties and has the right of access to books and accounts along with vouchers maintained by the branch office.

Right to Receive Branch Audit Reports

The company auditor has also the right to receive the audit report from the branch auditor for his consideration and deal with it in such a way, as he considers necessary while preparing his audit report on the accounts of the company.

Right to Receive Notices and to Attend General Meeting

Section 231 of the Companies Act entitles the auditors of a company to attend any general meeting of the company and to be heard on any part of the business, which concerns him as the auditor. He is also entitled to receive all notices and communications relating to any general meeting of the company.

Right to Make Representation

Pursuant to Section 225, the retiring auditor is entitled to receive a copy of the special notice intending to remove him or proposing to appoint any other person as auditor. The retiring auditor sought to be removed has a right to make his representation in writing and request that the same be circulated amongst the members of the company. In case, the same could not be circulated, the auditor may require that the representation shall be read out at the general meeting.

Right to Sign Audit Report

According to Section 229 of the Companies Act, only the person appointed as auditor of the company, or where a firm is so appointed only a partner in the firm practicing in India, may sign the auditor's report.

Right to Seek Legal and Technical Advice

The auditor of a company is entitled to take legal and technical advice, which may be required in the performance of conduct of audit or discharge of his duties [London and General Bank Case].

Right to be Indemnified

For different purposes, an auditor is considered to be an officer of the company. As an officer, he has the right to be indemnified out of assets of the company against any liability incurred by him in defending himself against any civil or criminal proceedings by the company, it he is not held guilty by the law.

Right to Receive Remuneration

On completion of his work, an auditor is entitled to receive his remuneration. The rights of the auditor cannot be limited by any resolution of the members passed in the general meeting [*Homer vs. Quitler*].

Right of Lien of Company Auditor

The right of 'lien' means right of one person to retain the property of another person who owes money to the former. The right of lien of an auditor of a limited company indicates his right to retain documents and records of the company for his unpaid fees. The Companies Act is silent about the right of lien of auditors on clients' documents and records. Also there are many conflicting legal judgments regarding this issue. The Institute of Chartered Accountants of England and Wales has issued a guideline in this regard.

Based on that guideline, the auditor's lien can be discussed under the following heads:

Lien on Books of Accounts

In the case, *Herbert Alfred Burleigh vs. Ingram Clark Ltd.* (1901), it was held that while an auditor acts as an accountant preparing books of accounts, he should have lien on such books of accounts for unpaid fees. But if he merely audits the books of accounts, he will not enjoy any right of lien on them.

But allowing auditor to enjoy right of lien on books of accounts prepared by him will conflict Section 209 of the Companies Act, which make it mandatory for every company to keep its books of accounts at its registered office or at such other place in India as the directors think fit. So, the auditor's lien would not be upheld on books of accounts, which the company has to keep in its possession as per the provisions of the Companies Act.

Lien on Working Papers

Audit working papers are those documents and records, which the auditors prepare in connection with his audit work. In fact, this question of ownership in respect to the working papers arose in the case of *Sockockingky vs. Bright Graham & Co.* (1938) in England. The question was whether the auditor had a right to retain the working papers as if it were their own property even after the payment of the audit fees. The court delivered judgment in favour of the auditors on the ground that they were independent contractors and not agents of the client.

Lien on Communication Documents

An auditor may communicate with third parties either as an agent on behalf of the client or independently in connection with his work. In this case, the communication documents will belong to the client. However, if the auditor makes correspondence with third parties not as an agent, but as a professional discharging his duties, the correspondence with the third parties will be his property.

Lien on Client's Money

The auditor should not have any lien on client's money, which may be kept with him. This is simply because he does not work on the money. He may be required to keep the money as a trustee only. So, if the auditor appropriates client's money towards his outstanding fees, he will be held liable.

General or Special Lien

An auditor has only lien on the particular document in respect of which he has rendered his professional service, but he has not yet been paid. He cannot have general lien, i.e., he cannot retain other documents with which he has not been concerned.

7.7.11 DUTIES OF A COMPANY AUDITOR

The duties of a company auditor can be described by classifying it in the following categories:

Statutory Duties

1. Duty to Report

According to Section 227 of the Companies Act, 1956, it is the duty of the company auditor to make a report to the members of the company on the accounts examined by him and on balance sheet and profit and loss account laid before the company in its general meeting.

2. Duty to Enquire

Sub-section (1A) of Section 227 of the Companies Act specifies six matters, which are required to be looked into by a company auditor. The statement on Qualifications in the Auditor's Report issued by the ICAI clarifies that the auditor is not required to report on the matters specified in sub-section (1A), unless he has any special comments to make on any of the items referred to therein.

3. Duty to Follow CARO

Under Section 227 (4A) of the Companies Act, the Central Government has the power to direct by a general or special order that in the case of specified companies, the auditor's report shall include a statement on such matters as may be specified in its order. In accordance with the provision, the Central Government issued revised order in 2003, namely Companies (Auditor's Report) Order. The auditor has the duty to follow the order.

4. Other Duties Under the Companies Act

The auditor has the following other duties under the Companies Act:

   i.   Duty of the auditor or a partner of a firm of Chartered Accountants practicing in India to sign audit report (Section 229).

   ii.   Duty of the auditor to report on prospectus on the accounting part (Section 56).

   iii.   Duty to assist the inspector appointed by the Central Government to investigate the affairs of the company (Section 240).

   iv.   Duty to report on profit and loss account for the period from the last closing date to the date of declaration of insolvency by the directors and also on balance sheet (Section 488).

   v.   Duty to certify the statutory report of the company in respect of shares allotted, cash received in respect of such shares and the receipts and payments of the company [Section 165 (4)].

Contractual Duties

A professional accountant may be hired by a company for purposes other than the statutory audit. In all such cases, the duty of the auditor will depend upon the terms and conditions of his appointment.

Duty to Have Reasonable Care and Skill

An auditor of a company must be honest and must exercise reasonable care and skill to perform his audit work; otherwise he may be sued for damages. It was observed in Kingston Cotton Mills Case (1896) that the auditor should perform his audit work with such care, skill and caution that is reasonably competent, careful and cautious auditor will use.

Duty of an Auditor Regarding Mandatory Accounting Standards

According to the decision of the Council of the Institute of Chartered Accountants of India, it has been resolved that while discharging their functions, it is the duty of the members of the Institute to ensure that the mandatory accounting standards are followed in the presentation of the financial statements covered by their audit report. In the event of any deviation from the standards, it is also be the duty of the auditor to make adequate disclosure in their reports so that the users of such statements may be aware of such deviations.

Section 227 (3) (d) of the Companies Act also states that the auditor's report shall state whether the company's balance sheet and profit and loss account comply with the Accounting Standards referred to in Section 211 (3C).

Duty to the Profession Itself

Every profession has its own code of conduct and professional ethics. The Institute of Chartered Accountants of India has also issued the required code of conduct and professional ethics, which has to be maintained by the members of the Institute. So, it is the duty of the company auditor to follow code of conduct and his professional ethics.

7.7.12 LIABILITIES OF COMPANY AUDITOR

The auditor holds a position of great responsibility and has to perform certain duties, statutory or otherwise, assigned to him. In performing his duties, he has to exercise reasonable care and skill. His client expects him to follow the generally accepted auditing standards and he may be held liable in case he does not act with reasonable care and skill required from him in a particular situation.

The liabilities of an auditor can be described by classifying them under the following categories:

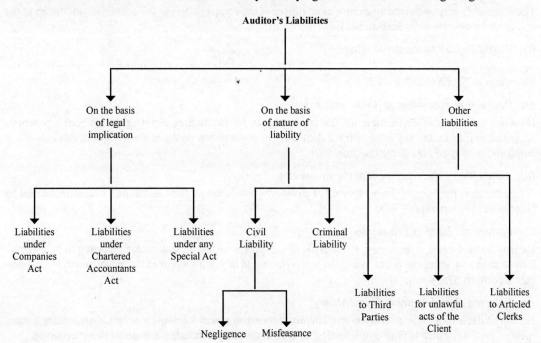

Liabilities on the Basis of Legal Implications

On the basis of legal implication, liabilities may be divided into three categories, namely:

Liabilities Under the Companies Act

Under the Companies Act, the liability of an auditor may arise in the following cases:

(a) Misappropriation and Retention of Client's Money

If an auditor has misapplied or retained or become liable or accountable for any money or property of the company, or has been guilty of any misfeasance or breach of trust in relation to the company, the court may compel him to repay or to restore the money or property of or any part thereof with interest at certain rate or to contribute such sum to the assets of the company by way of compensation *(Section 543)*.

(b) Mis-Statements in the Prospectus

He shall be liable with regard to mis-statements in the prospectus of the company under Section 62. The auditor is liable to pay compensation to every person who subscribes for any shares or debentures on the faith of the prospectus issued by the company for any loss or damage he may have sustained.

(c) False Statement in Returns, Reports, etc.

He shall be liable if he makes a false statement with material particulars in returns, reports or other statements knowing it to be false or omits any material fact knowing it to be material (Section 628).

(d) Intentional False Evidence

He shall be liable if he gives false evidence intentionally upon any examination upon oath or solemn affirmations, authorised under this Act or in any affidavit, deposition or solemn affirmations, in or about the winding up of any company under this Act (Section 629).

(e) Liability for Delinquency

The liquidators may prosecute an auditor as an officer of the company during the course of winding up of the company for delinquency (Section 545).

(f) Willful Default in Report Making

He will be held liable if he willfully makes a default in making his report to the shareholders according to the provisions of Sections 227 and 229 (Section 233).

(g) Destruction, Alteration of Books, etc.

If he is found guilty of destruction, mutilation, alteration, falsification or secreting of any books, papers or securities or if he makes any false or fraudulent entry in any register, books of accounts or documents of the company, he may be held liable (Section 539).

(h) Authorising False Statement in the Prospectus

If he authorises the issue of the prospectus of a company containing a false and untrue statement, he will be held liable (Section 63).

i. Party to the Issue of Prospectus

He may be held liable if he is party to the issue of prospectus including statement purporting to be made by him as an expert, unless he is not interested in the formation or promotion or in the management of the company (Sections 57, 58 and 59).

(j) Inducing Fraudulently to Invest Money

He will be liable if he induces a person fraudulently to invest money by knowingly or recklessly making a statement or promise, which is false or misleading, or if he dishonestly conceals the material fact (Section 68).

Liabilities Under the Chartered Accountants Act

The liability of Chartered Accountant, acting as an auditor, may be in the form of disciplinary proceedings under the Chartered Accountants Act, 1949. It may arise on account of professional misconduct on the part of the auditor.

There are separate provisions for professional misconduct in relation to (a) chartered accountants in practice (b) members of the Institute in service and (c) members of the Institute in general.

The Council, under Section 21, refers the case of professional misconduct on the part of the members to the Disciplinary Committee. The latter holds the enquiry and reports its findings to the Council. In case the Council finds, on the basis on its report that the member is guilty of professional misconduct, it gives chance to the member to explain his conduct. On the basis of hearing, the Council takes necessary fictions. But if the misconduct on the part of the member is other than that specified in the First Schedule of the Chartered Accountants Act, 1949, the Council has to refer the case to the High Court with its recommendations thereon.

Liabilities Under Any Special Act

In addition to the Companies Act and the Chartered Accountants Act, the auditor is also held liable under different special Acts, which are stated below:

(a) Under Banking Companies Regulation Act, 1940

i.   Under Section 46 of the Banking Companies Act, 1940, if an auditor in any return, balance sheet or other document, willfully makes a statement, which is false in any material particular, knowing it to be false, or willfully omits to make a material statement, he will be held responsible.

ii. Under Section 45G, an auditor of a banking company may be publicly examined in the winding up proceedings. On such examination, the High Court may make an order, if he is not found fit to act as an auditor, that he will not act as auditor of any company for such period not exceeding five years as may be specified in the order.

(b) Under the Life Insurance Corporation Act

Under Section 104 of the Life Insurance Corporation Act, 1956 an auditor may be sentenced to imprisonment or fine, or both, if he gives a false statement knowingly in any return, report or other such forms to be issued under the Act.

(c) Under the Indian Penal Code

Under Section 197 of the Indian Penal Code, if any person including auditor issues or signs a certificate required by law to be given or signed, or relating to any fact of which such certificate is by law admissible in evidence, knowing or believing that such certificate is false in any material point, he shall be punishable in the same manner as if he gave false evidence.

(d) Under the Income Tax Act

Under Section 278 of the Income Tax Act, 1961, if any person including an auditor abets or induces in any manner another person to make and deliver an account, statement or declaration relating to any income chargeable to tax which is false and which he either knows to be false or does not believe to be true, he shall be punishable.

Liabilities on the Basis of Nature of Liability

On the basis of nature of liability, it can be divided into two groups:

Civil Liability

The civil liability of an auditor can be for (a) negligence or (b) misfeasance. In these cases, he may be called upon to pay damages as decided by the court.

(a) Liability for Negligence

An auditor is appointed to perform certain duties. To the extent of his duties as an auditor, he acts as an agent of his client. In this capacity, he must exercise reasonable care and skill to perform his duties for which he is employed. If he acts negligently on account of which the client has to suffer loss, the auditor may be held liable and may be called upon to make good the damages, which the client suffered due to his negligence.

It should be noted that if an auditor fails to discover frauds, he might not be failing in his duty. In fact, fraud and other irregularities may not be disclosed by an annual audit and even a detailed audit may not discover certain types of fraud. Under such circumstances, whether the auditor will be held responsible that depends on the fact that whether the auditor should have been able to discover that fraud if he applies reasonable care and skill. If he could, he will be held responsible, otherwise not.

(b) Liability for Misfeasance

The term 'misfeasance' implies breach of trust or breach of duty. An auditor has to perform certain duties, which may arise out of a contract with the client as in the case of sole-proprietor or partnership or it may be statutory as laid down under various statutes. The duties of a company auditor have been statutorily laid down in the Companies Act, 1956. If the auditor does not perform his duties properly and as a result his client suffers, he may be held liable for misfeasance.

It should be noted that according to Section 543, the court might assess damages against delinquent director or other officers of the company, including an auditor for misfeasance or breach of trust. In the case of an auditor, who also comes within the definition of officer in Section 2 (30) for the purpose of this section, if he is guilty of neglect of duty or misfeasance, so as to causes loss to the company in any way, proceedings may be taken under this section against him either independently or other officers or jointly with them.

Criminal Liability

An auditor of a company can be held guilty of criminal offences, if he willfully makes a false statement in any report, return, certificate or balance sheet.

Under Section 628 of the Companies Act, "if an auditor in any report, certificate, Balance sheet, prospectus, statement or other document required by or for the purpose of any of this Act, makes a statement (a) which is false in any material particular, knowing it to be false or (b) omits any material fact, knowing it to be material, he will be held liable on criminal offence".

Again, Section 197 of the Indian Penal Code provides that whoever issues or signs any certificate required by law to be given or signed or relating to any fact which such certificate is by law admissible in evidence, knowing or believing that such certificate is false in any material point, shall be punishable in the same manner as he gave false evidence.

Other Liabilities

The other liabilities of an auditor may include the following:

Liability to Third Parties

There are several persons who completely rely upon the financial statements entitled by the auditor and enter into transactions with the company without any further enquiry. These parties may include creditors, the bankers, the tax authorities, the prospective investors etc.

In general, the auditor is not liable to third parties since no contractual obligation exists between the auditor and the third parties. Since they do not appoint him, he owes no duty to them and hence there is no question of any liability to them. He cannot be held liable unless he owes any duty to the persons, who hold him able for damages caused.

The third parties, however, can hold him liable, if there has been any fraud on the part of the auditor. Even if there is no contractual obligation between the auditor and the third parties, the latter can sue the auditor if the report of the auditor is of such a nature as amounts to fraud.

Liability for Unlawful Act of the Client

An auditor may obtain knowledge about the unlawful acts or defaults committed by his client during the course of his audit. The question arises whether he should form the proper authorities about it and whether he can be held liable if he does not do so. It is a difficult question indeed since it involves breach of confidence placed on him by his client.

Under such circumstances, he must act very carefully. He must not act in such a way, which unnecessarily injures the confidence of his client on him. If required, he should terminate his association with the client rather than open himself to such liability.

Liability to Article Clerks

The auditor may be held liable to his article clerks in the following circumstances:

i. If he does not act honestly with his article clerk.

ii. If he removes any of his article clerks without any prior notice.

iii. If he does not pay the required amount of monthly stipend to the article clerks.

iv. If he gives a false certificate of payment of stipend to his article clerks.

The auditor, however, cannot be held liable to his article clerks to pay compensation to them in case their services are terminated by the auditor. The question of payment of compensation to a retrenched or dismissed worker arises under the Industrial Dispute Act, 1956 only, which is not applicable to article clerks.

7.8 CASE STUDIES

CASE STUDY 1: ON APPOINTMENT OF AUDITORS

Modern Manufacturing Company is an old established private limited company, whose auditor Mr. Sharma has recently died. You have been approached by the directors with a request that your firm accepts appointment as auditor to the company and they have also asked if you, or one of your partners, would accept appointment as a director of the company and if a member of your staff would accept appointment as secretary of the company.

Discussion

a. What steps would be required to be taken by the company to establish your firm's appointment as auditors?
b. Which matters you feel should be included in a suitable letter of engagement?
c. Your proposed reply, giving your reasons, to the requests that you or one of your partners should accept appointment as a director and that a member of your staff should accept appointment as secretary.

CASE STUDY 2: ON APPOINTMENT OF AUDITORS

You have been approached by the partners of Somalia & Co., who carry on retail business, to audit the accounts of their business in place of D. Lochon and Company, who, you are informed, have resigned.

Discussion

You are required to state the following:

a. The action you would take before accepting the nomination, giving your reasons.
b. On the assumption that you accept the nomination, the information which you would require before commencing the detailed audit work for the first year.

CASE STUDY 3: ON APPOINTMENT OF AUDITORS

You have just been appointed as auditor of Hindalco Engineering Company Ltd. to fill up a casual vacancy created by the death of the previous auditor, Mr. V. K. Rattan, a sole practitioner. He has died after carrying out the audit of the company's accounts, but without having signed the audit report to the members for the accounting period.

Discussion

Set out the considerations which apply and the steps which you would take in these circumstances.

CASE STUDY 4: ON RELATED PARTY TRANSACTIONS

You are the auditors of Apollo Services Ltd. and you have recently been reading a report on a similar company that criticised the auditors for failing to comment on the existence of the material related party transactions.

Discussion

a. What do you mean by this term 'Related Party Transactions?'
b. What steps do you consider should be incorporated into your audit work to minimise the risk of similar criticism being levelled at your firm?
c. Illustrate your comment with examples of related parties and types of transactions.

◆ Suggested questions

A   Short-type questions

1.   Write short notes on:
      (a) Issue of shares at premium.
      (b) Payment of interest out of capital.
      (c) Reduction of share capital.
2.   What are the points you will consider at the time of examining the issue of right shares?
3.   State how an auditor should outline the programme suitable for a share transfer audit.
4.   How will you examine the following items while auditing the accounts of a limited company?
      (a) Re-issue of forfeited shares
      (b) Profit prior to incorporation
5.   How are the first auditors of a limited company appointed?
6.   Explain in brief the legal provisions as well as the Schedule VI Requirements regarding auditors' remuneration.
7.   Describe the qualifications of an auditor according to the Chartered Accountants Act, 1949.
8.   Discuss the status of an auditor in the company.
9.   How will you examine the following items while auditing the accounts of a limited company?
      (a) Redemption of preference shares.
      (b) Forfeiture of shares.
10.   State the circumstances when a person will be disqualified for being appointed as company auditor.
11.   How is the auditor of a government company appointed?
12.   Discuss the auditors' liability to third party?

B   **Essay-type questions:**

1.   What are the steps to be taken by a statutory auditor before commencement of an audit of a company?

2.   Mention important items for which auditor would refer to each of the following:

     (a) Minutes book of the Board Meeting

     (b) Minutes book of the Shareholders Meeting.

3.   What are the points to which you would direct your attention while accepting an appointment as an auditor of a company? State under what circumstances an appointed auditor can be removed from his office?

4.   State clearly the rights and duties of an auditor.

5.   'Under the Companies Act, an auditor may be held liable both for negligence and misfeasance'. Do you agree? Give reasons for your answer.

6.   Under what circumstances, an auditor can be appointed by the following:

     i. The Board of Directors

     ii. The Shareholders

     iii. The Central Government.

7.   (a) Discuss the circumstances in which bonus shares can be issued by a company.

     (b) Enumerate the procedures to be followed.

     (c) Explain the duties of the auditor in relation to the above.

8.   State the procedures an auditor should follow to verify the issue of share capital

     (a) for cash,

     (b) for consideration other than cash, and

     (c) for employees as 'sweat equity share'.

9.   Explain the statements:

     (a) "Information and means of information are by no means equivalent terms."

     (b) "An auditor is liable for any damages sustained by a company by reason of falsification, which might have been discovered by exercise of reasonable care and skill in the performance of audit."

10. Discuss the rights of lien of an auditor of a limited company.

Chapter 8

Divisible Profits and Dividends

8.1 MEANING OF DIVISIBLE PROFIT

The portion of profit, which can legally be distributed to the shareholders of the company by way of dividend, is called the 'divisible profit'.

The term 'divisible profit' is not defined in the Companies Act and the Act does not specify what is meant by 'profit'. Only Section 205 of the Act lays down that no dividend can be declared or paid by a company except out of current profits or past undistributed profits or both, arrived at after providing for depreciation or money provided by the government for payment of dividend in pursuance of a guarantee given by the government.

8.2 MEANING OF DIVIDEND

The dictionary meaning of 'dividend' is "sum payable as interest on loan or as profit of a company to the creditors of an insolvent's estate or an individual's share of it". But in commercial usage, however, dividend is the share of the company's profit distributed among the members. So, corporate earnings and profits not retained in the business and distributed among the shareholder share known as dividend. The term 'dividend' is also used to include distribution of the company's assets, in cash or in specie, which remain with the liquidator after he has realised all the assets and discharged all the liabilities, in the event of its winding up.

In *Commissioner of Income Tax vs. Girdhar Das & Co. (P) Ltd.* [1967] case, The Supreme Court defined the expression 'dividend' as follows:

> As applied to a company which is a going concern, it ordinarily means the portion of the profit of the company which is allocated to the holders of shares in the company. In case of winding-up, it means a division of the realised assets among creditors and contributories according to their respective rights.

Before introduction of sub-section 14 (A) in Section 2 of the Companies Act, the term was not defined. At present, according to this section, dividend includes any interim dividend. This definition assumes that the term should be understood only in its commercial sense.

The Institute of Chartered Accountants of India has defined dividend in its Guidance Notes on Terms Used in Financial Statements as "a distribution to shareholders out of profits or reserves available for this purpose".

8.3 CONCEPT OF PROFIT

The main objective of any business organisation is to earn profit, but the term 'profit' does not have any exact meaning in the accountant's language. Profit may be defined "as the increase in the net value of assets of a business over their net value at the commencement of a given period which has arisen other than by capital adjustment".

According to the viewpoint expressed by the Court in the *Spanish Prospecting Co. Ltd. (1911)* case, "the profit of an enterprise can be ascertained by computing the market value of its net assets at two accounting dates. The increase or decrease in the net worth is the profit or loss for the intervening period".

The Institute of Chartered Accountants of India has defined 'profit' in its Guidance Notes on Terms Used in Financial Statement*s* as "the excess of revenue of related costs".

8.4 PROFIT VERSUS DIVISIBLE PROFIT

All the profits of a company cannot be said to be divisible. Only those portions of the profit, which can be legally distributed to the shareholders of the company in the form of dividend, are called as divisible profits. A number of factors are required to be considered for the determination of divisible profit. Out of different important factors, the following four considerations govern the determination of divisible profit to a great extent:

   i.   Accounting Principles

   ii. Provisions of the Companies Act

   iii. Provisions of the Memorandum and Articles of Association and

   iv. Legal Judgments.

8.5 PRINCIPAL DETERMINANTS OF DIVISIBLE PROFIT

Several matters influence the determination of divisible profits. These arise from the provisions of law, case laws and provisions in the Articles of Association of the Company and the principles and policies involved in the determination of true and fair amount of profit. Section 205 of the Companies Act contains provisions relating to declaration of dividend and ascertainment of divisible profit. There are also certain provisions elsewhere in the Act connected with the question of divisible profit. All these provisions are stated below:

Profit After Providing for Depreciation
Dividend can be paid by a company only out of current profit and past profits remaining undistributed, both arrived at after providing for depreciation in accordance with the provisions of the Companies Act. However, the Central Government may, if it thinks necessary so to do in the public interest, allow any company to declare or pay dividend for any financial year out of the profits of the company for that year or any previous financial year or years without providing for depreciation.

As to how much depreciation should be provided for determining the divisible profit, Section 205 (2) provides that depreciation must be provided either:

   i.   to the extent specified in Section 350, or

   ii. in respect of each item of depreciable asset, for such an amount as is arrived at by dividing 95% of the original cost by the specified period, or

   iii. on any other basis approved by the Central Government by which 95% of the original cost of each such depreciable asset can be written off on the expiry of the specified period, or

   iv. in respect of other depreciable asset for which no rate of depreciation has been laid down by the Act or the Rules made there under, on such basis as may be approved by the Central Government by general or special order.

Grant by the Government

Dividend can also be paid out of money made available by the Central or State Government for the payment of dividend in pursuance of a guarantee given by the government.

Arrear Depreciation

If there is any arrear depreciation is respect of past years, it must be provided for out of current or past profits, before paying dividend for any financial year. In other words, where a company has not provided for depreciation for any financial year after the commencement of the Companies (Amendment) Act, 1960, this should be done before any dividend is declared. Such arrears of depreciation may be provided out of current profits or the profits of the previous financial years remaining undistributed.

Past Losses

Any past loss of the company must be set off against current or past profits or on both, to the extent required by the Companies Act, before paying dividend for any financial year. Where a company has incurred any loss in any previous financial year or years falling after the commencement of the Companies (Amendment) Act, 1960, then the lower of the following two amounts should be set off:

— the amount of the loss
— the amount of depreciation provided for that year or those years.

The amount should be set off against:

i. the profits of the company for the year for which dividends are proposed to be declared or paid, or
ii. the profits of the company for any previous financial year or years arrived at after providing for depreciation
iii. both.

Exemption from Depreciation

The Central Government may in the public interest allow any company to pay dividend out of current or past profits without making provisions for depreciation.

Transfer of Profits to Reserves

The current profit of a company arrived at after providing for depreciation can be applied for the payment of dividend only after transfer to reserves such a percentage of profit not exceeding 10% as may be prescribed by the Central Government.

After the commencement of the Companies (Amendment) Act, 1974 a company is required to transfer a prescribed percentage of its profit to its reserves before declaring dividend. However, there is no bar on a company to voluntarily transfer a higher percentage of its profits to the reserves in accordance with such rules as may be made by the Central Government in this context.

According to the Transfer to Reserve Rules, 1984 as framed by the Central Government, the following are the prescribed rates of profit to be transferred to reserve:

RARE OF PROPOSED DIVIDEND	AMOUNT TO BE TRANSFERRED TO RESERVES
Exceeding 10%, but not 12.5%	Not less than 2.5% of Current Profit
Exceeding 12.5%, but not 15%	Not less than 5% of Current Profit
Exceeding 15%, but not 20%	Not less than 7.5% of Current Profit
Exceeding 20%	Not less than 10% of Current Profit

However, no amount is required to be transferred to reserves, where the rate of proposed dividend is 10% or less.

Dividend from Reserves

Dividend can be paid out of the accumulated past profits of a company kept in reserves in accordance with the rules framed by the Central Government in this regard or with the previous approval of the Central Government [Section 328 (3)]. Section 205 (3) of the Companies Act, 1974 (as amended) requires that dividend can be declared out of reserves only in accordance with the rules framed by the Central Government. However, where a company wishes to declare a dividend otherwise than as per these rules, it may do so with the prior approval of the Central Government. The credit balance, if any, carried in the profit and loss account will be available for declaration of dividend without restriction if such balance was carried after charging depreciation, tax etc. in the previous year(s).

The rules framed by the Central Government in this regard provide that in the event of absence or inadequacy of profits in any year, dividend may be declared by the company out of accumulated past profits provided the following conditions are satisfied:

i.   The rate of dividend declared does not exceed the average of the rates at which dividend was declared by the company in the five years immediately preceding that year or 10% of its paid-up capital, whichever is less.

ii. The total amount to be drawn from the accumulated profits earned in previous years and transferred to the reserves does not exceed an amount equal to one-tenth of the sum of its paid-up capital and free reserves and the amount so drawn must first be utilised to set off the losses incurred in the financial year before any dividend in respect of preference or equity shares is declared.

iii. The balance of reserves after such withdrawal does not fall below 15% of its paid-up share capital.

iv. The amount in no way possible to be used to pay interim dividend.

Distribution of Profit Out of Capital Redemption Reserve Account

If Capital Redemption Reserve is created against redemption of preference shares, no dividend can be paid from this reserve in future (Section 80).

Premium on Redemption

The premium payable on redemption of preference shares shall be provided for out of the profits of the company or out of the securities premium account. (Section 80).

Other Determining Factors

(i) Provision for Taxation

No part of the net profit from business can be appropriated for payment of dividend without making necessary provision for taxation, as payment of income tax from business earnings is a legal obligation.

(ii) Dividend Out of Capital Profit

Excepting Securities Premium, profit from forfeiture of shares and profits prior to incorporation, capital profits can be applied for payment of dividend, subject to certain conditions, which include the following:

• Such profits must be realised profits.

• The Articles of Association of the company shall not contain any prohibitive provision relating to distribution of such profits as dividend, and

• Such profits must remain as a surplus after revaluation of all the assets of the company.

(iii) Capital Losses, Intangible Assets and Fictitious Assets

According to the accounting and commercial principles capital losses, intangible assets and fictitious assets should be written off from profits over a reasonable period and a company should have definite policies in respect of such writing off. Application of profit for payment of dividend can only arise after such regular annual write off.

(iv) Transfer of Additional Profits to Reserve

The directors of a company are empowered to transfer to reserves any additional amount of profit or carry forward any amount of profit, as they consider necessary, after statutory transfer of profits to reserves. Dividend can be paid only from the balance amount of profit.

8.6 PROVISIONS OF THE COMPANIES ACT RELATING TO PAYMENT OF DIVIDEND

The provisions of the Companies Act relating to payment of dividend are as follows:

i. Dividend shall only be payable in cash. But this will not prohibit capitalisation of profits or reserves of a company for the purpose of issuing fully paid-up bonus shares or paying up any unpaid amount of shares held by the members of the company [Section 205 (3)].

ii. Dividend payable in cash may be paid by cheque or dividend warrant. This has to be sent by post direct to the registered address of the shareholders entitled to the payment of the dividend or in the case of joint holders to the registered address of that one of the joint shareholders, which is first named in the Register of Members or to such person and to such address as the shareholder or the joint shareholders may in writing direct [Section 205 (4) (b)].

iii. The department of Company Affairs has clarified through its Circular No. 5/99 dated 12.5.1999 that dividend can also be transmitted electronically to the shareholders after obtaining their consent in this regard and asking them to nominate specific bank account number to which dividend due to them should be remitted.

iv. Dividend has to be paid to the registered holder of share or to his order or to his banker. In case a share warrant has been issued in respect of the share in pursuance of Section 114, dividend shall be paid to the bearer of such warrant or to his banker [Section 206].

v. Dividend has to be paid or the dividend warrant has to be posted within 30 days from the date of declaration of dividend, subject to certain exceptions. [Section 205 (4) (1)].

vi. Where a dividend has been declared by a company but has not been paid or the warrant in respect thereof has not been posted within 30 days from the date of the declaration to any shareholder entitled to the payment of the dividend, every director of the company shall, if he is knowingly a party to the default, be punishable with simple imprisonment for a term which may extend to three years and shall also be liable to fine of Rs. 1,000 for every day during which such default continues (Section 207). But the above provision is not applicable in the following circumstances:

(a) Where the dividend could not be paid by reason of the operation of any law,
(b) Where a shareholder has given direction to the company regarding the payment of the dividend and those directions cannot be complied with,
(c) Where there is a dispute regarding the right to receive the dividend,
(d) Where the dividend has been lawfully adjusted by the company against any sum due to it from the shareholder.

(e) Where, for any other reason, the failure to pay the dividend or to post the warrant within the period aforesaid was not due to any default on the part of the company.

vii. Any dividend, when declared, the amount thereof shall have to be deposited in a separate bank account within five days of declaration. The amount of dividend deposited in a separate bank account as above shall be used for the payment of interim dividend [Section 205 (1A)].

8.7 PROVISIONS OF THE COMPANIES ACT REGARDING UNPAID AND UNCLAIMED DIVIDEND

The provisions of the Companies Act regarding unpaid (unclaimed) dividend are as follows:

i. Where, after the commencement of the Companies (Amendment) Act, 1974 a dividend has been declared by a company but has not been paid or claimed within 30 days from the date of the declaration, to any shareholder entitled to the payment of the dividend, the company shall, within 7 days from the date of expiry of the said period of 30 days, transfer the total amount of dividend which remains unpaid or unclaimed to a special account to be opened by the company in that behalf in any scheduled bank to be called 'Unpaid Dividend Account' [Section 205A (1)].

ii. If the default is made in transferring the total amount referred to in sub-section (1) or any part thereof to the unpaid dividend account of the concerned company, the company shall pay from the date of such default, interest at the rate of 12% per annum and the interest accruing on such amount shall be used for the benefit of the members of the company in proportion to the amount remaining unpaid to them [Section 205A (4)].

iii. Any money transferred to the unpaid dividend account of a company in pursuance of this section, which remains unpaid or unclaimed for a period of 7 years from the date of such transfer shall be transferred by the company to the fund known as Investors Education and Protection Fund established under sub-section (1) of Section 205C [Section 205A (5)].

iv. If a company fails to comply with any of the requirements of this section, the company and every officer of the company, who is in default, shall be punishable with fine, which may extend to Rs. 5,000 for every day during which the failure continues [Section 205A (8)].

(a) Any person claiming to be entitled to any money transferred under sub-section (5) of Section 205A to the general revenue account of the Central Government may apply to the Central Government for an order for payment of the money claimed, and the Central Government may, if satisfied, whether on a certificate by the company or otherwise that such person is entitled to the whole or any part of the money claimed, make an order for the payment to that person of the sum due to him after taking such security from him as it may think fit [Section 205B].

8.8 PAYMENT OF DIVIDEND OUT OF CAPITAL PROFIT

Capital profits are profits that arise from capital sources and not from normal trading activity of a business. Capital profits are not frequently earned in a business. These profits are earned from capital transactions and assets revaluation.

Following are the examples of capital profits:

i. Profit prior to incorporation.

ii. Premium received on the issue of shares or debentures.

iii. Profit on forfeiture of shares and re-issue of forfeited shares.

iv. Profit made on sale of fixed assets.

v. Profit on revaluation of fixed assets.

vi. Profit on redemption of debentures at a discount.

Section 205 of the Companies Act provides that dividend can only be paid out of profits. Profits can be both revenue profits and capital profits. So the Companies Act does not provide any general restriction on the distribution of capital profit as dividend. But the following capital profits are not available for distribution of dividend:

Premium on Issue of Shares
As per Section 78 of the Companies Act, premium on issue of shares is available only for certain specified purposes and not for payment of dividend.

Profit on Re-Issue of Forfeited Shares
As per Part I of Schedule VI of the Companies Act, the amount of profit made on forfeiture of shares has to be shown by adding to the called up share capital of the company in its Balance Sheet and the amount of such profit finally left after re-issue of forfeited shares has to be transferred to Capital Reserve.

Profit Prior to Incorporation
A company comes into legal existence only from the date of incorporation. So, the profit earned during the period when the company was not in existence cannot be legally distributed as profit of the company.

Profit from Redemption of Debentures at a Discount
A capital profit earned from the redemption of debentures at a discount is not available for distribution as dividend as was held in the case *Wall vs. London and General Provincial Trust Co. Ltd.* (1930).

8.9   PAYMENT OF DIVIDEND OUT OF CAPITAL

According to the Companies Act, no dividend can be paid out of capital as it expressly provides in Section 205 that the dividend is payable only out of current profit or past undistributed profits, arrived at after providing for depreciation. Therefore, if the Memorandum or the Articles of Association even empower the company to declare dividend out of capital, such power becomes automatically invalid [*Verner vs. General and Commercial Investment Trust Ltd.* (1894)].

In the following circumstances, payment of dividend may amount to payment of dividend out of capital:

i. If dividend is paid out of the sale proceeds of fixed assets.

ii. If profits are inflated by:
  (a) charging revenue expenditure to capital,
  (b) making lower provisions for depreciation or liabilities,
  (c) overvaluing closing stock or investments,
  (d) excluding revenue expenditure from accounts,
  (e) any other way increasing profit.

iii. If a deficiency of capital exists and dividend is paid without making good such deficiency.

Payment of dividend out of capital indicates returning to the shareholders part of the paid-up share capital as dividend. The payment of dividend out of capital has the following consequences:

i. The Directors may have a right of indemnity against the members who knowingly received dividend out of capital. But they lose that right where the Directors represent that the dividend was paid out of profits [*Moxham vs. Grant* (1990)].

ii. In the absence of suspicious circumstances, the Directors are never wrong in accepting the reports and valuation of trusted·officers of the company [*Kingston Cotton Mills Co.* (1896)].

iii. The Directors are personally liable to make good the amount, which they have knowingly paid as dividend out of capital [*London and General Bank* (1895)].

iv. When the payment of dividend out of capital is subsequently made good out of profit, the directors can escape liability [*Boaler vs. The Watchmakers' Alliance and others* (1903)].

v. An auditor cannot held liable for negligence of duty for his inability to detect payment of dividend out of capital, if he has exercised reasonable skill and care and there is no suspicious circumstances for detection of deliberate enhancement of profit [*Kingston Cotton Mills Co. Ltd.* (1896)].

8.10 GENERAL GUIDELINES FOR DISTRIBUTION OF DIVIDEND

Following guidelines govern the distribution of profit as dividend by a company in general way:

i. Dividend can be declared and paid only if the cash position of the company is satisfactory.

ii. Shareholders' capital must not be utilised for the payment of dividend.

iii. A dividend should not be paid without making an adequate provision for depreciation on fixed assets.

iv. Capital profits may be distributed as dividend only if the following conditions are satisfied:
   (a) The Articles of Association of the company permit such a payment,
   (b) Such capital profits have been realised, and
   (c) The surplus remains even after the revaluation of all the other assets.

v. If there is a debit balance in the profit and loss account, dividend should not be distributed.

vi. If goodwill or other assets have been excessively written down in the past, the excess may be written back to profit and loss account and dividend can be distributed out of such profit.

vii. The company should adopt a steady dividend pay-out ratio. It need not distribute the whole of the profit among its shareholders as dividend.

viii. Provision of the Companies Act, Income Tax Act and the decisions of significant legal cases have to be observed and complied with while declaring dividend.

ix. Capital losses, intangible assets and fictitious assets should be written off over a period of time gradually to strengthen the financial position of the company.

x. The provisions of the Memorandum and Articles of Association must be complied with before distributing profit as dividend.

8.11 AUDITOR'S DUTY AS REGARDS PAYMENT OF DIVIDEND

Once dividend is declared, it constitutes an item of liability of the business. As specified above, the Regulation of Clause 85 of Table A of Schedule 1 to the Companies Act states that no dividend shall be paid in excess of the amount of dividend declared. But this does not mean that the company should pay less than what is declared. Accordingly, a company may be sued by the shareholders for such payment as was held in the case *Savern vs. Wye Railway Co.* (1896).

The duties of an auditor in connection with the payment of dividend are as follows:

i. He should examine the documents of the company to ascertain the various rights and privileges of the various categories of the members.

ii. He should also examine the minutes of both Director's and Shareholder's meeting regarding such payments.

iii. He should verify the rate of dividend and justify the rate in the context of the amount of profit earned.

iv. He should see that the unclaimed dividend have been transferred to a separate bank account.

v. He should obtain the Register of Members to justify whether dividend warrants have been sent to the appropriate persons.

vi. He should verify the Articles of Association to verify the authority for such payment.

vii. He should confirm that the declaration of dividend does not affect adversely the working capital position of the company.

viii. He should see that the provisions of the Companies Act relating to declaration and payment of dividend (Section 205) have been duly complied with before declaration and payment of dividend.

ix. He should ensure the basic principles of accounting and provisions regarding transfer of reserves have been duly adhered to while arriving at the distributable profit.

x. He should also consider the rate of interim dividend declared by the company and confirm that it has been considered in the declaration and payment of the final dividend.

8.12 PAYMENT OF INTERIM DIVIDEND AND THE ROLE OF AUDITORS

Interim Dividend is a dividend paid a year before the declaration of the final dividend. This means that it occurs between two annual general meetings and the declaration is done by the directors instead of the shareholders.

Sub-section 1 (A) of Section 205 of the Companies Act empowers the Board of Directors of a company to declare interim dividend. Clause 86 of Table A of Schedule 1 to the Companies Act provides that the Board may from time to time pay to the members such interim dividend as appeared to be justified from the profits of the company. Generally, the Articles of Association of a company gives this power to the Board of Directors. Till the passing of the Companies (Amendment) Act, 2000, there was no provision in the Companies Act (except Regulation 86 of Table A) relating to interim dividend. The Companies (Amendment) Act, 2000 has introduced sub-section 14 (A) in Section 2 whereby 'interim dividend' is now part of dividend and accordingly all provisions of the Companies Act relating to dividends have become applicable to interim dividend also.

To clarify all matters beyond doubt, Section 205 has also been amended to provide for the following:

i. The Board of Directors may declare interim dividend and the amount of dividend including interim dividend shall be deposited in a separate bank account within five days from the date of declaration of such dividend.

ii. The amount of dividend including interim dividend so deposited above shall be used for the payment of dividend including interim dividend.

iii. The provisions contained in Sections 205, 205A, 205C, 206, 206A and 207, as far as may be, also apply to interim dividend.

Often an auditor's advice is sought in the matter of payment of interim dividend. Following points are required to be considered by the auditor while giving advice to the management:

i. Interim profit and loss account should be prepared, if possible by a fair estimate of the closing stock.

ii.   Where the closing stock value at the end of the interim period cannot be fairly ascertained, a rough estimate of profit can be made by applying the gross profit percentage to sales and deducting from such gross profit the expenses to date.

iii. All adjustments on account of bad and doubtful debts, depreciation, outstanding liability, prepaid expenses etc. should be duly made to ascertain the fair profit for the interim period.

iv.   The proportion of interim profit to be applied to the payment of interim dividend should always be on the conservative approach after consideration of the forecasts for the future months and the allowances required for contingencies.

v.   A good cash balance should not be taken as an indicator of profit for the purpose of interim dividend. However, cash is also another deciding factor.

vi.   Future requirement of cash for expenses, asset replacement, loan repayment and working capital requirement should be fairly estimated. A good cash position does not always justify the payment of interim dividend, as the future cash requirement for those purposes may be quite substantial.

vii. It is the final dividend which has to be declared after the closing of the accounting year at a rate reasonably higher than the rate of interim dividend. Hence, it should be seen whether the company would be able to declare final dividend at a higher rate or not.

In paying interim dividend, the directors undertake certain amount of risk, because an interim dividend is, in fact, a dividend in respect of the whole year and if company makes a loss for the year, the payment of interim dividend will amount to payment of dividend out of capital, in case there are inadequate balances of reserves and surplus.

◆ Suggested questions

A   Short-type questions:

1.   What is dividend?

2.   What is interim dividend? When the question of interim dividend arises?

3.   State with reasons whether you, as an auditor, would approve the payment of dividend out of capital.

4.   Can dividend be paid out of current profit without writing off intangible and fictitious Assets?

5.   Can dividend be paid out of profit arising out of forfeited and re-issue of shares?

B   Essay-type questions:

1.   State the provisions of the Companies Act, 1956 regarding the declaration and payment of dividend.

2.   Can dividend be paid under the following circumstances:
     (a) Out of current profit without making good past losses?

     (b) Out of a capital profit.

     (c) Out of past profit when there is neither profit nor loss in the current year.

     (d) Realised capital profits.

3.   State the provisions of the Companies Act, 1956 regarding declaration and payment of interim dividend. What would be the duty of an auditor in connection with such a dividend?

4.   What do you understand by 'divisible profit'? State what considerations should be borne in mind before declaring dividend.

5. While examining the accounts of a company, you find the following items on credit side of profit and loss account:

   (a) Profit on revaluation of land.

   (b) Bounties received from Central Government.

   (c) Excess depreciation charged in the previous year now written back.

   (d) Unclaimed dividend.

   Would you have any objection as auditor in passing the accounts of the company? State with reasons.

Chapter 9

Audit Report and Certificate

9.1 DEFINITION OF REPORT

A report is a statement of collected and considered facts, so drawn up as to give clear and concise information to persons who are not in possession of the full facts of the subject matter of the report. According to Joseph Lancaster, "A report is a medium of expressing an opinion to persons concerned in order to give clear and summarised information based on collected facts and figures".

9.2 DEFINITION OF AUDIT REPORT

An auditor, under Section 227 (2) of the Companies Act, 1956, is required to make a report to the shareholders of the company whether the books of accounts examined by him exhibit 'true and fair' view of the state of affairs of the business.

The auditor submits his report to his client giving clear and concise information of the result of audit performed by him. The fact or information contained in the auditor's report is not available from any other source.

The statutory auditor of a company has to express his professional opinion about the truth and fairness of the state of affairs of the company as shown by the Balance Sheet and of the profit or loss as shown by the Profit and Loss Account in addition to other information in his report.

An auditor's report is, therefore, a written statement of the auditor, containing his independent professional opinion about the truth and correctness of accounts and financial statements examined by him and other specific information, which the auditor submits to his client at the conclusion of audit.

9.3 VALUE OF AUDIT REPORT

The auditor's report is of great value not only to the members of the company, i.e., the shareholders, but also to those persons who are interested in the affairs of the business, i.e., investors, creditors, employees, government and other financial institutions who require the audited Balance Sheet and Profit and Loss Account for the purpose of granting loans. The most important value of the auditor's report is reflected through its checking and verifying procedure as to accuracy and fairness of the facts and figures that appear in the books of accounts of the company. The audit report does not add anything more than what is provided in the books of accounts.

In view of changing socio-economic condition where the society demands more disclosure of accounting information, the auditor should insist on more disclosure by his clients to appraise the actual financial position of the business. It is a fact that the auditor makes his report on the available information supplied to him. So, his tests and examinations are confined to available information supplied to him. His duty is to report if certain items appear to him suspicious and he has no other motive.

9.4 ESSENTIALS OF GOOD AUDIT REPORT

The essentials of good audit report are as follows:

Simplicity
Simplicity should be one of the important characteristics of good audit report. It should be as clear as understandable. It implies that ambiguous terms and facts should not be included in the audit report.

Clarity
The term 'clarity' implies cleanness in audit report. This indicates that the audit report should not conceal material information, which is required for evaluating and appraising the performance of the business.

Brevity
The term 'brevity' signifies the conciseness in audit report. Repetition of facts and figures should be avoided in order to control the length of the report.

Firmness
The report should clearly indicate the scope of work to be done and should clearly indicate whether the books of accounts exhibit 'true and fair' view of the state of affairs of the business.

Objectivity
The report should be based on objective evidence. Opinion formed on the basis of information and evidences, which are not measured in terms of money, should not be incorporated in the audit report.

Consistency
Consistency in presenting accounting information is the basis of good audit report. A good audit report should take into consideration whether consistency, as to the method of stock valuation and depreciation charges, has been adhered to.

Accepted Principles
The audit report should be based upon the facts and figures that are kept in accordance with generally accepted accounting principles.

Disclosure Principles
The audit report should be unbiased. It should disclose all the facts and the truth.

9.5 SCOPE OF AUDIT REPORT

Sub-sections 2 and 3 of Section 227 provide that it is the duty of the auditor to report to the members of the company on the accounts examined by him and on the Balance Sheet and Profit and Loss Account and every other documents declared by the Act to be part of or annexed to the Balance Sheet and the Profit and Loss Account, laid before the company in general meeting during the tenure of his office, also that the report shall confirm the position, envisaged in the undermentioned manner in which the requirements are to be met.

Sub-section 2 specifically requires that the auditor should report whether in his opinion and to the best of his information and according to the explanations given to him, the said accounts give the information required by the Companies Act, 1956 in the manner so required and the Balance Sheet gives a true and fair view of the company's affairs at the end of the financial year and the Profit and Loss Account gives a true and fair view of the profit and loss for the financial year.

Sub-section 3 requires that the auditor should report on the following matters:

i. Whether he has obtained all the information and explanations which to the best of his knowledge and belief were necessary for his audit.

ii. Whether in his opinion, proper books of account as required by law have been kept by the company, so far as appears from his examination of those books and proper returns adequate for the purpose of his audit have been received from branches not visited by him.

iii. Whether in his opinion, the balance sheet and the profit and loss account comply with the accounting standards referred to in sub-section 3C of Section 211 of the Companies Act, 1956.

iv. Whether the company's balance sheet and profit and loss account dealt with by the report are in agreement with the books of account and returns.

v. Whether the report on the accounts of any branch office audited under Section 228 by a person other than the company's auditor has been forwarded to him as required by Section 228 (3) (c) and how he has dealt with the same in preparing the auditor's report.

The duty of any auditor for making a report on the statement of account also extends to matters reported upon by the directors to the shareholders in so far as information which is required to be given by the Act in the statements of account or can be given in a statement annexed to the accounts are contained in the report of directors (proviso to Section 222). For instance, the opinion of the Board of Directors as regards current assets, loans and advances, when contained in the directors' report, must be considered by the auditor.

9.6 SIGNING OF THE AUDIT REPORT

According to Section 229 of the Companies Act, only the person appointed as the auditor of the company or where a firm is so appointed, only a partner in the firm practicing in India may sign the auditor's report.

The Department of Company Affairs, Government of India, in a communication dated 29.7.1972 has expressed the view that when a single chartered accountant is practicing, there cannot be any question of any firm name. Further, it is stated that Section 229 of the Act clearly provides that if a firm of chartered accountants is appointed as auditor, only a partner in the firm may sign the auditor's report or sign or authenticate any other document required by law to be signed by the auditor. The practice of merely affixing the 'firm name' on the report or such other document is the correct approach in the eye of law.

According to Section 233 of the Companies Act, if an auditor's report or any document of the company is signed or authenticated otherwise than in conformity with the requirements of Section 229, the auditor concerned and the person, if any, other than the auditor who signs the report or signs or authenticates the document shall, if the default is willful, be punishable with a fine which may extend up to Rs. 1,000.

According to Section 230 of the Companies Act, the auditor's report must be read before the shareholders of the company in general meeting and should be kept open for the inspection of every member of the company.

According to Section 232, it is no part of duty of the auditor either to send a copy of his report to or allow inspection thereof by each member of the company individually; to see that the report is read before the company in general meeting. For non-compliance with any of the requirements of Section 225 to 231, the company and every officer of the company who is in default will be liable to a fine which may extend up to Rs. 500.

9.7 CONTENTS OF AUDIT REPORT

As per the provisions of Section 227 of the Companies Act, 1956 the following matters are required to be included in the auditor's report of a company:

i. Whether in his opinion and to the best of his information and according to the explanations given to him:

(a) The accounts of the company examined by him give the information required by the Companies Act in the manner so required.

(b) The accounts give a true and fair view of the state of company's affairs as at the end of its financial year in the case of the Balance Sheet.

(c) The accounts also give a true and fair view of the profit or loss of the company for its financial year in the case of the Profit and Loss account.

ii. Whether he has obtained all the information and explanations, which, to the best of his knowledge and belief, were necessary for the purpose of his report.

iii. Whether in his opinion, proper books of accounts as required by law have been kept by the company so far as appears from his examination of those books.

iv. Whether proper returns adequate for the purpose of his audit have been received from branches not visited by him.

v. Whether the report on the accounts of any branch office audited by a person other than the main auditor of the company has been forwarded to him.

vi. How he has dealt with the Branch Auditor's Report in preparing his audit report.

vii. Whether the Profit and Loss Account and Balance Sheet of the company are in agreement with the books of accounts and returns.

viii. Whether in his opinion the Balance Sheet and the Profit and Loss Account comply with the accounting standards.

ix. Where any of the matters in the auditor's report is answered in the negative or with a qualification, the reasons for such should also be stated.

x. A statement on such matters as may be specified in the Central Government orders. Presently the company auditors are required to make a statement on the matters specified in the CARO, 2003 issued by the Central Government, so far as they are applicable to a particular class of company.

9.8 FORMS OF AUDIT REPORT

International Auditing Guidelines issued by the International Federation of Accountants (first issued in 1983 and revised in 1989) provide guidance on the form and content of the auditor's report to be issued after the examinations of financial statements.

As per the guideline, the basic elements of the report are as follows:

Title

An appropriate title such as 'Auditor's Report' helps the reader to identify the report and to distinguish it from reports issued by others.

Address

The report should be properly addressed. Like in the case of a statutory audit of a company, the report is addressed to the shareholders and in case of special audit; it is addressed to the Government.

Identification of Financial Statements
The financial statements can be identified by including the name of the organisation and the date and period covered by the financial statements.

Reference to Auditing Standards and Practices
Such a reference ensures the compliance of the resolution of the ICAI and assured the readers that the accounting and auditing standards have been complied with.

Opinion on the Financial Statements
The report should clearly state the auditor's opinion on the financial position and operational result of the organisation.

Signature
The report should be signed in the name of the firm or personal name of the auditor or both.

Address of the Auditor
The report should give the address of the firm.

Date of the Report
It should be properly dated.

9.9 BASIC ELEMENTS OF AUDIT REPORT

As prescribed in Standards on Auditing-700, the auditor's report includes the following basic elements, ordinarily in the following layouts:

i.   **Title:** The auditor's report should have an appropriate title.

ii. **Addressee:** Generally, the auditor's report is addressed to the authority appointing the auditor.

iii. **Opening or introductory paragraph:** The report should include a statement that the financial statements are the responsibility of the management of the organisation and a statement that the responsibility of the auditor is to express an opinion on the financial statements based on the audit. In short, the opening paragraph shall include:
   (a) identification of the financial statements audited, and
   (b) statement of the responsibility of the organisation's management and the responsibility of the auditor.

iv. **Scope paragraph:** The auditor's report should describe the scope of the audit by stating that the audit was conducted in accordance with auditing standards accepted in India. The report should include a statement that the audit was planned and performed to obtain reasonable assurance whether the financial statements are free from material misstatement. In short, the scoping paragraph shall include:
   (a) a reference to the auditing standards generally accepted in India, and
   (b) a description of the work performed by the auditor.

v.   **Opinion paragraph:** The opinion paragraph of the auditor's report should clearly indicate the financial reporting framework used to prepare the financial statements and state the auditor's opinion as to whether the financial statements give a true and fair view in accordance with that financial reporting framework. In addition to an opinion on the true and fair view, the auditor's report may need to include an opinion as to whether the financial statements comply with other requirements specified by relevant statutes or law. In short, the opinion paragraph shall include:
   (a) a reference to the financial reporting framework used to prepare the financial statements, and
   (b) an expression of opinion on the financial statements.

vi. **Date of the report:** The date of report informs the reader that the auditor has considered the effect on the financial statements and on the report of the events and transactions of which the auditor became aware and that occurred up to that date.

vii. **Place of signature:** The report should name specific location, which is ordinarily the city where the audit report is signed.

viii. **Auditor's signature:** The report should be signed by the auditor in his personal name along with the membership number assigned by the Institute. Where the firm is appointed as the auditor, the report should be signed also in the personal name of the auditor and in the name of the audit firm.

9.10 AUDIT REPORT AND AUDIT CERTIFICATE

When an auditor certifies a financial statement, it implies that the contents of the statement are reliable as the auditor has vouched for the exactness of the data. The term 'certificate' is, therefore, used to mean confirmation of the truth and correctness of something after a verification of certain exact facts. An auditor may therefore certify the circulating figures of a newspaper or the value of imports and exports of a company.

The term 'certificate' should not be confused with the term 'report'. While a certificate affirms the truth and correctness of a fact, figure or a statement, a report is generally a statement of facts or an expression of opinion regarding the truth and fairness of the facts, figures and statements.

9.11 TYPES OF AUDITOR'S REPORT

Auditor's report can be of the following types:

Clean Report
An audit report is clean, where there is no qualified or adverse opinion or disclaimer of opinion in the report. A clean report indicates that the auditor is satisfied with all the points required to be stated in his report and states them in the affirmative, adding no reservation anywhere.

Qualified Report
When an auditor expresses an opinion in his report with a reservation or states anything in the negative, but its nature is such that it does not materially affect the true and fair picture shown by the accounts, then the auditor's report is said to be a qualified report.

Adverse Report
When the auditor expresses an adverse or negative opinion in his report about the principal point in the report for which audit is mainly intended, the report is called an adverse report.

Disclaimer of Opinion
When an auditor is unable to express an opinion due to certain reasons and states this in his report, it becomes a report with a disclaimer of opinion. A disclaimer of opinion is always required to be supported by the justified facts.

Piecemeal Report
Auditor's opinion in his report may not be on the entire financial statements. Such opinion may relate to some of the items contained in the statements on which only he can satisfactorily express opinion after audit.

Such an opinion as a part of the financial statement is a piecemeal opinion and the auditor's report containing such opinion is called a piecemeal report.

9.12 MODIFIED REPORTS

An auditor's report is considered to be modified when it includes:

   i.   Matters that do not affect the auditor's opinion

   ii.   Matters that do affect the auditor's opinion

9.12.1 MATTERS THAT DO NOT AFFECT THE AUDITOR'S OPINION

In certain circumstances, an auditor's report may be modified by adding an emphasis of matter paragraph to highlight a matter affecting the financial statements, which is included in a note to the financial statements that more extensively discusses the matter. The addition of such an emphasis of matter paragraph does not affect the auditor's opinion.

9.12.2 MATTERS THAT DO AFFECT THE AUDITOR'S OPINION

An auditor may not be able to express an unqualified opinion when either of the following two circumstances exists and in the auditor's judgement, the effect of the matter is or may be material to the financial statements:

   i.   there is a limitation on the scope of the auditor's work; or

   ii.   there is a disagreement with management regarding the acceptability of the accounting policies selected, the method of their application or the adequacy of financial statement disclosures.

The circumstances described in (a) above could lead to a qualified opinion or a disclaimer of opinion. The circumstances described in (b) above could lead to a qualified opinion or an adverse opinion.

9.13 TYPES OF AUDIT CERTIFICATE

The professional accountants are sometimes required to issue certificate on many occasions. In fact, the types of certificate depend on the purpose for which they are intended. The major types of certificates include the following:

Certificate for Tax Computation

The Chartered Accountants are sometimes required to certify certain incomes and expenses for obtaining exemptions from income tax, which is computed on the basis of provisions as contained in the Income Tax Act, 1961. The forms and contents of these types of certificates are usually provided under Income Tax Rules, as the appropriate wordings of the certificate depend on the nature and circumstances of individual cases.

Certificate of Import and Export

Import and Export Trade Control Rules and Procedures provide that the applicant applying for import or export license must furnish a certificate of import and/or export from a practicing qualified accountant. These certificates include the value of goods imported or exported, goods consumed by the organisation out of imported goods, goods supplied by the organisation for export out of own source and from other sources and the unutilised value of license on hand.

Certificate of Circulation

The Audit Bureau of Circulations Ltd., which is an association of advertisers and publishers, gives report of circulation figures of publication of its members. The association issues circulation certificate on the basis of audit report of the member. The auditor has to certify the circulation figure on the basis that he has checked and verified the books regarding newsprint consumption, distribution and unsold stock of publications as per the guidelines issued under A.B.C. Audit Procedure.

9.14   AUDITOR'S REPORT AND 'TRUE AND FAIR' VIEW

The Companies Act, 1956 has introduced the words 'true and fair' in place of the words 'true and correct' as appearing in the Companies Act, 1913. This is an important change and has far reaching effects.

The phrase 'true and correct' means that the financial statements are arithmetically correct and that they correspond to the figures in the books of accounts. But it does not specifically mean that the financial statements are representing the actual state of affairs and actual working results. In fact, at present the auditor is supposed to verify whether the books of accounts show a true and fair view of the state of affairs of the company as well as the true and fair view of the financial result of the company.

The phrase 'true and fair' thus signifies in the auditor's report that the financial statements are representing a fair and actual financial position of the company and profit and loss for the period. It means that the financial statements are disclosing all the relevant information as are required by various provisions of the Companies Act.

The major criticism of the phrase 'true and correct' was that in an accounting sense, there was insufficient distinction between the words 'true' and 'correct'. As such, every figure in the accounts could he justified and substantiated as both true and correct but, at the same time, the figures together could present a view to the person who reads the accounts, which could be misleading or even totally false when the accounts were read as a whole.

It was for this reason that the word 'fair' was used to replace 'correct', despite the inherent vagueness and absence of precision that the former word implies. The word 'fair', by definition, requires a judgement which can only be determined subjectively. This subjectivity and the related exercising of judgement provide the term with its true strength, at the same time it provides the auditor with his greatest challenge.

An auditor's assessment of whether accounts give a true and fair view, lacking as it does any legal or professional definition, necessitates a consideration of the accounts as a whole and the forming of an opinion concerning the overall impression conveyed by the accounts to the auditor and therefore to a reader. It also involves consideration of the substance of the information disclosed in the accounts as well as its form. In fact, the phrase 'true and fair' attempts to explain that accounts cannot be exact in all aspects due to the subjectivity of certain items, such as the valuation of closing stock and the provision for doubtful debts. The word 'fair' implies that the user should take an overall view of the financial statements and base interpretations on the figures as a set rather than an individual item. The word 'true' implies that the figures are decided on the facts as seen by the directors and the auditor but that other persons may draw different conclusions from the same facts. There is no attempt to make accounts precise in terms of mathematical accuracy as this is not possible due to need of estimation in certain cases. However, an attempt is made to ensure that the financial statements fairly reflect the company's result for the period and its state of affairs at the balance sheet date.

In view of the discussion as above, it can be stated that the concept 'true and fair' that are used in the auditor's report, is not appropriate in present day dynamic and complex nature of business environment. So, it is advocated that the audit report, which should be free from criticism as to nature and pattern of disclosing material information, should not use these equivocal words 'true and fair'. It is expected that the Companies Act should be duly amended for taking a special care in this matter.

9.15 SPECIMEN OF CLEAN AUDIT REPORT

To
The Shareholders
XYZ Company Ltd., Kolkata

Dear Members,

I/we have audited the annexed Balance Sheet of XYZ Co. Ltd. as at 31st March, 200x and also the Profit and Loss Account of the company for the year ended on that date and report that:

i.   We have obtained all the information and explanations which to the best of my/our knowledge and belief were necessary for the purpose of audit.

ii. In my/our opinion proper books of accounts as required by law have been kept by the company so far as appears from my/our examination of such books and proper returns adequate for the purpose of my/our audit have been received from the branches not visited by us.

iii. The accounts of Chennai branch office have been audited u/s 228 of the Companies Act by Subrata Renuka and Co. The report of the said accounts which has been forwarded to us has been dealt with by us, in the manner we have considered necessary, while preparing this report.

iv. The Balance Sheet and the Profit and Loss Account dealt with in this report are in agreement with the books of accounts.

v.   In my/our opinion and to the best of my/our information and according to the explanations given to me/us, the said accounts, together with the notes thereon, give the information required by the Act in the manner so required and give a true and fair view:

(a) In the case of the Balance Sheet of the state of the affairs of the company as at 31st March, 200x and

(b) In the case of Profit and Loss Account of the profit of the company for the year ended on that date.

Kolkata   For G. G. Basu & Co.
Date ....   Chartered Accountants
                                                             Signature ....
                                                             B. B. Basu (Partner)

9.16 SPECIMEN OF QUALIFIED AUDIT REPORT

To
The Shareholders
ABC Co. Ltd., Mumbai

Dear Members,

We have audited the annexed Balance Sheet of the ABC Co. Ltd. as at 31st March 200x and also the profit and loss account for the year ended on that date. We report that:

i. We have obtained all the information and explanations, which to the best of our knowledge and belief were necessary for the purpose of audit.

ii. In our opinion, proper books of accounts as required by law have been maintained by the company, kept in accordance with the accounting standards, so far as it appears from our examination of the books subject to the comments given here under:

    (a) The stocks of the company have been valued at a current replacement price, which is higher than the cost price to the extent of Rs. 1,03,000.

    (b) Provisions for bad and doubtful debts have not been taken into consideration, which should have been taken in view of the fact that some of the debts are quite old and time-barred.

    (c) In the absence of Stock Registers, adjustments relating to the balances on the register have been accepted on the basis of the decisions of the management.

iii. The Balance Sheet and Profit and Loss Account dealt with by the report are in agreement with the books of accounts and returns.

iv. Subject to the qualifications given above, in our opinion and to the best of information available and according to the explanations given to us, the said accounts, with the notes thereon and documents attached thereto give the information required by the law and accounting standards and gives a true and fair view:

    (a) In the case of the Balance Sheet of the state of affairs of the company as at 31 March, 200x and

    (b) In the case of the Profit and Loss Account of the profit for the year ended on that date.

Mumbai
Date ....

                     For B. K. Basu & Co.
                     Chartered Accountants
                     Signature ....
                     B. K. Basu (Partner)

◆ Suggested questions

A   Short-type questions

1. What do you mean by 'Auditor's Report'?
2. What is piecemeal report?
3. Distinguish between auditor's report and auditor's certificate.
4. Is there any difference between an adverse and a qualified report?
5. "Information and means of information are by no means equivalent terms". Explain.
6. What are the contents and format of an audit report?

B   Essay-type questions

1. (a) What is meant by auditor's report?

    (b) Discuss the characteristics of a good audit report.

    (c) What is the value of auditor's report?

2. State the matters required by the Companies Act, 1956 to be stated in auditor's report to the share-holders on the accounts of a company audited by such auditor.
3. What is a clean report? Give a specimen of a clean report of the auditor.
4. What is a qualified report? Give a specimen of a qualified report of the auditor.
5. How many types of audit report may be submitted by a company auditor and under what circumstances? Discuss briefly.
6. Under Section 227 (4A) of the Companies Act (1988), some additional information is to be given by the auditor in his report to the shareholders. State them.
7. What are the events that may occur after the preparation of Balance Sheet? Do you think that those events should be incorporated in the auditor's report?

Chapter 10

Audit of Banks

10.1 INTRODUCTION

A well-organised and efficient banking system is a pre-requisite for economic growth. Banks play an important role in the functioning of organised money markets. They act as a conduit for mobilising funds and channelising them for productive purposes. The Indian banking system, like the banking system in other countries, has played a significant role in the economic growth of the country. In order to meet the banking needs of various sections of the society, a large network of bank branches has been established. The volume of operations and the geographical spread of banks in India are steadily on the rise.

10.2 LEGISLATION RELEVANT TO AUDIT OF BANKS

Different legislative Acts are relevant to audit of different types of banks. An auditor should know the specific provisions of the Act(s) applicable to the type of bank under audit.

Following are the important Acts relevant for bank audit:

i.   Nationalised banks are governed by the provisions of the relevant Banking Companies (Acquisition and transfer of Undertakings) Act. Certain provisions of the Banking Regulation Act, 1949 also apply to nationalised banks.

ii. The non-nationalised banking companies are governed by the provisions of the Banking Regulation Act, 1949 and provisions of the Companies Act, 1956, which are not inconsistent with the provisions of the Banking Regulation Act, 1949.

iii. The Co-operative Societies Act, 1912, or the Co-operative Societies Act of the state in which they are situated, as well as Part V of the Banking Regulation Act, 1949, governs co-operative banks.

iv. The Regional Rural Banks Act, 1976, governs regional rural banks. The provisions of the State Bank of India Act, 1955 and State Bank of India (Subsidiary Banks) Act, 1959 apply to State Bank of India and its subsidiaries, respectively. Certain specified provisions of the Banking Regulation Act, 1949 are also applicable to regional rural banks as well as to State Bank of India and its subsidiaries.

Besides the above, the provisions of the Reserve Bank of India Act, 1934 also affect the functioning of banks. This Act gives wide powers to the Reserve Bank of India to give directions to banks.

10.2.1 LEGAL PROVISIONS RELATING TO ACCOUNTS

Section 29 of the Banking Regulation Act deals with the obligations of banks regarding maintenance of accounts and preparation of financial statements. According to the provisions of this section:

i.   Every bank has to prepare a balance sheet and a profit and loss account as on March 31 every year in the forms set out in the Third Schedule to the Act or as near thereto as the circumstances admit.

ii. The financial statements of banks are to be signed by the manager or the principal officer and by at least three directors.

iii. In case of banking companies, the provisions of the Companies Act, 1956 relating to financial statements are also applicable to the extent they are not inconsistent with the requirements of the Banking Regulation Act, 1949.

iv. As per the Third Schedule to the Banking Regulation Act, the balance sheet of a bank is to be prepared in vertical form and assets and liabilities will be classified as in the following manner:

CAPITAL AND LIABILITIES	ASSETS
1. Capital	1. Cash and balances with RBI
2. Reserves and surplus	2. Balances with banks and money at call and short notice
3. Deposits	3. Investments
4. Borrowings	4. Advances
5. Other Liabilities and Provisions	5. Fixed Assets
	6. Other Assets

Besides the above, contingent liabilities and bills for collection are also to be disclosed.

v. The profit and loss account is also required to be prepared in vertical form and it will show the main items of income (interest earned and other income), expenditure (interest expended, operating expenses and provisions) and appropriations.

Apart from the requirements of the Third Schedule to the Banking Regulation Act, 1949, the financial statements of a bank have to include additional disclosures required by Reserve Bank of India from time to time. The RBI has issued detailed notes and instructions for compilation of balance sheet and profit and loss account of banks. These notes and instructions are very useful to the auditor.

10.2.2 LEGAL PROVISIONS RELATING TO AUDIT

The legal provisions relating to bank auditors are as follows:

Appointment of Auditors

The auditor of a bank has to be a person who is duly qualified under law to be an auditor of a company. So, Section 226 of the Companies Act applies in case of appointment of an auditor of a bank. Previous approval of RBI is required for appointment of an auditor of a bank. The following are the appointing authorities of auditors of banks:

BANK	APPOINTING AUTHORITY
1. Nationalised Banks	Board of Directors
2. Banking Companies	Shareholders in AGM
3. State Bank of India	RBI in consultation with Central Government
4. Subsidiaries of State Bank of India	State Bank of India
5. Regional Rural Banks	Concerned Bank with the approval of Central Government

A detailed procedure is followed for appointment of central auditors as well as branch auditors of nationalised banks including State Bank of India and its subsidiaries. Each nationalised bank usually appoints four to six statutory central auditors and one auditor for each of its branches.

Procedure of Appointment

1. Central Statutory Auditors

The statutory central auditors are appointed by the bank concerned on the basis of the names recommended by RBI from out of a panel of auditors. The RBI formulates required norms on the basis of which a panel is formed by the Comptroller and Auditor General of India.

2. Branch Auditors

For the appointment of branch auditors in case of nationalised banks including State Bank of India and its subsidiaries, RBI maintains a panel, which is prepared by ICAI. ICAI invites applications for this purpose for empanelment. On the basis of these applications, ICAI prepares and sends the panel to RBI.

The remuneration of statutory central auditors as well as branch auditors is fixed on the basis of certain norms laid down by RBI.

Rights and Liabilities of Auditors

The auditor of a bank has the same rights and liabilities as those of a company auditor with the following exceptions:

1. Re: Right

The rights and powers of the auditors of a co-operative bank are governed by the relevant Co-operative Societies Act.

2. Re: Liabilities

If a person, in any return, balance sheet or other document, wilfully and knowingly makes a statement, which is false in any material particular or wilfully omits to make a material statement, he is liable for punishment with imprisonment for a term that may extend to 3 years and is also liable to fine: Section 46 of the Banking Regulation Act.

Special Audit

In addition to the normal audit, a special audit of a bank can be ordered by RBI under Section 30 (1B) of the Banking Regulation Act. If the RBI is of the opinion that it is necessary to do so in public interest or in the interest of the bank or its depositors, it can give the order for special audit.

For conducting the special audit, RBI may either appoint any person who is qualified to act as a company auditor or direct the statutory auditor of the bank to conduct the special audit.

10.3   APPROACH TO BANK AUDIT

Banks have the following characteristics, which distinguish them from most other commercial enterprises:

i.   **Rigorous Internal Control System:** They have custody of large volumes of monetary items, including cash and negotiable instruments, whose physical security has to be ensured. This applies to both the storage and the transfer of monetary items and makes banks vulnerable to misappropriation and fraud. They, therefore, need to establish formal operating procedures and well-defined limits for individual discretion and rigorous systems of internal control.

ii.   **Complex Accounting System**: They engage in a large volume variety of transactions in terms of both number and value. This necessarily requires complex accounting and internal system.

iii. **Greater Decentralisation of Authority:** They normally operate through a wide network of branches and departments, which are geographically dispersed. This necessarily involves a greater decentralisation of authority and dispersal of accounting and control functions, with consequent difficulties in maintaining uniform operating practices and accounting systems, particularly when the branch network transcends national boundaries.

iv.   **Off-Balance-Sheet Items:** They often assume significant commitments without any transfer of funds. These items, commonly called 'off-balance-sheet' items, may not involve accounting entries and, consequently, the failure to record such items may be difficult to detect.

v.   **Regulatory Requirements:** They are regulated by governmental authorities and the resultant regulatory requirements often influence accounting and auditing practices in the banking sector.

Special audit considerations arise in the audit of banks because of the following:

i.   **Risk Attachment:** The particular nature of risk associated with the transactions undertaken by banks.

ii.   **Scale of Banking Operation:** The scale of banking operations and the resultant significant exposures, which can arise within short periods of time.

iii. **Statutory Requirement Effect:** The continuing development of new services and banking practices, which may not be matched by the concurrent development of accounting principles and auditing practices.

The auditor should consider the effect of the above factors in designing his audit approach.

It is imperative that audit plan and schedule of audit work is to be prepared to ensure effective and timely completion of audit. The following action points would help the auditors to plan better and perform the task within the allotted time span.

i.   **Appointment:** Upon receipt of appointment letter, the auditor shall communicate with the previous auditor and later send his acceptance. Simultaneously, the branch head should be contacted to ascertain the quantum of business at the branch. This would help to plan the audit. The branch can be informed in writing as to when the audit would commence and a request should be made to keep the statements ready for audit. The auditor can send a questionnaire containing the details and information he wants from the branch for early completion of audit and also the various other information that need to be reported in LFAR, Tax Audit and other certifications.

ii.   **Planning for Audit:** The next step would be to carefully and thoroughly go through the appointment letter and list out the various documents like Audit Report, Trial Balance before and after closing, Balance Sheet and Profit and Loss Account, LFAR, Tax Audit etc. that need to be certified. The auditor has to prepare a checklist of documents to be certified and number of copies to be dispatched to each office.

iii. **Updating of Knowledge:** It is required to browse through RBI website and download relevant Master Circulars, which are the basis guide for conducting the audit. The audit team should also attend different workshops/seminars organised for bank audit and should go through the guidance notes issued by the ICAI on audit of banks.

iv.   **Audit Programme:** A comprehensive audit programme should be prepared in such a manner that all the aspects relating to the statutory audit, LFAR, Tax Audit and other certification work are covered in it.

v. **Conduct of Audit:** It is required to begin the work by seeking the following documents/books of accounts:

    (a) Trail Balance before and after closing.

    (b) Balance Sheet and Profit and Loss Account (if these are required to be certified).

    (c) Statement of NPA accounts.

    (d) Accounts closing circulars issued by the head office.

    (e) Branch Audit Report of the previous year, Concurrent Audit Reports, Internal/Inspection Audit Report and RBI Inspection Reports.

The following items will require special attention of the bank branch auditor at the time of conducting of audit:

Cash and Bank Balance

If possible, the auditor will verify the cash balance as on 31st March of each accounting year. If the verification is done on any later date, reconcile the cash balance from the date of verification to March 31 of that accounting year. The auditor should also obtain a certificate of balance from the branch on the date of verification. The auditor should verify the confirmation of balance received from other banks with books and check reconciliation statement.

Advances

The auditor should review the appraisal system and internal controls in place and the adequacy thereof. He should:

- check all files of large as well as critical borrowers, sanctions, disbursements, renewals, documentations, systems, securities etc.,

- check at random the sanctions, disbursements, renewals, documentations, systems, securities etc. in case of other advances,

- ensure the extent of compliance of terms and conditions detailed in the sanction ticket and whether the borrower is regular in submission of stock statements, book debt statements, financial statements etc. and whether penal interest is charged in case of default in submission of such documents,

- verify whether the branch has classified the advance in accordance with the prudential norms prescribed by the RBI,

- check whether classification and reporting is made properly such as secured loans, unsecured loans, priority, non-priority etc. and

- check whether unrealised interest on NPA accounts are reversed and not charged to such non-performing advance accounts.

Fixed Assets

The auditor should take into consideration the following points for verifying the fixed assets of the bank branch:

- Verify whether the Fixed Asset Register is maintained and also ascertain whether physical verification has been done around the balance sheet date.

- Verify the bills in case of additions and also confirm whether proper authorisation is available for such additions.

- Verify the depreciation charged and the rates and calculations thereof.

- If the branch premise is owned, verify the title deed. If it is on lease, verify the lease agreement.

Deposits

The transactions during the year shall be verified in respect of:

- new accounts opened and large sums of deposits placed,
- inoperative accounts,
- random checking of provisioning of accrued interest and
- compliance with the RBI directives on maintenance of NRI accounts.

Profit and Loss Items

To verify the correctness of items included in the profit and loss account, following points are required to be considered:

- Random checking of interest charge and levy of processing fee on advances accounts.
- Random check of interest paid on deposits accounts.
- Whether adequate provisioning for expenses has been made for interest accrued and not due, other recurring costs like rent, electricity, annual maintenance etc.
- Whether the branch has followed strictly the norms prescribed by the Reserve Bank of India regarding income recognition on non-performing advances.

Contingent Liabilities

The auditor should take into consideration the following points for verifying the contingent liabilities of the bank branch:

- **Letter of Credit Issued On Behalf of its Constituents:** Verify the Register maintained with the copies of the LC and the margin held. Obtain a certificate from the branch management that all letter of credits issued are recorded in the relevant register.
- **Bills Drawn by the Customers and Accepted By the Bank:** Verify outstanding bills accepted by the banks with the register maintained.
- **Guarantees Issued:** Verify the register of guarantees issued and look for any claims made. Whether the branch has reversed expired guarantees. Obtain a certificate from the branch management that all guarantees issued are recorded in the relevant register.
- **Claims Against the Bank Not Acknowledged as Debts:** To seek from the bank pending cases against the branch for claims made by third parties or constituents.

10.4   STAGE IN AUDIT OF BANKS

As in the cases of any other audit, the audit of banks involves the following stages:

i.   Preliminary work

ii. Evaluation of internal control system

iii. Preparation of audit programme for substantive testing and its execution

iv. Preparation and submission of audit report

10.4.1   PRELIMINARY WORK

Standards on Auditing (SA) 310 on 'Knowledge of the Business' requires that in performing an audit of financial statements, the auditor should have or obtain knowledge of the business sufficient to enable the auditor to identify and understand the events, transactions and practices that, in the auditors judgment, may have a significant effect on the financial statements or on the examination or audit report. The auditor's level of knowledge for an engagement would include a general knowledge of the economy and the industry within which the entity operates, and a more particular knowledge of how the entity operates. Knowledge of the business provides a frame of reference within which the auditor exercises professional judgment and assists him in assessing risks and identifying problems, planning and performing the audit effectively and efficiently, and evaluating the audit evidence.

The auditor should accordingly acquire knowledge of the regulatory environment in which the bank operates. Thus, the auditors should familiarise him with the relevant provisions of applicable law(s). He should be well acquainted with the provisions of the Banking Regulation Act, 1949, as well as any other applicable law(s) (e.g. Companies Act, 1956 in the case of audit of a banking company) particularly in so far as they relate to preparation and presentation of financial statements and their audit. The auditor should also possess an understanding of the various guidelines issued by Reserve Bank of India in so far as such guidelines have a bearing on his work. ·

The auditor should also acquire knowledge of the economic environment in which the bank operates. Similarly, the auditor needs to acquire good working knowledge of the services offered by the bank. In acquiring such knowledge, the auditor needs to be aware of the many variations in the basic deposit, loans and treasury services that are offered and continue to be developed by banks in response to market conditions. To do so, the auditor needs to understand the nature of services rendered through instruments such as letters of credit, acceptance, forward contracts, and other similar instruments. A bank's loan portfolio may have large concentration of credit to highly specialised industries, e.g., hire purchase and leasing, software, infra-structure, etc. Evaluating the nature of these may require knowledge of the business and reporting practices of those industries. Besides, there are a number of risks associated with banking activities, which, though not unique to banking, are sufficiently important in that they serve to shape banking operations. An understand-ing of the nature of these risks may help the auditor in perceiving the risk inherent in different aspects of a bank's operations and thus assist him in determining the degree of reliance on internal control and the nature, timing and extent of his other audit procedures.

The auditor should also obtain an understanding of the accounting system of the bank and the terminol-ogy used by the bank to describe various types of transactions and operations. Most banks have well-designed accounting and procedures manual, which can serve as an important source of information on these aspects.

In the case of joint auditors, it would be preferable that each joint auditor also obtains a general under-standing of the books and records, etc. relating to the work of other join auditors.

In addition to the above, the auditor should also undertake the following:

- Review relevant instructions issued by the bank, particularly those relating to closing of annual accounts. These instructions contain standardised accounting procedure required to be followed at head office, at regional offices, zonal offices and branches.

- Review the audit report for the previous year including the long form audit report. In case of branch auditors, the audit report on the financial statements of the branch for the previous year or for the audit last conducted should be reviewed. The purpose of his review is to understand the nature of observa-tions/comments made on the financial statements and for enquiring into the follow-up action taken on matters contained in such report.

- Review the revenue audit reports, internal audit reports, inspection reports and concurrent audit reports pertaining to the bank/branch, as the case may be.

The above review would help the auditor in gaining an understanding of the nature and volume of operations and the structure of assets and liabilities of the bank/branch as also of the nature of adverse feature observed in the past.

10.4.2 EVALUATION OF INTERNAL CONTROL SYSTEM

Internal control evaluation is an important element of audit process. In the case of audit of banks, it assumes even greater importance due to the enormous volume of transactions entered into by banks. Evaluation of design and operation of internal control system enables the bank auditors to perform more effective audits. The auditor should, therefore, study and evaluate the design and operation of internal controls. This would assist him in determining the nature, timing and extent of substantive procedures in various areas, depending upon whether the internal controls are adequate and observed in practice.

10.4.3 PREPARATION OF AUDIT PROGRAM FOR SUBSTANTIVE TESTING AND ITS EXECUTION

Having familiarised himself with the requirements of audit, the auditor should prepare an audit program for substantive testing, which should adequately cover the scope of his work. In framing the audit program, due weightage should be given by the auditor to areas where, in his view, there are weakness in the internal controls. The audit program for central auditors would be different from that of the branch auditors. At the branch level, basic banking operations are to be covered by the audit. On the other hand, the central auditors have to deal with consolidation of branch returns (both audited and unaudited), investments and items normally dealt with at the head office.

The auditor should ensure that the work is executed in accordance with the audit programme by persons having the requisite skills and competence.

10.4.4 PREPARATION AND SUBMISSION OF AUDIT REPORT

The audit report is the end product of the audit. It is through the medium of the audit report that the auditor conveys his observations/comments on the financial statements. The form and content of the audit report should be determined by the auditor taking into account his terms of engagement and applicable statutory, regulatory and professional requirements.

10.5 ADVANCES

In a bank branch, advances usually constitute the maximum amount of assets. Normally banks sanction advances against security of tangible assets. The bank may also require that the borrower should furnish guarantees of third parties for repayment of the advances. In some cases, the banks also grant advances without any security.

10.5.1 LEGAL PROVISIONS REGARDING ADVANCES

According to the Banking Regulation Act, certain restrictions are imposed against the granting of advances by the banks. This includes the following:

Section 20

A bank cannot make any loans or advances on the security of its own share. A bank is also not permitted to enter into any commitment for granting any loan or advance to or on behalf of:

   i.   any of its directors,

  ii.   any firm in which any of its directors is interested as a partner, manager, employee or guarantor,

 iii.   any company (except its own subsidiary or a company registered under section 25 of the Companies Act, 1956 or a government company) of which, or of a subsidiary of the holding company of which, any of its directors is a director, manager, employee or guarantor or in which he holds substantial interest or

iv. any individual in respect of whom any of its directors is a partner or guarantor.

Section 20A

A bank is prohibited from remitting the whole or any part of the debts due to it by certain persons (any director of the bank, any firm or company in which any such director is a director, partner or guarantor, and any individual of whom any director of the bank is a partner or guarantor) without the prior approval of RBI.

Section 21

RBI has the power to determine the policy in relation to advances to be followed by banks generally, or by any bank in particular and can give directions to bank regarding the purposes for which advances may or may not be given, the margins to be maintained, maximum amount of advances to any one party, the rate of interest and other terms and conditions of advances.

10.5.2 PRUDENTIAL NORMS OF RBI RELATING TO ADVANCES

RBI has prescribed the prudential norms relating to advances classification on the basis of record of recovery, creation of provision for doubtful advances and timing of recognition of income on doubtful advances. The important features of these norms can be stated as follows:

Classification of Advances

Advances are to be classified into two broad categories:

i. Standard Advances

ii. Non-performing Advances

A standard advance is an advance, which does not disclose any problems and does not carry more than the normal risk attached to the banking business.

A non-performing advance is an advance other than a standard advance. Non-performing advances are to be further classified into three sub categories, which are:

i. Sub-standard advances

ii. Doubtful advances and

iii. Loss advances.

A sub-standard advance is one, which has been classified as non-performing assets (NPA) for a period not exceeding 12 months.

A doubtful advance is one, which has remained in the sub-standard category for 12 months.

A loss advance is an advance identified by the bank or by its internal or external auditors or by RBI inspection but the amount has not been written off.

When Advances Become NPA

Once an advance is classified as NPA, adequate provision against the same has to be created. In addition to that income from such advances has not to be recognised until realised. Following norms have been prescribed to determine when an advance will become NPA.

1. Term Loans

A term loan account should be identified as NPA if interest and/or any installment of principal remain overdue for a period of more than 90 days. This is applicable for all term loans except agricultural advances.

2. Cash Credits and Overdrafts

A cash credit or overdraft account should be treated as NPA if it remains out of order. Cash credit or Overdraft account becomes out of order in the following circumstances:

  i. If the outstanding balance in the principal operating account remains continuously in excess of the sanctioned limit for 90 days as on the date of the balance sheet or

  ii. Though the outstanding balance is less than the sanctioned limit, there are no credits continuously for 90 days as on the date of the balance sheet or

  iii. The credits are not enough to cover the interest debited during the same period.

3. Bills Purchased/Discounted

A bill purchased/discounted should be treated as NPA if the bill remains overdue for a period of more than 90 days.

4. Agricultural Advances

A loan granted for short duration crops is to be treated as NPA, if the installment of principal and/or interest thereon remains overdue for two crop seasons.

A loan granted for long duration crops (longer than one year) will be treated as NPA if the installment of principal and/or interest thereon remains overdue for one crop season.

5. Other Accounts

Credit facilities other than those mentioned above should be treated as NPA if any amount in respect of such a facility will remain overdue for a period of more than 90 days.

Provision for Non-Performing Advances

The banks are required to make provisions against sub-standard advances, doubtful advances and loss advances. The norms in this regard are as follows:

1. Loss Advances

The entire advances should be written off. If the advances are permitted to remain in the books for any reason, 100% of the outstanding should be provided for.

2. Doubtful Advances

Provision has to be made for unsecured as well as secured portion as under-

  i. 100% to the extent to which the advance is not covered by the realisable value of the security to which the bank has valid recourse and the realizable value of which is estimated on a realistic basis should be provided for.

  ii. Provision in respect of the secured portion should be made as follows:

PERIOD FOR WHICH THE ADVANCE HAS BEEN CONSIDERED AS DOUBTFUL	PERCENTAGE OF PROVISION
(a) Up to one year	20
(b) One to three years	30
(c) More than three years (i) Outstanding stock of NPA as on 31 March 2004	— 60 with effect from March 31, 2005 — 75 with effect from 31 March 2006 — 100 with effect from 31 March 2007
(ii) Advances classified as doubtful—more than three years on or after 1 April 2004	— 100 with effect from 31 March 2005.

3. Sub-Standard Advances

A general provision of 10% of total outstanding should be made. The unsecured exposures, which are identified, as sub-standard would attract additional provision of 10%, i.e., a total of 20% on the outstanding balance.

4. Standard Advances

A general provision of a minimum of 0.25% should be made on standard advances on global loan portfolio basis. However, the provisions on standard advances should not be deducted for arriving at net NPA.

Provision for Bad and Doubtful Debts

The central auditor should examine the adequacy of provisions in respect of each of the categories under which advances are shown in the balance sheet of a bank. In evaluating such adequacy, the auditor specifically consider the guidelines issued by the Reserve Bank of India in this regard. The norms prescribed by the Reserve Bank of India provide a uniform and objective manner of determining the required provision.

According to the Guidance Note on Bank Audit as issued by ICAI, these norms should be considered as the minimum quantum of provision and if the situation demands a higher provision in the context of the threats to recovery, such higher provision should be made. So, the norms regarding the provisions for doubtful debts as prescribed by Reserve Bank of India do not influence the judgment of the auditor regarding the risks of non-recovery of advances and also the amount of provision required. The provisions of the Banking Regulation Act also support the necessity of Auditor's judgment regarding provision for doubtful debts. According to Section 15 of the said Act, the provision for doubtful debts is to be made to the satisfaction of auditors in the context of payment of dividends.

10.6   INCOME RECOGNITION

In line with the international practices and as per the recommendations made by the committee on the financial system, the Reserve Bank of India has introduced, in a phased manner, prudential norms of income recognition of the banks so as to move towards greater consistency and transparency in the published accounts.

The basis of income recognition in case of bank can be summarised in the following way:

Income from Advances

i.   In respect of advances against term deposits, National Savings Certificates eligible for surrender, Indira Vikas Patras, Kisan Vikas Patras and life insurance policies, interest may be recognised on due dates even where any amount in respect of such advances is overdue for the prescribed period. However, this interest can only be recognised if there is adequate margin available in the account.

ii. Fees and commissions earned by the bank as a result of re-negotiation or rescheduling of outstanding advances should be recognised on an accrual basis over the period of time covered by the re-negotiated or rescheduled period of credit.

Income from Non-Performing Assets

i.   Interest, fee, commission etc. pertaining to non-performing assets should not be recognised in the profit and loss account unless the same has been realised. Interest realised on a non-performing asset may be taken to the profit and loss account if the credits in the accounts towards interest are not out of fresh/additional credit facilities sanctioned to the borrower concerned.

ii. If any advance becomes NPA as at the close of any year, the amount of fees, interest, commission etc. credited to the profit and loss account in the corresponding financial year should be reversed or provided for, if the same has not been realised. In the case of assets given on finance lease, the finance charge component of finance income, which was accrued and credited to income account in the last accounting year before the asset became non-performing but which remains, should be reversed or provided for in the current accounting period.

iii. Banks are permitted to debit interest to an NPA account and take the same to Interest Suspense Account or to maintain only a record of such interest in pro forma account.

The bank should adopt a uniform and consistent policy regarding appropriation of partial recoveries in NPAs towards interest due and principal where there is no clear agreement between the bank and the borrower in this aspect.

10.7 BANK AUDIT REPORT

The bank auditor has to make his report directly to the bank. The contents of the auditor's report in the case of different types of banks are somewhat different. The report of the auditor of a nationalised bank is to be verified, signed and transmitted to the Central Government. The auditor has also to forward a copy of the audit report to the bank concerned and to RBI.

In addition to the matters, which the auditor is required to state in his report under the Companies Act, the auditor of a bank has also to state the following in his report:

In Case of Banking Companies

The auditor should include in his report:

i. Whether or not the information and explanations required by him have been found to be satisfactory;

ii. Whether or not the transactions of the company, which have come to the notice have been within the powers of the company;

iii. Whether or not the returns received from branches of the company have been found adequate for the purposes of his audit;

iv. Whether the profit and loss account shows a true balance of profit or loss for the period covered by such account;

v Any other matter, which he considers should be brought to the notice of the shareholders of the company.

In Case of Nationalised Banks

The auditor of a nationalised bank, State Bank of India or its subsidiary is required to report to the Central Government and has to state the following in his report:

i. Whether in his opinion the balance sheet is a full and fair balance sheet containing all the necessary particulars and is properly drawn up so as to exhibit a true and fair view of the affairs of the bank and in case he had called for any explanation of information, whether it has been given and whether it is satisfactory;

ii. Whether or not the transactions of the bank, which has come to his notice, have been within the powers of the bank;

iii. Whether or not the returns received from the offices and branches of the bank have been found adequate for the purpose of his audit;

iv. Whether the profit and loss account shows a true balance of profit or loss for the period covered by such account;

v. Any other matter, which he considers should be brought to the notice of the Central Government.

Apart from the audit report on the financial statements, the auditor of a nationalised bank, State Bank of India and any of its subsidiaries or a banking company including a foreign bank has also to prepare a long form audit report (LFAR).

10.7.1 LONG FORM AUDIT REPORT

The long form audit report highlights certain important aspects of the working of a bank and its branches. Guidance Notes issued by ICAI on Audit of Banks also deals with long form audit report. In case of branches, the auditors have to answer a detailed questionnaire formulated by the Reserve Bank of India.

Where any of the comments made by the auditor in his LFAR is adverse, he should consider whether a qualification in his main report is necessary. It should not however be assumed that every adverse comment in the LFAR would necessarily result in a qualification in the main report. In deciding whether a qualification in the main report is necessary, the auditor should use his judgment in the facts and circumstances of each case.

The main action points to be considered for this part include the following:

- First action point would be to collect the information required to be provided in the LFAR from the branch manager duly certified including the annexure to LFAR where the particulars of large borrowers are given in detail.

- Where branch maintains balance with other banks, verify confirmation of balances received from other banks with books and check reconciliation statement.

- While checking for investments held at the branch on behalf of head office, physical verification of scrips shall be made. Also check whether income and related tax deduction certificate received at the branch is accounted for accordingly.

- Whether lending is made for inventory held for more than 90 days or book debts exceeding 90 days.

- Ascertain whether the branch manager has read through the auditor's report and notes to accounts in case of corporate borrowers thoroughly before putting up the proposal for sanction/renewal, since this contain valuable information impacting the future plan of the company.

◆ Suggested questions

A   **Short type questions:**
1. What is Long Form Audit Report?
2. How an auditor of a bank is appointed?
3. What are the Acts relevant for bank audit?
4. What do you mean by Special Audit in case of bank?
5. What are the rights and liabilities of a bank auditor?
6. What are the different types of advances of a bank according to RBI prudential norms?
7. When an advance becomes NPA?

B   **Essay-type questions:**
1. State, in brief, the contents of an audit report of a bank.
2. Describe in brief the prudential norms of RBI relating to advances.
3. State, in brief, the relevant legal provisions in case of audit of banks.
4. Describe the main features of internal check suitable for a bank.
5. State the special features of a bank audit.

6. Discuss the different stages of conducting bank audit.

7. State the legal requirements of making provisions for non-performing assets.

8. State the duties of a bank auditor in writing Long Form Audit Report in respect of the following aspects:

   a. Cash

   b. Investments

   c. Advances

   d. Deposits

   e. Contingent liabilities

   f. Books and records

   g. Inter-branch accounts

   h. Audit and inspection

   i. Frauds

   j. Stamps and stationeries

9. State the practices that should be followed by the bank in respect to the following:

   a. Provision for doubtful debts.

   b. Income recognition.

Chapter 11

Audit of Insurance Companies

11.1 AUDIT OF COMPANIES CARRYING ON LIFE INSURANCE BUSINESS

Due to liberalisation of the economy, the economic policies of India have witnessed a significant transformation during the last decade. A new regulatory framework in the insurance sector has brought sweeping changes not only in terms of number of participants, but also in terms of portfolio of insurance business and the way the business is conducted.

The conduct of life insurance business is unique in the sense that the concept of 'Life Fund' and consequential segregation of Shareholders Fund from Life Fund and conditionalities of financial transactions between these two funds are not present in the conduct of any other business. This uniqueness brings about issues relating to recognition of revenue, preparation and presentation of accounts, valuation of assets and liabilities and measurement of taxable income requiring focus in specific manner.

The changing environment has made a strong case for better regulation on the insurance sector. An independent authority, Insurance Regulatory and Development Authority (IRDA), was constituted in the year 1999 to protect the interest of holders of insurance policies and to regulate, promote and ensure orderly growth of the insurance industry.

New companies have entered into life insurance business, and the organisational structure may differ from one insurance company to another. The Life Insurance Corporation of India (LICI) has a four-tier structure, i.e., head office, regional offices, divisional offices and branch offices, with each tier being responsible for performing the functions assigned by the head office.

11.1.1 IMPORTANT STATUTORY PROVISIONS FOR AUDIT

The important statutory provisions relevant to the audit of life insurance companies are included in the following Acts and Rules:

i. The Insurance Act, 1938.

ii. The Insurance Rules, 1939.

iii. The Income Tax Act, 1961.

iv. The Companies Act, 1956.

v. The Life Insurance Corporation Act, 1956.

11.2 AUDIT OF COMPANIES CARRYING ON GENERAL INSURANCE BUSINESS

The Indian economic environment is undergoing a significant transformation in view of economic reforms introduced since early 1990s. In the wake of these reforms, the privatisation of insurance sector is not only intended to mobilise long-term funds but also to make the insurance business more competitive and thus meet the fundamental security needs of various sections of the society.

The opening up of the general insurance sector enabled entry of various new companies and expanded the scope of general insurance coverage. The organisation structure may differ from one general insurance company to another. Most of the companies carrying on general insurance business have a four-tier structure, i.e., head office, regional offices, divisional offices and branch offices. Each tier of the structure is responsible for performing the functions assigned to it by the Head Office.

General insurance business usually involves fire, marine or miscellaneous insurance business, whether carried on singly or in combination of one or more of them. Some common types of miscellaneous insurance include motor vehicle insurance, credit insurance, burglary insurance, loss of profit insurance, health insurance, etc.

11.2.1 IMPORTANT STATUTORY PROVISIONS FOR AUDIT

The important statutory provisions relevant to the audit of general insurance companies are included in the following Acts and Rules:

   i. The Insurance Act, 1938.

  ii. The Insurance Rules, 1939.

 iii. The Income Tax Act, 1961.

 iv. The Income Tax Rules, 1962.

  v. The Companies Act, 1956.

 vi. The General Insurance Business (Nationalisation) Act, 1972.

 vii. The Motor Vehicles Act, 1988.

viii. Employees' State Insurance Act, 1948.

11.3 APPLICABILITY OF ACCOUNTING STANDARDS

The Accounting Standards as issued by the Institute of Chartered Accountants of India are applicable to the preparation of financial statements of a company carrying on insurance business, subject to Paragraph 1 of Part 1 of Schedule B to the IRDA (Preparation of Financial Statements and Auditor's Report of the Insurance Companies) Regulations, 2000.

The applicability of Accounting Standards to the insurance companies are discussed below:

Accounting Standard-3

According to the IRDA (Preparation of Financial Statements and Auditor's Report of Insurance Companies) Regulations, 2000, the Receipts and Payments Account of an insurer should be prepared using the 'Direct Method' as mentioned in Accounting Standard-3 on Cash Flow Statements.

Accounting Standard-4

Accounting Standard-4 on 'Contingencies and Events Occurring After the Balance Sheet Date' that deals with accounting treatment of contingent losses and gains and events occurring after the balance sheet date, excludes from its applicability the liabilities of companies carrying on insurance business in view of special considerations applicable to such liabilities. The Standard excludes, from its applicability, the liabilities arising out of policies issued and not other liabilities, which do not arise out of policies issued by the insurance companies such as liabilities arising out of income tax dispute. Thus, the Standard applies to such other liabilities.

Accounting Standard-9

Accounting Standard-9 on 'Revenue Recognition' does not apply to revenue of insurance companies arising from insurance contracts, in view of the fact that revenue recognition from insurance contracts requires special considerations. The Standard is applicable to the insurance companies only in respect of income not earned from the insurance contracts such as interest, dividend, rent etc.

Accounting Standard-13

Under paragraph 2(c) of Accounting Standard-13 on 'Accounting for Investments', it has been provided that the Standard does not deal with the investments of insurance enterprises.

Accounting Standard-17

So far as the applicability of Accounting Standard-17 on Segment Reporting is concerned, the regulations have disregarded the applicability clause contained in the Standard by providing that irrespective of the fact that the securities of the company are traded or not, Accounting Standard-17 would be applicable to an insurer carrying on life or general insurance business.

11.4 BOOKS AND REGISTERS TO BE MAINTAINED

An insurance company is required to maintain the following books of accounts and returns:

11.4.1 REGISTERS

Register of Policies

Under Section 14 of the Insurance Act, 1938 every insurer is required to maintain a register or record of policies containing the details regarding every policy issued by the insurer, name and address of the policy holder, the date of effect of the policy, record of any transfer, assignment or nomination of which insurer has a notice.

Register of Claims

Every insurer is also required to maintain a register or record of claims containing the details on date of claim made, name and address of the claimant, date of discharge of each claim and in case the claim is rejected, the date of rejection along with grounds there for.

11.4.2 BOOKS OF ACCOUNTS

The insurance companies generally maintain the following books of accounts:

- ➢ Cash book (for receipts and payments)
- ➢ Ledger
- ➢ Subsidiary records (accounts of claims, premium, commission, assets, liabilities etc.)
- ➢ Control register

In addition to that the provisions under Section 209 of the Companies Act, 1956 regarding books of accounts are also applicable to the insurance companies.

11.4.3 SUBMISSION OF REPORTS AND RETURNS

Under Section 18 of the Insurance Act, 1938 every insurer is required to furnish to the Authority, a certified copy of every report on the affairs of the concern, which is submitted to the members or policyholders of the insurer immediately after its submission to the members of policyholders, as the case may be.

The audited accounts and statements referred to in Section 11 or Section 13 (5) and the abstracts and statements referred to in Section 13 shall be printed and four copies thereof shall be furnished as returns to the Authority, in the case of the accounts and statements referred to in Section 11 or Section 13 (5) within six months and in case of the abstracts and statements referred to in Section 13 within nine months from the end of the period to which they refer.

11.5   AUDIT OF ACCOUNTS

Under Section 12 of the Insurance Act, 1938 the financial statements (Balance Sheet, Profit and Loss Account and appropriations there from) and Revenue Accounts of every insurer are required to be audited annually. Section 2 (4) of the Insurance Act, 1938 defines the term 'auditor' as a person qualified under the Chartered Accountants Act, 1949 to act as an auditor of a company.

The provisions of Section 12 of the Insurance Act, 1938 apply only in a case where the financial statements of the insurer are not subject to audit under the Companies act, 1956. A company carrying on life and general insurance business is, therefore, subject to audit requirements laid down under the Companies Act, 1956.

Further, Section 12 of the Insurance act, 1938 does not cover the requirement for audit of the Receipts and Payments Account of an insurer. But the IRDA Act, 1999 inserted a new sub-section (1A) in Section 11 of the Insurance Act, 1938, overriding sub-section (1) of Section 11, prescribing the financial statements to be prepared by an insurer. The new sub-section requires that after the commencement of the IRDA Act, 1999, every insurer, in respect of insurance business transacted by him and in respect of his shareholders funds, should, at the end of each financial year, prepare a Balance Sheet, a Profit and Loss account, a separate Account of Receipts and Payments and a Revenue Account in accordance with the regulations laid down by the Authority.

The Authority, in exercise of the powers conferred by the Insurance Act, 1938 issued the IRDA (Preparation of Financial Statements and Auditor's Report of Insurance Companies) Regulations, 2000. These regulations also require the auditor of an insurance company to report whether the Receipts and Payments Account of the insurer is in agreement with the books of accounts and returns. The auditor is also required to express an opinion as to whether the Receipts and Payments Account has been prepared in accordance with the provisions of the relevant statutes and whether the Receipts and Payments Account give a true and fair view of the receipts and payments of the insurer for the period under audit. It implies that the auditor is required to audit the Receipts and Payments Account of the insurer.

The IRDA Act, 1999 also inserted the third proviso to Section 2C (1) of the Insurance Act, 1938. The proviso requires that no insurer other than an Indian insurance company can commence any class of insurance business after the commencement of the IRDA Act, 1999. Under the circumstances, an Indian insurance company would be subject to the audit requirements laid down under the Companies Act, 1956.

11.5.1   Qualification of an Auditor

A chartered accountant fulfilling the requirements of the Companies Act, 1956 can be appointed as an auditor of an insurer. According to Section 226 of the Companies Act, 1956 a chartered accountant or a firm of chartered accountants or a restricted state auditor can be appointed as auditor of a company.

However, the following persons cannot be appointed as auditor of a company:

   i.   a body corporate;

  ii.   an officer or employee of the company;

 iii.   a person who is a partner, or who is in the employment of an officer or employee of the company;

iv. a person who is indebted to the company for an amount exceeding Rs. 1,000 or who has given any guarantee or provided any security in connection with the indebtedness of any third person to the company for an amount exceeding Rs. 1,000;

v. a person holding any security of the company carrying voting rights.

It may be noted that the Insurance Act, 1938 mentions that the auditor of an insurer should be a chartered accountant qualified under the Chartered Accountants Act, 1949. Therefore, a restricted state auditor cannot be appointed as an auditor of an insurance company and only chartered accountants can be appointed as auditors of insurance companies.

A person is not qualified for appointment as auditor of a company if he is disqualified for appointment as auditor of any other body corporate, which is that company's subsidiary or holding company or a subsidiary of that company's holding company or would be so disqualified if the body corporate were a company.

It may also be noted that in case of indebtedness in excess of the specified limit as mentioned above, the chartered accountant concerned becomes disqualified to audit any branch of the insurer and the disqualification is not only confined to appointment as auditor of the particular branch to which the debt is owed.

11.5.2 APPOINTMENT OF AUDITOR

The Insurance Act, 1938 is silent on the procedure for appointment of auditors of insurance companies. Therefore, the provisions of the Companies Act, 1956 would apply in so far as appointment of auditor is concerned. The auditor of an insurance company is to be appointed at the annual general meeting of the company. The approval of the Authority is required before the appointment is made. The central statutory auditors of insurance companies are appointed by the insurance company concerned on the basis of the names recommended by the Authority from out of a panel of auditors. For this purpose, the Authority formulates detailed norms on the basis of which the panel is prepared.

11.5.3 REMUNERATION OF AUDITOR

The remuneration of auditor of insurance company is fixed in accordance with the provisions of Section 224 of the Companies Act, 1956, i.e., the remuneration of the auditor is fixed by the company in general meeting or in such manner as the company in general meeting may determine.

11.5.4 POWERS OF AN AUDITOR

The auditor of an insurance company has the same powers as those of a company auditor in the matter of access to the books of accounts, documents and vouchers. He is also entitled to require from the officers of the insurance company such information and explanations as he may think necessary for the performance of his duties. In the case of an insurance company, he is entitled to receive notice relating to any general meeting. He is also entitled to attend any general meeting and to be heard thereat on any part of the business, which concerns him as the auditor.

11.5.5 AUDITOR'S REPORT

The Authority has prescribed the matters to be dealt with by the Auditor's Report under Schedule C of IRDA (Preparation of Financial Statements and Auditor's Report of Insurance Companies) Regulations, 2000.

The auditors are required to make a report to the members of the company on the following matters:

i. (a) Whether they have obtained all the information and explanations, which, to the best of their knowledge and belief, were necessary for the purposes of their audit and whether they have found them satisfactory;

(b) Whether proper books of accounts have been maintained by the insurer so far as it appears from an examination of those books;

(c) Whether proper returns, audited or unaudited, from branches and other offices have been received and whether they were adequate for the purpose of audit;

(d) Whether the Balance Sheet, Revenue Accounts and Profit and Loss Account dealt with by the report and the Receipts and Payments account are in agreement with the books of account and returns;

(e) Whether the actuarial valuation of liabilities is duly certified by the appointed actuary including a statement to the effect that the assumptions for such valuation are in accordance with the guidelines and norms, if any, issued by the Authority, and/or the Actuarial Society of India in concurrence with the Authority.

ii. The auditors are also required to express their opinion on:
  (a) (i) Whether the Balance Sheet gives a true and fair view of the surplus or the deficit for the financial year/period;
  (ii) Whether the Revenue Accounts give a true and fair view of the surplus or the deficit for the financial year/period;
  (iii) Whether the Profit and Loss Account gives a true and fair view of the profit or loss for the financial year/period;
  (iv) Whether the Receipts and Payments Account gives a true and fair view of the receipts and payments for the financial year/period;
  (b) Whether the financial statements stated at (a) above have been prepared in accordance with the requirements of the Insurance Act, 1938, the Insurance Regulatory and Development Authority Act, 1999 and the Companies Act, 1956, to the extent applicable and in the manner so required.
  (c) Whether investments have been valued in accordance with the provisions of the Act and Regulations.
  (d) Whether the accounting policies selected by the insurer are appropriate and are in compliance with the applicable Accounting Standards and with the accounting principles, as prescribed in these Regulations or any order or direction issued by the Authority in this behalf.

iii. The auditors are required to further certify that:
  (a) They have reviewed the management report and there is no apparent mistake or material inconsistency with the financial statements; and
  (b) The insurer has compiled with the terms and conditions of the registration stipulated by the Authority;

iv. A certificate signed by the auditors certifying that:
  (a) they have verified the cash balances and the securities relating to the insurer's loans, reversions and life interests and investments;
  (b) the extent, if any, to which they have verified the investments and transactions relating to any trusts undertaken by the insurer as trustee; and
  (c) no part of the assets of the policyholders' funds has been directly or indirectly applied in contravention of the provisions of the Insurance Act, 1938 relating to the application and investments of the policyholders' funds.

11.5.6 OTHER IMPORTANT PROVISIONS RELATING TO AUDIT

Every insurance company, in the management report, has to furnish a responsibility statement in connection with the existence and effective operation of an internal audit system. It implies that every insurance company should have in place an internal audit system commensurate with its size and nature of the business.

Section 40B and 40C of the Insurance Act, 1938 provides for the limitations on expenses of management in life and general insurance companies, the rules in respect of which have been specified under Insurance Rules, 1939. Every insurer is required to incorporate in the Revenue Account a certificate signed by the chairman and two directors and by the principal officer of the insurer, and by the auditor certifying that all expenses of management, wherever incurred, directly or indirectly, in respect of the business referred to in this section have been fully debited in the Revenue Account as expenses.

11.5.7 AUDIT AT BRANCH/DIVISIONAL OFFICE LEVEL AND AT HEAD OFFICE LEVEL

Under the restructuring of the insurance sector, insurance business can be run by Life Insurance Corporation of India or by General Insurance Corporation of India or public sector companies or private companies. The concept of divisional office may not be relevant in case of private companies but may continue to be of relevance in case of Life Insurance Corporation of India and General Insurance Corporation of India. Wherever the reference is made to the divisional office, it may be understood as branches or any other offices where those operations are carried out in case of private companies.

Further, the Life Insurance Corporation of India and General Insurance Corporation of India may call for trial balances or other relevant returns from the branches and then the same may be consolidated at the head office level. There is a significant difference in the scope of audit at a branch or divisional office of an insurance company and at head office as well as other controlling offices such as regional offices. The difference stems from the fact that the insurance business—receiving premiums and selling claims—as well as most other insurance related operations take place at the branch level or divisional office level.

In the normal course, the head office and the regional offices do not conduct any insurance business except reinsurance transactions. They are generally responsible for administrative and policy decisions which are executed at the branch/divisional office level.

Audit at Branch/Divisional Level
Audit of branches of insurance companies is required under Section 228 of the Companies Act, 1956. It is, thus, obligatory for an insurance company to get the financial statements of each of its branch offices audited except branches under the Companies (Branch Audit Exemption) Rules, 1961.

The branch auditor has the same powers and duties in respect of audit of financial statements of the branch as those of the central statutory auditors in relation to audit of head office.

The branch auditors furnish their audit reports on the branch financial statements to central statutory auditors with a copy to the management of the company. Branch returns include Balance Sheet, Profit and Loss Account, Revenue Account and other information relevant for preparation of financial statements of the insurance company such as particulars of premiums/claims and also include the returns from unaudited branches. Audited as well as unaudited branch returns are consolidated at the head office. The returns pertaining to a region may be sent by the branches or divisional office to the regional office concerned and are consolidated there. The returns received from various regions may then be consolidated at the head office.

Audit at the Head Office Level
The central statutory auditors, apart from examining consolidation of branch returns, look into specific matters, which are normally not dealt with at the branch level. These may include the following:

- Depreciation on assets like premises, etc., where the recording of the relevant fixed assets is centralised at the head office.
- Valuation of investments and provisions for diminution in value thereof.
- Provisions in respect of non-performing loans and doubtful elements of other current assets.
- Accounting for reinsurance transactions.

- Provisions for gratuity, pension and other retirement benefits.
- Provision for payment of bonus or ex-gratia in lieu of bonus.
- Provision in respect of losses arising from frauds discovered.
- Provision for taxation.
- Provision for audit fee.
- Provisions to meet any other specific liabilities or contingencies the amount of which is material.
- Transfers to reserves.
- Dividends.
- Any other matters dealt with at the head office.

Another area, which is of utmost importance for the central statutory auditors in the present day context, is that related to inter-office reconciliation. Such reconciliation is mostly centralised at the Head Office. Each company has laid down methods and procedures for reconciling the transactions between the various offices of the company.

The central statutory auditors also have to consider the observations made in the branch auditors' reports. They have to judge whether the observations appearing in the branch auditors' reports, though considered material at the branch level are material in the context of the financial statements of the company as a whole.

11.6 PREPARATION FOR THE AUDIT

Following are the stages through which the auditors of insurance companies can prepare themselves for conducting audit:

Preliminary Work

The auditor's knowledge for an engagement would include general knowledge of the economy and the industry within which the entity operates. The auditor should, accordingly, acquire knowledge of the regularity environment in which an insurance company operates. He should familiarise himself with the relevant provisions of the applicable laws and ascertain the scope of his duties and responsibilities in accordance with such laws.

Evaluation of Internal Control System

Evaluation of the internal control system assumes greater importance in case of audit of insurance companies due to the enormous volume of transactions entered into by these companies. The auditor should study and evaluate the design and operation of internal control.

Preparation of Audit Programme

The auditor should prepare an audit programme for substantive testing, which should adequately cover the scope of his work. In framing the audit programme, the auditor should give due importance to the areas where, in his view, there are weaknesses in internal controls. The audit programme for central statutory auditors would be different from that of branch auditors. The central statutory auditors have to deal with consolidation of branch accounts, investments and items normally dealt with at head office level, while the branch auditors have to deal with basic operations.

Communication with the Previous Auditor

The objective of communicating with the previous auditor is to provide the proposed auditor with an opportunity to know the reasons for the change. When communicating with the previous auditor, the incoming auditor should find out whether there is any professional or other reason why he should not accept the appointment.

Letter of Engagement

An audit engagement letter is aimed at documenting and confirming the acceptance of appointment as auditor. The branch auditor should send an audit engagement letter to the appointing authority before the commencement of the audit.

Co-ordination with Branch Management

Co-ordination between the auditor and the branch management is essential for an effective audit. The branch auditor should send a formal communication to the branch management specifying the books, records and other information that would be required while conducting the audit.

11.7 INTERNAL CONTROLS

The existence and effective operation of an adequate system of internal control is an essential pre-requisite for efficient and effective functioning of any enterprise. Specific internal control procedures are to be followed in an enterprise depend upon variety of factors. However, as in the case of other enterprises, the generic internal controls in insurance companies generally fall under following categories:

11.7.1 SEGREGATION AND ROTATION OF DUTIES

One of the fundamental features of an effective internal control system is the segregation and rotation of duties in a manner conducive to prevention and timely detection of frauds and errors.

The functions, typically, segregated are

- authorisation of transactions;
- execution of transactions;
- physical custody of related assets; and
- maintenance of records and documents.

11.7.2 AUTHORISATION OF TRANSACTIONS

The management of an enterprise delegates authority to different levels and to particular persons in the enterprise to execute specified kinds of transactions in accordance with the prescribed conditions. Authorisation may be general or it may be specific with reference to a single transaction. It is necessary to establish procedures, which provide assurance that authorisations are issued by persons acting within the scope of their authority and that the transactions conform to the terms of the authorisations.

The following procedures are usually established in insurance companies for this purpose:

- The financial and administrative powers of key officials are approved and noted in the Board meetings and other committee meetings.
- The financial and administrative powers of each official are fixed and communicated to all persons concerned.
- All financial decisions at any level are required to be reported to the next higher level for confirmation and information.
- Any deviation from the laid down procedures requires confirmation from/ intimation to higher authorities.

- Branch managers have to send periodic confirmation to their controlling authority on compliance of the laid down systems and procedures.

11.7.3 MAINTENANCE OF ADEQUATE RECORDS AND DOCUMENTS

The prime objective of accounting controls is to ensure that the transactions are recorded at correct amounts and in the accounting periods in which they are executed and that they are classified under appropriate accounts. The procedures adopted by insurance companies to achieve these objectives are quite similar to other commercial enterprises and include the following:

- All records are maintained in accordance with the prescribed regulations and furnish the information as required.
- Books are reviewed periodically by responsible official and balanced and reconciled where necessary.
- Inter-office transactions are reconciled within a specified time frame.
- Records are duly updated to ensure accountability and safeguarding of assets.
- Proper returns are received from branches at the corporate level for necessary accounting and reconciliation.

11.7.4 ACCOUNTABILITY FOR AND SAFEGUARDING OF ASSETS

Accountability of assets starts at the time of their acquisition and continue until their use and disposal. It is achieved by maintenance of records of assets and their periodic comparison with the related assets. To safeguard the assets, it is also necessary that the access to assets is limited to authorised personnel. This covers not only direct physical access, but also indirect access through preparation and processing of documents that authorise the use or disposal of assets. Significant controls in this regard generally followed in the insurance companies are as follows:

- All the assets held physically by custodians are duly verified/confirmed on a periodic basis and verified with the underlying records as stated above. Any discrepancies need to be promptly dealt with.
- The assets are reviewed for impairment at the time of verification as stated above to reflect to the appropriate valuation in respect thereof.
- Sensitive items such as cash on hand, cheque books, electronic fund transfer access control to be under the responsibility/ custody of at least two officers who have been instructed on the importance of such responsibility.

◆ Suggested questions

A   Short-essay type questions

1. What are the Acts and Rules govern the accounts of companies carrying on general insurance business?
2. What are the registers to be maintained by an insurance company?
3. Name the books of accounts required to be maintained by a company carrying on life insurance business.
4. Who can be appointed as auditors of an insurance company?
5. How the auditor of a company carrying on life insurance business is appointed?
6. How the remuneration of auditor of a company carrying on general insurance business is fixed?

7. State the powers of an auditor of an insurance company.

8. State the important matters, the central statutory auditor looks into, while conducting audit at the head office level.

B   **Essay-type questions**

1. State the important provisions of the IRDA regulations, 2000 governing the audit of an insurance company.

2. State the applicability of Accounting Standards to the preparation of financial statements of insurance companies.

3. What are the provisions of the Insurance Act, 1938 regarding submission of reports and returns by the insurance companies?

4. State the provisions as contained in Schedule C of IRDA Regulations, 2000 regarding Auditor's Report of an insurance company.

5. How the auditors prepare themselves before undertaking audit of an insurance company?

6. Discuss, in detail, the internal control procedures, that should be adopted by an insurance company.

Chapter 12

New Areas of Auditing

12.1 INTRODUCTION

Auditing in its modern form adopts a multidimensional approach. At present, the scope of auditing is not only restricted to financial audit under the Companies Act. The purpose of auditing has been extended to cost accounts, managerial policies, operational efficiencies, system applications, social implications of business organisations and also environmental aspects. Even non-business organisations avail the services of qualified auditors and audit their accounts. At present, field of audit also covers:

i. checking cost accounting records and verifying the cost accounting principles that have been adopted in preparing and presenting cost accounting data i.e., cost audit;

ii. comprehensive examination and review of managerial policies and operational efficiency, i.e., management audit;

iii. checking the performance of the organisation and comparing it with the overall performance of the industry in which the organisation belongs, i.e., performance audit;

iv. critical examination and analysis of the contribution of the organisation for the benefit of the society, i.e., social audit;

v. Evaluation and measurement of efficiency of the human resources in the organisation and comparing it with the expected utilisation of the human resources as a whole, i.e., human resource audit;

12.2 COST AUDIT

Under Section 233B of the Companies Act, the Central Government may, if it considers necessary, direct by an order that a cost accountant within the meaning of the Cost and Works Accountants Act shall conduct the cost audit in such manner as may be specified.

Thus, the Central Government may order an audit of cost accounts for specified companies and that audit is to be conducted by a cost accountant. This cost audit is in addition to the financial audit conducted by an auditor appointed under Section 224 of the Companies Act. If the Central Government orders for the cost audit, it requires the company concerned to conduct cost audit every year till further orders.

12.2.1 DEFINITION

Cost audit was introduced in 1965 for the first time in India when the Central Government added Clause (d) to Sections 209 and 233B of the Companies Act. Cost audit is an effective means of control in the hands of management and it is a check on behalf of the shareholders of the company, consumers and the government.

In fact, cost audit is an audit process for verifying the cost of manufacture or production of any article on the basis of accounts taking into consideration utilisation of material or labour or other items of costs, maintained by the company.

According to the definition provided by the Institute of Costs & Works Accountants of London, "Cost audit is the verification of the correctness of cost accounts and adherence to the cost accounting plans". Smith and Day define cost audit as "the detailed checking of costing system, techniques and accounts to verifying correctness and to ensure, adherence to the objectives of cost accounting".

So, from the above-mentioned definitions, we can say in the simple words that cost audit is the detailed checking as well as the verification of the correctness of the costing techniques, systems and cost accounts.

12.2.2 OBJECTIVES

Every branch of study or knowledge aims to achieve specific objectives. It is quite natural that cost audit should have specific objectives. A branch of study cannot develop without objectives.

The following are the main objectives of cost audit:

i. To detect any error or fraud that might have been done intentionally or otherwise.

ii. To ensure that the cost accounting procedures, which have been laid down by the management is strictly followed.

iii. To verify the accuracy of costing data by checking the arithmetical accuracy of cost accounting entries in the books of accounts.

iv. To have a full control on the working of costing department of the organisation and to suggest ways and means for its smooth functioning.

v. To introduce an effective internal cost audit system in order to reduce the burden of detailed checking work of the external auditor.

vi. To help the management in taking correct and timely decisions on cost of production and cost variations.

vii. To verify the adequacy of the books of account and records relating to cost.

viii. To value accurately the value of work-in-progress and closing stock.

ix. To advice the management for the adoption of alternative courses of action by preparing cost plan.

x. To report to appropriate authority as to the state of cost affairs of the organisation.

12.2.3 ADVANTAGES

From the discussion of the objectives of cost audit, it appears that cost audit not only serves the management of the business and the shareholders but it serves the consumers as well as the society in a broader sense. The advantages of cost audit can be described in the following way:

To the Management

i. It helps in controlling different elements of cost.

ii. It can assess the profitability of the organisation.

iii. It helps to have a better inter-firm comparison.

iv. It is a basis of evaluation of the inter-divisional performance.

v. It helps in obtaining licenses for either expansion or diversification of the various product lines of the business.

vi. It can also check to control high inflationary trend of cost.

vii. It helps the management in finding out the correct cost of production.

viii. It can increase the productivity by detecting the weaker areas of cost of production.

ix. The inefficiencies of the employees working in the cost department may be revealed.

x. Errors and frauds may be detected through efficient conduct of cost audit.

To the Shareholders

i. It gives guarantee of the proper maintenance of cost records.

ii. It can stop the capital erosion by maintaining a constant monitoring with regard to the better plant utilisation, discontinuing uneconomic product lines and elimination of wastage.

iii. Through cost audit, the decision makers get timely and proper information, which results in better performance by the organisation.

iv. Cost audit also ensures fair return to shareholders on their investments.

To the Consumers

i. Cost audit helps in the fixation of fair prices.

ii. It helps the consumers indirectly in increasing their standard of living.

To the Government

i. It forms a basis for the assessment of income tax.

ii. It helps the government in fixing and regulating prices.

iii. It gives guidelines to improve working of uneconomic industrial units.

iv. It gives information to the government regarding fraudulent intentions of any company.

To the Society

i. Cost audit provides guidelines to the industries for improving its workings and thus renders a great service towards the society.

ii. It saves the customers from exploitation by revealing them the actual cost and to know the market price of product is fair or not.

iii. It helps the industries to improve their efficiencies and production and to reduce the prices of the product.

12.2.4 DISADVANTAGES

Cost audit may have some limitations. In fact, these limitations do not relate to the objectives for which it has been introduced. The limitations may arise due to limited scope of application of cost audit in the related field of operation. However, cost audit is criticised on the following grounds:

i. It introduces unnecessary interference in the normal working of companies.

ii. It leads to duplication of work because large areas of working of financial and cost audit are common.

iii. It may be considered as a burden to the company because of the additional cost to be incurred on cost audit.

iv. Conduct of cost audit by outsiders may be harmful to the interest of the company itself as the confidentiality of cost accounts may not be maintained.

v. By introducing cost audit in certain industries, more restrictions have been imposed on the functioning of the organisations by the government.

12.2.5 APPOINTMENT

According to sub-section (2) of Section 233 (B), a cost auditor shall be appointed by the Board of Directors of the company in accordance with the provisions of sub-section (IB) of Section 224 and with the previous approval of the Central Government. Further, it has been provided that before the appointment of any cost auditor is made by the Board, a written certificate shall be obtained by the Board from the auditor proposed to be appointed to the effect that the appointment, if made, will be in accordance with the provisions of sub-section (IB) of Section 224.

Such a company is required under Clause (d) of sub-section (I) of Section 209 of the Companies Act to include in its books of accounts, the particulars, referred to therein. The cost audit is in addition to and independent of the normal financial audit carried out pursuant to the appointment under Section 224 of the Act. The cost auditor shall have the same powers and duties as are prescribed under Section 227 (1) of the Act for the auditors appointed under Section 224.

A firm of cost accountants can be appointed as a cost auditor if all the partners of the firm are practicing cost accountants and the firm itself has been constituted with the previous approval of the Central Government as required by the regulations framed under the Cost and Works Accountants Act, 1959.

12.2.6 QUALIFICATION

Under the provisions of Section 233B, such an audit is to be conducted by a cost accountant within the meaning of the Cost and Works Accountants Act, 1959. But if the Central Government is of opinion that sufficient number of cost accountants within the meaning of the Cost and Works Accountants Act, 1959 are not available for conducting the audit of the cost accounts of companies generally, the Government may, by notification in the Official Gazette, direct that, for such period as may be specified in the said notification, a Chartered Accountant within the meaning of the Chartered Accountant's Act, 1949, as possesses the prescribed qualifications, may also conduct the audit of the cost accounts of companies, and thereupon a chartered accountant possessing the prescribed qualifications may be appointed to audit the cost accounts of the company.

12.2.7 DISQUALIFICATION

A person will be considered disqualified to be appointed as cost auditor:

  i.   if he is disqualified according to the provisions of Section 226 (3) and 226 (4) of the Companies Act as applicable in case of appointment of company auditor,

 ii.   if he is holding appointment as the statutory auditor under Section 224 of the Companies Act and

iii.   on becoming subject to any of the disqualifications mentioned in (i) and (ii) above after being appointed as the cost auditor.

12.2.8 COST AUDIT REPORT

According to sub-section (i) of Section 233 (B), the auditor appointed under that sanction is expected to conduct the audit in such manner as may be specified in the order issued by the Central Government. Further, as per Section 233 (B) (4), the cost auditor must forward his report to the Central Government and to the company within 120 days of the closing of the year to which the audit related. The report is to be given in the form prescribed for the purpose.

The Central Government has issued Cost Audit (Report) Rules, 1968 specifying the form of the report and the additional information, which should be included therein in the form of annexure. The rules have also set down the various points on which the auditor should make his observations and gives his conclusions. The rules have been superseded by a Cost Audit (Report) Rules, 1996.

The auditor must further report on the adequacy of cost accounting records maintained by the company as prescribed by the Government under Section 209 (1) (d) of the Act to confirm that they give a true and fair view of the cost of production, processing, manufacturing or mining activities, as the case may be. If the auditor's report contains any qualification, the company must furnish to the Central Government full explanation on any such qualification within 30 days of the receipt of such report.

In the cost audit report, the cost auditor is supposed to mention the following points:

i.   Whether proper records of fixed assets in detail are mentioned or not.

ii. Whether the assets have been properly revalued during the year and what was the basis of revaluation.

iii. Whether all the assets are properly verified and discrepancies, if any, are properly dealt with in the books of accounts.

iv. Proper accounting records as required by Section 209 (l) (d) have been kept or not.

If there is any additional information that the auditor would like to furnish, he may include in the annexure to the report.

12.2.9 DISTINCTION BETWEEN FINANCIAL AUDIT AND COST AUDIT

POINTS OF DIFFERENCE	FINANCIAL AUDIT	COST AUDIT
1. Concept	Financial audit is an audit of financial accounts, supporting vouchers or documents and financial statements.	Cost audit is an audit of cost accounts, cost statements and cost accounting plans.
2. Inter-relationship	It is not necessary for a financial auditor to examine cost accounts except for the purpose of valuation of inventory.	As the source of cost accounts is financial accounts, the cost auditor has to make a detailed checking of expenses.
3. Objective	The primary objective of financial audit is to see whether necessary accounts, records and documents have been maintained by the organisation and whether the profit and loss account and the balance sheet give a true and fair view of the profit and loss and state of affairs, respectively.	The primary objects of cost audit are to verify whether costs have been ascertained on the basis of cost accounting principles, whether cost records have been properly maintained and whether the cost of production and sale have been correctly worked out.
4. Nature	Financial audit is somewhat a post-mortem examination. It looks back to the past.	Even though cost audit also refers to the past, it creates thinking for the future. It is therefore forward-looking to a great extent.

POINTS OF DIFFERENCE	FINANCIAL AUDIT	COST AUDIT
5. Verification of stock	The financial auditor has only to see whether all categories of stock have been included in the accounts in true quantities and values.	The cost auditor has not only to check the cost of each item of stock, but also to check whether the stocks are maintained at proper level or not.
6. Purpose	Financial audit is essentially an audit on behalf of the proprietors or shareholders.	Cost audit is a tool in the hands of the management. Statutory cost audit is, however, conducted as per order of the Central Government.
7. Compulsion	Financial audit is compulsory for each company in each financial year as per the Companies Act.	As per the Companies Act, statutory cost audit is only required for the year if it is so ordered by the Central Government.
8. Submission of report	The financial auditor submits his report to his clients. In case of company, such report is required to be submitted to the shareholders.	Cost auditor also submits his report to his clients. In case of statutory cost audit, such report is required to be submitted to the Central Government.

12.2.10 CEILING ON NUMBER OF AUDITS

Section 233B (2) of the Companies Act provides that the cost auditor shall be appointed by the Board of Directors of the company as per the provisions of Section 224 (1B) and with the previous approval of the Central Government. According to Section 224 (1B), the number of audit that an auditor or a firm of auditors can undertake has certain maximum ceiling. This ceiling is as follows:

In Case of a Firm of Cost Accountants
Twenty companies (other than private companies) for every partner of the firm who is not in full time employment. Not more than ten out of the twenty companies should have a paid up share capital of Rs. 25 lakhs or more.

In Case of an Individual Cost Accountant Which is in Full-Time Employment
Twenty companies (other than private companies) of which not more than ten out of the twenty companies should have a paid up share capital of Rs. 25 lakhs or more.

In Case of an Individual Cost Accountant Who is Not in Full-Time Employment
There is no limit on the number of companies that such a person can audit.

The board of directors should obtain a written certificate from the person proposed to be appointed as cost auditor that he is not violating the aforesaid ceiling.

12.3 MANAGEMENT AUDIT

It has been advocated in recent years that accountants should become more concerned with the efficiency of their clients, rather than concentrating their attentions almost exclusively on the accuracy of accounting records and financial statements relating to past periods. This could entail a professional firm's undertaking what has become known as a management, operations or efficiency audit in addition to fulfilling its basic statutory duties.

Management audit reveals irregularities and defects in the working of management and suggests the ways to improve the efficiency of management. It concentrates on results and does not examine whether procedures have been followed or not.

12.3.1 Definition

Management audit is performed to examine, review and appraise the various policies and functions of the management on the basis of certain standards. It attempts to evaluate the performance of various management processes of an organisation.

According to Taylor and Perry, "Management audit is the comprehensive examination of an enterprise to appraise its organisational structure, policies and procedures in order to determine whether sound management exists at all levels, ensuring effective relationships with the outside world".

According to the Institute of Internal Auditors, management audit is "a future oriented, independent and systematic evaluation of the activities of all levels of management for the purpose of improving organizational profitability and increasing the attainment of the other organizational objectives".

So, from the above definitions, it can be simply stated that ''[m]anagement audit is that type of audit which examines, reviews and appraises the various policies and actions of the management on the basis of established norms and standards".

12.3.2 Objectives

The following are the main objectives of management audit:

i. To reveal any irregularity or defect in the process of management and to suggest improvements to obtain the best results.

ii. To assist all levels of management from top to bottom through constant monitoring of all operations of the organisation.

iii. To review the performance of the management through close observation of inputs and outputs.

iv. To assist management in achieving co-ordination among various departments.

v. To assist management in establishing good relations with the employees and to elaborate duties, rights and liabilities of the entire staff.

vi. To recommend changes in the policies and procedures for a better future.

vii. To ensure most effective relationship with the outsiders and the most efficient internal organisation.

viii. To recommend for better human relation approach, new management development and overall organisational plans and objectives.

12.3.3 Importance

Management audit is concerned with assessment of efficiency and soundness of management to lead the business to its goal. It critically reviews all aspects of management performances and prescribes ways and means for its improvement.

Management audit is very important for the following reasons:

Reviews Plans and Policies

The management holds periodical meetings for the review of the organisation's performance and for the assessment of their operations to ascertain whether these are performed according to the plans and policies adopted by them. But if the plans and policies are defective, the assessment will be of no use. Hence, there should be some independent review of the plans and policies as formulated by the management. The functions are performed by the management auditors.

Identification of Management Weaknesses
Management audit properly spots the inefficiencies and weaknesses of management. It assesses the soundness of plans adopted and the adequacy of control system for making the plans successful.

Proper Advice to the Management
Management audit does not rest simply on identifying shortcomings. To provide proper solution for removal of these shortcomings is one of the major functions of management auditors.

Advising the Prospective Investors
Management audit can also be useful to a prospective investor who is considering a big investment in the organisation. The management auditor engaged by him can collect such information from the organisation as will be useful in evaluating the investment decision.

Taking Over of Sick Industry
Before deciding to take over a sick organisation, the government can order a management audit in such an organisation and understand the actual causes of failure. On the basis of the recommendations from the management auditors, the government can take proper steps accordingly.

Helping in Foreign Collaboration
In case of industrial collaboration, the foreign collaborators can collect useful information about the management and the future of the collaborating unit through management audit and can take right decision.

Guides the Bank in Sanctioning Loan
Before granting loan or participating in the equity capital of a company, a bank or financial institution may perform management audit to ensure that their investment in the company would be safe and secured in the hands of the management.

Guard against Short-sighted Project
As the tenure of the directors is very short, they become prone to take decisions keeping in view only short-term profit, ignoring its adverse effect on the company in the long run. Management audit can act as a guard against such possibility.

12.3.4 SCOPE
The following are the important areas fall within the normal terms of reference of management audit:

i.   Whether the basic aims and objectives of the enterprise are being fulfilled in practice.

ii. Whether the enterprise is being successful in adapting itself to technological change.

iii. Whether the management structure is suitable.

iv. Whether management is efficient at all levels and to extent to which economies are possible.

v.   Whether the policies with regard to staff recruitment and training are adequate, and whether staff morale is satisfactory.

vi. Whether there is a proper communication system both upwards and downwards throughout the enterprise including a proper management information system.

vii. Whether the enterprise's share of the market is increasing or declining and how it compares with its main competitors.

viii. Whether the return on capital employed is satisfactory and how it compares with other companies in the same industry.

ix. Whether the management has been able to establish good relations with the employees and how it compares with other companies.

x. Whether its relationship with the outside world is effective and whether its corporate image in the eyes of outsiders is satisfactory.

12.3.5 STEPS

Management auditors are appointed to help the management obtain suggestions from the auditors for improving efficiency of the entire organisation or the specific areas assigned to them. Management audit, therefore, comprises of three basic steps. These are as follows:

i. Examination of management performance

ii. Reporting defects and irregularities

iii. Presenting suggestions for improvement

These basic steps can further be broken down into the following stages: (1) study of the activities, (ii) detailed diagnosis, (iii) determination of purpose and relationship, (iv) looking for deficiencies, (v) analytical balance, (vi) testing of effectiveness, (vii) searching for problems, (viii) ascertainment of solutions, (ix) determination of alternatives, (x) seeking out methods of improvement.

The auditors conducting management audit begin their work with discussions with the management executives and employees; then they note down their findings and make out their probable recommendations on the basis of those findings. Finally, they submit their final report along with their recommendations.

12.3.6 ADVANTAGES

The importance of management audit can be understood if the advantages of the management audit is studied. There is no denying the fact that the management audit is result-oriented. It provides the following advantages:

i. It helps the management in preparing plans, objectives and policies and suggests the ways and means to implement those plans and policies.

ii. The inefficiencies and ineffectiveness on the part of the management can be brought to light.

iii. The techniques of management audit are not only applicable to all factors of production, but also to all elements of cost.

iv. Proper management audit techniques can help the business to stop capital erosion.

v. It increases the overall profitability of a concern through constant review of solvency, profitability and efficiency position of the organisation.

vi. It helps the top management in arriving at correct management decision without any delay.

vii. It helps the management in strengthening its communication system within and outside the business.

viii. It can help management in the preparation of budgets and resource management policies.

ix. It can also help the management in training of personnel and marketing policies.

12.3.7 DISADVANTAGES

The disadvantages of management audit can briefly be stated as follows:

i. The introduction of management audit technique involves heavy expenditure.

ii. Managers will hesitate to take initiative, as the management auditor will always pinpoint some short-comings in the action.

iii. Managers will always try to keep the records up to date rather than improving efficiency and reducing the costs.

iv. Due to ineffectiveness and inefficiency of the management auditor, in all cases, management audit cannot provide result-oriented service.

v. Management auditors are sometimes engaged in some activities detrimental to social objects of audit-ing, for example, evasion of tax.

12.3.8 APPOINTMENT

A group of auditors should be appointed to conduct management audit, as it is not expected that an individual auditor have all the expertise in all fields of management to conduct this type of audit effectively. Hence a group is formed taking experts from each area of management field for this purpose. The internal auditors must also be included in this group as they are familiar with internal affairs of the organisation and management.

Management audit involves an appraisal of activities of the management of the organisation. So, the auditors must study the organisational activities and its plan of action in detail. Further, the management auditors should get full co-operation from the top-level management to enable them to conduct the audit effectively. But the effectiveness of management audit will depend on the scope of audit, which the management has to decide.

12.3.9 QUALITIES OF MANAGEMENT AUDITORS

The task of performing the management audit cannot be assigned to an ordinary person. The management auditor should have sufficient experience and knowledge about the functions of management. In fact, he should have the ability to understand different management activities of the organisation, viz., internal control system, production planning and control, personnel management techniques, etc. The different qualities that the management auditor should possess are stated below:

i. The management auditor should have the ability to understand the problems of the organisation.

ii. He should have a clear understanding as to the nature, purposes and objectives of the organisation.

iii. He should have the ability to determine the progress of the organisation.

iv. He should be tactful in dealing with different employees and officers of the organisation.

v. He should have pleasing and dynamic personality.

vi. He should have general understanding of different types of laws, particularly the Income Tax Act and the Companies Act.

vii. He should have a sound knowledge in preparing various reports presented to management.

viii. He should be able to assess and examine the internal control system of the organisation.

ix. He should be familiar with various principles of management, viz., planning, control, management by exceptions, etc.

x.   He should have good knowledge of financial statement analysis techniques like fund flow analysis, ratio analysis, standard costing etc.

12.3.10 Management Auditor's Report

After conducting management audit, the management auditors are required to prepare a report to be submitted to the management of the organisation. On the basis of findings and definite information, the auditors prepare a report making recommendations for improvement in the functioning of the management. He should not hesitate in criticising the management in case some deficiencies are found. His recommendations should be constructive and adequate for the improvement of the overall efficiency of the organisation.

Nevertheless the report must be clear and unambiguous, either making the point that efficiency is such that no change is advocated, or if reorganisation is considered advisable, then the management auditor must be sufficiently confident of his own ability to have assessed the situation that he can make adequate proposals, which will lead to improvement and increased profitability.

12.3.11 Difference Between Management Audit and Cost Audit

Cost audit is the detailed checking as well as the verification of the correctness of the costing techniques, systems and cost accounting data. On the other hand, management audit is the detailed examination of an organisation to appraise its organisational structure, policies and procedures of management in order to determine the existence of effectiveness of management system in the organisation.

The following are the points of differences between management audit and cost audit:

POINTS OF DIFFERENCE	MANAGEMENT AUDIT	COST AUDIT
1. Scope of audit	Management audit is a comprehensive review of all aspects of management functions.	Cost audit is the verification of correctness of cost accounting data, costing techniques and system.
2. Legal compulsion	Management audit is not a statutory requirement.	In certain industries, cost audit is compulsory and a statutory requirement.
3. Qualification of auditor	The management auditor must be a person having wide expertise in the field of management and accountancy.	The cost auditor must possess prescribed qualifications as per the provisions of the Companies Act.
4. Area of audit	The management auditor critically examines the policies, procedures and the techniques of management adopted and report on their effectiveness.	The cost auditor checks the cost accounting data only.
5. Periodicity	It covers wide area of activities of the management and may be for more than one financial year.	The cost audit is conducted for every financial year separately.

POINTS OF DIFFERENCE	MANAGEMENT AUDIT	COST AUDIT
6. Submission of audit report	There is no time limit for the submission of management audit report.	There is a stipulated time limit within which cost audit report has to be submitted.
7. Regularity	Management audit is not a regular feature. Whenever need arises, the management may decide to conduct management audit.	It is a regular feature and required to be conducted year after year.
8. Accountability	The management auditor is accountable to the management only.	The cost auditor is accountable to the shareholders as well as to the Central government.

12.3.12 Dɪꜰꜰᴇʀᴇɴᴄᴇ Bᴇᴛᴡᴇᴇɴ Mᴀɴᴀɢᴇᴍᴇɴᴛ Aᴜᴅɪᴛ ᴀɴᴅ Fɪɴᴀɴᴄɪᴀʟ Aᴜᴅɪᴛ

Management audit is an examination of efficiency of management at all levels throughout the organisation in order to ascertain whether sound management prevails, thus facilitating the most effective relationship with the outside world and the most efficient organisation.

On the other hand, financial audit is an audit of financial accounts, supporting vouchers or documents and financial statements. So, financial audit and management audit may be distinguished on the following lines:

POINTS OF DIFFERENCE	FINANCIAL AUDIT	MANAGEMENT AUDIT
1. Concept	Financial audit is an examination of financial accounts and financial statements.	Management audit is a comprehensive and constructive examination of the efficiency of management at all levels throughout the organisation.
2. Objectives	The primary objectives of financial audit are to ascertain whether all the transactions have been properly accounted for in the books of accounts and whether the financial statements of the organisation give a true and fair view of the financial result and financial position.	The primary objectives of management audit are to make an evaluation of the efficiency of management at different levels and make useful suggestions for removal of inefficiencies of management functions.
3. Continuity	Financial audit is required to be done every year.	Management audit is not required to be conducted every year.
4. Scope	The scope of financial audit is quite narrow.	The scope of management audit is much broader.

POINTS OF DIFFERENCE	FINANCIAL AUDIT	MANAGEMENT AUDIT
5. Efficiency of employees	The efficiency of employees is not assessed in financial audit.	The efficiency of the employees is assessed in management audit.
6. Auditor	Only professional accountants are competent to perform financial audit.	Management audit can be performed by a group of experts, consisting of management experts, professional accountants, engineers etc.
7. Cost involvement	Financial audit involves less cost.	Management audit is quite costly.
8. Duration	Financial audit covers the accounts of only one year.	Management audit covers accounts and other aspects of management activities for a number of years.

12.4 HUMAN RESOURCE AUDIT

12.4.1 CONCEPT OF HUMAN RESOURCE

Of all the elements that result in profit generation of an organisation, the most important factor is the human resource factor. The growth and development of the organisation including increase in productivity, profitability and expansion of the organisation is dependent on the performance and efficiency of all the workers and employees of the organisation in general and the dynamism on the part of the top management in particular. All these human factors, which contribute in the growth and expansion of the business, either directly or indirectly, may be termed as human assets or human resources.

12.4.2 CONCEPT OF HUMAN RESOURCE ACCOUNTING

Touche Ross and Co., a Canadian CPA firm has introduced for the first time the concept of human resource accounting as a part of its management information system in the belief that a good human resource accounting system can provide information of vital importance for short term as well as long-term decision-making and performance measurement.

According to Eric Flamholtz, "Accounting for people as an organizational resource involves measuring the costs incurred by business firms and other organizations to recruit, select, hire, train and develop human assets",

12.4.3 CONCEPT OF HUMAN ASSET AUDIT

The decision of the investor to invest in the company is greatly influenced by the working of the managerial staff of the company. So, disclosure of information regarding human capital in the annual report of the company may help prospective investors in forming an opinion whether to invest in the organisation or not. This may remove the standing criticism of the financial reporting that 'one of the outstanding omissions is information concerning the human capital employed.'

But before including human capital employed as a part of annual account, it has to be ensured that the human capital as included is reliable and computed on the basis of generally accepted principles for the valuation of human capital. In order to get reliable value of human resources, the necessity of human resource audit is felt. The Human Resource Audit examination should not relate the rightness to the process of valuation of the asset, but it should see that the information upon which the calculations are based upon are reliable and authentic.

So, the definition of human resource audit may be given in the following way:

"Examination of the human asset figure that appears in the balance sheet through checking, inspecting and appraising the various facts and figures which are based on the estimated value of human assets, is called human resource audit."

12.4.4 STEPS FOR HUMAN RESOURCE AUDIT

The following steps may be suggested for the purpose of audit of human resources:

i.   The nature of the organisation should be thoroughly examined to know whether it is a firm of professionals or of the general business.

ii.   Interview with the top managerial personnel should be taken to acquire information regarding the valuation of human resources.

iii. It should be seen that provision for depreciation of human assets has been adequately provided.

iv.   It should be confirmed that the correct value has been placed in the balance sheet.

v.   The internal control system as regards various information of human resources should be reviewed to evaluate its effectiveness.

vi.   It should also be ensured that all contingencies that have the effect on the valuation of human resources are duly considered in the value measurement of human resources.

12.4.5 PROBLEMS OF HUMAN RESOURCE AUDIT

Though the auditor is not an expert for the human resource valuation, yet he has to be intimately connected with the measurement of human resources. For this, the auditor has to appraise the values that are placed in the balance sheet either in the form of investment against human resources or in the form of Net Value of Human Assets. But there are certain problems, which may be encountered by the auditor while verifying the value of human resources. These are as follows:

i.   It is not possible to determine the value of an individual with perfection. Therefore, the audit procedure under this system of audit is bound to give unrealistic approach to the direction.

ii.   It is difficult for the auditors to measure the value of the employees who are trained by the methods suggested by the accountants or the valuers.

iii. As there is a scope for a subjective judgment in valuing the resource, the audit procedure may not give the guarantee as to the reliability of the data.

iv.   It is difficult for the auditor to collect the required correct information upon which the human resource valuation is based.

v.   As the concept of audit under the name, 'human resource audit' has not attained much popularity and its use is not found so far widely in organisations, the auditor may be put into the dilemma as to the course of action to be followed for the purpose of audit.

12.4.6 ADVANTAGES OF HUMAN RESOURCE AUDIT

In spite of the existence of various problems that stand on the way of conducting an efficient audit of human resources, the audit procedure adopted for this purpose may provide the following advantages:

   i.   The audited figure may be taken by the management as reliable for taking any decision on the matter.

   ii. The actual audit of this figure may help the auditor to give his audit report about the true and fair view of the state of affairs of the business.

   iii. It may invite the investor to invest more funds in the business.

   iv. Thorough enquiry as to allocation of resources among various competitive opportunities made by the company can be made possible through this system of audit.

   v.   The audit of human asset may rightfully justify whether expenditure incurred in this regard is reasonable.

   vi. The audited figure of human resource may form a valuable basis in the preparation of social accounts.

12.5 SOCIAL AUDIT

12.5.1 CONCEPT OF SOCIAL RESPONSIBILITY

Corporate entities are now regarded as a great social force. They are not expected to be only engaged in profit earning activities and paying dividend to the shareholders. They have an important role to play in the social well-being. They have high responsibility to the society. Such responsibilities can be identified in two directions:

Internal Social Responsibility
It includes:

   i.   Extending staff benefits comprising of indirect monetary benefits like provident fund, gratuity, bonus, insurance, leave salary, medical benefits, housing facility, recreation and entertainment for employees and workers and other benefits.

   ii. Keeping the environment of the factory and its surrounding area clean and non-hazardous.

   iii. Paying the statutory dues in time.

   iv. Supplying quality products at fair prices and

   v.   Giving fair return to investors commensurate with risk.

External Social Responsibility
It includes:

   i.   community development through creation and maintenance of roads, parks, playgrounds and provision for drinking water facilities,

   ii. tree plantation for the improvement of environment,

   iii. growth and expansion of the business and thereby creating new job opportunities,

   iv. setting up plants in backward areas.

12.5.2 CONCEPT OF SOCIAL ACCOUNTING

In recent years, a school of thought has developed a new concept, which advocates that as large companies have responsibilities to persons other than their shareholders, so information relevant to such groups should be provided.

For instance, it has been suggested that information should be given dealing with such matters as:

i. Remuneration of employees and fringe benefits.

ii. Retirement arrangements for employees.

iii. Health and safety measures.

iv. Staff training programmers.

v. Industrial relations.

vi. Pricing policies in respect of goods and services provided.

vii. Quality control over products sold.

viii. Integrity of advertising campaigns.

ix. Pollution controls.

x. Energy conservation.

Social accounting is a system of accounting, which indicates how, and in what way a business organisation performs the above-mentioned obligations for the society. So, "Social Accounting can be defined as a method of measurement and reporting, internal and external, of the information concerning the impact of an entity and its activities on society".

According to the National Association of Accountants (NAA) of the United States, social accounting is the "identification, measurement, monitoring and reporting of the social and economic effects of an institution on society. It is intended for both internal managerial and external accountability purposes and is an outgrowth of changing values that have led society to redefine its notion of a corporation's social responsibility".

12.5.3 CONCEPT OF SOCIAL AUDIT

The term 'social accounting' and 'social audit' are used sometimes in the literature interchangeably. But social accounting is concerned with the development of measurement system to monitor social performance, and social audit is the use of an independent auditing system to verify a firm's records of social performance. John Crowhurst in his book *Auditing Guides to Principles and Practice* has clearly explained these two terms. According to him, '[s]ocial accounting is the process of determination of social performance of an organization", while 'social audit' is the enquiry into the corporate social accounting records by an outside agency that can opine with a view to attestation and authentication of such results and reports.

So, social audit may be defined as "assessment of the performance of an industry as a whole vis-à-vis its total responsibility". But social responsibility in the present day is not a total concept relating to a single industry. Each organisation forming part of an industry is considered to have specific social responsibility. Social audit, may therefore, be rightly defined as "the assessment of social performance of an organization".

12.5.4 OBJECTIVES OF SOCIAL AUDIT

The social audit is a very new and growing area of audit. The modern accountants have developed several approaches and techniques for the effective conduct of social audit. Social audit techniques, in fact, are to be framed by the accountants taking the following objectives of social audit into consideration:

i. To make an assessment of social performance by an organisation.

ii.   To inform the management of an organisation of the accuracy and fairness of its social accounts.

iii. To evaluate the socio-economic contributions made by an industry.

iv.   To bring to light for public knowledge how far an organisation has discharged its responsibility to the society.

v.   To advise the management in the preparation of social accounts.

vi.   To evaluate with the help of financial data, various social actions of an organisation and describe them in properly analyzed form in the absence of socio-economic performance statement.

vii. To check whether various social actions of an organisation have be evaluated under proper categories like products, employees, local community, environment, public in the social income statement.

viii. To examine the correctness of 'value added statements' when the contribution of an enterprise to the national economy is described through such statements.

ix.   To verify the assets shown in the social balance sheet and check their values.

x.   To examine the correctness of amount shown as social equity in the liability side of the social balance sheet.

12.5.5 IMPORTANCE

Social audit is a new concept and has emerged out of the growing awareness of the responsibility of the business towards the society. In the changing socio-economic scenario, the social audit has assumed a special significance. In fact society now demands something more from the auditing profession. Apart from expecting the traditional services from audit, i.e., ensuring reliability and fairness of accounts, the society now requires audit to become society-oriented for safeguarding the interest of various elements of the society. So, social audit is very important in the present business environment. The importance of social audit can be stated in the following way:

Assessment of Social Contribution
Social audit assesses the social performance of a business enterprise. Only through social audit one can get a correct picture of the contributions made by an enterprise to the society.

Presentation of Annual Social Accounts
In order to conduct social audit, social accounts are also required to be prepared. Attention is given at present for the development of suitable social accounting system with standards for measurement of social performance and presentation of annual social accounts.

Guide to the Management
The social auditors may guide the management in the measurement of social performance, proper keeping of social accounting records and presentation of social statements. Their specialised knowledge may be of immense value to the management.

Contribution of the Industry
Social audit has also an important role to play in relation to an industry, as it can also successfully assess the overall contribution made by an industry to the society and the national economy.

Allocation of Scarce Resources
To ensure effective allocation of scarce resources, evaluation of different social projects should be done from the viewpoint of their social costs and social benefits. This evaluation is done through social audit.

12.5.6 SOCIAL AUDIT IN INDIA

When the Central Government issued Manufacturing and Other Companies (Auditor's Report) Order in 1975 and when it is implemented as social audit by Company Law Board by the introduction of Section 227(4A) of the Companies Act, 1956, it becomes compulsory for the company auditor to give report on several additional matters of social importance. A number of audit experts described these steps by the Central Government as the introduction of social audit in India. But it is not at all a social audit, as social audit is not an audit for expressing auditor's opinion on the matters of internal control, propriety and compliance. However, this can be considered a right step in keeping the companies aware of their social responsibility and accountability to the society.

For the first time in India, the Tata Iron and Steel Company published the report of their Social Audit Committee in the year 1980. The Committee had to make an assessment of the social performance of the company in the light of specific provision contained in the Articles of Association regarding its responsibility to the society. But the report of the committee was mere description of socio-economic contributions made by the company. No socio-economic activity wise operating statement showing costs and benefits of various social actions was prepared.

In India, audit of social accounts is not yet in practice and the term 'social audit' is still in a conceptual stage in the country. There are two basic reasons for this situation:

i. There is no statutory provision in any act attempted to make it compulsory the keeping of social accounting and conducting the audit thereof.

ii. In our country, no standard for the preparation of statement of social performance and socio-economic operating statement have not yet developed.

So, in India, the concept of social audit is still a vision in reality.

12.6 TAX AUDIT

12.6.1 DEFINITION

Statutory audit is conducted mainly keeping in view the information requirement of the shareholders. But there are also other parties who are interested in the financial information of the organisation. One such interested party in the Tax Authority, which needs information on the correct income of the assessee for the tax provisions point of view. With this objective, the Income Tax Act of 1961 has included a number of provisions, which require audit of statements prepared for tax purposes.

So, the term 'tax audit' refers to the audit of income and expenses or specific claims of deductions and exemptions that are required to be computed as per the provisions of the Income Tax Act. Tax audit is a specific requirement under the Income Tax Act. It is required in addition to financial audit, which does not fulfill the specific requirement of the tax authority.

12.6.2 TYPES OF TAX AUDIT

There are three types of tax audit under the Income Tax Act. These are as follows:

i. Compulsory tax audit under Section 44AB.

ii. Tax audit for claiming exemptions or deductions.

iii. Selective tax audit under Section 142 (2A).

12.6.3 Tax Auditor

Only an accountant as defined in the explanation to Section 288(2) of the Income Tax Act can conduct a tax audit under any of the provisions of the Act. A person eligible for the appointment as auditor of a company under Section 226(2) of the Companies Act, 1956 is also included in the definition of accountant. A chartered accountant, to conduct tax audit, must however, be a practicing chartered accountant holding a certificate of practice as required under the Chartered Accountants Act, 1949.

In the case of companies, the tax audit can be conducted by the statutory auditor or by any other chartered accountant in practice. The appointment of tax auditor can be made by the management of the organisation. Thus, in case of a company, the board of directors or the officer so authorised by it can appoint the tax auditor. Similarly, a sole proprietor or a partner of a firm or any other authorised person can appoint the tax auditor.

12.6.4 Compulsory Tax Audit Under Section 44AB

Since the assessment year 1985–86, certain provisions under Section 44AB of the Income tax Act, 1961 was added to provide that certain persons have to get compulsory tax audit of their accounts. This section provides that every person:

i.   carrying on business, if his total sales or gross receipts in the previous year exceeds Rs. 40 lakhs or

ii. carrying on profession, if his gross receipts exceeds Rs. 10 lakhs in the previous year shall get his accounts of the previous year audited by an 'accountant' before the 'specified date' and obtain before that date the report of such audit in the prescribed form duly signed and verified by such accountant. 'Specified date' means 31st day of December of the assessment year, where the assessee is a Company and 31st day of October of the assessment year in any other case.

So, unlike statutory audit, tax audit under this section is not confined to company only. The approach of tax auditor is similar to that of statutory auditor. He applies the same generally accepted principles for conducting audit and can rely on the technique of selective verification. However, he is to keep in mind the requirement of Income Tax Act and various judicial pronouncements in this area of application.

12.6.5 Penalty for Non-Compliance

Section 271B of the Income Tax Act, 1961 prescribes a penalty of a sum equal to 0% to 5% of the total sales or gross receipts, as the case may be or Rs. 1,00,000, whichever is lower, for a person, where he fails to get his accounts audited as per Section 44AB or to furnish such report with his return of income. But, if a person can show reasonable cause against his failure, no such penalty may be imposed.

12.6.6 Tax Audit Report

The tax auditor is required to express his opinion in the tax audit report about the tax computation method adopted by the enterprise. He has to express in his report as to:

i.   Whether or not the financial statements give a true and fair view of the profit or loss and the state of affairs, if the accounts of the assessee are not subjected to audit under any other law.

ii. Whether or not the prescribed particulars contained in the statement annexed to the audit report are true and correct.

Rule 6G of the Income Tax Rules prescribe the formats in which the auditor has to submit his audit report. The various formats are-

Form 3CA + 3CD

In the case of a person who carries on business or profession and who is required under any other law to get his accounts audited, the tax auditor has to give his report in Form 3CA and annex with the audit report a statement of particulars in form 3CD.

Form 3CB + 3CD

In the case of a person who carries on business but whose accounts are not audited under any other law, the tax auditor has to give the audit report in form 3CB and annex thereto a statement of particulars in Form 3CD.

12.7 VAT AUDIT

12.7.1 CONCEPT OF VAT AUDIT

The implementation of state-level Value Added Tax (VAT) System for Commodity Taxation in 21 States of India effective from 1.4.2005 is seen as a major change in the Commodity Taxation System. The state legislatures providing for VAT audit by Chartered Accountants have reaffirmed the faith and confidence reposed by the society in Chartered Accountants.

Though the basic principles of audit remain the same for all type of audit yet the audit differs to a great extent so far as reporting requirements are concerned. The purpose of audit under the Companies Act is different than the purpose of audit under the Income Tax Act. The above two audits may also differ from the audit under VAT Law as all the three audits are undertaken with different objectives, which are divergent from each other.

The audit under the VAT Law differs from the earlier two audits to a great degree in the sense that so far as the books of accounts etc. are concerned the auditor gives his opinion as to whether the financial statements give a true and fair picture and whether they are in conformity with the books of accounts or not at the same time it also certifies the turnover of sales and purchases, calculation of output tax, the various exemptions and the deductions claimed, the certification of input tax credit etc. Therefore, the audit under the VAT Law is far more complicated.

12.7.2 ROLE OF VAT AUDITOR

The role of VAT auditor in the initial years of implementation of VAT would be that of an advisor to the taxpayers. In playing the advisory role, the auditor will have to help in devising a proper accounting system as will generate the required information regarding the output tax, input tax credit etc.

The role of VAT auditor vis-à-vis the VAT administrator is that the auditor while discharging his functions finds out whether the turnover of sales/purchases is shown correctly in the returns and backed up by the accounts and other relevant documents. The deductions claimed by the taxpayer from the turnover of sales are genuine and supported by valid documents. The claim of Input Tax Credit has been properly made, i.e., it has not been claimed on the higher side or on such purchases, which are not eligible for grant of Input Tax Credit.

12.7.3 PREPARATION FOR VAT AUDIT

A VAT auditor has to make certain preliminary preparation before actual execution of VAT audit under the VAT Law. The major steps required to be undertaken foe preparation are as follows:

i. After accepting the audit assignment, the audit should get first familiar with the business as given in (SA 310). The auditor should make himself familiar with the process of production so also the distribution channel. Similarly, the sources of purchase, the items sold should be listed out. Further it should be ascertained whether the auditee has opted for composition scheme or not.

ii. The auditor should obtain a complete list of all the accounting records relating to sale/purchase of goods and stock and also the various source of documents in which the entries are recorded in the books of accounts and the process of their generation.

iii. The auditor should know the major accounting policies based on which the accounting is done. If there is any significant change in the accounting policy giving rise to some material effect on the tax liability, the same should be invariably reported.

iv. Before determining the extent of audit checks to be applied, the auditor should ascertain whether there in internal check system in operation in the entity. He should particularly find out how the purchase/sale gets initiated and materialised. If the internal control is reliable, the extent of audit may be reduced and should be focused only on those areas whether the auditor feels that greater degree of audit risk is involved.

v. The auditor should have thorough knowledge of the State VAT Law under which the audit is to be conducted. The auditor should also have some knowledge about the judicial pronouncements made by the Tribunals and the Courts on the various facets of these laws.

12.7.4 APPROACH TO VAT AUDIT

While designing the audit programme, the auditor has to ensure that the programme includes the performance of such audit checks as will enable the auditor to get the information which he needs to be analysed for reporting. He should also ensure that:

- The turnover of sales/purchases of goods have been properly determined keeping in view not only the generally accepted accounting principles but the definition of turnover of sales in the relevant VAT Law.

- The turnover of purchases should be tested by applying audit checks as will enable the auditor to get the purchases eligible for grant of input tax credit segregated from other purchases.

- The auditor is also required to comment on the timely filing of the returns under the VAT Law. For this purpose, the auditor is expected to list out the due dates of filing of returns and find out the reasons for delay in filing the returns if any.

- The auditor has to give his report on the tax deducted at source (TDS). Therefore, such tests are to be applied as will enable him to report on the applicability of TDS provisions, the accuracy of the amount deducted and paid, timely issue of TDS certificate, and filing of TDS returns.

- The auditor is also expected to check the consolidation of the returns filed for all the periods covered in the year under audit.

So the audit approach of the VAT auditor under the VAT System is more or less similar to the approach adopted by the auditor while conducting the tax audit under the provisions of Section 44AB of the Income Tax Act, 1961. However, the reporting requirements vary to a considerable extent.

12.7.5 AUDIT REPORT UNDER VAT

The auditor is expected to give his opinion on the adequacy of accounting records, correctness and completeness and arithmetical consistency of returns filed. Further he has to state the basis of his opinion, i.e., the accounts, financial statements and documents verified by him to arrive at the above conclusion.

So far as the comment on the variation of tax liability is concerned, the auditor has to quantify exactly the amount by which the liability increases or decreases. Therefore, he has to state either the tax liability shown in the return is correct or it is incorrect by what extent. Thus, an amount of certification of tax liability is involved therein, which casts greater responsibility on the auditor. Fortunately the VAT audit under VAT laws is to be conducted on yearly basis. A time period of about six to eight months is given in the VAT Laws to get the audit done and submit the audit report. This time can be utilised by the profession in preparing for the VAT Audits by sharpening their tools.

12.8 GREEN (ENVIRONMENTAL) AUDIT

Environmental audit is an excellent management tool for relating productivity to pollution. The Environment (Protection) Act, 1986 under the Rule 14 requires an industry to submit annual environmental statement by the 30th of September every year, from 1993 onwards, to the relevant State Pollution Control Board. Rule 14 is applicable to any industry or organisation, which possesses or requires consent or authorisation under Water (Prevention & Control of Pollution) Act, 1974, Air (Prevention & Control of Pollution) Act, 1981 and/or Hazardous Waste (Management & Handling) Rules, 1989.

12.8.1 DEFINITION

Environmental audit is the examination of the correctness of environmental accounts. In broader sense, environmental auditing is the examination of accounts of revenues and costs of environmental and natural resources, their estimate, depreciation and values recorded in the books of accounts.

In the words of N. Rajaraman, "Environmental auditing is a series of activities undertaken on the initiative of an organization's management to evaluate its environmental performance".

The International Chamber of Commerce defines "[e]nvironmental auditing as a basic management tool comprising a systematic, documented, periodic and objective evaluation of how well environmental organization, management and equipment are performing with the aim to safeguard the environment".

So, environmental audit is an excellent management tool to assess the activities of an industry from a pollution viewpoint and measure the efficiency and the adequacy of control measures.

12.8.2 OBJECTIVES

The following are some of the objectives of environmental auditing:

i.   To see that the natural resources are properly utilised.

ii. To control the costs incurred on procuring the natural resources and to ensure that they have been properly classified.

iii. To see that natural resources have been properly shown in a nation's balance sheet as they are the nation's valuable assets.

iv. During production process, when natural resources are utilised, some adverse environmental effects are produced and pollution is created. So, the objective of such an audit is to see that proper steps are taken to control or to prevent such adverse effects like pollution.

v.   To ensure that the natural resources are utilised for industrial development and for national progress.

vi. To see that proper steps have been taken for maintaining health and welfare of the community and also for disposal of harmful wastes and social risks.

12.8.3 Stages of Environmental Audit

As green consciousness is growing and developing, more companies are beginning to evaluate both its commercial implications and the impact of their operations. The environmental audit is essentially a management tool. It implies that companies should not wait for restrictive legislation to bring about changes.

Environmental audit comprises the following stages:

➤ Existing legislative requirements, health and safety practices and forthcoming regulatory developments are analysed.

➤ Internal procedures and external requirements are examined, compared and constructed. The implications of external requirements on production processes and equipments are assessed and the impact in terms of waste and emission are evaluated.

➤ The organisational structure, administration and communication process of the company are analysed to determine the extent to which management is informed of the environmental impact of the company's activities. Gaps are identified and remedies suggested.

12.8.4 Environmental Audit Practice in India

The development of environmental audit can be traced back to the early 1970s. Oil spill off the British South Coast, Bhopal Gas Leak, Chernobyl disaster, pollution of different rivers etc. have lead to increased concern in industrial environmental management. The United States Environmental Protection Agency published their environmental audit policy in 1986, followed by International Chamber of Commerce booklet on Environmental Auditing (1988) and UNEP published their technical report on environmental audit.

In India, recognising the importance of Environmental Audit, its procedure was first notified under the Environment (Protection) Act, 1986 by the Ministry of Environment and Forests. Under this Act, every person carrying on an industry, operation or process requiring consent under Section 25 of the Water (Prevention & Control of Pollution) Act, 1974 or under Section 21 of the Air (Prevention & Control of Pollution) Act, 1981 or both or authorisation under the Hazardous Wastes (Management and Handling) Rule of 1989 issued under the Hazardous (Protection) Act, 1986 is required to submit an environmental audit report. The Environmental Audit Report has been renamed as Environmental Statement in 1993. This statement is required to be submitted to the concerned Pollution Control Boards.

The Environmental Statement should not be treated as a substitute for Environmental Audit, rather as a database for Environmental Audit. The analysis of the data and necessary suggestions for improvement in the environment and efficiency is not outlined in the Environmental Statement. Most of the developed countries like the United States, the United Kingdom, Canada, Australia have already taken up environmental audit for their corporate sector. As of now, any disclosures on the environmental matters in the annual report of an Indian company are voluntary in nature. Environmental audit is conducted by a very limited number of companies in India.

12.9 CORPORATE GOVERNANCE THROUGH AUDIT COMMITTEES

12.9.1 Introduction

The efficiency of a Board depends on the overall performance of its functions, composition and structure of the Board and the procedures followed by it. Ideally, in mid-size to large-size Boards, the Board of Directors constitute sub-committees as part of the Board only to discuss certain issues at Board level in a much detailed and focused manner.

Clause 49 prescribes only two committees as mandatory ones. These are:

i.   Audit Committee

ii. Shareholder's Grievances Committee

Section 292A of the Companies Act, 1956 contains a provision relating to establishment of Audit Committee by every public company having paid up capital of Rs. 5 crores or more. Clause 49 of the uniform listing agreement prescribed by SEBI is applicable to all listed companies. Clause 49 of the listing agreement deals with corporate governance and prescribes the setting up of a qualified and independent Audit Committee.

12.9.2 Area of Work

As per Section 292A of the Companies Act, 1956, Audit Committee should have discussions with the auditors periodically about internal control systems, scope of audit including the observations of auditors and review of the half-yearly and annual financial statements before submission to the Board and also ensure compliance of internal control system. It shall have the authority to investigate into anything in relation to such matters and shall have full access to information contained in the records of the company.

As per Clause 49 of the listing agreement, Audit Committee is empowered to investigate any activity within terms of reference, seek information from any employee, obtain outside advice and secure attendance of outsiders, if necessary. Its role shall include recommending appointment and removal of external auditor, fixation of audit fees, approval of payment for other services, review with the management of the annual financial statements before submission to the Board, reviewing the adequacy of internal control system, oversight of the financial reporting process of the company and disclosure of its financial information to ensure that financial statements are correct, sufficient and credible, reviewing the adequacy of internal audit function, reviewing the financial and risk management policies of the company, reviewing the functioning of the whistle blowing policy and looking into reasons for substantial defaults etc.

12.9.3 Relevant Provisions Regarding Audit Committee

As required by Section 292A of the Companies Act, 1956 every public limited company (listed or unlisted) having a share capital of at least Rs. 5 crores shall constitute a committee of the Board to be known as Audit Committee. The provisions in respect of Audit Committee are as follows:

➢   The Committee shall have at least three (3) members (directors).

➢   Two-third (2/3) of the members shall be non-executive directors.

➢   The Board of Directors shall prescribe the terms of reference of the Committee in writing.

➢   The statutory auditor, the internal auditor and director-in-charge of finance shall attend every meeting of the audit committee but shall not have the right to vote.

➢   Half-yearly and annual accounts should be discussed by the Audit Committee with auditors before presenting the same to the Board.

➢   The Audit Committee shall have the right to investigate any matter covered under the broad terms or reference.

The recommendations of the Audit Committee will be binding on the Board. Though the Board is a superior body, yet it cannot override the recommendations of the Committee. In case the Board does not accept the recommendations of the Audit Committee, it will have to record the reasons and communicate the same to the shareholders.

The other relevant provisions relating to Audit Committee include the following:

➢   The chairman of the Audit Committee shall attend the annual general meeting to provide clarifications on matters relating to audit.

➤ The constitution and composition of the Audit Committee is to be disclosed in the annual report of the company.

➤ Auditors, internal and external, and Director (Finance) shall attend the meeting but not have the right to vote.

➤ Audit Committee should discuss internal control systems, scope of audit, observations of auditors, review of periodic financial statements etc. and compliance of internal control system.

➤ The minutes of the Audit Committee are required to be placed before the next Board Meeting.

Any default in complying with the provisions of Section 292A may attract imprisonment up to one year or fine up to Rs. 50,000 or both. The company and every officer of the company who is in default are liable for prosecution. The offence is compoundable under Section 621A.

12.9.4 FUNCTIONS OF THE AUDIT COMMITTEE

The Audit Committee constituted under this section shall act in accordance with the terms of reference to be specified in writing by the Board. The Audit Committee should have periodic discussions with the auditors about the following matters:

  i.   Internal control system.

 ii.   Scope of audit including the observation of auditors.

iii.   Review the half-yearly and annual financial statements before submission to the Board.

 iv.   Compliance of internal control system.

The Audit Committee shall also have authority to investigate into the matters in relation to the items specified in this section or matters referred to it by the Board of Directors. To carry out such investigation, the Audit Committee will have full access to information contained in the records of the company and the external professional advice, if necessary.

12.9.5 AUDIT COMMITTEE UNDER CLAUSE 49

Revised clause 49 of the listing agreement provides for specific requirements of an Audit Committee. The companies shall be required to comply with the requirements of Clause 49 in relation to Audit Committee, viz.

Qualified and Independent Audit Committee

A qualified and independent audit committee shall be set up by all eligible companies giving the terms of reference, subject to the following stipulations:

  i.   The Audit Committee shall have minimum three directors as members. Two-third of the members of the Audit Committee shall be independent directors.

 ii.   All members of the Audit Committee shall be financially literate and at least one member shall have accounting or related financial management expertise.

iii.   The Chairman of the Audit Committee shall be an independent director.

 iv.   The Chairman of the Audit Committee shall be present at Annual General Meeting to answer the shareholder's queries.

Meeting of Audit Committee

The Audit Committee should meet at least four times in a year and not more than four months shall elapse between two meetings. The quorum shall be either two members or one-third of the members of the Audit

Committee, whichever is greater, but there should be a minimum of two independent members present. There is no bar on the maximum number of sittings an Audit Committee can have.

Powers of Audit Committee

The Audit Committee shall have powers, which should include the following:

i. To investigate any activity within its terms of reference.

ii. To seek information from any employee.

iii. To obtain outside legal or other professional advice.

iv. To secure attendance of outsiders with relevant expertise, if it considered necessary.

Role of Audit Committee

According to Clause 49, the role of the Audit Committee shall include the following:

➤ Oversight of the financial reporting process of the company and the disclosure of its financial information to ensure that the financial statement is correct, sufficient and credible.

➤ Recommending the appointment and removal of external auditor, fixation of audit fee and also approval for payment for any other service.

➤ Reviewing with management the annual financial statements before submission to the Board.

➤ Reviewing with the management, external and internal auditors the adequacy of the internal control systems.

➤ Reviewing the findings of any internal investigations by the internal auditors into matters where there is suspected fraud or irregularity or a failure of internal control systems as a material nature and reporting the matter to the Board.

➤ Reviewing the adequacy of internal audit function, including the structure of the internal audit department, staffing and seniority of the official heading the department, reporting structure coverage and frequency of internal audit.

➤ Discussion with the internal auditors on any significant findings and follow up thereon.

➤ Discussion with the external auditors before the audit commences about the nature and scope of audit as well as post audit discussion to ascertain any area of concern.

➤ Reviewing the financial and risk management policies of the company.

Apart from the above, if the company has set up an Audit Committee pursuant to the provisions of the Companies Act, then such Audit Committee shall have such additional functions and features as contained in the listing agreement.

Review of Certain Information by Audit Committee

It is mandatory for the Audit Committee to review the following information:

➤ Financial statements and draft audit report, including quarterly/half-yearly financial information.

➤ Management discussion and analysis of financial condition and results of operations.

➤ Reports relating to compliance with laws and to risk management.

➤ Management letters/letters of internal control weaknesses issued by statutory/internal auditors.

➤ Records of related party transactions.

> ➤ Appointment, removal and terms of remuneration of the chief internal auditor shall be subject to review by the Audit Committee.

From the above discussion, it can be said that the Audit Committee of any Board is like the central fulcrum of the management. While it is imperative to have Audit Committee to ensure good corporate governance, it is also true that one cannot think of corporate governance without a functional Audit Committee.

12.10 ACCOUNTING STANDARDS

12.10.1 CONCEPT

Accounting standards are the written policy documents issued by the Government or other regulatory body or expert institute covering various aspects of recognition, measurement, treatment, presentation and disclosure of accounting transaction in the financial statements.

Companies (Amendment) Act, 1999 has inserted new sub-section (3C) in Section 211, which defines "Accounting Standards to mean standards of accounting recommended by the Institute of Chartered Accountants of India, constituted under the Chartered Accountants Act, 1949, as may be prescribed by the Central Government in consultation with the National Advisory Committee on Accounting Standards established under Section 415(1).

All over the world, accounting standards are drafted, framed and implemented by professional accounting bodies. While accounting standards in India are framed by Accounting Standard Board of the Institute of Chartered Accountants of India, International Accounting Standards (IAS) are pronounced by the International Accounting Standard Committee comprised of representatives of member institutes of professional accountants.

12.10.2 OBJECTIVES/IMPORTANCE

The objective of accounting standards is to standardise the diverse accounting policies and practices with a view to eliminating, to the extent possible, the non-comparability of financial information and to produce reliable accounting statements acceptable in the country.

The use of accounting standards is well established and no one can deny the importance of accounting standards. It is utmost necessary that these statements are compiled on the basis of accounting standards. Legislative attempts have been made to have accounting standards prescribed under different statutes. For example, Companies (Amendment) Act, 1999 lay down prescribing accounting standards.

The globalisation of business, promotion of external trade, internationalisation of financial institutions etc. necessitated the development of accounting standards. So the importance of accounting standards can be described in the following way:

Globalisation of Business

Business is global in the modern society now. Multinational companies are working in different countries with different currency, rules and accounting practices. If every country is allowed to follow its own practice, external trade cannot flourish. Confusion will be created as a result. The smooth and fair flow of the global business needs international accounting standards.

Uniform Presentation of Accounts

Financial accounting is not very exact science. To some extent, it is subject of interpretation. The presence of different concepts, conventions, customs, traditions and practices created confusion and checked free, fair and smooth flow of financial activities. It necessitated uniformity in the concepts, conventions and practices.

Removal of Ambiguity

Accounting is one of the important parts of business activities. It does not show the actual financial status of the business by indicating net profit or loss only, but it also forecasts the future trend of the business. But certain accounting terms and practices are ambiguous and confusing, e.g., valuation of stock, methods of depreciation etc. Accounting standards are needed to remove these different types of ambiguity.

Prevention of Accounting Scandals

Ambiguity, confusion and inexactness in the meaning of accounting terminology generate accounting scandals lead to the failure of the business. As such, standardisation of accounting terminology is necessary for preventing misuse of accounting terminology.

Internationalisation of Financial Institutions

Banks and financial institutions have assumed global status in the present day scenario. Their activities are not restricted to one country alone. Banks have to operate their branches in the foreign countries also. The successful implementation of these activities needed that the financial accounting must be standardised internationally.

12.10.3 ACCOUNTING STANDARDS AND THE AUDITOR

While discharging their attest function, the auditors are required to ensure that the accounting standards issued and made mandatory by the Institute of Chartered Accountants of India are implemented in the presentation of financial statements covered by their audit reports. In the event of any deviation form the standards it will also be their duty to make adequate disclosure in their reports so that the users of the financial statements are made aware of such deviations.

According to amendment made in Section 227 of the Companies Act, 1999 additional duties has been given to the auditors to state in their reports whether in their opinion, the profit and loss account and the balance sheet comply with the accounting standards provided in Section 211 (3C) and also the reasons for any adverse comments or qualifications in this regard.

12.11 AUDITING AND ASSURANCE STANDARDS

12.11.1 BACKGROUND

The International Federation of Accountants (IFAC) came into existence in 1977 and constituted International Auditing Practices Committee (IAPC) to formulate International Auditing Guidelines. These guidelines were later on converted into International Standards on Auditing (ISA). Considering the development in the field of auditing at international level, the need for issuing Standards and Guidance notes in tandem with international standards but conforming to national laws, customs, usages and business environment was felt. With the objective, the Institute of Chartered Accountants of India constituted the Auditing Practices Committee (APC) on September 17, 1982, to spearhead the new framework of Statements on Standard Auditing Practices (SAPs) and Guidance Notes (GNs) inter alia to replace various chapters of the old omnibus Statement on Auditing Practices issued in 1964.

In July 2002, the Auditing Practices Committee has been converted into an Auditing and Assurance Standards Board by the Council of the Institute to be in line with the international trend. A significant step has been taken aimed at bringing in the desired transparency in the working of the Auditing and Assurance Standards Board through participation of representatives of various segments of the society and interest groups, such as regulators, industry and academics. The nomenclature of SAPs has also been changed to Auditing and Assurance Standards (AASs).

12.11.2 CONCEPT

In India, the Institute of Chartered Accountants of India issues the auditing procedures/practices and these are called Auditing and Assurance Standards (AAS), previously known as Standard Auditing Practices (SAP). The Institute of Chartered Accountants of India has recently made a new classification of Auditing and Assurance Standards and these are now termed mainly as Standards on Auditing. In fact, AAS are the benchmarks by which the quality of audit performance can be measured and the achievement of objectives can be documented. By using these standards, an auditor can determine the professional qualities necessary for effective audit performance. In simple words, AAS are auditing standards which prescribe the way the auditing should be conducted to maintain audit quality.

Quality in audit through Auditing and Assurance Standards provide a reasonable assurance to the concerned regulatory authority and leads to improved systems and procedures for the business as a whole and particularly to the subject matter of the audit. It provides reasonable professional satisfaction to the auditor and acts as a guide to the successor. In short, it helps in better presentation of information.

12.11.3 SCOPE

The Auditing and Assurance Standards are applicable whenever an independent audit is carried out, i.e., in the independent examination of financial information of any entity, whether profit oriented or not, and irrespective of its size, or legal form (unless specified otherwise) when such an examination is conducted with a view to expressing an opinion. The Auditing and Assurance Standards may also have application, as appropriate, to other related functions of auditors. Any limitation on the applicability of a specific standard is made clear in the introductory paragraph of the concerned standard.

Various professional bodies of accountants in different countries have issued pronouncements on accepted auditing practices for the guidance of their members. These pronouncements on auditing practices relate not only to financial audit but also to other types of audit namely propriety audit, internal audit, peer review etc. In India, the Institute of Chartered Accountants of India has been issuing a series of statements of AAS on independent financial audit.

12.11.4 OBJECTIVES AND IMPORTANCE

Auditing and Assurance Standards refer to general guidelines given by the professional bodies of accountants for conducting audit. They indicate principles and techniques of auditing to be followed by the auditors while conducting audit in different audit environment. Based on the collective deliberations and views, the professional bodies prescribe principles and techniques of auditing. The aim of prescribing these guidelines is to ensure sound and effective auditing practices.

The importance of Auditing and Assurance Standards can be outlined in the following way:

Codification of Auditing Practices

These professional pronouncements attempt to codify the auditing practices expected to be applied while conducting audit.

Ensure Effective Auditing Practices

These professional principles and techniques of auditing are generally accepted as standard. The objective of prescribing these guidelines is to ensure sound and effective auditing practices.

Guidance to the Auditors

These standards refer to general guidelines given by the professional bodies of accountants for conducting audit. They indicate the principles and techniques of auditing to be followed by the auditors while conducting audit.

Uniform Presentation of Accounts

Auditing is not a very exact science. To some extent it is the subject of interpretation. The presence of different concepts, conventions, customs, traditions and practices created confusion and checked free, fair and smooth flow of auditing activities. It necessitated uniformity in the concepts, conventions and practices.

Prevention of Accounting Scandals

Ambiguity, confusion and inexactness in the meaning and interpretation of auditing terminology generate accounting scandals leading to the failure of the business. As such, standardisation of auditing terminology is necessary for preventing misuse of auditing terminology.

12.11.5 PROCEDURES FOR ISSUING STANDARDS

Broadly, the following procedure is adopted for the formulation of Auditing and Assurance Standards:

- The AASB determines the broad areas in which the AASs need to be formulated and the priority in regard to the selection thereof.

- In the preparation of AASs, the AASB is assisted by Study Groups constituted to consider specific subjects. In the formation of Study Groups, provision is made for participation of a cross-section of the members of the Institute.

- On the basis of the work of the Study Groups, an exposure draft of the proposed AAS is prepared by the Committee and issued for comments by members of the Institute.

- After taking into consideration the comments received, the draft of the proposed AAS is finalised by the AASB and submitted to the Council of the Institute.

- The Council of the Institute considers the final draft of the proposed AAS, and, if necessary, modifies the same in consultation with the AASB. The AAS is then issued under the authority of the Council.

12.11.6 AAS AND THE AUDITOR

It is the duty of the auditor to ensure that the audit is conducted in accordance with the auditing and assurance standards and if there is any material departure from the standards, the auditor should report thereon. The auditor becomes liable to the disciplinary preceding of the Institute of Chartered Accountants of India under clause (9) of part I of Second Schedule to the Chartered Accountants Act, 1949.

The auditors in their audit report have to mention that they have conducted the audit in accordance with the 'generally accepted auditing standards'. The generally accepted auditing standards in Indian context mean the Auditing and Assurance Standards as issued by the Institute of Chartered Accountants of India.

◆ Suggested questions

A   Short-type questions

1. Define 'propriety' audit. What are its objectives?
2. Define 'efficiency' audit. What are its objectives?
3. Who can conduct cost audit under the Companies Act, 1956?
4. Do you justify the introduction of social audit in India?
5. What is Tax Audit? Who can be appointed as tax auditor?
6. Write short notes on compulsory tax audit.
7. What do you mean by human resource audit?

8. Define performance audit. What is its importance?
9. What are the contents of cost audit report?
10. Define operational audits. What are its objectives?

B **Essay-type questions**

1. What is social audit? Give your views on the objectives of social audit. Discuss the position of social audit in Indian scenario?

2. What is environmental audit? State the objectives of environmental audit. What is the position of environmental audit at present in India?

3. Discuss the concept and objective of cost audit. What are the advantages of cost audit from the viewpoint of the management? Distinguish between cost audit and management audit.

4. What is management audit? State the uses, limitations and importance of management audit.

5. Define human resource audit. State its advantages and limitations. How does it differ from human resource accounting?

Chapter 13

Special Audit

13.1 INTRODUCTION

The main aspects of the auditor's work are common to all types of audit, but as every organisation will have its own peculiar facets, it will be necessary for the auditor to apply his skill and judgment individually in carrying out his audit work. There are, however, certain types of organisations that will require special treatment, either owing to the exceptional nature of work or to their being covered by statutes, which require the investigation and presentation of certain information.

While framing audit programme concerning the audit of specialised enterprises, the auditor should ask himself the following questions:

    i.   Are there any special statutory regulations covering the enterprise?

    ii.   Are there any special regulations governing the accounts?

    iii.   What is the enterprise's basic internal regulatory document?

    iv.   What is the nature of the enterprise's business, and what transactions arise from its business?

    v.   What are its main sources of income and expenditure?

    vi.   What are its main assets and liabilities?

    vii.   Are there any special audit points that should be considered?

Hence, audits requiring special treatment are mentioned as follows:

13.2 AUDIT OF CHARITABLE SOCIETY

A charitable society is performing its operations for rendering social services. Its main sources of revenue are donations and legacies. The object of audit of this type of society is to ensure that its revenue is being utilised for the purpose for which the society has been established and it is being operated in conformity with its rules and regulations.

The auditor should pay attention to the following points, while auditing the accounts of a Charitable Institution:

13.2.1 GENERAL MATTERS

Study of the Constitution

The constitution of the charitable institution has to be studied first and important rules and regulations are to be noted down for consideration of detailed auditing of the institution.

Examination of Activities

The activities of the institution should be identified and it should be examined whether these activities are within the constituted objectives of the institution.

Review of Internal Control System

The internal control system regarding the cash receipts and cash disbursement should be reviewed.

Inspection of the Minutes Book

The auditor should inspect the minutes book of the meetings of the Managing Committee and identify the resolutions having bearing on accounts and audit.

Study of Financial Power of Executives

The financial power of different executives and officers as well as the members of the managing committee should be noted.

13.2.2 RECEIPTS

Subscription and Donations

Subscriptions and donations, which are the main sources of income of a charitable institution, should be checked and verified with references to entries in the cash book with the help of receipts counterfoil, registers of subscription and donations, list of members, rates of subscription for different classes of membership and other relevant documents.

Grants

Grants received or receivable from the government or any local authority should be checked with the help of relevant correspondence, minutes book etc.

Interests and Dividend

Interest and dividend from the deposits and investments should be checked with the relevant vouchers. In addition to that, the interest on such deposits and dividends, either ex-dividend or cum-dividend should be checked to see whether these are recorded properly in the books of accounts.

Rent and Other Income from House Property

Rent and other income from properties of the institution should be checked with the help of counterfoils of receipts and other relevant documents.

Receipts from Charity Show, etc.

Receipts from charity shows or other special functions should be checked with the counterpart of the tickets sold, statement of cash collection and entries in the cash book.

13.2.3 PAYMENTS AND EXPENSES

Distinction Between Capital and Revenue Expenditure

The auditor should see that proper distinction has been made in the accounts between capital expenditure and revenue expenditure.

Vouching of Expenses

He should check all expenses with reference to the entries in the cash book with the help of bills, receipts, etc. In addition to that, special attention should be given for the checking of expenses relating to charity shows and other functions.

SPECIAL AUDIT | **13.3**

Grants Made by the Institution
Grants made by the institution constitute the major expenses of the institution. So the auditor should pay special attention to check these payments. The auditor should ensure himself that all grants have been made for admissible purposes and they are properly authorised.

Purchase and Sale of Assets and Investments
Purchase and sale of movable as well as immovable properties and investments should be verified with the help of relevant documents. The auditor should assure himself about their existence through physical verification at a particular point of time.

13.2.4 ASSETS AND LIABILITIES

Verification of Assets and Liabilities
The auditor should verify all assets and liabilities with the help of relevant documents. He would confirm about their physical existence either through physical verification or through confirmation from the concerned parties.

Utilisation of Fund
In this type of organisation, different types of funds are created for some specific purposes. The auditor should ensure the proper utilisation of these funds for the purposes specified.

13.2.5 INCOME TAX

Taxability of Income
The auditor should see whether the income of the institution is exempt from income tax according to the provisions of Section 11 of the Income Tax Act, 1961 and if so, whether refund of income tax deducted at source from interest income, if any, has been claimed from the tax authority.

13.2.6 FINANCIAL STATEMENT

True and Fair View
The auditor should examine the financial statements and see whether they give a true and fair view of the surplus or deficit and of the state of affairs of the institution.

13.3 AUDIT OF CLUBS

Clubs are the associations of group of persons with common interest and these are basically established with non-profit motive. The main activities of the clubs include provision for amusement and recreation and constructive work for the welfare of the society. From the legal point of view, clubs can be of two types:

  i.   Government-registered clubs.

  ii. Unregistered clubs.

Government-registered clubs are required to get their accounts audited at regular intervals for renewal of their registration. Besides, in order to avail different government grants the clubs are required to submit audited accounts. But this is not required for unregistered clubs.

The auditor should pay attention to the following points, while conducting audit of accounts of a club:

13.3.1 General

Study of the Constitution
First of all, the auditor shall acquaint himself with rules, regulations, by-laws and constitution of the club, particularly in respect of accounts.

Inspection of the Minutes Book
The auditor should inspect the Minutes Book of the executive committee and take note of resolutions passed having bearing on accounts and audit.

Noting of Financial Power of Executives
The financial powers of different executives and of different committees have to be noted.

Review of Internal Control System
The auditor should also study the internal check and internal control system in respect of purchases, receipts, stock of foodstuff etc.

13.3.2 Receipts

Subscriptions and Entrance Fees
The main source of income of a club is subscription from the members. The auditor should vouch all the receipts from entrance fees and subscriptions from members with the help of counterfoils of receipts and Register of members.

Arrear Subscriptions
Any subscriptions in arrear should be verified from the schedule received from the club, which should be certified by the executive committee. He should also look into the reasons for non-payment of subscriptions and steps taken for their recovery.

Sale of Refreshment, etc.
He should vouch the sale of refreshments, wines, cigars and billiard room and swimming receipts etc. He should also see that proper records are maintained for the stock of refreshments, wines, cigars, swimming costumes etc.

Donations
If donations are received by the club, it should be ensured that such donations are utilised by the club for the specified purposes for which it is received.

Receipts from Cultural Functions
Receipts from special functions or cultural functions should be vouched with the counterfoils of tickets, statement of collections etc. Expenses of the functions should also be checked with the related vouchers.

13.3.3 Payments and Expenses

Distinction Between Capital and Revenue Expenditure
The auditor should see that proper distinction has been made in the accounts between capital expenditure and revenue expenditure.

SPECIAL AUDIT | **13.5**
SPECIAL AUDIT | **13.5**

Vouching of Expenses
He should vouch all expenses with reference to the entries in the cashbook with the help of bills, receipts etc. He should vouch the payments made on account of purchases of crockery, wines, furniture etc.

Depreciation of Fixed Assets
The auditor should examine whether proper depreciation has been charged on all assets of the club including furniture, sports equipments and crockeries.

13.3.4 ASSETS AND LIABILITIES

Verification of Assets and Liabilities
The auditor should verify all assets and liabilities with the help of relevant documents. He should confirm about their physical existence either through physical verification or through confirmation from the concerned parties.

Creation of Reserve Fund
The club has to create a number of reserve funds for different purposes. The auditor should ensure that proper appropriation of surplus generated has been made for this purpose.

13.3.5 INCOME TAX

Taxability of Income
The auditor should check the tax liabilities of the club as regards sales tax and income tax. He should verify that whether tax return is submitted on regular basis along with the amount of tax.

13.3.6 SPECIAL ACCOUNTS

Special Services to the Members
The auditor should vouch debits to members for special services, e.g., billiards, tennis court reservations, dinners etc., with member's signatures in the respective registers.

Individual Activity Accounts
Individual accounts maintained for various activities like games and sports, social functions, charity shows, etc. should be carefully examined, and particularly he should check the arrangement for meeting the expenses of teams for participation of the club in different tournaments.

13.3.7 FINANCIAL STATEMENTS

True and Fair View
The auditor should examine the financial statements and see whether they give a true and fair view of the surplus or deficit and of the state of affairs of the club.

13.4 AUDIT OF CO-OPERATIVE SOCIETIES

The co-operative movement in India is not a recent event. The co-operative sector in India has been developed as a result of government initiative and effective measures. The Co-operative Societies Act was passed in the year 1912. The co-operative societies in India are established and governed by this Act.

To monitor the day-to-day activities of the society, a group of members are selected to form the 'management committee'. This committee usually consists of Chairman, Secretary and Treasurer. In every annual general meeting, the members of this committee are elected.

On the basis of liability of members, co-operative societies can be of two types:

i. Limited Liability Societies.

ii. Unlimited Liability Societies.

The provisions regarding the maintenance of books of accounts and records are also governed by the Indian Co-operative Societies Act, 1912. According to Section 17 of this Act, the accounts of these types of societies are required to be audited by the auditors of the Department of Co-operative Societies. A chartered accountant can also conduct audit of this type of society. It may be noted in this context that the Companies Act, 1956 is not at all relevant and applicable in case of audit of co-operative societies. In general, three types of audit are conducted in a co-operative society, namely continuous audit, annual audit and re-audit. The auditors of co-operative societies are appointed by the Registrar of Co-operatives.

The auditor should pay attention to the following points, while auditing the accounts of a big co-operative society:

13.4.1 General

Study of the Act
The auditor should go through the Co-operative Societies Act, 1912 and the rules and regulations relating to accounts to see that the books of account are kept with the provisions as contained in the Act.

Inspection of the Minutes Book
The auditor should obtain the minutes of the Board Meeting to see any specific resolutions relating to accounts. He should also see that the resolutions of the meetings of the Board have been properly implemented.

Review of the Internal Control System
The auditor should review the internal control system to see whether it is commensurate and compatible with the requirements of co-operative society. He should examine its effectiveness in preventing frauds and misapplication of assets.

Restrictions on Functions of the Society
The auditor should examine the compliance of the following restrictions as imposed by the Act:

i. If the liability of members is limited by share, no member other than a co-operative society can hold a number of shares exceeding the prescribed number of shares as per the Act.

ii. No member of a society registered with limited liabilities can transfer his shareholdings violating the regulations of the Act.

iii. A registered society cannot give loan to a person other than a member.

iv. A registered society can take loan from non-members only to such extent as may be prescribed by the provisions of the Act.

13.4.2 Receipts

Recovery of Loan
The auditor should see that the receipts of instalment money have been properly entered in the cash book and accordingly member's account is credited to that extent.

Interest on Loan
The auditor should check the interest receipt by reference with the agreement of loan with the borrower.

13.4.3 PAYMENTS AND EXPENSES
Loan Payments
The auditor should vouch the payment of loan granted with the agreement of loan with the borrower as well as from the money receipts of the borrower.

Provisions for Depreciation
The auditor should see that adequate provision for depreciation have been provided for all the fixed assets owned by the society.

Appropriation of Profit
He should ensure that proper appropriation of profits to different funds viz. Reserve Fund and Welfare Fund have been made as per the provisions contained in the Act.

Payment of Dividend
The auditor should confirm that dividend declared and paid to the members are in accordance with the rules and regulations of the society and see that the dividend should not exceed the permissible limit.

13.4.4 ASSETS AND LIABILITIES
Capital Structure
The auditor should examine the capital structure of the society. He should ensure that no individual member should hold more than the prescribed limit of the authorised share capital of the society.

Loan Obtained
He should vouch the loan from Central Co-operative Banks and other financial institutions by reference to cash book, correspondences and other documentary evidences.

Investment of Surplus
The auditor should see that the surplus funds of the society are invested either in government securities or in such banks as deposits as approved by the registers of societies.

Physical Verification of Assets
The auditor should verify the assets of the society physically. He should verify cash and investment by reference with cash counting and statement of investments.

Overdue Debts
He should verify whether or not there is any overdue debts and whether or not assets and liabilities have been properly valued.

Irregularity in Granting Loan
He should examine whether there is any material impropriety or irregularity in sanctioning loan to any member or in the realisation of loans from any member.

13.4.5 INCOME TAX

Taxability of Income

The Central Government is empowered to exempt any registered co-operative society from income tax, stamp duty and registration fees. The auditor will see whether necessary application has been made to the Central Government for arrangement of their exemption.

13.4.6 FINANCIAL STATEMENT

True and Fair View

The auditor should verify whether books of accounts have been maintained as per rules framed and whether financial statements have been prepared in accordance with the prescribed form.

13.5 AUDIT OF EDUCATIONAL INSTITUTION

Educational institutions include schools, colleges, training centres and universities. The main activities of these types of institutions are more or less similar to each other. As a result, the types of problems the auditor usually face in conducting audit of these types of institutions are also same. However, on the basis of financial support and affiliation from the government, the educational institutions can be divided into four types, which include

- i. Government institutions.
- ii. Government-aided and -affiliated institutions.
- iii. Government-affiliated institutions.
- iv. Private institutions.

On the basis of the nature of the institutions, the activities and mode of maintenance of books of accounts and records may also differ and the auditor will take into consideration these deviations at the time of his audit.

The auditor should pay attention to the following points, while auditing the accounts of educational institutions:

13.5.1 GENERAL

Study of the Constitution

The auditor should go through the Trust Deed or Regulations to find out provisions affecting accounts and should ensure that the books of accounts are kept with the provision as contained in the Deed or Regulation.

Inspection of the Minutes Book

The auditor should inspect the minutes of the meetings of the Managing Committee or Governing Body, noting resolutions affecting accounts and ensure that these have been duly complied with, specially the decisions as regards the operation of bank account and sanctioning of expenditure.

Review of the Internal Control System

The auditor should check the names entered in the Students Fee Register for each term with the respective Class Registers, showing names of students on rolls and check the amount of fees charged. In this way, he should ensure that there operates a system of internal check which is effective.

13.5.2 RECEIPTS

Tuition Fees Received

The auditor should check the fees received by comparing counterfoils of receipts granted with entries in the cash book and should trace the collection in the Fees Register to confirm that the revenue from this source has been duly accounted for.

Admission Fees Received

He should check admission fees with admission slips signed by the head of the institution and confirm that the amount has been credited to a Capital Fund, unless the Managing Committee has taken a decision to the contrary.

Government Grants

He should verify the grant from the government or any local authority with the memo of grant. If any expense has been disallowed for purposes of grant, the auditor should ascertain the reasons thereof.

Fine for Late Payments etc.

The auditor should check that the time for late payment or absence etc. have been either collected or duly accounted for under the proper authority.

Income from Other Sources

The auditor should check income from other sources, viz., rental income from landed property, interest and dividends from investments etc. with reference to documentary evidence available.

13.5.3 PAYMENTS AND EXPENSES

Distinction Between Capital and Revenue Expenditure

The auditor should see that proper distinction has been made between capital expenditure and revenue expenditure in the accounts.

Vouching of Expenses

He should check all expenses with reference to the entries in the cash book with the help of bills, receipts etc.

Purchase of Fixed Assets

Purchase of fixed assets should be verified with the help of relevant documents. The auditor should assure himself about their existence through physical verification at a particular interval of time.

Depreciation of Fixed Assets

The auditor should examine whether proper depreciation has been charged on the fixed assets of the institute including furniture and buildings.

13.5.4 ASSETS AND LIABILITIES

Arrears on Account of Fees

The auditor should report on any old and heavy arrears on account of fees, hostel rents etc. to the Managing Committee.

Caution Money and Other Deposits

The auditor should confirm that caution money and other deposits paid by the students on admission have been shown as liability in the balance sheet and not transferred to revenue, unless they are not refundable.

Accumulated Investments

He should note the investments representing endowment funds for prizes are kept separate and any income in excess of the cost of prizes has been accumulated and invested with the original fund.

Maintenance of Different Funds

The auditor should verify the annual statements of account and while doing so, he should ensure that separate statements of accounts have been prepared as regards, Poor Students Fund, Games Fund, Library Fund etc.

13.5.5 INCOME TAX

Tax Liability on Income

The auditor should confirm that the refund of taxes deducted from income from investment has been claimed and recovered since the institutions are generally exempted from income tax liability.

13.5.6 FINANCIAL STATEMENTS

True and Fair View

The auditor should examine the financial statements and see whether they give a true and fair view of the surplus or deficit and of the state of affairs of the institution.

13.6 AUDIT OF HOTELS

The business of running a hotel is very much dissimilar to running of any other organisations. It is a service-oriented business and may have some element of production of foodstuff and sales thereof. However, this business is characterised by handling of liquid cash, stocking and providing a large variety of items, keeping watch on customers to ensure that satisfactory services being provided to them etc.

In view of these, the following matters deserve special attention of the auditor in auditing hotel businesses:

Internal Control System

The internal control system of the hotel should be reviewed first. The auditor should ensure himself that effective internal control is in operation and for this purpose, he should evaluate the following:

i. Effectiveness of arrangement regarding receipts and disbursement of cash.

ii. Purchase procedure and stocking of various commodities and provisions.

iii. Billing procedures for the customers.

Cash Collections

Control of cash assumes great importance in any hotel. The auditor should reconcile the total sales reported with the total bills issued. Billing may be done room-wise as well as customer-wise. The auditor should see that there exists numerical control over the bills to ensure that all bills are included in the total.

Stocks

The stocks in any hotel are both portable and saleable particularly the food and beverage stock. It is, therefore, extremely important that all movements and transfer of such stocks should be properly documented. Control over stocks can be imposed from the point of two directions:

i. *Control Over Movements*: The area where stocks are kept should be locked under the supervision of the departmental manager. The auditor should see that the movements of goods in or out of the stores take place only after proper authorisation and recording.

ii. *Control Over Valuation*: Although valuation of stocks is made by the experts appointed by the management, it is important that the auditor satisfies himself that the amount included for such stocks are reasonable. The auditor can also attend at the physical stock taking and check certain pricing calculations.

Fixed Assets

The accounting of fixed assets is likely to differ from hotel to hotel. Certain hotels may consider its utensils as a stock item while others may treat it as fixed assets. A comprehensive definition of the stock should be there and the auditor should see whether the same have been clearly followed or not. Regarding auditing of fixed assets; the auditor should ensure himself that:

i. all the fixed assets are physically verified and properly valued at the end of the accounting period and

ii. adequate provisions have been made for depreciation on all fixed assets for the accounting year.

Compliance with Statutory Provisions

A number of statutory provisions are required to be complied with in running a hotel business. All types of hotels are governed by various rules and regulations by different authorities, which include the following:

(a) Foreign Exchange Regulatory Authority

In large hotels, it is very common to have facility of exchanging foreign currency into Indian Rupees. There are provisions for foreign exchange transactions.

(b) Department of Tourism

The Department of Tourism also prescribes various conditions to be fulfilled by the hotels.

(c) Local Authority

Approval of the local authority and license are required for running hotel business. The auditor should see that various applicable regulations and conditions are duly complied with by the hotel.

Dealings with Traveling Agents

It is very common that the hotels get their bookings through travel agents or other booking agencies. The auditor should ensure that money is recovered from travel agents as per the terms of credit allowed. Commission, if any, paid to travel agents should be checked by reference to the agreement on that behalf.

Vouching of Receipts and Expenses

The auditor should vouch all receipts and expenses with reference to the entries in the cash book with the help of documentary evidence. He should pay special attention to the following points:

i. Consumption shown in various physical stock accounts may be traced to customers' bill on a sampling basis, wherever practicable to ensure that all issues have been billed or accounted for.

ii. All payments made to foreign collaborator, if any, are in accordance with the terms of agreement.

iii. Expenses and receipts may be compared with the figures of the previous year having regard to the average occupancy of visitors and changes in the rates.

iv. Special receipts on account of letting out of the auditorium space and other spaces for shops and for special exhibitions etc. should be verified with reference to the respective agreements.

v. Customer's Ledger should be examined on a sample basis but in depth to check that all charges that should be made to the customers are in fact made.

vi. Proper reserves are required to be maintained for redecoration and renovation of buildings and other structural facilities.

Other Points
In addition to the above important points regarding the workings of the hotel, the auditor should also take into consideration the following points:

i. *Taxability of Income*: The auditor should check the assessment of tax aspect of the hotel in order to verify that whether the tax return is submitted by the hotel on regular basis along with the amount of tax.

ii. *Deposit of Sales and Entertainment Tax*: The auditor should examine whether the sales and entertainment tax collected by the hotel is duly deposited to the proper authorities with the prescribed limit of time.

iii. *True and Fair View*: The auditor should also see whether the financial statements give a true and fair view of the profit or loss and of the balance sheet of the hotel for the accounting period.

13.7 AUDIT OF HOSPITALS
The hospitals are usually established with the fund provided by the government, local authorities, municipalities and similar other types of funds. On the basis of ownership, hospitals can be government hospitals or private hospitals or a joint venture of public-private partnership. As the nature of activities of a hospital are totally different from that of other organisations or institutions, the audit programme to be followed for conducting audit of these types of organisations will also differ.

The auditors pay attention to the following points, while auditing the accounts of a hospital:

13.7.1 GENERAL MATTERS
Legal Status
The auditor should see relevant documents to ascertain the legal status of the hospital. He should examine the constitution of the management and provisions affecting annual accounts for consideration of auditing techniques to be used.

Inspection of the Minute Book
If there is a managing committee or a governing body, the auditor should go through the minutes of their meetings in order to note decisions concerning financial matters, especially engagement of staff, acquisition and sale of fixed assets and investments, delegation of authority regarding expenditure etc. and to see that the resolution affecting accounts have been duly complied with.

Internal Check System
The auditor should examine the internal check as regards the issue and receipts of stores, linen, apparatus, clothing, instruments etc. so as to ensure that purchases have been properly recorded in the stock register and that issues have been made only against proper authorisation.

Examination of Activities

The activities of the hospital should be identified and the auditor should ensure himself that all the activities as decided to be undertaken being actually performed by the hospital.

13.7.2 Receipts

Cash Collections

The auditor should check the cash collections as entered in the cash book, with the receipt counterfoils and other evidence. He should also check the bill registers of patients to see that the bills have been correctly prepared.

Free Bed Facility

He should see that bills have been issued to all patients from whom any amount was recoverable according to the rules of the hospital. He should also ensure that free bed facilities were extended to the patients only according to the hospital regulations.

Income from Property and Investments

The auditor should refer to the Properties and Investment Registers to see that all the incomes that should have been recovered by way of rent from properties, dividend and interest on securities etc. have been collected.

Legacies and Donations

He should also ascertain that legacies and donations received for a specific purpose have been so utilised.

Grants Received

The auditor should verify that the grants received, if any, have been duly accounted for. He should also ensure that the refund in respect of taxes deducted has been claimed.

Income from Other Sources

The auditor should verify the income of the hospital from any other sources, with reference to the source of income, e.g., X-rays Lab, Blood Testing Lab, etc.

13.7.3 Payments and Expenses

Distinction Between Capital and Revenue Expenditure

The auditor should see that proper distinction has been made in the accounts between capital expenditure and revenue expenditure.

Purchase and Sale of Assets

Purchase and sale of movable as well as immovable properties should be verified with the help of relevant documents. The auditor should assure himself about their existence through physical verification at a particular point of time.

Vouching of Expenses

The auditor should vouch all the expenses including the capital expenditure. He should verify that the capital expenditure has been incurred only with the prior sanction of the Managing Committee.

Depreciation on Fixed Assets

He should see that depreciation at appropriate rates has been written off against all the fixed assets.

13.7.4 ASSETS AND LIABILITIES

Verification of Assets and Liabilities

The auditor should see that all fixed assets have been acquired under proper authority and that proper registers are maintained to record their particulars. He should also confirm about their physical existence either through physical verification or through confirmation from the concerned parties.

Stock-in-Trade

The auditor should obtain inventories of stocks and stores at the end of the year and check a percentage of them physically. He should also verify Stock Register in respect of stock and stores such as medicines, test tubes, cleaning materials etc. and see that management has carried out a periodical inspection of all such store items.

13.7.5 INCOME TAX

Taxability of Income

The auditor should see whether the income of the hospital is exempt from income tax according to the provisions of the Income Tax Act, 1961 and if so, whether refund of income tax deducted at source, if any, has been claimed from the tax authority.

13.7.6 FINANCIAL STATEMENT

True and Fair View

The auditor should examine the financial statements and see whether they give a true and fair view of the financial results as well as of the financial position of the hospital.

13.8 AUDIT OF HIRE PURCHASE AND LEASING COMPANIES

13.8.1 INTRODUCTION

The financing of credit transactions has been a growth industry in recent years. Such transactions take various forms; the principal ones are as follows:

i.   Hire purchase transactions are entered into where the title to the goods or assets remains with the seller, until a specified number of instalments are paid.

ii. Leasing agreements are made where the goods are leased to the hirer. The title of the goods remains with the finance company.

In relation to these transactions, there are two audit considerations of paramount importance. One is that the interest or profit is correctly apportioned over the financial periods to which the transactions relate and the other is that adequate provision is made for bad debts.

There have been cases in the past where finance companies have not paid due regard to the 'prudence concept' when accounting for the profit on credit transactions and have taken too much profit immediately on the transaction being entered into. The auditor must ensure that such profits are apportioned according to a sound accounting policy that is consistently applied.

By their nature, credit transactions must entail the risk of substantial bad debts, particularly in times of economic recession. The auditor must ensure that there is a proper and consistent accounting policy for provision for bad debts. At every audit, he should carefully consider the adequacy of the provision being made for bad debts.

13.8.2 AUDIT OF HIRE PURCHASE TRANSACTIONS

Hire purchase system refers to that system where the buyer undertakes to pay the price of the goods but by instalments including interest for the delayed payment to acquire the possession immediately, but the title passes to the buyer only on the payment of the last instalment.

There are two parties involved in the hire purchase agreement—(1) the purchaser and (2) the hire purchase vendor. In order to sale the goods or assets under hire purchase system, the hire purchase vendor prepares an agreement with some stipulated terms and conditions of selling the goods or assets on hire purchase basis to the interested purchaser and if the intended purchaser agrees to the terms and conditions of the agreement, he will sign it and the hire purchase vendor delivers him the goods or assets.

Usually in the hire purchase agreement, an option to purchase the goods or assets is given to the purchaser and the agreement generally includes the following:

i.   Possession of goods or assets is delivered by the hire purchase vendor to the purchaser on condition that such person pays the agreed amount in periodical instalments.

ii. The property in the goods or assets is to pass to the purchaser on the payment of the last instalment.

iii. The purchaser has a right to terminate the agreement at any time before the property so passes.

13.8.3 AUDITOR'S DUTY

While checking the hire purchase transactions, the auditor should take into consideration the following two aspects of the transactions, viz.

i.   Hire purchase Agreement.

ii. Payment of Instalment.

Hire Purchase Agreement

The auditor should check the following points in order to assess the propriety and fairness of the hire purchase agreement:

i.   Whether the hire purchase agreement is in writing and signed by all parties involved in the agreement.

ii. Whether the agreement clearly specifies the hire purchase price of the goods or assets to which it relates.

iii. Whether it is mentioned in the agreement the cash price of the goods, i.e., the price at which the goods may be purchased by the purchaser for cash.

iv. Whether the agreement clearly mentions the date on which the agreement shall be deemed to have commenced.

v.   Whether the description of the goods have been mentioned in the agreement in a manner sufficient to identify the goods or assets to purchase.

Payment of Instalments

The auditor should ensure the following points in order to ensure the payment of instalment against the purchase of the goods or assets:

i.   Whether the payments are being received by the hire purchase vendor regularly as per agreement.

ii. Whether it is clearly mentioned in the agreement the number of instalments by which the hire purchase price has to be paid, the amount of each of those instalments and the date or the mode of determining the date upon which it is payable and the person to whom and the place where the amount is payable.

13.8.4 AUDIT OF LEASE TRANSACTIONS

Lease can be of two types: operating lease and finance lease. An operating lease is a simple arrangement, where in return of rent, the lessor allows the lessee to use the asset for a certain period. On the other hand, in a finance lease, a party acquires the right to use an asset for an agreed period of time in consideration of payment of rent to another party. In this type of lease, the legal ownership of the asset remains with the lessor (the leasing company), but in substance, all the risks and rewards of ownership of the asset are transferred to the lessee.

Steps in Lease Transactions

A normal finance lease transaction usually passes through the following steps:

Step 1: Before the Agreement

i. *Selection of asset*: The lessee will select the equipment and satisfy himself about the functional fitness and specifications. The lessor has no participation at this stage.

ii. *Approach to the lessor*: Having finalised the type of equipment, the lessee approaches a lessor, either directly or through a lease- broking agency.

iii. *Negotiation*: The lease agreements are subject to negotiation and the amount involved in the agreement is finalised.

iv. *Procurement of the asset*: The lessor places an order to the manufacture or the supplier to supply the asset as selected by the lessee.

v. *Delivery of asset*: The manufacturer or the supplier delivers the ordered assets at the disposal of the lessee and on receiving the asset the lessee informs the lessor about the acceptance of the asset.

Step 2: During the Lease Period

The lease agreement containing the details terms and conditions of the lease is signed between the parties. During the tenure of the lease period, the lessee:

i. will pay the lease rent regularly at periodical intervals as agreed upon,

ii. will maintain the asset in good working condition and regular repairs and maintenance of the assets will have to be undertaken,

iii. will claim the manufacturer or the supplier's warranties or after-sales services.

Step 3: End of Lease Period

At the end of the lease period, the asset shall retreat to the lessor. The lessee may, however, enjoy the right to renew the lease agreement or may be given the option to purchase the asset if the lessor intends to sale the asset. Usually no purchase option is included in the lease agreement itself, so that the lessee may get the right to acquire the asset.

13.8.5 AUDITOR'S DUTY

The duty of an auditor in respect of leasing transaction can be grouped under the following categories:

Lessor, i.e., Leasing Company

i. The auditor should go through the objective clause of the leasing company to check whether the company is set up to deal with the leasing of assets as well as whether the company can undertake financing activities or not.

ii. The auditor shall also see the Board resolution to check whether a particular director has been authorised to execute the lease agreement.

Lease Agreement

i. The auditor should note down the amount of lease rent, tenure of lease period, dates of payments, late fine charges, deposits or advances etc.

ii. The auditor should ensure that the description of the lessor, the lessee, the asset and the location where the asset will be delivered are included in the lease agreement.

iii. The auditor should also check whether the asset shall be returned to the lessor on termination of the lease agreement and whether it is clearly mentioned in the lease agreement that the cost of returning the asset is to be borne by the lessee.

iv. He should check whether the agreement prohibits the lessee from assigning the subletting of the asset and authorises the lessor to do so.

Lessee

i. The auditor should check whether there exists a procedure to ascertain the credit worthiness of the lessee, i.e., whether the lessee will be able to pay the lease rent regularly as per the commitment given in the lease agreement.

ii. The auditor should examine the acceptance letter obtained from the lessee indicating that the asset has been received in order and is acceptable to the lessee.

Others

i. The auditor should examine the lease proposal form submitted by the lessee requesting the lessor to provide him the asset on lease.

ii. He should ensure that the invoice is retained safely as the lease is a long-term contract.

iii. He should see the copies of the insurance policies have been obtained by the lessor for his records.

Note: It is not possible to consider every possible types of entity that could be the subject of an examination question, but it is proposed in this chapter to set out the more important points relating to a number of enterprises. Students should see to establish for themselves the approach that they would adopt in tackling such questions.

◈ Suggested questions

A   Short-type questions

1. In framing the audit programmes of specialised enterprises, what additional factors are required to be considered by the auditor?

2. Draft an audit programme covering eight special points for examining the accounts of a:

   (a) sports club,

   (b) medical college,

   (c) traveling agent,

   (d) college hostel,

   (e) publishing company.

B   **Essay-type questions**

1. Draft an audit programme for examining the accounts of either a hotel or a cinema hall.
2. Prepare audit programme of any one organisation from the following two:
   (a) Nursing home.
   (b) Co-operative society.
3. What special points the auditor has to consider in conducting audit in the following institutions:
   (a) Charitable institution.
   (b) Educational institution.

Chapter 14

Audit of the Accounts of Governments and Public Sector Undertakings

14.1 INTRODUCTION

The audit of government accounts and the accounts of public sector undertakings has a special significance and importance in view of the public accountability of government and innumerable transactions involving large sums of public money. Government audit is totally different from audit of commercial firms and the audit of public sector undertakings, but has the features of both commercial audit and government audit.

14.2 AUDIT OF PUBLIC SECTOR UNDERTAKINGS

Special statutes have set up several public sector undertakings. In many of such undertakings, the Comptroller and Auditor General of India (CAG) has to conduct statutory audit. In some of the undertakings, though professional accountants conduct the statutory audit, the CAG is empowered to conduct separate audit, independent of statutory audit. Moreover, in government companies, which are governed by the Companies Act, the CAG has the power to direct the manner in which the accounts shall be audited by the statutory auditor and the CAG can conduct test audit or supplementary audit in government companies.

In fact, public sector undertakings are of three different types, which are as follows:

i.   Departmental commercial undertakings

ii. Statutory corporations

iii. Government companies.

Departmental commercial undertakings are directly controlled by a ministry or department of the government. Examples of these are Indian Railways, Post and Telegraph, Bharat Sanchar Nigam Limited etc. Statutory corporations have been set up by special Acts of Parliament and they are governed by such Acts. Examples of such corporations are the Life Insurance Corporation of India, the Reserve Bank of India, the State Bank of India, and the nationalised banks etc. Government companies is the third type of public sector undertakings. These companies are registered under the Companies Act and are also governed by the said Act. There are innumerable Central and State level public sector undertakings in India.

14.2.1 SOME SPECIAL FEATURES OF PUBLIC SECTOR UNDERTAKINGS

The public sector undertakings differ from private sector undertakings in many ways and it is necessary to keep them in mind before actually undertaking the audit of such undertakings. Some important features of public sector undertakings affecting audit are as follows:

Different Forms

These undertakings have been set up mainly in three forms, viz., departmental commercial undertakings, statutory corporations and government companies. All these three forms differ substantially from the point of view of their establishment, operations and operational autonomy.

Governing Acts and Provisions

A majority of these undertakings have been set up as government companies under the Companies Act, 1956 just like any other company in the private sector. These companies are governed by the provisions of the Companies Act. A few undertakings have been set up as departmental undertakings and their operational autonomy is quite limited as they are under the direct control of the government. Statutory corporations are governed by the special statute and Act.

Profit Motive

These undertakings are desired to observe business and commercial principles and are also required to earn profits. However, the profit motive cannot be such overriding factor in their case as it is in private companies.

Managerial Personnel

Several managerial personnel in these undertakings came from the government departments and not from the commercial or industrial field. As a result, the approach of the management is not the same as we find in case of private commercial undertakings.

Accountability

The autonomy of the management of these undertakings is severely restricted due to stricter control and accountability of the management to the government and to the Parliament and several other agencies. The managing director of a public sector undertaking is not as free to act as in case of a private undertaking.

Government Policy

For several matters, the management of these undertakings is guided and directed by the concerned ministry. The minister in charge of the ministry concerned controls them formally as well as informally. The government is empowered to lay down policies, issues directions, appoint or replace top officials, approve capital expenditures beyond a prescribed limit, sanction of borrowings and investments etc.

Reporting

Every undertaking is required to submit its annual report in detail in the Parliament every year. There is a Parliamentary Committee known as Committee on Public Undertakings, which examines their workings in detail. On the basis of report submitted to the Parliament, action has to be taken on it within the stipulated period. The report on action taken is also submitted in the Parliament.

Audit

The professional accountants normally undertake the audit of these undertakings, but the CAG has the power to conduct an efficiency-cum-propriety audit of these undertakings.

14.2.2 Distinction Between Audit of Public Sector Undertakings and Audit of Private Sector Undertakings

The auditor should keep in mind the distinction between the audit of private sector undertakings and that of public sector undertakings. This is quite necessary, as the professional accountants are required to audit the accounts of both the types of undertakings.

The auditor of a private sector undertaking is, in general, required to undertake the verification audit and has to give his opinion as to whether the profit and loss account and the balance sheet exhibit true and fair state of affairs of the undertakings. He has nothing to do with the impropriety of the actions of the management. He is not required to question the points of inefficiency of the management.

The auditor of a public sector undertaking has to adopt some of the techniques of the government audit and at the same time should follow the standard practices and techniques of audit of a private company. It seeks to verify whether the expenditure conforms to the various provisions of the law and the rules and whether every officer has exercised the same vigilance in respect of expenditure incurred from public money, as a person of ordinary prudence would exercise in respect of expenditure of his own money. It also seeks to verify whether the expenditure was necessary and whether the individual items of expenditure give the best results.

It has been found in practice that the auditors of the public sector undertakings have been adopting bolder approach as compared to those of private sector undertakings. A qualified report by the auditors of private sector undertakings is given only in very exceptional circumstances and is rare. But it is not so in case of public sector undertakings.

We have three forms of public sector undertakings as already mentioned earlier. They are departmental commercial undertakings, statutory corporations and the government companies. Let us discuss the provisions and procedures of audit of these different types of undertakings separately:

14.2.3 AUDIT OF DEPARTMENTAL COMMERCIAL UNDERTAKINGS

Several Central Government commercial undertakings have been set up in India as departmental commercial undertakings. They are administered as a part of the department, like any government department. The departmental commercial undertakings have been defined as companies, which are maintained mainly for the purpose of rendering services or providing supplies of certain special kinds on payment for the services rendered or the articles supplied. They are required to work to a financial result determined through accounts maintained on commercial principles. The examples of these undertakings are: Indian Railways, Indian Security Press, Chittaranjan Locomotive Works, Post and Telegraph Department etc.

The main features of departmental commercial undertakings are:

i.   The enterprise is financed by annual appropriations from the Treasury and a major share of its revenue is paid into the Treasury.

ii. The enterprise is subject to the budget, accounting and audit controls applicable to other government activities.

iii. The enterprise is generally organised as a major sub-division of one of the central departments of government.

iv. The employees of these types of enterprises are civil servants.

v.   The enterprise possesses the sovereign immunity of the State and be sued without the consent of the Government.

Under Article 149 of the Constitution of India, the CAG is empowered to conduct audit of departmental undertakings. The audit is primarily in the nature of commercial audit, but it is extended to include the examination of the regularity and propriety of transactions, authority of expenditure etc. The commercial audit of the CAG mainly aims at verifying the adoption of commercial principles in the preparation and presentation of statements showing financial result and financial position of the undertaking, the completeness and accuracy of the preparation and presentation, the correctness of the allocation of expenditure between capital and revenue, the fairness of the valuation of the assets and liabilities, the adequacy of the provisions for depreciation and bad debts etc.

The function of the auditor in this case is also to ensure that the subsidiary accounts are so prepared as to render it possible to compare the relative efficiency of government trading and manufacturing institutions with one another or with similar non-government institutions. The audit of such undertakings is more than the verification audit and efforts are made to analyse the workings of these undertakings in details so that weaknesses, if any, may be brought to light and remedial measures may be taken in future.

14.2.4 AUDIT OF STATUTORY CORPORATIONS

A few statutory corporations have also been set up in the country to undertake the commercial and industrial activities. For the establishment of these corporations, special Acts have to be enacted through Parliament. There are several corporations in financial areas, such as Reserve Bank of India, State Bank of India, Life Insurance Corporation of India. Some of these corporations are also working in the non-financial areas such as Oil and Natural Gas Commission, Air India etc.

The main features of statutory corporations are as follows:

i.   It is generally established by a special law defining its powers, duties and obligations.

ii.   It is wholly owned by the State.

iii. As a body corporate, it has a separate entity for legal purposes.

iv.   Statutory corporations are usually independently financed.

v.   It is not ordinarily subject to the budget, accounting and audit laws and procedures, applicable to non-corporate agencies.

The enabling statutes of these corporations have made provision for the audit of these corporations. In some cases, the Auditor General is fully empowered to undertake their audit and in some cases, the audit is undertaken by the professional accountants. In fact, the audit of each statutory corporation is conducted as per provisions contained in the applicable Act and such provisions vary from one corporation to another.

The form and the contents of the audit report, as prescribed for different corporations, are similar to those prescribed under the Companies Act, 1956. Besides, the nature of audit and the powers and responsibilities of the auditor in the case of statutory corporations are almost similar to those as in case of company audit.

14.2.5 AUDIT OF GOVERNMENT COMPANIES

A government company is one in which not less than 51% of the paid up share capital is held by the Central Government, one or more State Governments or jointly by the Central Government and one or more State Governments.

Audit of Government Companies is governed by Section 619 of the Companies Act, 1956. The important provisions relating to the audit of Government Companies as contained in Section 619 are given below:

Appointment of Auditor

The auditor of a government company is appointed or reappointed by the Central Government on the advice of the CAG [Section 619 (2))].

The limits of company audit as specified in sub-sections 1B and 1C of Section 224 also apply in relation to the appointment or reappointment of an auditor of a government company.

Remuneration

The Act is silent about the fixation of remuneration of an auditor of a government company. As the Central Government is the appointing authority, it is natural that the remuneration of the auditor will be fixed by the Central Government.

Audit Procedure

The CAG requires the auditor to give specific answers to questions, which are contained in a questionnaire that the auditor gets from the CAG. This is in addition to the report to be submitted by the auditor under Section 227 of the Companies Act. In fact, the CAG has the power the direct the manner in which the accounts of the government companies shall be audited by the auditor and to give such instructions in regard to any matter relating to the performance of his functions as such [Section 619 (3) (a)].

The direction of the CAG as per Section 619 (3) (a) in questionnaire form includes specific questions on the following matters:

i. System of accounts and book keeping.

ii. Internal control.

iii. Manufacturing and production accounts.

iv. Profit and Loss Account.

v. Balance Sheet.

vi. General review.

vii. Accounting policies.

viii. Financial notes.

Therefore, the auditor of a government company first of all conducts a full company audit, which concludes in giving a report as per provisions of Section 227 of the Companies Act. In addition to the audit report, the auditor is required to send a special report containing the answers to the questions of the questionnaire of the CAG only. This is not within the scope of company audit or duties of the company auditor under the Companies Act.

Supplementary Audit by the CAG

The CAG has the power to conduct the supplementary audit of the accounts of the government companies by his authorised person [Section 619 (3) (b)]. The CAG also conducts another type of audit in government companies on a regular interval on the basis of the power under Section 619 (3) (b). This audit is in the nature of propriety-cum-efficiency audit under which the activities of the company, its performance, various transactions, utilisation of assets and other facilities, managerial effectiveness etc. are examined.

Audit Report

The statutory auditor of these types of companies has to submit a copy of his audit report to the CAG who has the right to comment upon the report. Any comments of the CAG to the audit report are required to be placed before the annual general meeting of the company at the same time and in the same manner as the audit report [Section 619 (5)].

14.3 GOVERNMENT AUDIT

Government audit means the audit of accounts of departments and offices of the Central Government, the State Governments and the Union Territories. Under Article 149 of the Constitution of India, the CAG is empowered to conduct complete audit of accounts of governments and of those undertakings, which are directly under a ministry or government department.

14.3.1 OBJECTIVES

An Introduction to Indian Government Accounts and Audit, a book issued under the authority of the CAG, states that the main objectives of the government audit are to ensure:

i. that there is provision of funds for the expenditure duly authorised by a competent authority;

ii. that the expenditure is in accordance with a sanction properly accorded and is incurred by an officer competent to incur it;

iii. that the payment has, as a fact, been made and has been made to the proper person and that it has been so acknowledged and recorded that a second claim against the government on the same account is impossible;

iv.   that the charge is correctly classified and that if a charge is debitable to the personal account of a contractor, employee or other individual, or is recoverable from him under any rule or order, it is recorded as such in a prescribed account;

v.   that in the case of audit of receipts sums due are regularly recovered and checked against demand and sums received are duly brought to credit in the accounts;

vi.   that in the case of audit of stores and stock, where a priced account is maintained, stores are priced with reasonable accuracy and that the rates initially fixed are reviewed from time to time, correlated with market rates and revised when necessary;

vii.   that the articles are counted periodically and otherwise examined for verification of the accuracy of the quantity balances in the books and that the total of the valued account tallies with the physical numerical balance of stock materials at the rates applicable to the various classes of stores; and

viii.   that expenditure conforms to the following general principles, which have for long been recognised as standards of financial propriety, namely

    (a)   that the expenditure is not prima facie more than the occasion demands, and that every government servant exercises the same vigilance in respect of expenditure incurred from public moneys as a person of ordinary prudence would exercise in respect of expenditure of his own money,

    (b)   that no authority exercises its powers of sanctioning expenditure to pass an order which will be, directly or indirectly, to its own advantage,

    (c)   that public moneys are not utilised for the benefit of a particular person or section of the community unless
   - the amount of expenditure involved is insignificant, or
   - a claim for the amount could be enforced in a court of law, or
   - the expenditure is in pursuance of a recognised policy or custom, and

    (d)   that the amount of allowances granted to meet expenditure of a particular type is so regulated that the allowances are not, on the whole, sources of profit to the recipients.

        In a nutshell, government audit encompasses two main elements. These are the following:

    (a) Fiscal accountability: Audit of provision of funds, sanctions, compliance and propriety; and

    (b) Managerial accountability: Audit of efficiency, economy and effectiveness.

14.3.2 Distinction Between Government Audit and Commercial Audit

The government audit is not same as commercial audit. Certain special aspects are required to be covered under government audit, which are not at all required for commercial audit.

The distinction between government audit and commercial audit can be outlined in the following way:

POINTS OF DISTINCTION	GOVERNMENT AUDIT	COMMERCIAL AUDIT
1. Nature of audit	Government audit is conducted almost continuously throughout the year, because the number of transactions is many and involves large sums of money.	Commercial audit is mostly periodical in nature.
2. Auditor	The audit officers of the Indian Audit and Accounts Department conduct government audit.	Professional chartered accountants mostly conduct commercial audit.

POINTS OF DISTINCTION	GOVERNMENT AUDIT	COMMERCIAL AUDIT
3. Dominating factor	Propriety-cum-efficiency audit is predominant in Government audit.	This aspect is not strictly adhered in case of commercial audit.
4. Preparation of accounts	In this case, the Indian Audit and Accounts Department including its field offices prepares or compiles the major part of government accounts and also audits the accounts.	In commercial audit, the auditor audits the accounts prepared by others. The auditor is not at all responsible for the preparation and/ or compilation of accounts.
5. Method of accounting	In government audit, the auditor has to see whether the accounts have been prepared according to the prescribed rule of Government Accounts.	In commercial audit, the auditor has to see whether the accounts have been prepared on the basis of double entry system.
6. Objective	Government audit is concerned with examining the propriety of expenditure.	The primary objective of this audit is to see whether the Balance Sheet prepared gives a true and fair view of the state of affairs of the enterprise and the Profit and Loss Account gives a true and fair view of the profit or loss of the enterprise.
7. Vouching of payment	Government spending is done by the Treasury Officer or Disbursement Officer, who makes a detailed scrutiny of the bills before payment. So, government auditor is relieved of detailed checking of payments.	In commercial offices, the cashier does not have to make such a scrutiny before payment. So, payments require proper vouching in commercial audit.

In fact, the government auditor, unlike the independent financial auditor, is concerned with examining the economy, efficiency and effectiveness (i.e., three E's) of various schemes or projects. The government auditor seeks to get the following answers:

i. Whether the projects have been completed at the minimum cost, i.e., whether the project cost is economical or not.

ii. Whether the project has efficiently been completed, i.e., whether the projects are not suffering from deficiencies.

iii. Whether the projects have been performed in the most effective way, i.e., whether the projects become successful projects or not.

It can, thus, be seen that the objectives of government audit are much wider than those of independent financial audit. In government audit, there is a greater emphasis on examining compliance with standards of financial propriety, compliance with rules and procedures and the efficiency and performance of various projects or schemes than in an independent financial audit. The difference in objectives of audit generates from the consideration of public interest and the urge to exercise stringent financial controls over public money.

14.4   COMPTROLLER AND AUDITOR GENERAL OF INDIA

Under the Constitution of India, the position of the CAG is similar to that of the Judge of the Supreme Court of India. He enjoys an independent status under the Constitution of India. The CAG is appointed as per constitutional provision and his terms and conditions of service, powers and duties, rights and responsibilities are governed by the relevant Act of Parliament.

The Constitution of India gives a special status to the CAG and contains provisions to safeguard his independence. Following are the important provisions with regard to CAG:

Appointments and Removal
Article 148 of the Constitution provides that the CAG shall be appointed by the President of India and can be removed from the office only in a like manner and on the like grounds as a Judge of the Supreme Court. Thus, the CAG can be removed only on the ground of proven misbehaviour or incapacity and only through an order of the President of India after each House of Parliament has recommended the removal by the required majority.

Remuneration
The salary and other terms of service of the CAG are determined by the Parliament. His term of office is six years, unless within this term he reaches the age of 65 years, in which case his term will extend only up to 65 years. However, he can resign from his office at any time by submitting a resignation letter to the President of India.

Duties
The Act assigns the CAG the following duties with regard to audit:

i.   To audit and report on all expenditures from the Consolidated Fund of India and the Consolidated Fund of each state/union territory with a legislative assembly.

ii. To audit and report on all receipts, which are payable into the Consolidated Fund of India and Consolidated Fund of each state/union territory with a legislative assembly.

iii. To audit and report on all transactions of the union and of the states relating to Contingency Funds and Public Accounts.

iv. To audit the accounts of stores and stocks kept in any office or department of the union or of a state.

v.   To audit and report on all trading, manufacturing and profit and loss accounts, balance sheets and other subsidiary accounts kept in any department of the union or of a state.

vi. To audit and report on all receipts and expenditures of any body or authority if it is substantially financed by grants or loans from the Consolidated Fund of India or from the Consolidated Fund of any state/union territory that has a legislative assembly, subject to the provisions of any applicable law in force.

vii. To scrutinise the procedure by which the sanctioning authority satisfies itself regarding the fulfilment of the conditions of any grant or loan given for any specific purpose from the Consolidated Fund of India or from the Consolidated Fund of any state/union territory that has a legislative assembly.

viii. To audit the accounts of government companies and corporations in accordance with the provisions of the Companies Act, 1956 or other relevant legislation.

ix. To audit the accounts of certain other bodies or authorities at the request of the President of India/ Governor of any state/Administrator of a union territory having a legislative assembly.

x. To conduct audit in any body or authority not within his auditing jurisdiction, if he considers that such an audit is necessary in view of substantial government investment or advances. However, it has to be proposed to the President of India or Governor of the concerned state or Administrator of the concerned union territory in public interest and get the approval before such audit takes place.

Powers

To discharge the above duties, the CAG has been given the following powers:

i. He can visit any office of the Government, where principal or subsidiary accounts are kept.

ii. He can require that the books of accounts, supporting papers and documents relating to the transactions under audit are to be sent to a place to be specified by him for the purpose of examination.

iii. He can call for any information from appropriate persons, which he may require for the performance of his duties.

iv. He can make any such queries or observations to the persons in charge of affairs in an office, as he may consider necessary.

v. In carrying out the audit, the CAG has the power to dispense with any part of detailed audit of any accounts and class of transactions and to apply such limited checks in relation to such accounts or transactions as he may determine.

Audit Report

Article 151 of the Constitution requires that the audit reports of the CAG relating to the accounts of the central/state government should be submitted to the President of India/Governor of the concerned state who shall cause them to be laid before the Parliament/respective state legislature.

◆ Suggested questions

A   Short essay-type questions

1. How is the auditor of a government company appointed?
2. What are the basic features of statutory corporation?
3. State the objectives of government audit.
4. Who conducts the government audit? How is he appointed?
5. What is a government company?
6. What do you mean by 'supplementary audit' by CAG?
7. State the main features of departmental undertakings.
8. State the appointment procedure and terms of office of CAG of India.

B   Essay-type questions

1. Describe how the government accounts and the accounts of public sector undertakings are audited.
2. How does government audit differ from commercial audit? Describe the broad objectives of government audit.

3. Indicate the main features of public sector undertaking. How it is different from private sector undertakings?

4. Define government company. How is the auditor of a government company appointed and removed? What are the powers and duties of the auditor?

5. Describe the manner in which the CAG controls the audit of government companies.

6. State the objectives of audit of government accounts and compare them with those of the audit under the Companies Act.

7. Describe the provisions of the Companies Act relating to the audit of government companies.

8. Describe the main features of public sector undertaking, which affect its audit.

9. Describe the procedure for audit of (a) departmental undertakings and (b) statutory corporations.

Chapter 15

Audit in CIS Environment

15.1 INTRODUCTION

In recent years, there has been a rapid development in the use of computers to generate financial information. This development has created certain problems for the auditor in that although general auditing principles have not been affected, it is sometimes necessary to use specialised auditing procedures and techniques. As a result of this, within the accounting profession, a group of electronic data processing (EDP) audit specialists have emerged, equipped with sufficient technical expertise to make an intelligent analysis of complex computer audit situations. The intention of this chapter is to outline the various factors that need to be taken into consideration in evaluating internal control within EDP systems and to draw attention to the modifications in audit procedures, which may be required in certain circumstances.

The basic objective and nature of an audit does not change in a computer information system (CIS) environment. However, the use of computers in maintaining the books of accounts and records affects the processing, storage, retrieval and communication of financial information and may require changing the accounting and internal control systems employed by the organisation.

As given in SA-401, the auditor should evaluate the following factors to determine the effect of computer information system environment on the audit:

   i.   The extent to which the computer information system environment is used to record, compile, and analyse accounting information,

   ii.   The system of internal control in existence in the entity with regard to:
      (a) Flow of authorised, correct and complete data to the processing centre;
      (b) Processing, analysis and reporting tasks undertaken in the installation; and

   iii.   the impact of computer-based accounting system on the audit trial that could otherwise be expected to exist in an entirely manual system.

The auditor should have sufficient knowledge of the computer information systems to plan, direct, supervise, control and review the work performed. He should also consider whether any specialised skills are required in the conduct of audit in a computer information system environment. In planning the portions of the audit which may be affected by the computer information system environment, the auditor should obtain an understanding of the significance and complexity of the computer information system activities and the availability of the data for use in the audit. When the computer information systems are significant, the auditor should also obtain an understanding of the computer information system environment and whether it may influence the assessment of inherent and control risks.

The auditor should document the audit plan, the nature, timing and extent of audit procedures performed and the conclusions drawn from the evidence obtained. In an audit in computer information system environment, some of the audit evidence may be in the electronic form. The auditor should satisfy himself that such evidence is adequately and safely stored and is retrievable in its entirety as and when required.

15.2 GENERAL APPROACH TO AN EDP-BASED AUDIT

It is usual for the auditor to base his approach to an EDP based audit upon two completely separate types of review:

15.2.1 ORGANISATIONAL REVIEW

Organisational review is the review of the organisational controls within the computer installation itself. This review seeks to examine the internal control within the computer installation, to ensure that:

i. An acceptable standard of discipline and efficiency is maintained.

ii. An adequate division of duties exists, thus preventing any undue concentration of functions.

Serious weaknesses in internal control within the EDP department itself can throw doubt on the validity of all the data it produces.

15.2.2 SYSTEM REVIEW

System review is a detailed review of the controls operating within each computer-based accounting system. This review seeks to establish that controls operate within each individual system which, inter alia, ensure that:

i.   All data is completely and accurately processed.

ii. Permanent data is adequately protected.

iii. A satisfactory 'audit trial' exists.

Both types of review are carried out by the use of questionnaires and these questionnaires are based on the 'key question' principle. It is necessary to evaluate both the general and computer questionnaires together to obtain a proper understanding of the system and to access the significance of individual controls.

15.3 COMPUTER INSTALLATION REVIEW

The organisational review seeks to establish that there are no serious internal control weaknesses within the installation, which could throw doubt on the validity of the information produced.

Adopting this approach, the auditor should seek to establish that six key controls operate within the installation. These controls are as follows:

Controls by Management Over the Activities of the EDP Function

The degree of control which general management should exercise over the EDP department will depend both upon the nature and complexity of the business and the complexity of the computer installation.

The following minimum standards should, however, apply:

i. The EDP Manager should report directly to senior management.

ii. All significant aspects of EDP activity should be regularly reported.

It should therefore be ascertained that the person to whom the EDP Manager reports is a member of the senior management team and has sufficient authority to ensure that the department will receive adequate support and effective management.

The auditor should also enquire into the manner in which the activities of the department are reported to senior management. Ideally, a monthly control report should be prepared, which should include the following information:

i. An analysis of computer usage, showing productive and non-productive time separately.

ii. A manpower allocation report.

iii. A report on projects under development.

iv. An analysis of expenditure against budget.

Controls to Ensure the Continuing Existence of EDP Facilities

Arrangements should exist within every EDP installation, which attempt either to eliminate or to minimise the possibilities of EDP facilities being completely destroyed by any reason. These arrangements are significant in that the loss of certain vital information could seriously disrupt an organisation's general business and profitability.

The auditor should enquire into the existence of the following controls:

(a) Insurance Cover

The following risks should be insured:

i. Loss of equipment.

ii. Loss of file devices.

iii. Reconstruction of files (i.e., the cost of reconstituting the data from external sources).

iv. Consequential loss.

v. Employee fidelity.

(b) Emergency Precautions

The operating area should be fitted with fire detection equipment and also with fire-fighting equipment. The computer operators should also be fully aware of the emergency procedures to be adopted in the event of fire. Adequate security measures should also exist to ensure that authorised persons only would gain access to key areas within the department.

(c) Stand-by Facilities

Arrangements should exist where by data can be processed at another installation in the event of machine failure. These arrangements are particularly important where certain systems are time-critical (e.g., payrolls).

It is unfortunately rather common for these arrangements to be made only on a casual basis, since most machine breakdowns are only of a temporary nature. The auditor should therefore enquire into the stand by arrangements in some detail. In particular, he should direct his attention to the following points:

i. Whether the arrangements are verbal, written or contractual.

ii. Whether or not the stand-by equipment is fully compatible and whether any recent changes have been made.

iii. Whether significant running time would be available if prolonged use of the stand-by facility were necessary.

(d) Back-up Copies of Files, Programs and Documentation

Processing arrangements should be such that a recent copy of all master files and programs are available in the event of the current copy being either lost, corrupted or destroyed. Similarly, a copy of all system flowcharts and program listings should also be maintained, so that loss of the originals would not destroy all evidence of programme details.

The nature of the back-up arrangements and the frequency to which copies should be made will vary between installations and also different systems within an installation. It is considered, however, that the following minimum standards should apply:

i. **Programs and Systems Documentation:** A back-up copy of each program should be maintained and stored under secure conditions in a place remote from the computer room. This will minimise the risk of both original and copy being destroyed. Similarly, a backup copy of system documentation should also be maintained. Arrangements should also exist which ensure that copy programs and documentation are regularly updated with amendments.

ii. **Master Files:** At least one recent copy of each master file should always be stored under secure conditions off the premises. Security is further strengthened by means of processing files on a generation basis. Under this system, a copy of the file can always be re-created before the live edition of the file is updated with current transaction data.

(e) Equipment Maintenance

The equipment should be subject to maintenance as recommended by the manufacturer. The auditor should enquire into the maintenance arrangements and ensure that they comply with the manufacturer's recommendations.

15.3.1 SAFEGUARDING OF THE CLIENT'S RECORDS

The division of duties within the EDP department and the general procedural arrangements should be such that the records of the client are not exposed to any undue risk of loss or corruption, either accidental or deliberate.

The auditor should therefore direct his attention to the following aspects of internal control:

(a) Division of Duties within the EDP Department

In common with other departments of the organisation, the extent to which duties can be divided between the staff within the EDP department depends to a very large extent upon the size of the department.

Ideally, the following duties should be carried out by separate individuals-

i. Data initiation (outside the EDP department).
ii. Data control (within the EDP department).
iii. Data preparation (entering and verifying).
iv. Job scheduling.
v. Operation of the computer.
vi. Maintenance of programs and the file library.
vii. Systems development.
viii. Programming of new systems.

It should be emphasised that the full division of duties as listed above will only be found in very large institutions. Small installations, for example, rarely employ a file librarian and frequently combine the activities of systems development and programming.

(b) Storage of Information, Files and Programs

Procedural controls should be such that files and input and output data should not be accessible to unauthorised persons. The following matters warrant particular attention:

i. Files should always be stored securely, preferably in a separate file library.
ii. Access to the files should be limited to authorised personnel only.

iii.   Output should not be accessible to visitors to the department.

iv.   Systems and programme documentation should be stored securely.

(c) Processing of Files

As stated, files should always be processed on a generation basis, thus ensuring that a copy can always be re-created should be the current edition of the file be either lost or destroyed.

The auditor should enquire into the number of generations of master files that are kept and should access the adequacy of the storage arrangements for each generation.

(d) Procedures to Prevent Accidental Overwriting of Files

Operating procedures should incorporate controls designed to prevent the accidental overwriting of files. The auditor would normally expect to find the following procedures in operation:

i.   Files should be subject to retention periodical checks on set-up, i.e., the file label has a date imprinted on it, before which the file may not be overwritten or erased.

ii.   Files should be written both internally and externally.

iii.   Files should be stored in an orderly fashion to prevent the accidental selection of the incorrect file.

iv.   Operators should be given details of files labels before processing, so that operating problems can be resolved.

(e) Amendments to Programs

Strict control should be exercised over amendments made to existing programs. This is not only to safeguard fraudulent manipulation or suppression of data, but also to ensure that costly amendments are not made without first establishing that they are both desirable and necessary.

The auditor should establish that:

i.   operators are instructed only to accept amendments, which have been authorised, by either the EDP manager or the operations manager,

ii.   amended versions of programs are thoroughly tested before implementation and

iii.   all program amendments are recorded in the relevant programme documentation, the back-up documentation and also in a central record of all amendments.

15.3.2 Control Over the Data Passing Through the **EDP** Department

Control over data submitted for processing is of vital concern to the auditor. The controls established within each system, such as control total checks and validation checks should be examined in detail by means of separate audit reviews of each individual system. Additionally, the auditor should examine as part of his installation review the general standard of controls, which are in operation within the EDP department, particularly within the data control section.

There are three main areas of control to which the auditor should direct his attention:

(a) Controls Maintained by User Departments

In all batch-processing installation, it should be regarded as a cardinal rule that all user departments should maintain strict input controls over the data, which they submit for processing.

The type of control maintained will clearly vary according to the nature of the business and the individual requirements of each system. During his installation review, the auditor should therefore ascertain whether or not:

i.   all data is batched before it is submitted for processing,

ii.   user departments are required to maintain Input/Output controls in the form of batch total summaries and

iii.   there are indications that these user controls are effective.

(b) Data Control Function within the EDP Department

A data control section invariably exists in all but the smallest of installations. Its functions are to receive data from user departments, assemble it into a state ready for processing and to monitor its progress through the various stages of processing.

Again, the auditor will review the activities of this section in detail during each of his reviews. During his installation review, however, he should seek to establish that:

i.   a data control section does exist within the EDP department,

ii.   staff within the data control section does not have other duties, which give rise to internal control weaknesses,

iii. authorisation controls exist, which ensures that all authorised data is received form users and that only authorised data is accepted for processing,

iv. a record is maintained of all data received and of its progress through processing,

v.   control totals are balanced to output after processing and

vi. the data control section exercises anticipatory control over the receipt of data from users.

(c) Storage Arrangements within the EDP Department

There should be secure storage arrangements, both during and outside normal working hours, for

i.   unprocessed data in the data control section,

ii.   data in the record room,

iii. data in the job assembly area (if any),

iv. input documents after processing,

v.   output documents after processing and

vi. undistributed output.

15.3.3 CONTROLS OVER THE OPERATION OF THE COMPUTER

The procedural controls relating to the operation of the computer should also be reviewed, the objective being to ensure that there is no internal control weaknesses, which could give rise to the mis-processing of data.

The points to be considered during this aspect of the review are as follows:

(a) Number of Operators Present During Processing

Ideally, there should always be two operators present during processing. This means that collusion would have to exist before data could be deliberately copied, manipulated or destroyed. If two or more operators are employed, the auditor should ensure that adequate cover arrangements exist in the event of holidays, sickness, extended shifts and lunch or tea breaks. In such a situation, the rotation of operators' duties is also of significance.

If it is not the standard practice for at least two operators to be present during processing, the auditor should seek to assess other controls, which may exist and which may compensate for the absence of control over operators' activities.

(b) 'Hands-on' Testing

There should invariably be a rule, within all expect the smallest of installations, that system analysts and programmers are not allowed access to the computer operating area, other than for 'hands-on testing'. Hands-on testing is the term used to describe the situation where the programmer tests out, on the computer, programs which he is writing and developing.

It should also be a rule that during hands-on testing, at least one operator should be present, who alone operates the computer. If no operator is present, special precautions should exist which ensure that the programmer or the analyst cannot access live files and programs.

(c) File Library

From an internal control point of view, it is clearly preferable that files and programs are stored in a separate file library. Where such library exists, it should be under the control of a file librarian. Operators should not have access to this library.

Where such a library does exist, the auditor should establish that it is a requirement that all files are stored in this library when not in use. He should inspect other areas within the operations suite to confirm that this requirement is being observed.

(d) Review of Operators' Activities

It should be an accepted principle within the installation that operators' activities should be recorded and reviewed. The manner in which this is carried out will vary according to the nature of the installation.

(e) Access to the Operating Area

Clearly, access to the operating area should be subject to rigid security.

The auditor should therefore ensure that

i.   unauthorised persons cannot gain access to the operating area either during or outside normal working hours,

ii.   checks exist, which ensure that operators do not bring unauthorised files or work into the operating area and

iii. it is not possible for operators to remove files or work from the operating area without authorisation.

15.3.4 CONTROL OVER THE RESOURCES, ASSETS AND LIABILITIES OF THE EDP DEPARTMENT

To contribute his review of the computer installation, the auditor should conduct a review of the internal control surrounding the general activities of the EDP department. The points that should be covered within this area of review are as follows:

(a) Protection of Confidential Information

Controls should exist which ensure that confidential information is adequately protected. Such controls will take one or other of the following forms:

i.   Attendance of users during the processing of sensitive applications.

ii.   Security grading of printouts, with a corresponding restriction of distribution.

iii. If machine time is sold, special precautions relating to the protection of files, programs and data whilst visitors are in the operating area.

(b) Development of New Systems and Applications

Procedures within the department should ensure that computer systems are only developed in situations where there is a genuine need for them and that they are developed along practical and commercial lines.

The controls surrounding systems development should therefore ensure that:

i.   feasibility studies are always carried out before new applications are authorised and undertaken. Such studies should have regard to all the relevant factors including: obtaining users co-operation; proving a need for the application; setting realistic time scales for implementation etc.,

ii. systems and programs under development are reviewed at critical stages during their development. It is clearly essential that systems, when developed, are acceptable to all concerned. Reviews should therefore be carried out as follows:

➤ Users should approve the system before development begins.

➤ Auditors should be involved before programming begins to ensure that acceptable control standards are incorporated into the system.

➤ The system analysts should review all programs before they are compiled.

➤ The programmer should extensively test the programs.

➤ The analyst should review the results of program testing.

➤ The user department should formally authorise the system as ready for implementation.

(c) Sale of Machine Time/Data Conversion Facilities

If computer time and/or operating facilities are sold on anything more than an occasional basis, controls should exist to ensure that all income is duly received. The auditor should therefore enquire into the following:

i. The system surrounding the invoicing and collection of revenue.

ii. The rates charged and the comparison of these rates against commercial bureau charges.

(d) Cost Control Over the Activities of the EDP Department

The auditor should establish that there is an adequate form of review over the activities of the EDP department. As a corollary to this enquiry, it is appropriate to enquire under this heading into the detailed mechanics of cost control. In particular, the attention should be paid to the following:

i. Any cost accounts prepared by the EDP department.

ii. The reconciliation of these cost accounts to the main financial accounts.

iii. The comparison of actual costs against budget.

iv. The means by which management review variances.

15.4 COMPUTER SYSTEM REVIEW

Having completed his review of the installation and satisfied himself as to the adequacy or otherwise of the design and operation of the various procedural controls, the auditor will be in a position to review in detail the design and operation of each of the individual systems.

His approach to this task will be similar to that employed in any other system based audit, which include the following:

Documenting the System

The task of documenting a computer system is not dissimilar from that of documenting any other accounting system. In fact, the auditor is invariably aided in his work in that he will normally find that the system has already been well documented by the analysts who designed the system.

The amount of documentation, which will be available, will clearly vary from installation to installation. It some cases, it will be necessary to supplement the documentation with the auditor's own notes and flowcharts, whereas in other cases the notes and flowcharts provided by the client will prove sufficient.

The documentation will need to be assembled in a manner, which will facilitate an evaluation of the system on the 'key question' principle. Clearly, no hard and fast rules can be laid down, but it will normally be convenient to use the outline system flowchart as the principal record of the system and to supplement this flowchart with the following four main schedules:

   i.   Schedule of input types

  ii.   Schedule of master files

 iii.   Schedule of intermediary files

  iv.   Schedule of reports printed.

The outline system flowchart, together with the four main supporting schedules should provide the auditor with the bulk of the information, which he requires for his evaluation of the system.

Evaluating the System

Having completed his documentation of the system, the auditor can proceed with his evaluation of the internal controls operating within the system. He will do this by means of an internal control questionnaire. The questionnaire should seek to establish that the following seven key controls operate:

   i.   That it is possible to trace transactions through each stage of processing, i.e., a satisfactory audit trial exists.

  ii.   That there are controls, which prove prima facie that transaction data, is processed correctly.

 iii.   That there are adequate controls to protect standing data.

  iv.   That controls exist to ensure that all authorised, and only authorised data is processed.

   v.   That adequate is exercised over rejections and resubmission of corrected data for reprocessing.

  vi.   That the system provides adequate management information and that it is broadly suited to its purpose.

 vii.   That the system is adequately documented.

Designing the Audit Programme

Having documented the system and having evaluated the controls operating within the system, the auditor will be in a position to design his audit programme. It should be emphasised that the principles involved are identical to those in any other system-based audit, namely, that the auditor is seeking to assess and test the operation of the system, so that he can rely on the information produced by the system.

If he can satisfy himself as to the reliability of the system, this does not of course obviate the necessity for balance sheet verification work. Thus, even though the auditor is satisfied as to the operation of the computer systems, it will still be necessary to verify, for example, purchase ledger balances against circulars and statements and stock ledger balances against physical stock counts.

A.   Transaction and Weakness Test

The principles to be employed in designing computer system audit tests are again similar to those employed in designing audit tests in respect of manual or mechanised systems. If the answer to a key question is positive and the auditor is satisfied that no fundamental internal control weakness exists, and then he imposes a transaction test to establish that the system is operating satisfactorily. If, however, the answer to a key question is negative, he imposes special weakness test to assess the significance of that weakness. If at the conclusion of those tests he is satisfied that no major error could occur, he reports the weakness to the management and continues with normal balance sheet verification work. If he thinks that a major error could occur, he must then impose additional verification tests or perhaps qualify the audit report.

It is not practical to specify a standard audit programme, which can be used in all cases where no major weakness has been identified. It is, however, possible to give an indication of the normal tests, which would be included in a transactions audit programme where there is no loss of audit trial.

B. Loss of Audit Trial

The tests indicated above deal with the basically simple situation where all information is processed in batch form and where it is possible to link the input directly with output.

However, losses of and changes in traditional audit trials are encountered increasingly in the more advanced computer applications. A typical example would be a large public company with a sales ledger comprising over half a lakh balances. It would be impractical to print out a full list of balances each month, so the control totals are printed, together with certain exception reports, such as overdue balances. There is, therefore, no output report against which the auditor can compare input.

A commonsense approach should be adopted to losses of audit trial of this nature. The auditor must adapt his technique to suite the situation. A number of choices are open to him, including some sophisticated techniques.

Techniques used in these circumstances include:

i. Arranging for special printouts of additional information for the auditor's use. This often involves an additional suite of programs, which are activated at the auditor's request.

ii. Clerical re-creation, i.e., to verify a sales total when no detailed listings have been produced, the copy invoices can be add-listed and the totals compared against the computer reports.

iii. Testing on a total basis, ignoring individual items.

iv. Use of a computer audit programme to directly interrogate the magnetic file and printout information specifically selected by the auditor.

v. Use of a test pack to test the correct processing of data.

vi. Relying on alternative tests.

15.5 APPROACHES TO EDP AUDITING

Rapid changes in hardware and software have changed the conceptual approach to auditing in an EDP environment. In earlier times, audit approach consisted of ignoring the existence of computer and treating it as a black box and audit is conducted around the computer. However, the increasing developments of computers has since led to computers being used in two different ways:

i. As a tool to the auditor in conducting audit such as printing confirmation requests, and

ii. As the target of the audit where data are submitted to the computer and the results are analyzed for processing reliability and accuracy of the computer system.

The auditor must plan whether to use the computer to assist the audit or whether to audit without using the computer. These two approaches are commonly known as 'auditing around the computer' and 'auditing through the computer'.

15.5.1 AUDITING AROUND THE COMPUTER

Auditing around the computer involves arriving at a conclusion through examining the internal control system for computer installation and the input and output only for application systems. On the basis of the quality of the input and output of the application system, the auditors take decision about the quality of the processing carried out. Under this approach, the auditor considers the computer as a black box and as a result, the application system processing is not examined directly.

Usually the auditors adopt this approach of auditing around the computer, when any of the following conditions are fulfilled:

i. The system itself is very simple.

ii. The system is batch oriented and

iii. The system uses generalised software, which is well tested and used widely by many concerns.

For these well-defined systems, generalised software packages often are available. For example, software vendors have already developed packages for value-added tax calculation. If these software packages are provided by a recognised vendor, have received widespread use and appear error-free, the auditor may decide not to test directly the processing aspects of the system. However, the auditor must ensure that the installation has not modified the package in any way and that adequate controls exist to prevent unauthorised modification of the package.

The basic advantage of auditing around the computer is its simplicity. The auditors having little technical knowledge of computers can be trained easily to perform the audit.

However, this approach is also not free from defects. There are two major limitations to this approach. Firstly, the type of computer system where it is applicable is very restricted. It should not be used in those systems having complexity in terms of size or type of processing. Secondly, the auditor cannot assess very well the likelihood of the system degrading if the environment changes. The auditor should be concerned with the ability of the organisation to adjust with a changed environment. Systems can be designed and programs can be written in certain ways so that a change in the environment will not disturb the system to process data incorrectly or for it to degrade quickly.

15.5.2 Auditing Through the Computer

The auditor can use the computer to test: (a) the logic and controls existing within the system and (b) the records produced by the system. Depending upon the complexity of the application system being audited, the approach may be fairly simple or require extensive technical competence on the part of the auditor.

Following are the situations where auditing through the computer must be used:

i. The logic of the system is complex and there are large portions that facilitate use of the system or efficient processing.

ii. The application system processes large volumes of inputs and produces large volumes of output that makes extensive direct examination of the validity of input and output difficult.

iii. Because of cost–benefit considerations, there are substantial gaps in the visible audit trial.

iv. Significant parts of the internal control system are embodied in the computer system.

The main advantage of this auditing approach is that the auditor has increased power to effectively test a computer system. The range and capability of tests that can be performed increases and the auditor acquires greater confidence that data processing is correct. By examining the system's processing, the auditor also can assess the system's ability to cope with environment change.

The main disadvantages of this approach are the high costs sometimes involved and the need for extensive technical expertise when systems are complex. However, these disadvantages are really spurious if auditing through the computer is the only viable method of carrying out the audit.

15.6 SPECIAL TECHNIQUES FOR AUDITING IN AN EDP ENVIRONMENT

As in the case of manual systems, the basic approach to auditing in an EDP environment is to:

i. study and evaluate the system through which the information under audit is generated, including the various internal controls in the system and

ii. carry out appropriate substantive procedures.

Due to the special characteristics of an EDP environment, auditors often use the computer for performing several compliance procedures as well as substantive procedures. The techniques, which involve the use of the computer for audit purposes, are known as computer-assisted audit techniques (CAATs).

15.6.1 WHAT ARE CAATs?

Computer-assisted audit techniques involve the use of computers in the process of an audit rather than limiting it to an entirely manual approach. CAATs are defined as computer-based tools and techniques, which facilitate auditors to increase their personal productivity as well as that of audit function. CAATs are software tools for auditors to access, analyse and interpret data and to draw an opinion for an audit objective.

15.6.2 NEED FOR CAATs

Standards on Auditing-401(SA-401) states that effectiveness and efficiency of audit procedures may be improved through use of CAATs. CAATs may be used in performing various auditing procedures, including the following:

➤ Tests of details of transactions and balances;

➤ Analytical procedures;

➤ Tests for general controls;

➤ Sampling programs to extract data for audit testing;

➤ Tests of application controls;

➤ Re-performing calculations performed by the organisation's accounting system.

Guidance note on CAAT issued by the Institute of Chartered Accountants of India describes CAATs as important tools for the auditor in performing audits. During the course of audit, auditor is to obtain sufficient, relevant and useful evidence to achieve the audit objectives effectively. Audit findings and conclusions are to be supported by appropriate analysis and interpretation of the evidence.

In auditing a computerised environment where all significant operations are computerised, it may be impractical to perform audit completely and with assurance unless the auditor uses CAATs for collection and evaluation of audit evidence by performing both compliance and substantive tests. By using CAATs, it is possible for the auditor to perform audit more effectively and efficiently and also have greater assurance on the audit process.

15.6.3 CONSIDERATIONS IN THE USE OF CAATs

When planning an audit, the auditor may consider an appropriate combination of manual and computer-assisted audit techniques. In determining whether to use CAATs, the factors to consider include:

➤ the IT knowledge, expertise and experience of the audit team;

➤ the availability of CAATs and suitable computer facilities and data;

➤ the impracticability of manual tests;

- ➤ effectiveness and efficiency; and
- ➤ time constraints.

Before using CAATs, the auditor considers the controls incorporated in the design of the entity's computer system to which CAAT would be applied in order to determine whether, and if so, CAAT should be used.

15.6.4 TYPES OF CAATS

CAATs can be broadly categorised into the following three types:

Generalised Audit Software (GAS)

These are also referred as package programs. GAS refer to generalised computer programs designed to perform data processing functions such as reading data, selecting and analysing information, performing calculations, creating data files and reporting in a format specified by the auditor. GAS is standard off-the-shelf audit software, which can be used across enterprises and platforms.

Specialised Audit Software (SAS)

These are also referred to as purpose-written programs. They perform audit tasks in specific circumstances. These are specifically written for performing audit tests for specific type of applications. These programs may be developed by the auditor, the business entity being audited or an outside programmer hired by the auditor. In some cases, the auditor may use an entity's existing programs in their original or modified state because it may be more efficient than developing independent programs.

Utility Software

These are used by an entity to perform common data processing functions, such as sorting, creating and printing files. Utility software also includes utility programs available in system programs for performing debugging or analysis of various aspects of usage/access. These programs are generally not designed for audit purposes but can be used for performing specific tests.

CAATs and more specifically audit software have the potential to enable auditors to recognise computer as a tool to assist them in the audit process. Audit softwares give auditors access to data in the medium in which it is stored, eliminating the boundaries of how it can be audited. Once the auditors accept and learn how to use audit software, they will be in a better position to create value addition in their audit. The greatest barrier in promoting use of audit software is failure to recognise opportunities to use audit software for audit. Understanding and recognising how CAATs can be used and knowing how to use audit software is most critical to its effective use.

Using audit software enhances the effectiveness of audit and enables auditor to provide better assurance to their clients. In an increasingly computerised environment, it is critical for the auditor to move from ticks to clicks and learn to harness the power of computers for audit. Using audit software as their tool for auditing digitised data, auditor can shift focus from time-consuming manual verification audit procedures to intelligent analysis of data to provide assurance to clients and manage audit risks.

CASE STUDY

Your client is considering computers to replace his existing manual accounting system and has asked for your advice on the matter.

Discussion

a. Briefly outline the stages in the development of the new computer application.
b. Indicate the extent to which you, as an external auditor, need to be involved in the developments in order to make the changeover as smooth as efficient as possible and to simplify your audit procedures.

◈ Suggested questions

A   **Short-essay type questions**

1. What are the features of an EDP environment that affect the nature, timing or extent of audit procedures?

2. What do you mean by the term 'computer-assisted audit techniques'? State the factors to be considered before using these techniques.

3. Describe briefly the common types of computer-assisted audit techniques?

4. Write short notes on:

    a. Batch total

    b. Test data

    c. Check digit

5. State the primary purpose of generalised audit software.

B   **Essay-type questions**

1. You have been appointed as the auditor of a company, which maintains its accounts on computers. Write in detail the audit approach that you would follow in the case of the company.

2. Describe the similarities and differences in the approach of an auditor to conduct audit of accounts maintained manually and those maintained on computers.

3. State the controls that can be applied over inputs and processing of data in a computerised accounting environment.

4. Write notes on the following:

    a. Hands-on testing

    b. Files library

    c. Auditing around the computer

    d. Utility software

5. Describe the steps to be followed in reviewing computer installation.

Annexure A

Important Case Decisions

1. Allen Craig & Co. (London) Ltd. (1934)

Subject: The company auditor's responsibility to submit the audit report of the company to the concerned officials.

Fact: The company made a loss in each year of its existence, and there was as deficiency of assets to meet liabilities of over £40,000. In submitting the accounts for the year to 30th June 1924, the auditor sent a letter to the company drawing attention to the serious position of the company, this being quite apart from the normal audit report. In 1927, in submitting the accounts for the years to 30th June 1925 and 1926 respectively, the auditor sent further letters, showing that there was a deficiency as regards creditors of nearly £11,000.

The Liquidator of the company took out a summon for misfeasance against the former managing director and the auditor asking for a declaration that such parties were liable for the debts of the company incurred after 30th June, 1925.

Legal view: It was held that the duty of the auditors, after having signed the report to be annexed to a balance sheet, is confined only to forwarding that report to the secretary of the company. It will be for the secretary or the directors of the company to convene a general meeting and send the balance sheet and report to members entitled to receive it. The auditor, in no way, will be held liable in this situation.

2. *Ammonia Soda Co. Ltd. v. Arthur Chamberlin and Others* (1918)

Subject: Payment of dividend without meeting the deficiency of capital.

Fact: An action was brought by the company against the former two directors, asking them to refund to the company a sum amounting to £1268 14s. 4d., which was illegally paid as dividend during the years 1912 to 1915. The company was incorporated as a private limited company in July 1908. Thereafter, by a special resolution, passed in October 1911, it was converted into a public limited company. The company's profit and loss account showed a debit balance amounting to £19,028, 5s. 4d. The directors were entrusted to value the land and accordingly it was valued at £79,166 and the addition of expenses for the innovation of new bed of rock self amounting to £20,542. 2s. 4d. was added to the value of land. The sum was credited to reserve account and was used to write off the following:

i. The debit balance of the profit and loss account amounting to £12,970. 18s. 3d,

ii. Goodwill for £1,500.

iii. Cash bonus for £1,980.

and the balance of £4,091. 4s. 5d. was transferred to reserve account.

During half year ended 31.01.1912, the company made net profit of £7,348. 13s. and the value of the land was increased in the balance sheet to the extent of £16,450 18s. 3d. and thus eliminating the credit balance for £4091 4s. 5d., which was left to the credit of the reserve account. During the years 1912 to 1915, dividends amounting to £1,268. 14s. 4d. were paid to the preference shareholders.

Legal view: The court decided that the assets of the business may be written up as a result of bona fide revaluation and that the current profits may be divided without making good past losses of the business.

However, the decision of this case in no way holds good in India after the introduction of Section 205 (1) (b) of the Indian Companies Act, 1956.

3. *Armitage v. Brewer & Knott* (1932)

Subject: Auditor's negligence in duty for non-detection of fraud.

Fact: A lady bookkeeper has embezzled a large sum of money by manipulating the wage sheets. She had complete control over the books, vouchers, wage sheets and other documents. There was no system of internal check in force. The auditors were appointed to conduct a continuous and a detailed audit. The charge against them was that they failed to exercise reasonable care and skill in the course of examination of documents, i.e., they failed to vouch and verify book entries. The defense put forth by the auditors was that the frauds could not possible to be detected by the exercise of ordinary and reasonable care.

Legal view: The case was decided against the auditors and they were ordered to pay damages amounting to £1,259 to the plaintiff. It may be remembered that according to the instructions issued to the auditor, it was clear that there was a suspicion that fraud had been committed and hence the auditor ought to have been extra careful.

4. *Arthur E. Green & Co. v. the Central Advance & Discount Corporation Ltd.* (1920)

Subject: Auditor's duty and liability in regard to bad and doubtful debts.

Fact: The case concerned the failure of the company to make adequate provision for bad and doubtful debts. The auditors relied upon the bad debt provisions made by the managers, despite the fact that many debts not provided for were old and some of them were even statute-barred. The auditors were found to have been negligent.

Legal view: The decision indicates that the auditors must exercise proper skill and care in carrying out their own tests to establish the value of material assets. They were not adequately performing their duties by relying on a certificate provided by a responsible official.

5. *Bolton v. Natal Land and Colonisation Co. Ltd.* (1892)

Subject: Payment of dividend out of current profits without writing off Capital Loss.

Fact: The business of the company consisted of buying, selling, letting, cultivating and otherwise dealing with land in South Africa. In the year, 1892, the company, under peculiar circumstances, debited to its profit and loss account £70,000 as bad debt and credited in the same profit and loss account with an equal amount arising from revaluation in the value of land over and above the cost price. Accordingly, the profit and loss account was balanced. Subsequently, the company earned working profit and declared dividend from the said source in respect of arrear dividend of 1885.

Legal view: An action was brought before the court against the company restraining it to capitalise a part of the reserve that has been created by revaluation of assets of the company. The basic reason behind such action was that the profits of the business were not realised. But it was held that surplus of capital assets resulting from bona fide revaluation of assets, even though it is unrealised, may be available for issuing bonus shares.

However, the application of this decision cannot be made possible in India after the introduction of the Indian Companies Act, 1956.

6. *Bond v. Barrow Haematite Steel Co. Ltd.* (1912)

Subject: Transfer of profits to reserves; payment of dividend before making good loss of capital.

Fact: Empowered by the Articles of Association, the Directors carried forward the entire credit balance of the Profit and Loss Account of a year to reserves. For certain years, no depreciation was provided in the accounts in respect of building, works, plant and mining leases and subsequently it was discovered after revaluation that the company's capital was considerably reduced. The transfer of profits to reserves without payment of dividend was intended to make good this loss of capital. An application was also made to the court for capital reduction, but this was rejected. After these, some preference shareholders brought actions against the company to compel it to pay dividend out of current profits without transfer of profits to reserves for making good the loss of capital.

Legal view: It was held that when the Articles empower the Directors to transfer profits to reserves before payment of dividend and the Directors do so to the extent it is necessary to make good loss of capital, preference shareholders cannot restrain the Directors from such an action in order to get dividend from current profit.

7. *Colmer v. Merrett, Son and Street* (1914)

Subject: Gross negligence of an auditor to detect falsification of accounts.

Fact: Mr. Colmer, an engineer, claimed damages from the defendant, the auditor, for the losses sustained by him by investing heavy sum of money on the reliance of his report. In fact, the auditor was given only three days time to prepare the annual accounts. Therefore, he did not undertake the complete audit or investigation. The report was based on approximation.

Legal view: It was held that assessment of financial position along with the preparation of animal accounts for the purpose of investigation was not possible within a period of two or three days. What the investigating auditor has done that he has taken only the readymade information into consideration. He has not checked the truth and fairness of the accounting records. So, he was held liable for gross negligence in his duty.

8. *Commissioner of Income Tax, Madras v. G. M. Dandekar* (1952)

Subject: Liability of an auditor to a third party.

Fact: Mr. Dandekar, a Chartered Accountant, was appointed by A. Mohammed & Co. to prepare the statement of accounts and income tax returns. He examined the books of accounts and signed a few statements including the Trading and Profit and Loss Account and the Balance Sheet. He also forwarded the statements of account of the firm to the Income Tax Department stating that the accounts were verified by him. But the Income Tax Department later discovered that the profits shown in the above statements were incorrect and false. The department, therefore, brought legal action against the auditor for his negligence in duty.

Legal view: The case was decided in favour of the auditor and he was not held guilty for negligence. It was held that the role of an auditor to the assessee is just like a lawyer or an advocate in a court. It is the responsibility of the Income Tax Officer to investigate the accounts. The auditor owed no duty to the Income Tax Department (third party) and as such, no question of negligence in duty could arise.

9. *Chas Fox and Son v. Morris Grand & Co.* (1918)

Subject: Liability of accountants for non-examination of Bank Passbook.

Fact: The auditors were employed to check the books and prepare accounts. But they did not examine the bank passbook, for which they could not detect defalcations. Their defense was that they acted as accountants and not as auditors and for the preparation of accounts and checking the arithmetical accuracy of books, examination of passbook was unnecessary.

Legal view: The auditors were held liable for damages. The Court held that it was the implied duty of the accountants to see that 'Cash at Bank', which they had inserted in the Balance Sheet, actually existed.

10. *Foster v. New Trinidad Lake Asphalte Co. Ltd.* (1901)

Subject: Payment of dividend out of capital profit.

Fact: The company along with the assets of the other company took over a debt of £1,00,000 secured by promissory note, at its formation. At that time, the debt was considered valueless. Later on, the debt was paid in full together with an interest accrued amounting to £26,258,16s. The directors proposed to distribute the amount as dividend as the directors treated the said amount as capital profit. But one shareholder brought an action before the court restraining the company to pay dividend on the ground that the decrease in the value of other assets should have been considered.

Legal view: It was held in this case that the question of what is profit available for dividend depends upon the results of the whole accounts taken fairly for the year, capital as well as profit and loss, and though dividends may be paid out of earned profits in proper cases, not withstanding depreciation of capital, a realised accretion to the estimate value of one item of capital asset cannot be deemed to profit divisible among the shareholders without reference to the result of the whole accounts fairly taken. So, the realised appreciation in the value of book debts should not be considered as profit available for dividend.

11. *Irish Woolen Co. Ltd. v. Tyson and Others* (1900)

Subject: Liability of an auditor for his failure to detect falsification of accounts.

Fact: The auditor was found to have been negligent in that he had failed to discover that the company's liabilities were understated due to the suppression of creditor's invoices. This fraud would have been discovered if the auditor had either checked the ledger balances against the creditor's statements or scrutinised the dates entered in the first few weeks of the next period.

Legal view: This case again shows the courts refusing to accept that the auditor had discharged his duties by checking the arithmetical accuracy of the entries in the books. He must exercise due skill and care in checking the validity of these entries. The auditor was, therefore, liable for damages sustained by the company by reason of his negligence.

12. Kingston Cotton Mills Co. Ltd. (1896)

Subject: Auditor's right in accepting stock certificate from the management.

Fact: In this case, the accounts had been manipulated by the overvaluation of stock by the managing director, who had certified the stock valuation to the auditor. It was held in the court of appeal that it was not the duty of the auditor to take stock, and that in the absence of suspicious circumstances, he was not guilty of negligence in accepting the certificate of a responsible official with regard to the value of stock.

Legal view: As far as the main question is involved, whether the auditor could place total reliance on the stock certificate of a responsible official with regard to the value of stock in the absence of suspicious circumstances, this case is now of historical interest only. At present, the Companies Act, 1956 requires that auditors should state whether accounts show a true and fair view. The professional accountancy bodies have issued statements regarding detailed audit work to be carried out in relation to stock verification and valuation and attendance by the auditor at stock-taking.

It was held at that time that there was no breach of duty on the part of the auditor. An auditor is not supposed to take stock himself and in the absence of suspicious circumstances, he can accept a stock certificate issued by a trusted official of the company. However, in the present context, it does not seem that the auditor could simply accept a stock certificate from a responsible official, where stock was a material item and then plead this case in justification when defending the inevitable action for misfeasance or negligence.

13. *Lee v. Neuchatel Co. Ltd.* (1889)

Subject: Requirement of charging depreciation of wasting assets.

Fact: The Articles of Association of the company provided for the distribution of profit on preference shares and ordinary shares at the rate of 7% and 4%, respectively. For this, the consent of the shareholders is a must. Moreover, the Articles of Association of the company contained a clause that does not bind the directors to make reserve for replacement on renewal of any property. The directors decided to declare dividend out of profits of the company to the preference shareholders without making good the loss of depreciation of wasting assets, i.e., mines and other assets of the company. One of the ordinary shareholders Mr. Charles John Lee brought an action against the directors of the company restraining them to pay dividend without making good the depreciation of assets of the business.

Legal view: It was held that the company may distribute dividend without making good the depreciation on wasting assets if it is authorised by its Articles of Association to do so. In fact, the object of charging depreciation is for the replacement of assets, but when the wasting assets are subject to exhaustion, the company is formed to go into liquidation, the question of replacement does not arise.

However, under the Indian Companies Act, depreciation on all depreciable assets must be provided including on wasting assets before declaration or payment of dividend from profits.

14. *Leech v. Stokes Bros.* (1937)

Subject: Auditor's liability for non-detection of frauds, when he acts only as an accountant.

Fact: The defendants had prepared accounts for a number of years for a firm of solicitors for the purpose of submission to the Inspector of Taxes. No balance sheets were ever prepared. The instructions were given by one of the partners, Dublin and on his death, a new partner then admitted employed another accountant to audit the accounts, as a result of which defalcations by the cashier of the client's money were discovered. Action for damages on the ground of negligence was brought against the defendants.

Legal view: The negligence alleged were:

   i.   failure to prepare a balance sheet,

   ii.   failure to vouch or test certain fees brought into the accounts and

   iii.   failure to reconcile the bank account and cash.

The defendants were able to prove that they were not employed to audit the accounts, but only to prepare a profit and loss account for Income Tax.

The courts found that there was no negligence in not preparing a balance sheet or in not refusing to prepare a profit and loss account until the books were written up to enable them to prepare a balance sheet.

15. *Leeds Estate Building and Investment Co. v. Shepherd* (1887)

Subject: Auditor's liability for not studying the Articles of Association of the company.

Fact: In this case, the auditor had not discovered that certain payments relating to dividends, directors' fees and bonus were irregular. This was because he had not concerned himself with the company's Articles of Association. He was held liable for damages.

Legal view: This case had established that it is not sufficient for an auditor to concern himself with the arithmetical accuracy of the books and accounts. He has a duty to ensure that the transactions are in order. When an auditor takes over a company audit, one of his first actions is to obtain a copy of the memorandum and articles and note important points therein affecting the accounts. So, the auditor was held guilty of negligence for not satisfying himself that certain transactions were ultra vires the Articles of Association of the Company.

16. London and General Bank Ltd. (1895)

Subject: Information and means of information are by no means equivalent terms. Auditor's duty is to give correct information to the shareholders and not means of information.

Fact: The company, in this case, had not made adequate provision for bad debts. The auditor had discovered that debts were doubtful and had clearly reported the situation to the directors, but, when the directors failed to make provisions, instead of reporting the fact equally clearly to the shareholders, he simply made the statement that "the values of the assets are dependent upon realization". It was held that the auditor had failed in his duty to convey information clearly in his report and he was held liable for certain dividends improperly paid.

Legal view: This case is important, because it was stated unequivocally that an auditor has a duty to convey facts clearly to the shareholders. It was held in this case that "a person whose duty is to convey information to others does not discharge that duty by simply giving them so much information as is calculated to induce them or some of them to ask for more".

This case established the fact that an auditor who shrinks from fully and clearly disclosing all the material facts known to him is putting himself at risk. The court also discussed the basic duty of an auditor. It was laid down that he must exercise reasonable care and skill, but that he in no way acts as an insurer and does not guarantee the accounts.

17. *Lubbock v. British Bank of South America* (1892)

Subject: Payment of dividend out of capital profit.

Fact: The bank was carrying its business in Brazil and in some other countries. It sold its business in Brazil to a Brazilian company. Subsequently it repurchased its business from that Brazilian Company and in the process of sale and repurchase gained £2,05,000. The directors wanted to credit this sum to profit and loss account and distribute the same as dividend. Thereupon, the plaintiff on behalf of himself and other shareholders brought an action, which was of a friendly character, to restrain the directors from distributing the sum on the ground that it represented accretion of capital assets and thus paying it out as dividend would amount to payment of dividend out of capital.

Legal view: The court gave its verdict in favour of directors stating that the sum was profit on capital and not part of capital itself. This is because there was surplus on the asset side after putting capital and external liabilities on one side of the balance sheet and the assets on the other. It was held that the directors were justified in carrying the amount to the profit and loss account for distribution as dividend as the Articles of Association of the company did not prohibit the distribution.

18. *Newton v. Birmingham Small Arms Co. Ltd.* (1906)

Subject: Power of the Articles of Association to impose restriction on the statutory duties of an auditor.

Fact: The fact of the case was that the Articles of Association of the company was amended through a special resolution authorising the directors to create secret reserve and use the same in the interest of the company in future. However, the most serious matter was that the amendment also imposed restrictions on the auditor from disclosing the existence and mode of utilisation of secret reserve. The validity of the resolution was challenged by one of the shareholders, A. J. Newton in the court.

Legal view: It was held that any provision in the Articles of Association, curbing the auditor's statutory duties relating to his report to the shareholders is ultra vires, as being accepted canon of law. Hence, Articles of the company, under no circumstances, can restrain the auditor from reporting to shareholders the creation of secret reserve and its utilisation. The auditors are required to report the true and fair state of affairs of the company. So, any regulation precluding the auditors from discharging his duty is inconsistent with the Act.

In our country, also the Companies Act requires the balance sheet reflects a true and fair view of the state of affairs of the company. The balance sheet will not definitely present a true and fair view if secret reserve exists in the accounts. So, creation of secret reserve is not possible in our country under the existing law subject to certain exceptions.

19. *Regina v. Wake and Stone* (1954)

Subject: Liability of the Directors and the Auditors for false statement in the prospectus.

Fact: The prospectus of the defendant company Wake and Stone contained the figures for stock and work-in-progress, which was duly certified by the auditor of the company, was subsequently proved to be false, deceptive and misleading. A case was filed by the plaintiff against the company and its auditors for inflating the stocks and work-in-progress figure. It was pleaded on behalf of the auditor that he relied on the statement given by the managing director.

Legal view: Both the managing director and the auditor were found guilty. But the nature of punishment in two cases was different. The managing director was sentenced to imprisonment and the auditor was fined £200 or in the alternative six months imprisonment for having signed the report for the prospectus recklessly.

20. *Short and Compton v. Brackett* (1904)

Subject: Auditor's negligence in duty for non-detection of fraud during the period of investigation.

Fact: The plaintiff sued for the fees for having investigated the books of the defendant firm in respect of the proposed admission of partner in the firm. It was subsequently revealed that an employee of the firm defrauded the firm by defalcation of wage sheet. The important point to be noted in this case that a part of the fraud was made by an employee during the period of investigation. A counter sue was made by the defendant against the plaintiff to the original case for alleged negligence in failure to discover the fraud.

Legal view: It was proved by the court that when the plaintiff checked the wage sheet, it was correct at that time. Therefore, the counter-claim was dismissed by the court.

21. *Smith v. Sheard* (1906)

Subject: Auditor's liability for non-detection of fraud, when he acts only as an accountant.

Fact: The plaintiff had incurred losses owing to the defalcations of an employee. The actual contract with the accountant was in question. The defendant denied that he had ever agreed to audit the books; he was only instructed to check the postings in order to make out a balance. But in sending the bill of charges, his clerk had inadvertently used the word 'audit', instead of 'auditing of posting'. The balance sheet and the accounts sent in did not contain any signature or certificate.

Legal view: It was held that the accountant was held liable for damages. The jury found that there was a contract to audit, though the decision was very much against the opinion of the judge.

22. *Sockochinsky v. Bright Graham & Co.* (1938)

Subject: Right of auditor to retain working papers prepared by him to carry out the assignment.

Fact: In this case, an important and pertinent question had raised as to who is the owner of the working papers. Sockochinsky, the auditor, claimed that he has collected the information for the purpose of discharging his duties; therefore he is entitled to the possession of these papers. On the other hand, the client had claimed that the auditor has acted as agent of the business and he should surrender these papers to the client as every other agent does. The auditor had also argued that in case he is charged by his client of negligence, he could produce these papers as evidence in his defense.

Legal view: It was held that the working papers belonged to the auditor, because they were independent contractors and not agents of the clients in this context. So, an auditor as an independent professional is entitled to the working papers prepared by him.

23. S. P. Catterson and Sons Ltd. (1937)

Subject: Inadequacy of internal check system and the duty of the auditor.

Fact: In this case, the company had a poor system for dealing with sales in that the same invoice book was used for both cash sales and credit sales and this led to defalcations. The auditors had drawn attention of the directors to the shortcomings of the system, but no action had been taken. The auditor was acquitted of negligence on the ground that the primary duty for exercising control vested with the directors.

Legal view: The auditors had reported about the weaknesses in the system rightly to the directors. This should now be done formally in 'Internal Control Letters' (Letters of Weaknesses). So, the auditor was not held liable.

24. *Stepley v. Red Brothers* (1924)

Subject: Writing off the debit balance of profit and loss account from revaluation profit and payment of dividend out of current profit.

Fact: The company had written off the balance of goodwill account (£51,000) out of reserve. In a later year, the profit having being found inadequate for both setting off the debit balance of the profit and loss account and paying dividend on preference shares including arrear dividend, the directors decided to write up goodwill by £40,000, being the conservative value of goodwill and credit the sum to Reserve Account, which could be utilised for writing off the debit balance (£25,500) of the profit and loss account and paying the dividend. A shareholder, thereupon, moved the court for an injunction to restrain the directors from writing back £40,000, which was previously written off out of reserves created from profit.

Legal view: It was held that a company could write up at a fair value the goodwill, which was written off excessively in the earlier years and utilise the sum for writing off the debit balance of the profit and loss account and distribute the current profit as dividend.

25. The City Equitable Fire Insurance Co. Ltd. (1924)

Subject: Window dressing of balance sheet and auditor's inability to detect the manipulation of accounts.

Fact: This case concerned various alleged frauds in relation to the accounts of the company. The most important of these with regard to auditing principles was that securities owned by the company were deposited with its stock brokers. The auditors accepted a certificate from the stock brokers in respect of such securities for a very material amount. Had they insisted on inspecting the securities, these could not have been produced as they had been pledged by the stock brokers. An additional complication was that the chairman of the company was also a partner in the firm of stock brokers.

The auditors escaped liability because the company had a clause in its Articles of Association, which provided that the directors, auditors and officers of the company should be indemnified by the company except in the case of willful default.

Legal view: The importance of this case was that it demonstrated the importance of auditors actually inspecting documents of title by third parties held. Only where such documents are held by one of the major banks or are not very substantial and are held in the ordinary course of a business by another independent third party should the auditor accept a certificate. Moreover, if the auditor entertains the slightest doubt of the desirability of accepting a certificate, it would always be wise to insist on actual inspection.

26. *The London Oil Storage Co. Ltd. v. Seear, Hasluck & Co.* (1904)

Subject: Auditor's liability for not verifying petty cash.

Fact: This was another case where the auditors had concerned themselves only with the entries in the books and not with the verification procedures. The balance sheet showed cash balance of almost £800, which agreed with the books, but the actual balance was only £30, the difference having been misappropriated. The auditor was held to have been negligent in not verifying the balance. However, damages of only five guineas were awarded against the auditor, because the court held that the director responsible for supervising the fraudulent employee, who was the person primarily responsible for the loss.

Legal view: There are two important aspects to this case. The first is that the court again held that the auditors have a duty to verify assets and not merely to check bookkeeping entries. The second and the very important is that the auditors are responsible for the loss resulting directly from their negligence and thus are not responsible where the loss has resulted from other causes.

27. Thomas Garrand and Sons Ltd. (1967)

Subject: Liability of an auditor for his failure to detect falsification of accounts.

Fact: The accounts of this company had allegedly been manipulated in the following ways:

   i.   The stock figures were inflated.

   ii. Purchases relating to the current period were charged in the succeeding period.

   iii. Sales made after the accounting date were credited in the earlier period.

The auditors were found liable for misfeasance in respect of dividends paid by the company, where had the accounts not been manipulated, no profit would have been available. The auditors' negligence arose primarily from their failure to follow up the alterations of the purchase invoices. They had discovered the alterations, but accepted explanations too easily.

Legal view: Two main conclusions can be drawn from this case. Firstly, the need for sound audit tests on the year-end cut-off procedures and secondly, the fact that once the auditors have discovered suspicious circumstances in this case, the alteration of the dates on the invoices – they have a duty to probe the matter thoroughly, and must not be easily satisfied by explanations provided by directors or officials.

28. *Trustees of Apfel v. Annan Dexter and Co.* (1926)

Subject: The difference between the work of an accountant and that of an auditor and the liability of an auditor.

Fact: Mrs. Apfel had a business in which her two sons were managers. These managers misappropriated the assets of the business gradually. Consequently, she had become insolvent. In order to submit the accounts of the business to the Tax Authority, she appointed M/s. Annan Dexter & Co., Chartered Accountants. After her insolvency, the trustees brought an action against the auditors demanding a compensation of £28,600. It was pointed out that the auditor had acted negligently and that is why they did not trace out the fraud of the managers.

Legal view: The court declared that the auditors were innocent. The auditors proved that they were asked to prepare the accounts and not to audit them. Hence, they were not responsible and no action could be taken against any person who was appointed to work of accountants and not of auditors.

29. Westminster Road Construction and Engineering Co. Ltd. (1932)

Subject: Auditor's liability for failure to detect omission of liabilities from balance sheet and overvaluation of work-in-progress.

Fact: This case concerned misfeasance by the auditor of a company, which had subsequently gone into liquidation. The auditor was held to have been negligent for failing of detect the omission of liabilities from the balance sheet in circumstances where their omission should have been apparent and for failing to detect the overvaluation of work-in-progress in circumstances where there was available evidence to have enabled him to do so.

Legal view: This case again underlined the need for sound verification procedures and with regard to the work-in-progress underlined the need for the auditor to make use of all available records and information.

30. *Wilmer v. McNamara Co. Ltd.* (1895)

Subject: Payment of dividend without writing off depreciation of fixed assets.

Fact: In the annual general meeting, a resolution was passed declaring dividend to the preference shareholders from profit without making any provision for depreciation of fixed assets. Mr. Wilmer, an ordinary shareholder, thereupon moved the court to prevent the company from giving effect to the resolution. The plaintiff contended that the loss of capital must first be made good and particularly because the company had provided for full depreciation on its assets in the earlier years.

Legal view: It was held that a company could not be restrained from declaring a dividend out of current profits merely because no provision had been made for the depreciation on fixed assets.

However, the decision of this case in no way hold good in India after the introduction of Section 205 (1) (b) of the Indian Companies Act, 1956.

Annexure B

Objective Type Questions

1. **Auditing refers to**
   a. Preparation and checking of accounts
   b. Examination of accounts of business units only
   c. Examination of accounts by professional accountants
   d. Checking of vouchers

2. **Auditing is a branch of**
   a. Natural Science
   b. Social science
   c. Abstract Science
   d. None of them

3. **Statutory audit means**
   a. Compulsory audit
   b. Audit as required by law
   c. External audit
   d. All of them

4. **The main objective of auditing is**
   a. Detection of errors
   b. To find out whether Profit & Loss accounts and Balance Sheet show true and fair state of the affairs of the company
   c. Detection of frauds
   d. Detection and prevention of frauds and errors

5. **Auditing is luxury for a**
   a. Joint stock company
   b. Partnership firm
   c. Small shopkeeper
   d. Government company

6. **The limitation of audit is**
   a. That it does not reveal complete picture
   b. That it does not guarantee accuracy of accounts
   c. That auditor may be biased
   d. All of the above

7. **Auditing is compulsory for**
   a. Small-scale business enterprises
   b. All partnership firms
   c. All joint stock companies
   d. All proprietary concerns

8. **Propriety audit refers to**
   a. Verification of accounts
   b. Examination of accounts of proprietary concerns
   c. Enquiry against justification and necessity of expenses
   d. Audit of government companies

9. **Propriety audit is normally undertaken in case of**
   a. Joint stock company
   b. Government company
   c. Statutory corporation
   d. Government departments

10. **Government may order for Special Audit under Section ... of the Companies Act, 1956.**
    a. Section 227
    b. Section 233A
    c. Section 233B
    d. Section 224

11. Special Audit is necessary for
   a. Manufacturing company
   b. Processing company
   c. Inefficient company
   d. Trading company

12. Government may order for Cost Audit under
   a. Section 227
   b. Section 233A
   c. Section 233B
   d. Section 224

13. Central Government may order for Cost Audit of
   a. Trading companies
   b. Mining companies
   c. Insurance company
   d. Non-processing companies

14. Interim audit refers to
   a. Examination of accounts continuously
   b. Examination of accounts intermittently
   c. Audit work to find out and check interim profits of a company
   d. Carrying on audit for bonus purposes at the end of year

15. Final Audit implies
   a. Audit of accounts at the end of the year
   b. Finally checking of accounts to reveal frauds
   c. Audit for submitting report immediately
   d. Audit of banking companies at the end of year

16. A continuous audit is specially needed for
   a. Any trading organisation
   b. Smaller organisations
   c. Banking companies
   d. Any manufacturing company

17. Alteration of figures after audit is a limitation of
   a. Final audit
   b. Continuous audit
   c. Interim audit
   d. None of the above

18. Management Audit means
   a. Audit undertaken on behalf of the management
   b. Evaluating performance of various management processes and functions
   c. Audit undertaken on behalf of government to punish management
   d. Compulsory audit of company management

19. Systems Audit implies
   a. Systematic examination of auditing systems
   b. Audit undertaken to improve accounts
   c. Investigating accounting and control systems
   d. Checking the performance of management

20. Internal Audit means
   a. Audit undertaken to ascertain truth and fairness of state of affairs of the company
   b. Audit undertaken internally to evaluate management functions
   c. Audit by independent auditor to improve internal affairs of the company
   d. Audit undertaken by employees of the organisation to check financial irregularities

21. Internal Audit is
   a. Compulsory for a company with paid-up capital of Rs. 50 lakhs and above
   b. Voluntary for a company
   c. Not necessary for a company
   d. Necessary for a company

22. Internal Audit is undertaken
   a. By independent auditor
   b. Statutorily appointed auditor
   c. By a person appointed by the management
   d. By a government auditor

23. Internal auditor is appointed by the
   a. Management
   b. Shareholders
   c. Government
   d. Comptroller and Auditor General of India

24. **The scope of work of Internal Audit is decided by the**
   a. Shareholders
   b. Management
   c. Government
   d. Law

25. **The scope of work of Statutory Audit for a company is decided by the**
   a. Shareholders
   b. Management
   c. Government
   d. Law

26. **The objective of Internal Audit is**
   a. To prevent errors and fraud
   b. To detect errors and frauds
   c. To improve financial control
   d. All of the above

27. **Internal auditor can be removed by the**
   a. Government
   b. Shareholders
   c. Management
   d. Company Law Board

28. **Control and management of audit profession is in the hands of**
   a. Government
   b. Comptroller and Auditor General of India
   c. Institute of Charted Accountants of India
   d. Institute of Cost and Work Accountants of India

29. **Institute of Chartered Accountants of India was established on**
   a. April 1, 1956
   b. April 1, 1949
   c. July 1, 1956
   d. July 1, 1949

30. **Internal check refers to**
   a. Checking of record by the cashier
   b. Checking of accounts by the internal auditor
   c. Checking of work of one person by another automatically
   d. Managerial control internally over the subordinates

31. **The objective of internal check is to**
   a. Control wastages of resources
   b. Prevent errors and frauds
   c. Verify the cash receipts and payment
   d. Facilitate quick decision by the management

32. **Effective internal check system reduces**
   a. The liability of auditor
   b. Work of auditor
   c. Both work as well as liability of auditor
   d. Responsibilities of an auditor

33. **Internal check is a part of**
   a. Internal audit
   b. Internal accounting
   c. External audit
   d. Internal control

34. **Internal check is carried out by**
   a. Special staff
   b. Internal auditor
   c. Accountant
   d. None of the above

35. **Internal check is suitable for**
   a. Larger organisations
   b. Smaller organisations
   c. Petty shop keepers
   d. None of the above

36. **Internal check involves**
   a. Reduction of work of a cashier
   b. Division of responsibilities of members of staff
   c. Verification of inventory
   d. Collusion among the members of staff

37. **Internal audit is carried out by**
   a. Staff specially appointed for the purpose
   b. Internal auditor
   c. The members of the staff among themselves
   d. Supervisor of the staff

38. Internal check is essential for
   a. Petty traders
   b. Cash transactions in a large concern
   c. An organisation using automatic equipments
   d. None of the above

39. Misappropriation of goods may be checked by
   a. Proper supervision over stock
   b. Punishment of employees
   c. Checking of employees
   d. None of the above

40. Window dressing implies
   a. Curtailment of expenses
   b. Undervaluation of assets
   c. Checking wastages
   d. Overvaluation of assets

41. Falsification of accounts is undertaken by
   a. Auditors
   b. Clerks
   c. Accountants
   d. Responsible officials

42. Errors of omission are
   a. Technical errors
   b. Errors of principle
   c. Compensating errors
   d. None of the above

43. Valuation of assets on wrong basis is a
   a. Technical error
   b. Clerical error
   c. Error of principle
   d. Compensating error

44. Test checking refers to
   a. Testing of accounting records
   b. Testing of honesty of employees
   c. Intensive checking of a selected number of transactions
   d. Checking of all transactions recorded

45. Test checking should not be applied to
   a. Purchases Book
   b. Sales Book
   c. Stock Book
   d. Cash Book

46. Test checking should not be applied to
   a. Sales Book
   b. Purchases Book
   c. Bank Reconciliation Statement
   d. Bills Book

47. Cost of removal of business to a more convenient place is a
   a. Capital expenditure
   b. Revenue expenditure
   c. Deferred revenue expenditure
   d. None of the above

48. Expenses on experiments are
   a. Revenue expenses
   b. Capital expenses
   c. Deferred revenue expenses
   d. None of the above

49. Vouching implies
   a. Inspection of receipts
   b. Examination of vouchers to check authenticity of records
   c. Surprise checking of accounting records
   d. Examining the various assets

50. Payment for goods purchased should be vouched with the help of
   a. Creditors statement
   b. Correspondence with the suppliers
   c. Cash memos
   d. Ledger accounts

51. Payment for wages should be vouched with the help of
   a. Piece Work Statement
   b. Wages Sheets
   c. Minutes Book
   d. Bank Pass Book

52. Commission paid should be vouched with the help of

a. Salary Book

b. Wages Sheet

c. Creditors Statement

d. Commission Book and related agreements

53. The most reliable voucher is one that originates

a. In the organisation

b. Outside the organisation

c. Outside the organisation and sent directly to the auditor

d. In the organisation and sent directly to the auditor

54. Sales proceeds from machine should be vouched with the help of

a. Cash Book

b. Sale Contract

c. Brokers' Statement

d. None of the above

55. Payment for building purchased should be vouched with he help of

a. Title Deed

b. Correspondence with the brokers

c. Building Account

d. Cash Book

56. Partner's drawing should be vouched with the help of

a. Stock Book

b. Cash Book

c. Memorandum Drawing Book

d. Agreement Deed

57. Investment should be vouched with the help of

a. Commission Book

b. Brokers' Book

c. Sales Deeds

d. Minutes Book

58. Receipts from debtors should be vouched with the help of

a. Counterfoil Receipts and Cash Book

b. Supplier's Statement

c. Sales Deeds

d. General Ledger

59. Bad debt recovered should be vouched with the help of

a. Debtors Statement

b. General Ledger

c. Dividends Book

d. Counterfoils of dividend warrants

60. Receipts from sale of investment should be vouched with the help of

a. Brokers' Budget Notes

b. Brokers' Sold Notes

c. Minutes Book

d. Inventory of investment

61. Purchase Returns should be vouched with the help of

a. Bought Notes

b. Credit Notes

c. Goods Inwards Book

d. Cash Book

62. Payment for bills should be vouched with the help of

a. Debtors' Statement

b. Creditors' Statement

c. Bills Returned

d. Bills with the suppliers

63. Verification refers to

a. Examination of journal and ledger

b. Examination of vouchers related to assets

c. Examining the physical existence and valuation of assets

d. Calculation of value of assets

64. The objective of verification is

a. Physical verification of assets

b. Checking value of assets

c. Examining the authority of their acquisition

d. All of the above

65. Which of the following statement is correct?
a. Valuation is a part of verification
b. Verification is a part of valuation
c. Valuation is a valuer's responsibility
d. Valuation has nothing to do with verification

66. Stock should be valued at
a. Cost
b. Market value
c. Cost or market price, whichever is lower
d. Cost less depreciation

67. Valuation means
a. Calculating value of assets
b. Checking the value of assets
c. Checking the physical existence of assets
d. Examining the authenticity of assets

68. "Auditor is not a Valuer" was stated in
a. Kingston Cotton Mills case
b. London and General Bank case
c. Lee v. Neuchatel Co. Ltd. case
d. London Oil Storage Co. case

69. Fixed assets are valued at
a. Cost
b. Market value
c. Cost or market price, whichever is less
d. Cost less depreciation

70. Plantation products are valued at
a. Cost
b. Market
c. Cost or market price, whichever is lower
d. Net amount subsequently realised

71. Incomplete contracts should be valued on the basis of
a. Net profit of the period
b. Two-third of net profit of the period
c. Two-third of estimated profit of the period
d. None of the above

72. Joint Audit implies
a. Audit of two companies together
b. Audit of joint stock companies
c. Audit of joint sector companies
d. Audit by two Chartered Accountant firms

73. Loans given should be verified with the help of
a. Statement of loans
b. Schedule of book debts
c. Inspection of agreement
d. Certificate from the bank

74. Book Debts should be verified with the help of
a. Balance Sheet
b. Amount received from Debtors
c. Debtors' schedule
d. Certificate from the management

75. To verify Goodwill, the auditor should check
a. Sales Deed
b. Purchase Agreement
c. Balance Sheet
d. Certificate from the management

76. Investments in hand should be verified with the help of
a. Schedule of Investments
b. Balance Sheet
c. Inspection of securities
d. Certificate from the bank

77. First auditor of a company is appointed by the
a. Shareholders
b. Central Government
c. Company Law Board
d. Board of Directors

78. Which of the following persons is qualified to be a company auditor?
a. An employee of the company
b. A body corporate
c. A person who is indebted to the company for Rs.10,000
d. A person who is a member of a private company

79. Which of the following person is not qualified to be a company auditor?
a. A body corporate
b. An employee of the company
c. A man of unsound mind
d. All of the above

80. The first auditor of company will hold office
a. For a period of one year
b. Till holding of statutory meeting
c. Till the conclusion of first annual general meeting
d. Till a new auditor is appointed

81. The following cannot be appointed as an auditor of the company
a. A Chartered Accountant
b. A Chartered Accountant firm
c. A body corporate
d. None of the above

82. Normally, a company auditor is appointed by the
a. Central Government
b. Shareholders
c. Board of Directors
d. Comptroller and Auditor General of India

83. An auditor in a casual vacancy is appointed by the
a. Central Government
b. Shareholders
c. Board of Directors
d. Comptroller and Auditor General of India

84. If an auditor, not appointed at general meeting, he is appointed by the
a. Central Government
b. Shareholders
c. Board of Directors
d. None of them

85. A vacancy caused by resignation of the auditor is filled only
a. By Board of Directors
b. At the general meeting of shareholder

c. By the Central Government
d. By the Company Law Board

86. A Special Auditor is appointed by the
a. Shareholders
b. Board of directors
c. Central Government
d. Comptroller and Auditor General of India

87. A Government auditor may be appointed by the
a. Central Government on the advice of Comptroller and Auditor General of India
b. Shareholders
c. Board of directors
d. Comptroller and Auditor General of India

88. A company auditor can be removed before expiry of his term by
a. Shareholders
b. Board of Directors
c. Central Government
d. State Government

89. Remuneration of a company auditor is fixed by the
a. Shareholders
b. Board of Directors
c. Central Government
d. Appointing authority

90. A company auditor, in general, has to submit his report to
a. Shareholders
b. Board of directors
c. Central Government
d. Comptroller and Auditor General of India

91. An auditor of government Company has to submit his report to the
a. Shareholders
b. Ministry concerned
c. Central Government
d. Comptroller and Auditor General of India

92. Amount of share premium may be utilised for
a. Payment of dividend
b. Writing off of preliminary expenses
c. Routine expenses
d. Purchase of fixed assets

93. Shares can be issued at premium under Section ... of the Companies Act, 1956.
a. 76
b. 78
c. 79
d. 80

94. Dividend cannot be paid out of
a. Capital profits
b. Capital receipts
c. Revenue receipts
d. None of above

95. A Chartered Accountant sent circular letter soliciting his work. He will be liable for
a. Misfeasance
b. Negligence
c. Professional misconduct
d. None of the above

96. Civil liability of an auditor implies liability for
a. Fraud
b. Misappropriation of cash
c. Incorrect reporting
d. Misfeasance

97. An auditor, working in honorary capacity, is
a. Liable
b. Not liable
c. Criminally liable
d. None of the above

98. A company auditor should see that the dividend has been paid
a. After provisioning for depreciation
b. Out of capital profit
c. Out of accumulated profit
d. None of the above

99. In his audit report, the company auditor should state
a. Correct state of affairs
b. True state of affairs
c. Fair state of affairs
d. True and fair state of affairs

100. Companies Auditor's Report Order (CARO) is applicable to
a. Banking companies
b. Trading companies
c. Insurance companies
d. None of the above

101. Under the Companies Act, 1956, annual audit is compulsory for
a. Private limited companies
b. Public limited companies
c. Companies listed on a stock exchange
d. All companies

102. The Companies Auditor's Report Order does not cover the following:
a. An overseas branch of an Indian company
b. Indian branch of a company incorporated outside India
c. The head office of a company incorporated outside India
d. All of them

103. The branch auditor of a limited company can be appointed by
a. Board of directors of the company
b. Statutory auditor if authorised by the company in general meeting
c. Company itself in general meeting
d. None of the above

104. Cost Audit Report is to be furnished to
a. The Central Government with a copy to the company
b. The Central Government only
c. The company only
d. The shareholders of the company

105. **All the books of account and supporting vouchers of a company are seized by the tax authorities. The auditor would most likely to express**
   a. A qualified report
   b. An adverse report
   c. A disclaimer of opinion
   d. None of the above

106. **A control procedure often used in cases where computer files can be accessed from terminals is the use of**
   a. Check digit
   b. Password
   c. Batch total
   d. System analyst

107. **An error report, containing erroneous data detected by programmed control procedures, should be reviewed and followed up by**
   a. System analyst
   b. Computer programmer
   c. Check digit control
   d. EDP internal auditor

108. **The values of certain artwork held as investments by the enterprise have been estimated by a qualified valuer engaged by the enterprise. As an auditor, you should**
   a. Accept the valuation
   b. Engage another valuer for valuation
   c. Reject the valuation
   d. Disclaim an opinion

109. **The most common audit procedure for verification of ownership of land is**
   a. Examination of correspondence concerning purchase of land
   b. Examination of title deed of the land
   c. Examination of minutes of the board meeting concerning purchase of land
   d. Physical verification of land

110. **To discover unrecorded disposal of fixed assets, the auditor should check**
   a. Examination of insurance policies
   b. Review of repair and maintenance expenses
   c. Examination of invoices relating to additions to fixed assets
   d. Scrutiny of Cash Book

111 **Independent financial audit can best be described as**
   a. A branch of accounting
   b. A legal requirement
   c. A tool to protect the shareholders interest
   d. A function of attestation

112. **Following type of audit is not statutorily required for companies in India:**
   a. Cost audit
   b. Tax audit
   c. Annual financial audit
   d. Internal audit

113. **The audit involves examining the effects of the activities of an enterprise on environment is known as**
   a. System audit
   b. Green audit
   c. Cost audit
   d. None of them

114. **Following audit aims at measuring the efficiency with which an enterprise has used energy:**
   a. Environmental audit
   b. Management audit
   c. Energy audit
   d. None of them

115. **In case of payments, the most reliable evidence is**
   a. Receipts sent by the person to whom payment is made
   b. Entry relating to payment in the bank pass book
   c. Entry relating to payment in the cash book
   d. None of the above

116. **Direct confirmation procedure can be applied to**
   a. Debtors only
   b. Creditors only
   c. Both
   d. None of them

117. **An audit engagement letter should preferably be sent**
   a. Before the commencement of audit
   b. Immediately after the commencement of audit
   c. Any time before the completion of audit
   d. After the completion of audit

118. **Internal check usually operates**
   a. Before the processing of a transaction
   b. As a part of the processing of a transaction
   c. After the processing of the transaction
   d. At all stages of the transaction

119. **The scope of internal audit of a company is determined by**
   a. Shareholders
   b. Management
   c. Provisions of the Companies Act, 1956
   d. All of them

120. **Statistical sampling involves the use of statistical techniques for**
   a. Determination of sample size
   b. Selection of sample
   c. Interpretation of sample results
   d. All of them

121. **Statistical sampling techniques can be employed by an auditor in carrying out**
   a. Compliance procedures
   b. Substantive procedures
   c. Both the procedures
   d. None of them

122. **The following document would be considered most reliable in case of receipts from customers:**
   a. Daily cash receipts statement
   b. Copy of acknowledgement sent to the customers
   c. Bank pay-in-slip
   d. Bank statement

123. **The general accepted basis of valuation of fixed assets is**
   a. Net realisable value
   b. Historical cost less depreciation
   c. Replacement cost
   d. None of the above

124. **An auditor finds that fictitious sale have been recorded to inflate profit. The auditor**
   a. Ignores it
   b. Allows it
   c. Qualifies his audit report
   d. None of the above

125. **The auditor did not check the adequacy of provision for bad and doubtful debts. He can be**
   a. Held liable for it
   b. Not liable for it
   c. Liable criminally for it
   d. None of the above

Index